CHARLEY'S
WAR

BLUE'S STORY

CHARLEY'S WAR: Blue's Story

ISBN 1 84576 323 8
ISBN-13 9781845763237

Published by
Titan Books
A division of Titan Publishing Group Ltd
144 Southwark Street
London SE1 0UP

Charley's War is © 2007 Egmont Magazines Ltd. All rights reserved. No portion of this book may be reproduced or transmitted, in any form or by any means, without the express written permission of the publisher.

A CIP catalogue record for this title is available from the British Library.

This edition first published: October 2007
2 4 6 8 10 9 7 5 3

Printed in Italy.

Also available from Titan Books:
Charley's War: 2 June 1916 – 1 August 1916 (ISBN: 1 84023 627 2)
Charley's War: 1 August 1916 – 17 October 1916 (ISBN: 1 84023 929 8)
Charley's War: 17 October 1916 – 21 February 1917 (ISBN: 1 84576 270 3)

Grateful thanks to Pat Mills, Trucie Henderson, Neil Emery, Yvonne Oliver and Dan Todman for their help and support in the production of this book.

Cover photo used by permission of the Imperial War Museum, London (Q27724).
Poppy artwork © 2005 Trucie Henderson.

Introduction © 2007 Tariq Goddard.
The Battle of Verdun feature © 2007 Steve White.
Strip commentary © 2007 Pat Mills.

Photo credits: Page 6: Erich von Falkenhayn – Robert Carlson.
Page 7: Firefighters in Verdun, Joseph Joffre; Page 9, Robert Nivelle
– The Literary Digest History of the World War (London, 1920)
Page 8: Ruins of Fort Vaux – Stan Parry
All other photos used are taken from the Photos of the Great War website,
www.gwpda.org/photos/greatwar.htm

What did you think of this book? We love to hear from our readers.
Please email us at : readerfeedback@titanemail.com, or write to us
at the above address.

To receive advance information, news, competitions, and exclusive Titan offers online,
please register as a member by clicking the "sign up" button on our website:
www.titanbooks.com

Much of the comic strip material used by Titan in this edition is exceedingly rare. As such, we hope that readers appreciate that the quality of the materials can be variable.

CHARLEY'S WAR

BLUE'S STORY

PAT MILLS
JOE COLQUHOUN

TITAN BOOKS

INTRODUCTION

by Tariq Goddard

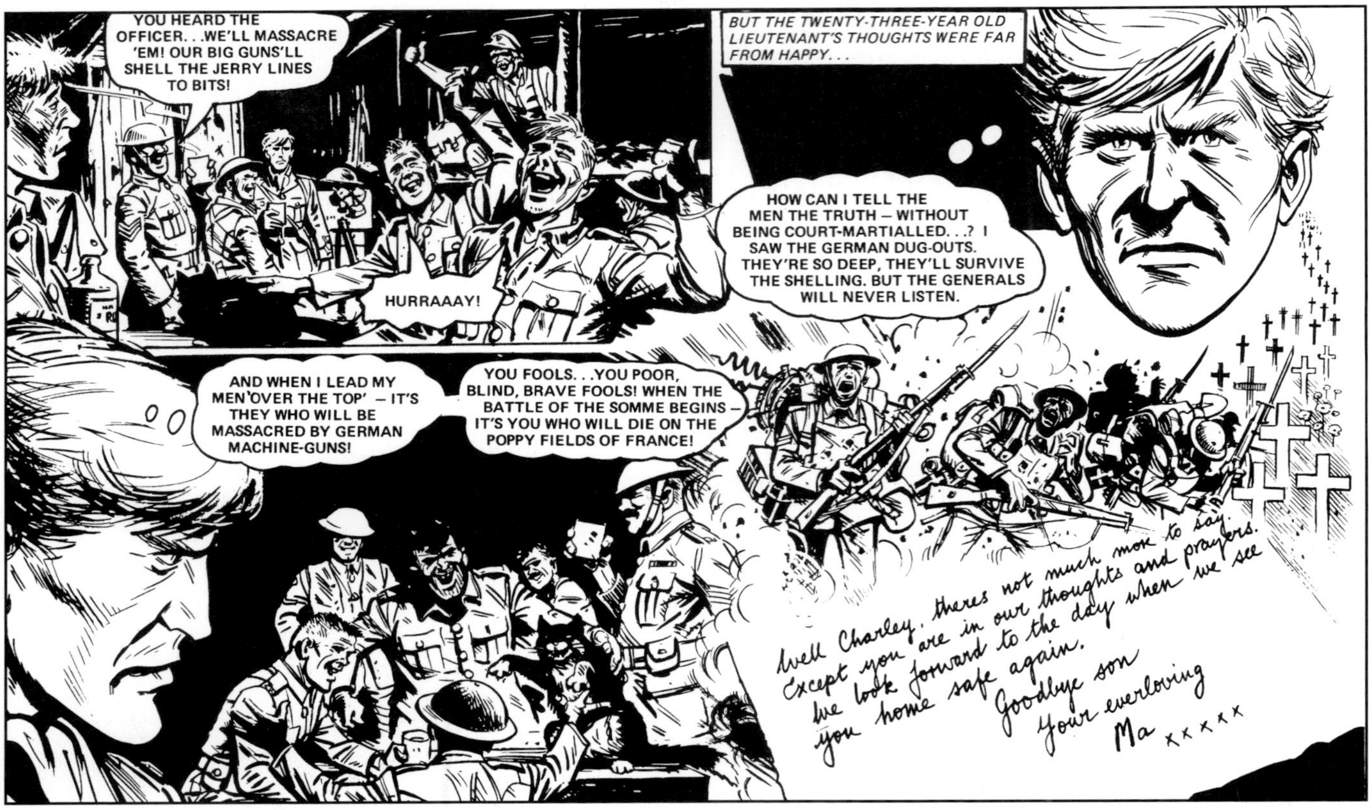

YOU HEARD THE OFFICER. . .WE'LL MASSACRE 'EM! OUR BIG GUNS'LL SHELL THE JERRY LINES TO BITS!
HURRAAAY!
BUT THE TWENTY-THREE-YEAR OLD LIEUTENANT'S THOUGHTS WERE FAR FROM HAPPY. . .
HOW CAN I TELL THE MEN THE TRUTH – WITHOUT BEING COURT-MARTIALLED. . .? I SAW THE GERMAN DUG-OUTS. THEY'RE SO DEEP, THEY'LL SURVIVE THE SHELLING. BUT THE GENERALS WILL NEVER LISTEN.
AND WHEN I LEAD MY MEN 'OVER THE TOP' – IT'S THEY WHO WILL BE MASSACRED BY GERMAN MACHINE-GUNS!
YOU FOOLS. . .YOU POOR, BLIND, BRAVE FOOLS! WHEN THE BATTLE OF THE SOMME BEGINS – IT'S YOU WHO WILL DIE ON THE POPPY FIELDS OF FRANCE!
Well Charley, theres not much more to say.
Except you are in our thoughts and prayers.
We look forward to the day when we see
you home safe again.
Goodbye son
Your everloving
Ma xxxxx

When I grew up, war comics were another country, in which things were done differently. I was drawn to them at six through my father, an ex-serviceman whose interest developed in tandem with my own, reading them to me instead of bedtime stories. Until we experienced *Charley's War* in *Battle*, war stories were mostly fought by gentlemanly amateurs and their working-class sidekicks, often on uneven terms, against two-dimensional hate machines, usually German or Japanese; a necessary role that subsequently fell to aliens and other extra-terrestrials whose slaughter could not be objected to on the grounds of political correctness[1].

Charley's War was in many ways my first encounter with a wholly adult reality, like a blast of shrapnel from a parallel world – a world my father had no difficulty recognising, but one I barely grasped the character of. Although other stories in *Battle* had softened the blow, it was *Charley's War* that took a generation of comic readers' innocence from them and replaced it with something very like an infant political sensibility. What I find most revealing is that even though the strip was bleak and sometimes upsetting (comic plots and illustrations tended to occupy a comic reality, whereas *Charley's* sought to emulate a living one), I could tell that this was a story concerned with truth in a way that others were not.

Charley's War was populated by a democratic ensemble cast: Charley – the hero not because of who he was but by virtue of what he saw – represented decency and was thus appalled by war, which was crucial, as war had never seemed indecent to me or my friends before. Certainly there had been the odd "cad", or good German, written in to a story to provide it with a twist, but nowhere had injustice been featured as a character in its own right. Every week serial injustices were perpetrated by "our" side against "our" soldiers, a battle not between English and German but between the leaders and led, thus introducing another character to war comics, "the System". The industrial slaughter of the Western front had already been blamed on this or that general, but Mills went further in identifying patterns and pointing the finger at the real off-page villain: the system responsible for a series of treaties, kept secret from Parliament and the public, ending in a needless and avoidable cataclysm that left 8.5 million dead and 21 million wounded. Mills' skill was in allowing this to emerge out of the story, retaining the dramatic elements of war comics, whilst

[1] This was a convention Mills would later challenge in *2000 AD*'s *Nemesis the Warlock*, where the humans were cast as the aggressors and aliens as the victims.

mounting surprise attacks on their underlying conventions that would have clashed with his role as a propagandist.

This operation could not have been as effective as it was, were it not for the magnificent artwork of Joe Colquhoun. The symbiosis and complementary relationship between him and Mills was so complete that I initially believed they were the same person. Colquhoun possessed a range and talent vivid enough to draw an army of faces that were different from one another, a deceptively simple feat. To compare his work with that of his peer group demonstrates what a revolutionary leap this was, for his characters were no action-men carved of wood, but creations equal to life and its complexities. Every person, even the most marginal, was as dextrous and excessive as Mills' script required them to be, from the doomed nobility of Lieutenant Thomas to the embittered Bolshevik warlord Spinrov; the Russian Civil War sequence that this last character featured in is arguably the most underrated in British comics. Even Colquhoun's depictions of civilian life on the home front carried something of the war in them: the narrow streets of London's East End resembling the trenches of the Western Front, and the lines of Tommies blinded by mustard gas the dole queues of the '20s.

Though I did not know that I was absorbing lessons that one day would provide me with a grounding as a novelist, I learnt the distinction between flat and rounded characters from Charley's War, and the way social types and ciphers could still be people in their own right; an incredibly difficult feat to pull off within the restrictions of the comic medium. That you could imagine these characters having a life off-page, that – crucially – did not resort to fantasy (no reader wrote to the letters page asking for Charley's spent cartridges in the way they might have asked for Captain Hurricane's beret) proved that the story transgressed its genre and medium, operating like literature, something that is now taken for granted in the better graphic novels.

Disquietingly – and contrary to Mills' intentions – I believe that *Charley's War* can also be read completely straight, that is from the point of view that war, however bloody and violent, is necessary. Certainly my father was pleased that an accurate depiction of war had surfaced, so that the general reader would appreciate how gritty it was, rendering the final victory an even greater triumph. After *Saving Private Ryan* it is clear that graphic accounts of death in combat have not put everyone off the idea, suggesting that though crude imperialism may now be discredited, the heroic ideal is still far from dead amongst the martially inclined. Which takes nothing away from a story that was always too ambitious and emotional to be restricted to a tidy interpretation, its belligerent mix of pride and anger a fitting and accurate reflection of the feelings of the soldiers it depicted and dignified. ✢

Tariq Goddard
April 2007

Tariq Goddard is the Whitbread prize-nominated author of *Homage to a Firing Squad*. His other works include *Dynamo* and *The Morning Rides Behind Us*. He is currently working on his fourth novel, *War Pigs*.

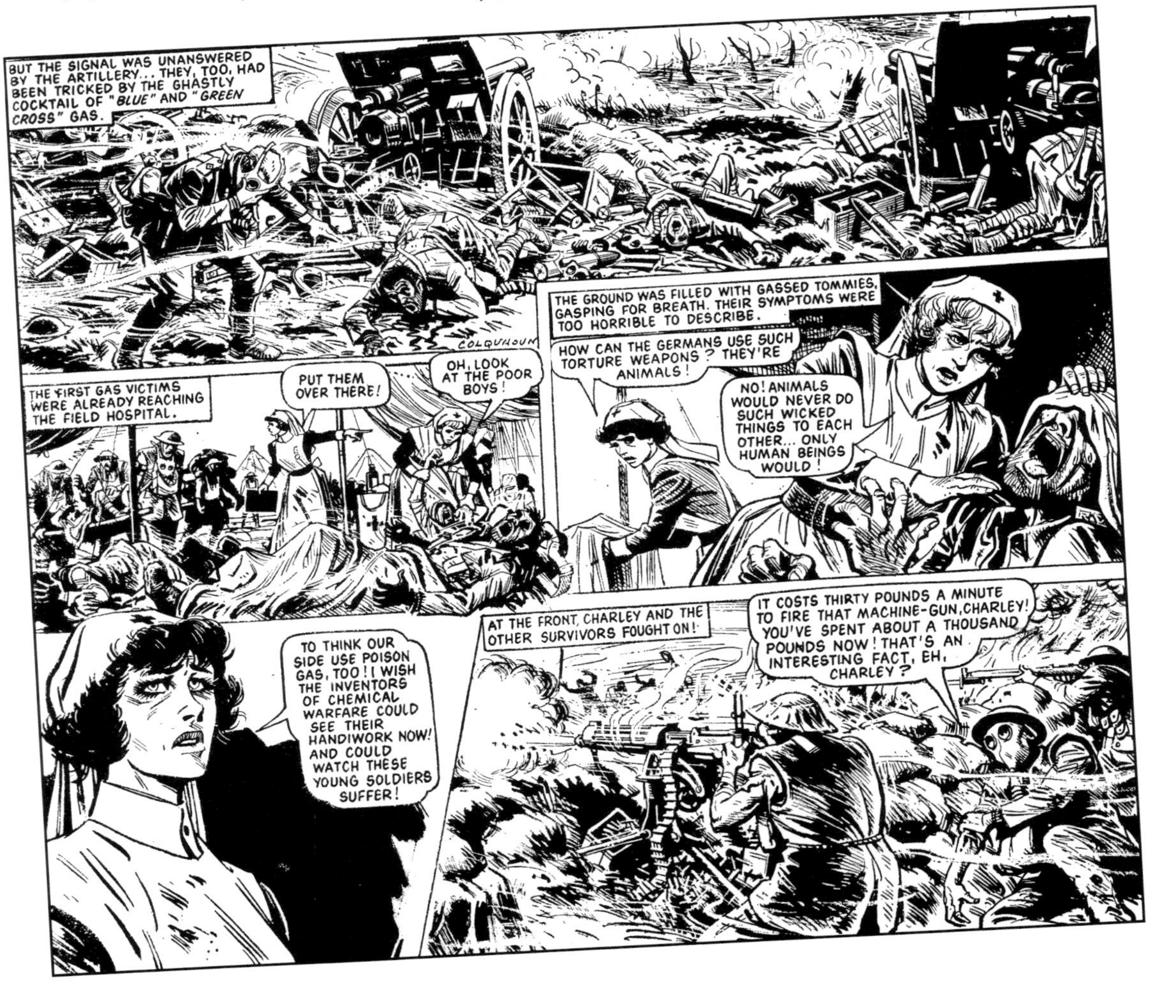
BUT THE SIGNAL WAS UNANSWERED BY THE ARTILLERY... THEY, TOO, HAD BEEN TRICKED BY THE GHASTLY COCKTAIL OF "BLUE" AND "GREEN CROSS" GAS.
COLQUHOUN
THE FIRST GAS VICTIMS WERE ALREADY REACHING THE FIELD HOSPITAL.
PUT THEM OVER THERE!
OH, LOOK AT THE POOR BOYS!
THE GROUND WAS FILLED WITH GASSED TOMMIES, GASPING FOR BREATH. THEIR SYMPTOMS WERE TOO HORRIBLE TO DESCRIBE.
HOW CAN THE GERMANS USE SUCH TORTURE WEAPONS? THEY'RE ANIMALS!
NO! ANIMALS WOULD NEVER DO SUCH WICKED THINGS TO EACH OTHER... ONLY HUMAN BEINGS WOULD!
TO THINK OUR SIDE USE POISON GAS, TOO! I WISH THE INVENTORS OF CHEMICAL WARFARE COULD SEE THEIR HANDIWORK NOW! AND COULD WATCH THESE YOUNG SOLDIERS SUFFER!
AT THE FRONT, CHARLEY AND THE OTHER SURVIVORS FOUGHT ON!
IT COSTS THIRTY POUNDS A MINUTE TO FIRE THAT MACHINE-GUN, CHARLEY! YOU'VE SPENT ABOUT A THOUSAND POUNDS NOW! THAT'S AN INTERESTING FACT, EH, CHARLEY?

"THEY SHALL NOT PASS!"

The Battle of Verdun

by Steve White

THE BOCHE ARE SHELLING *THE GAUNTLET* EVERY *NINETY* SECONDS... IT WILL TAKE YOU ABOUT *EIGHTY-FIVE* SECONDS TO PASS THE DANGER ZONE... THE NEXT SHELL WILL BE YOUR *STARTING SIGNAL! GOOD LUCK!*

GOOD EVENING, GENTLEMEN! I AM YOUR *FERRYMAN!*

EN AVANT! **RUN FOR YOUR LIVES!**

TOP: Blue's unit prepare to run the gauntlet.

ABOVE: Erich von Falkenhayn, the German Chief of Staff.

The Battle of Verdun is considered the longest battle in history. Officially lasting from 21 February to 18 December 1916, the ten months of the battle cost the lives of around a quarter of a million men. For the French, Verdun took on a similar resonance as the Somme for the British, encompassing the same sense of horror and relentless, grinding attrition that forms the cultural backbone of the First World War.

The fighting centred around the ancient town of Verdun-sur-Meuse, in the Lorraine region of north-east France. The town had a long, interesting history long before being swallowed up by the Western Front. Founded by the Gauls, its position on the river Meuse and astride the road to Paris gave it a strategic importance which led to its being overrun by the Romans, Attila the Hun and the Prussians. At the outbreak of World War One in 1914, Verdun was one of the strongest positions in France, ringed by a powerful line of fortifications. The Germans quickly recognised its value when the town held out against their initial invasion. As the front line settled, the town formed a bulge – a salient – into German-occupied territory, a boil the Germans could not lance even by pounding it with their heaviest artillery.

The roots of the battle lay with the German Chief of Staff, Erich von Falkenhayn. He was concerned that the stalemate on the Western Front could no longer be broken by breakthrough attacks. All three of the major combatants – France, Britain and the opposing Germans – had failed miserably, leaving no change in the status quo other than in the horrific casualties sustained.

Von Falkenhayn offered a different solution to breaking the deadlock. The key to winning the war lay not in defeating the Russians in the East, whom he believed – rightly, as it turned out – would soon be forced out of the war by impending revolution. Instead, the cornerstone of his strategy lay in forcing Britain out of the fighting. Falkenhayn believed Britain was the real muscle behind the Allied war effort; he suggested Germany lift all restrictions on its war against shipping bringing supplies across the Atlantic to the UK, despite the inherent risks this entailed in bringing the USA into the fighting (many ships were American). This merciless assault on Britain's supply lines would starve the country into submission and was one half of his strategic goal.

The second was a knockout blow to the French: a blow that would leave the burden of the fighting on Britain's sagging shoulders, forcing it to seek a peaceful settlement. The French Army's destruction was to take place at Verdun. Von Falkenhayn's decision was based around a number of factors. The salient meant that Verdun was surrounded on three sides; the French could only receive supplies up a single road, which also left communications to their rear in a poor state. Conversely, a railhead was only 12 miles from the German positions – supplies could be moved easily to the front. But uppermost in von Falkenhayn's mind was the powerful psychological importance of Verdun to the French. The salient had become a potent symbol of French resistance. There were many alive who remembered that Verdun was the last fortress town to fall in the Franco-Prussian War of 1870-71. As such, the French High Command would do everything it could to keep the town from falling, compelling them, von Falkenhayn believed, "to throw in every man they have." In this way he hoped to exsanguinate France's army.

The German Fifth Army, led by Crown Prince Wilhelm, was given the task of taking the town. Originally planned to begin on 12 February, the assault, codenamed 'Juggernaut', was held up by poor weather, a frequent problem around the salient. The British newspaper baron, Lord Northcliffe, wrote in his dispatches from the front, "The district of Verdun lies in the coldest and also the most misty sectors of the long line between Nieuport and Switzerland."

However, the French now knew an attack was imminent. As Northcliffe commented, "[The Germans] announced that something large was pending by closing the Swiss frontier." French intelligence services also received warnings, prompting reinforcements to

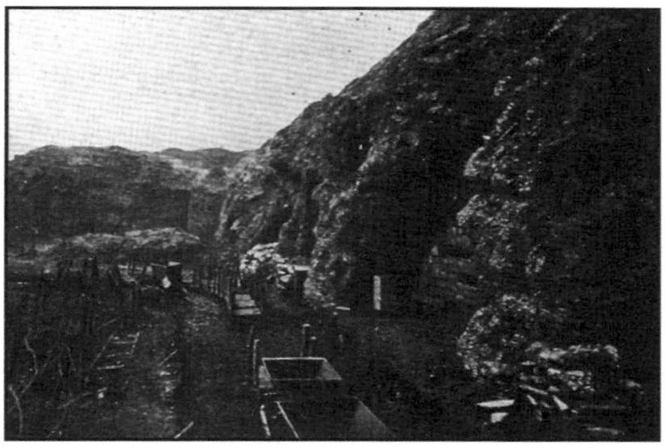

be fed into Verdun's defences. In Verdun itself, efforts were made to improve fortifications and strengthen the line. Even so, the 200,000 defenders faced the best part of a quarter of a million Germans, supported by 1200 artillery pieces and 168 aircraft – the largest concentration of warplanes in history at the time.

The weather finally cleared enough for the attack to get underway on 21 February. Six miles of the French line received a 21-hour preliminary bombardment, the shells falling at a rate of 100,000 an hour. As one French soldier wrote, "Men were squashed, cut in two or divided from top to bottom. Blown into showers; bellies turned inside out..." During the day, German scouts optimistically reported half the French defenders out of action, but Wilhelm, exercising caution, did not instigate a full frontal assault – choosing instead to remain behind the artillery barrage.

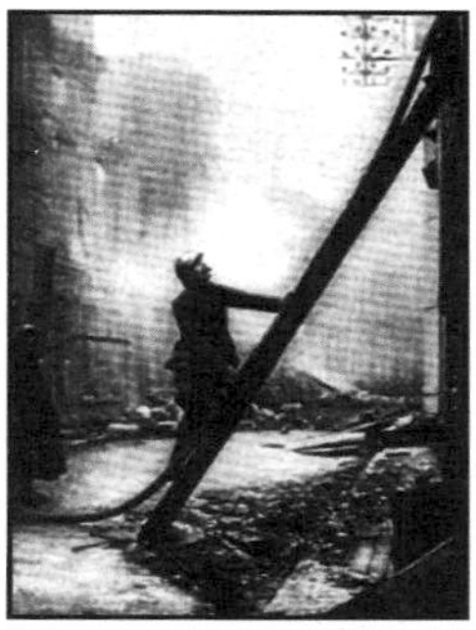

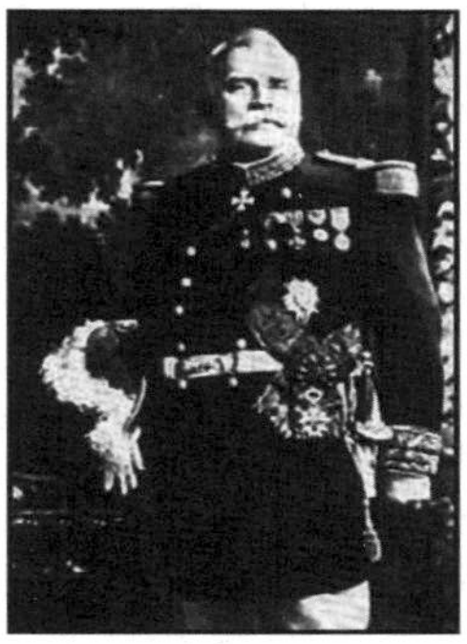

TOP MIDDLE: The underground endtrance to Fort Douaumont.

TOP: Firefighters at Verdun.

ABOVE: Joseph Joffe.

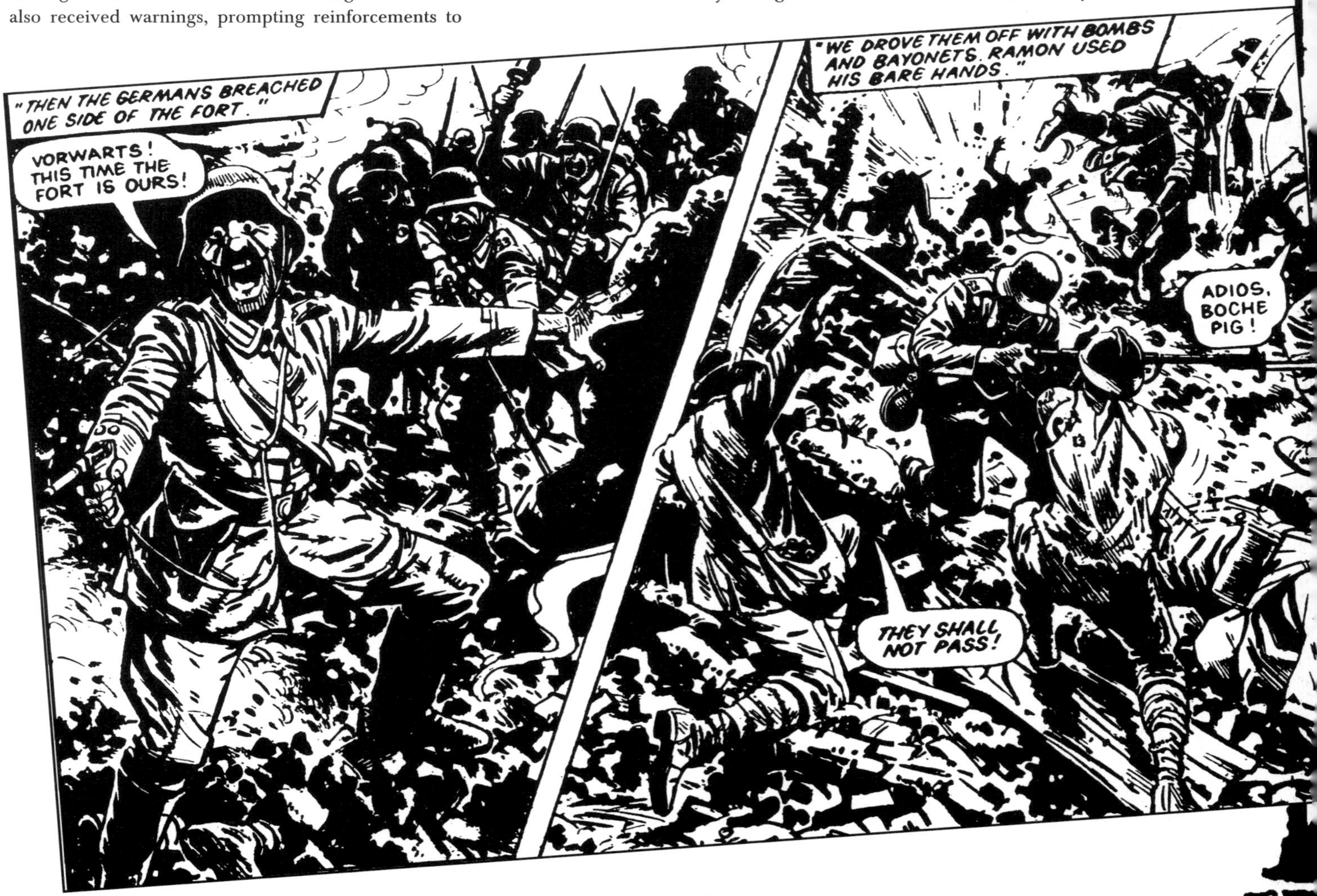
"THEN THE GERMANS BREACHED ONE SIDE OF THE FORT."
VORWARTS! THIS TIME THE FORT IS OURS!
"WE DROVE THEM OFF WITH BOMBS AND BAYONETS. RAMON USED HIS BARE HANDS."
ADIOS, BOCHE PIG!
THEY SHALL NOT PASS!

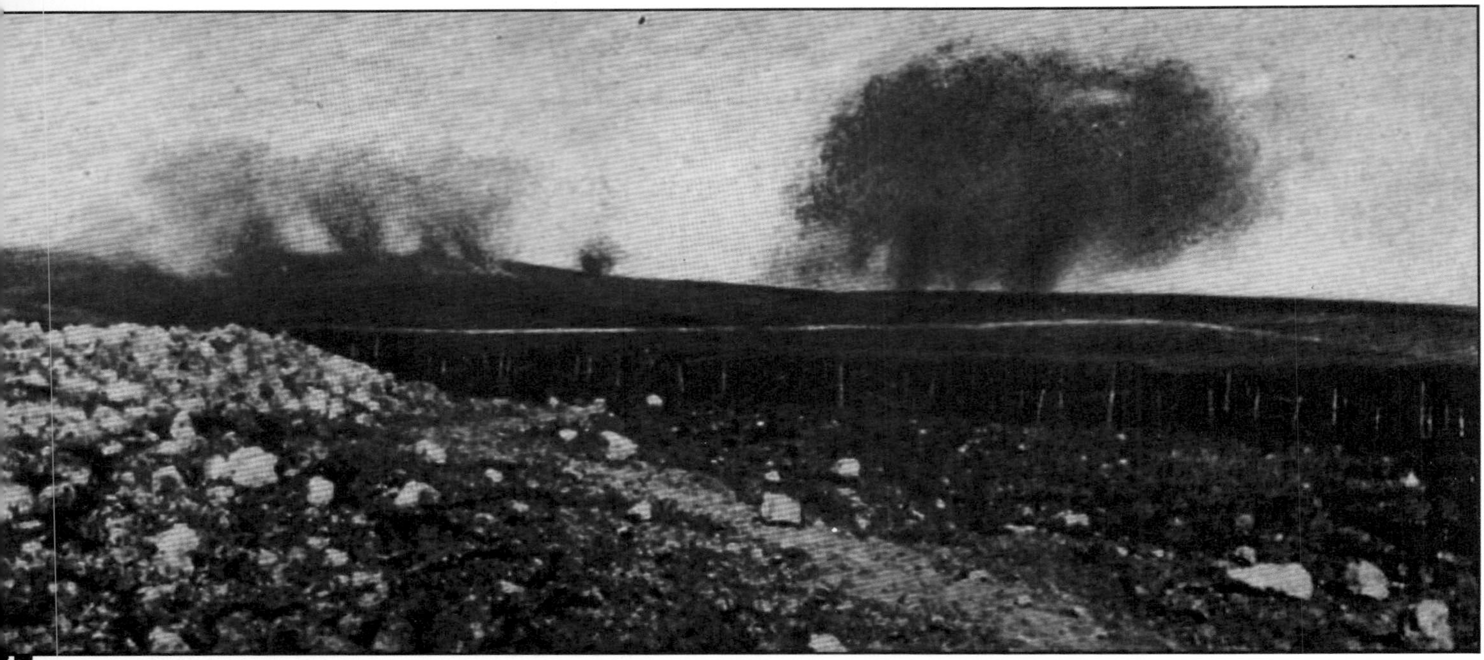

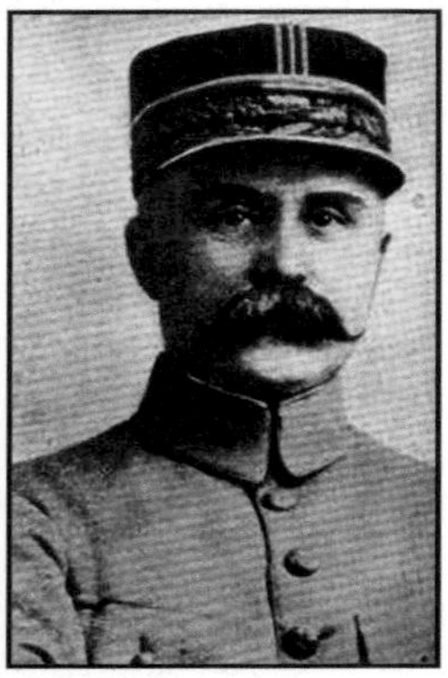

TOP: The artillery assault on Mort-Homme and Hill 287.

ABOVE: Henri Pétain.

BELOW: Fort Souville, May 1917.

By the end of 21 February, the Germans had only managed to capture the first line of French trenches, cleared out with the help of flamethrowers – their first use in the history of war. The initial cautious showing by the Germans still did not alter the fact that the French situation at Verdun was dire, a fact that eluded the High Command due to the poor communications predicted by von Falkenhayn.

24 February saw the fall of Fort Douaumont, only five miles from Verdun, to the Germans. Just 56 elderly soldiers manned this powerful fortification, and its capture caused consternation and outrage amongst the French. In fact, its downfall was at first withheld from French papers. Propaganda instead reported that the battle was going well for France, but as word spread, demands mounted for the recapture of the fort. The French Commander-in-Chief, Joseph Joffe, was now bound by popular demand to hold Verdun at all costs – again, as von Falkenhayn had foreseen. Joffe ordered that any commander who retreated would be court-martialled, dismissing Verdun's commander, General Langle de Cary, for already doing so.

Verdun's defence was now handed over to General Henri-Phillip Pétain (later to achieve notoriety as the leader of Vichy France under Nazi German rule). Pétain did not hold the prevailing view of 'attack at all costs', believing that technology – artillery, the machine gun, chemical weapons – would lead to disaster in the face of such recklessness. This left his career on the slow track, but Pétain remained a level-headed commander despite the perilous situation now handed to him.

The single road into Verdun was a mere 20 feet wide so that vehicles could barely pass. Yet it was christened 'Voie Sacreé' – the sacred road – and units of French troops were assigned the task of keeping the road open at all times, repairing it, and keeping it clear so that the supplies flowed. They had to, for the road was the lifeline to Verdun, with 25,000 tons and 90,000 troops passing up it to the defenders. Securing the supply route, Pétain also ordered the commanders at Verdun to hold on – playing right into the hands of von Falkenhayn.

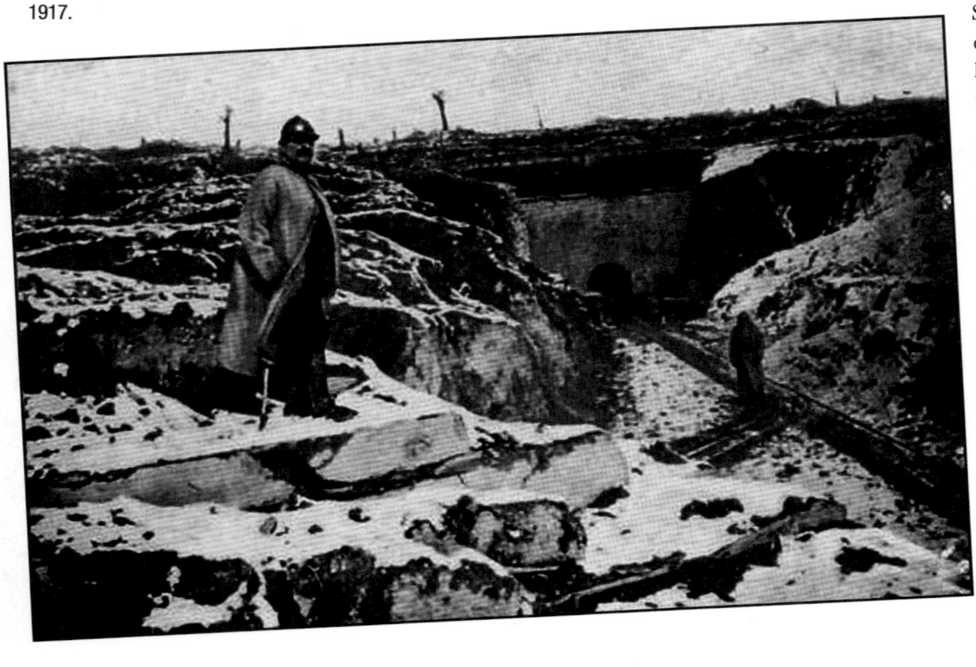

However, events began to conspire against the Germans. Pétain knew French casualties would be heavy, but this didn't stop him and his superiors feeding the Second Army into the sector. Tough French resistance also held up the Germans, compounded by heavy snowfall that added to the suffering inflicted by war. As Northcliffe wrote, "It is one of the most gruesome facts in the history of war that the French, peering through the moonlight at what they thought to be stealthily crawling Germans, found them to be wounded men frozen to death."

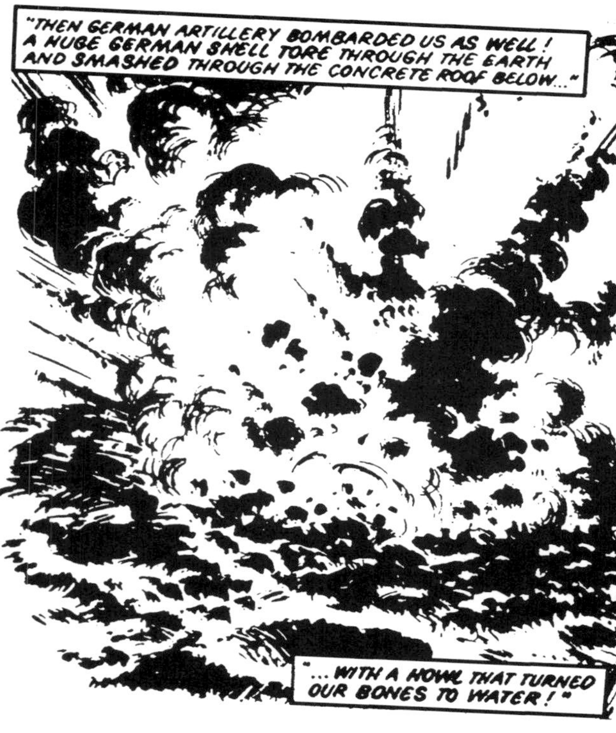
"THEN GERMAN ARTILLERY BOMBARDED US AS WELL! A HUGE GERMAN SHELL TORE THROUGH THE EARTH AND SMASHED THROUGH THE CONCRETE ROOF BELOW..."
"... WITH A HOWL THAT TURNED OUR BONES TO WATER!"

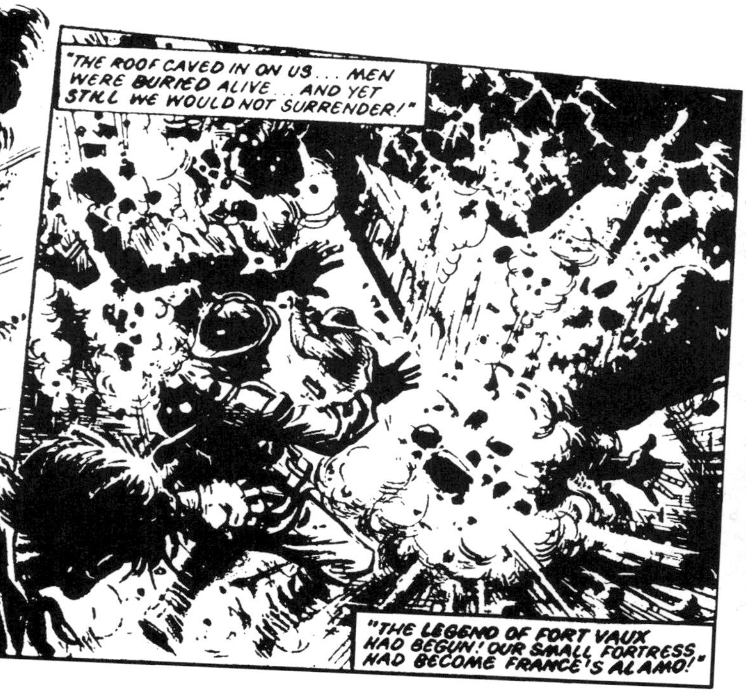
"THE ROOF CAVED IN ON US... MEN WERE BURIED ALIVE... AND YET STILL WE WOULD NOT SURRENDER!"
"THE LEGEND OF FORT VAUX HAD BEGUN! OUR SMALL FORTRESS HAD BECOME FRANCE'S ALAMO!"

The German advance had also taken them beyond the secure umbrella of their artillery, whilst moving them into range of the French guns.

Successive German attacks saw ever-increasing losses. The village of Douaumont finally fell on 2 March, but left four German regiments destroyed.

With fresh artillery now deployed and their frontal assault faltering, the Germans launched a new attack against a hill on the left bank of River Meuse called Le Mort-Homme (appropriately, 'the Dead Man'), and on the 8th at Fort Vaux. The fighting was savage, the Germans halted by French counter-attacks, only to mount repeated assaults against the French reinforcements being fed into the Fort. Losses on both sides were horrendous. A French officer recalled the fighting on the 20-24 May: "There are slopes on Hill 304 where the level of the ground is raised several metres by mounds of German corpses. Sometimes it happens that the third German wave uses the dead of the second as ramparts and shelters."

The Germans managed to capture the villages of Chattencourt and, on 29 May, Cumieres-le-Mort-Homme – one of nine villages completely destroyed by the fighting and declared, 'died for France'. Fort Vaux finally fell on 2 June.

But the price for the Germans as well as the French was heavy: 120,000 German casualties, 133,000 French, by the end of April. As a French soldier put it, "An artery of French blood was split on February 21st and it flows incessantly in large spurts." Another said, "You eat beside the dead; you drink beside the dead, you relieve yourself beside the dead and sleep beside the dead." Pétain asked for more men but was denied due to the impending Somme Offensive (see *Charley's War: 2 June – 1 August 1916*.) His concerns over casualties led to a more defensive strategy, so that on 1 May he was promoted and replaced by General Robert Nivelle.

The latter's views were sumurised by a quote often attributed to Pétain: "They shall not pass." Nivelle turned defence into offence.

The grim irony was that just 150 miles away, in Paris itself life carried on in relative normality. The French government's suppression of the stark reality of the Battle of Verdun meant civilians neither knew nor cared about the horrors their fellow countrymen on the front line were experiencing, soldiers being paid sixty times less than the average factory worker. By 1917, the soldiers' mounting dissatisfaction would become outright mutiny.

1 June saw the Germans unleash a new offensive against Verdun, pushing to within two and a half miles of the town itself. Assaults were mounted against Fort Souville, the attack opening with a bombardment of French positions with Germany's newest WMD – diphosgene gas, which when inhaled, turned to hydrochloric acid in the lungs. Although they took the outlying positions at Thiaumont and Fleury, the fort held out until 6 September.

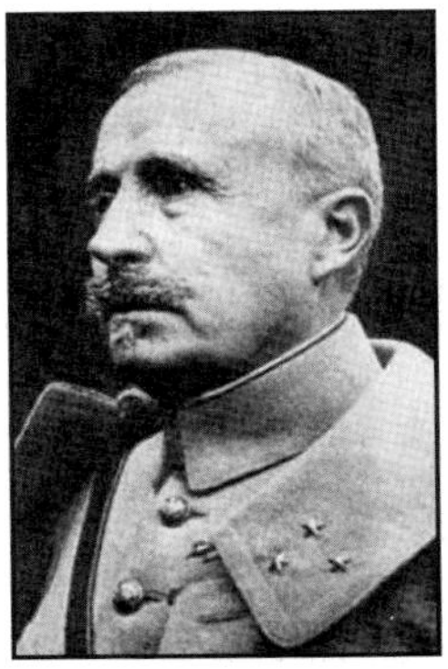

TOP: Blue recounts the shelling of Fort Vaux.

ABOVE: Robert Nivelle.

BELOW: Between firefights in the tunnels below Fort Vaux.

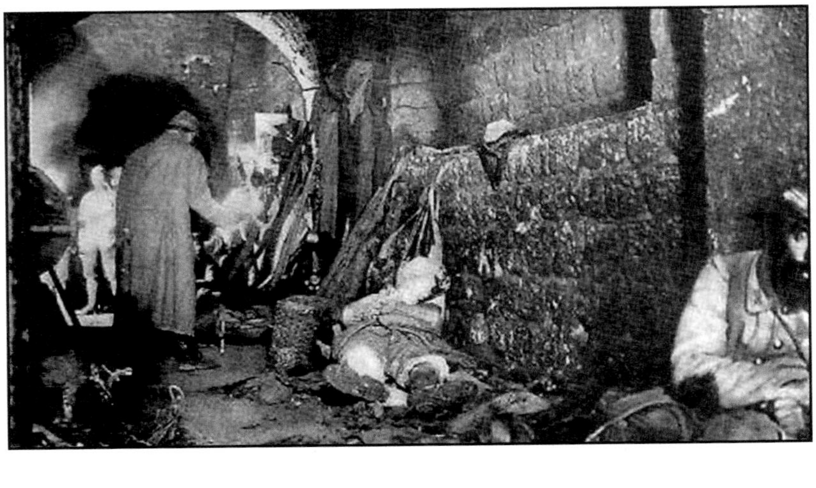

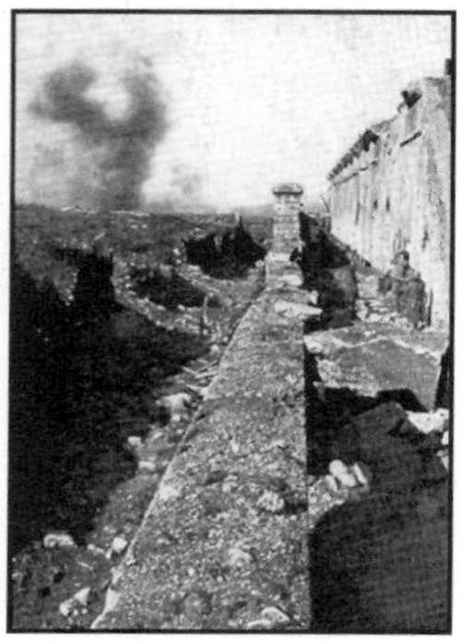

ABOVE: The moat at Fort Vaux.

BELOW: An aerial photograph of the ruins of Fort Vaux.

Elsewhere, events began to unfold that were to have a profound influence on the fighting. Preparations had been underway by the Allies to open a new offensive at the Somme. The exhausted French hoped the push would help bring relief at Verdun. Joffe even urged the British to open the attack a month early and on 24 June, the preliminary bombardment began. The attack required the Germans to re-deploy some of its artillery to help counter the British offensive. They were also forced to send fifteen divisions to the Eastern Front to help halt a Russian offensive.

By the end of summer, the Germans were spent. Von Falkenhayn was increasingly criticised for his lack of success. His battle of attrition was proving as costly to the Germans as to the French. Finally on 29 August he was dismissed from the Western Front and sent off to the Transylvanian Front. His replacement was one of his harshest critics, Paul von Hindenburg.

The French switch to the offensive manifested itself as a counterattack on 21 October. Supported by new, giant 400mm guns and air cover, three French divisions re-took Fort Douaumont on the 24th from seven German divisions. On 2 November, Fort Vaux was recaptured. The fighting left behind a devastated moonscape. A French officer noted: "Our modern battles afford no spectacle; they are cruel and mysterious. There are big empty spaces clotted with shell holes and cut with long furrows which mark the soil as the veins make marble patterns on the hand." The battle rumbled on into December until, on 11 December, a final French offensive drove the Germans back to their original start line, leaving 11,000 prisoners and 115 artillery pieces behind.

Von Hindenburg finally dispensed with von Falkenhayn's strategy, bringing the battle to an end on 18 December. Losses on both sides were grievous. "The Mincing Machine of Verdun" claimed over a million casualties, but accurate figures remain unknown, with estimates varying between 360,000 and 550,000 French, and 340,000 and 434,000 German casualties, of which around half were fatalities.

As with the Somme, such horrific losses left scar tissue across the national psyche. Verdun came to represent an exercise in futility for the nations concerned. Ten months of appalling losses resulted in no significant strategic gain. Von Falkenhayn is said to have envisaged Verdun as an effort to "bleed France white." Apocryphal or not, his claim proved only half right. He managed to do the same to his own army as well. ✛

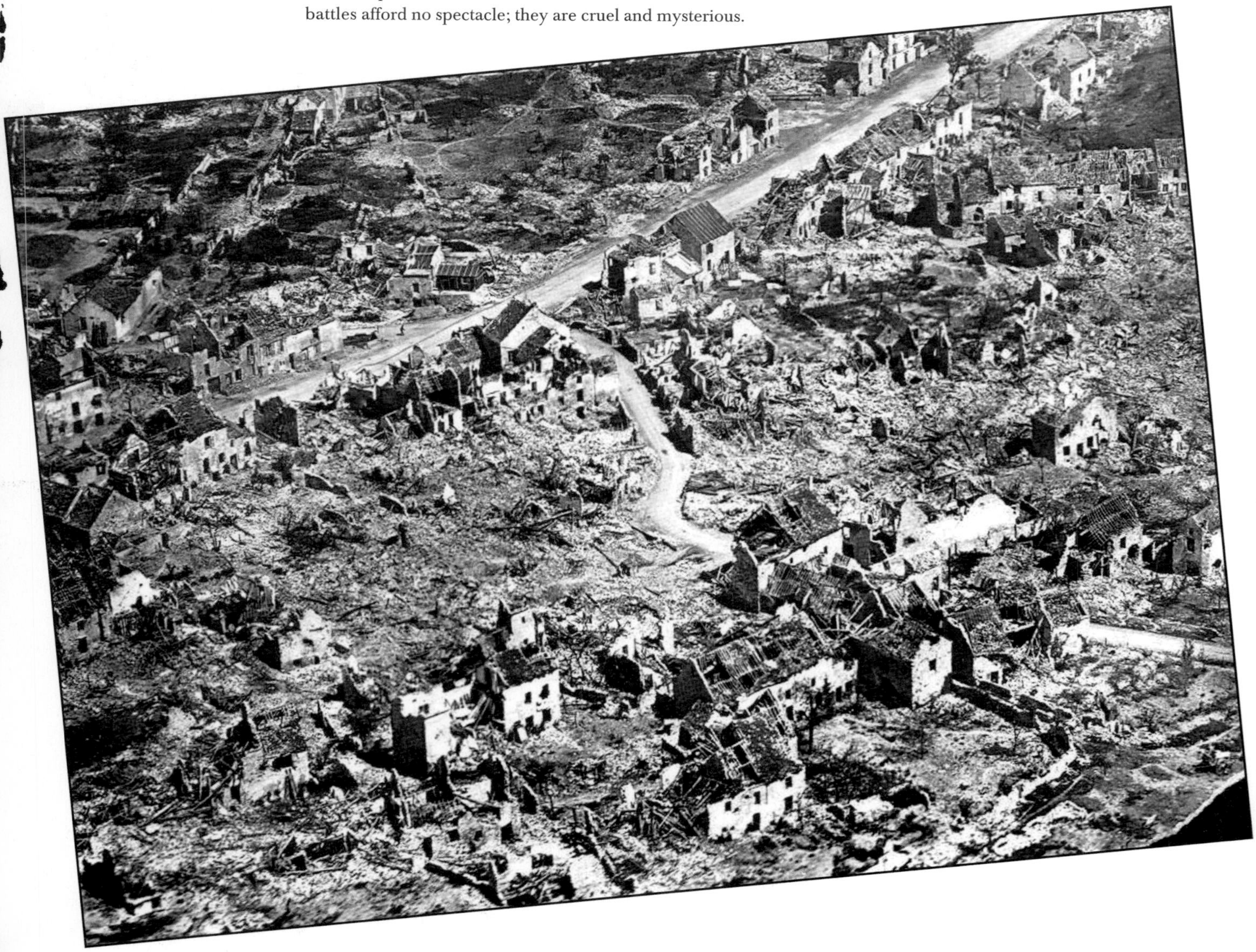

PREVIOUSLY IN *CHARLEY'S WAR*

2 June 1916: Charley Bourne, who has joined the army aged sixteen (two years less than the official conscription age), is sent with his unit to France, several weeks before the Battle of the Somme.

1 July 1916: The Battle of the Somme begins. Charley and his comrades spare a German soldier they find, but he is shot in cold blood by Lieutenant Snell.

2 July – 14 July 1916: Charley, "Ginger" Jones and "Lonely" are captured. "Lonely" reveals the secret of the lost platoon, his old unit. During the escape, Charley inhales poison gas and becomes gravely ill.

14 July 1916: Charley, Ginger and "Lonely" meet a group of British cavalrymen. "Lonely" bravely sacrifices himself during a German attack.

1 August 1916: On Charley's seventeenth birthday, the British forces accidentally begin shelling their own side. Charley volunteers to be a communications runner to try to end the bombardment, but is delayed by Snell. Lieutenant Thomas orders Charley's unit to retreat, and is later arrested for cowardice.

August 1916: Charley refuses his order to execute Lieutenant Thomas (who is killed in any case, aged 22). Charley and his comrade "Weeper" are sentenced to fourteen days' punishment, strapped to the wheel of a field gun.

September 1916: "Ginger" is killed by a stray shell, causing Charley to suffer a temporary breakdown. Charley's unit is reinforced by tanks, and on 15 September Charley is joined by his cowardly brother-in-law, "Oiley". Oiley deliberately injures himself to be sent home, and Charley covers for him.

October 17, 1916: Colonel Zeiss, a German commanding officer, unleashes the "Judgement Troopers". These 'dirty tricks' soldiers use concealed weapons and gas attacks in defiance of the established conventions of war.

October 1916: Charley is wounded during the battle against the "Judgement Troopers", but sent back to the lines. Eventually, Colonel Zeiss' plan is halted by the German High Command, but before he can celebrate, Charley is badly injured by shrapnel from a stray shell.

November 1916: Charley, an "unknown soldier" suffering from amnesia, is recuperating in a military hospital when Sergeant Tozer arrives and recognises him.

February 18, 1917: Charley survives a U-Boat attack on the *York Castle*, the hospital ship returning him home.

February 20, 1917: A huge, Zeppelin-launched German air-raid targets Silvertown, Charley's East End home and location of several munitions factories. Desperately trying to warn his mother, Charley rushes into the factory, as a German firebomb falls towards it… ✛

BELOW: Charley and his mother are in grave danger during the Zeppelin raid on Silvertown.

BOTTOM: A devastated Charley buries his friend 'Ginger'.

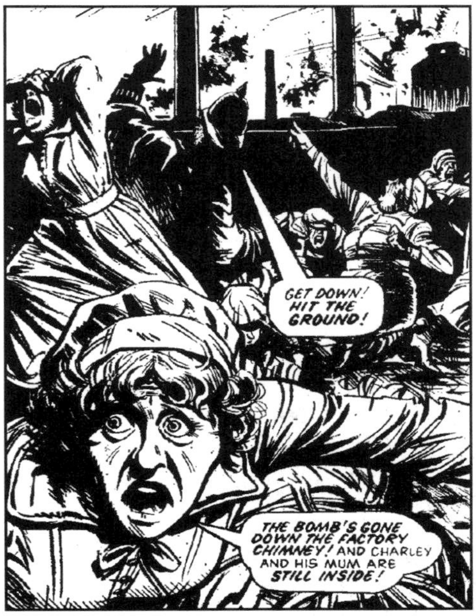
GET DOWN! HIT THE GROUND!
THE BOMB'S GONE DOWN THE FACTORY CHIMNEY! AND CHARLEY AND HIS MUM ARE STILL INSIDE!

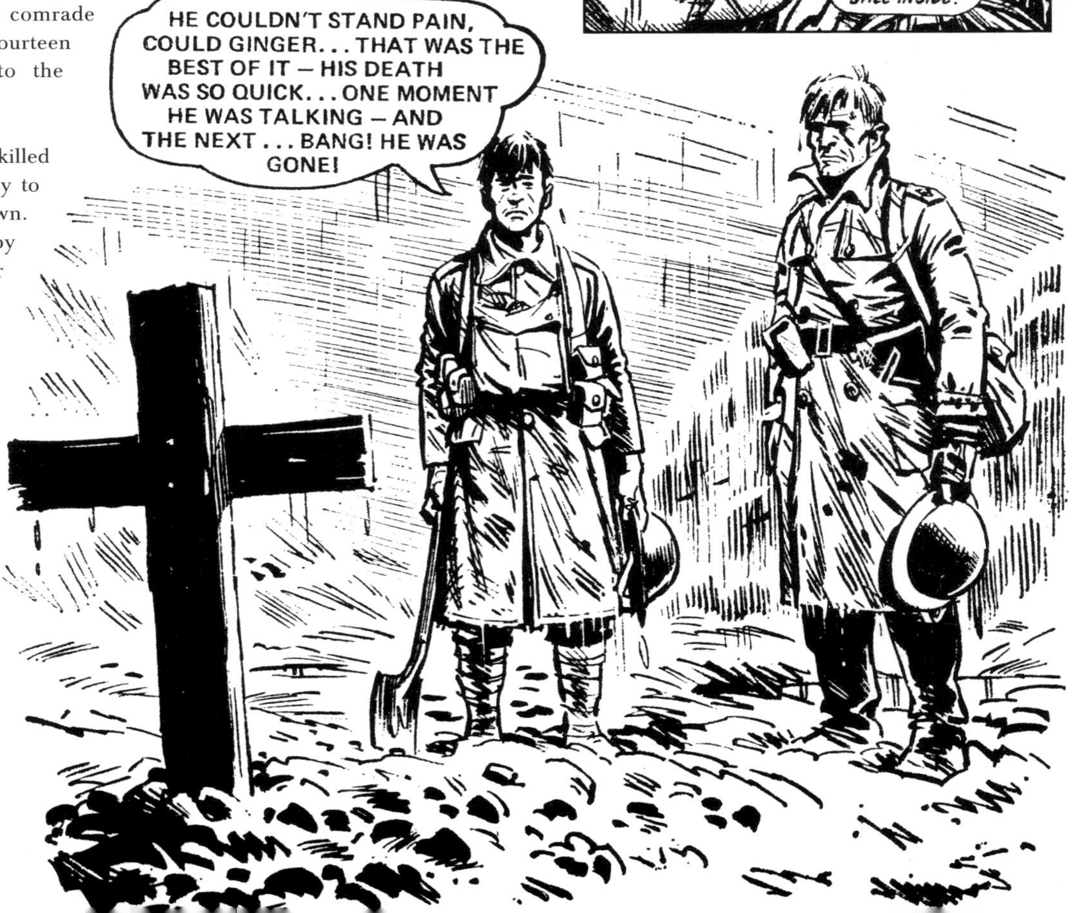
HE COULDN'T STAND PAIN, COULD GINGER... THAT WAS THE BEST OF IT — HIS DEATH WAS SO QUICK... ONE MOMENT HE WAS TALKING — AND THE NEXT ... BANG! HE WAS GONE!

Charley's War

FEBRUARY 1917. A ZEPPELIN RAID ON LONDON HAD BEGUN AND THE MUNITION FACTORIES IN LONDON'S EAST END WERE AMONG THE AIRSHIPS' MAIN TARGETS. *CHARLEY BOURNE* WAS INSIDE ONE OF THE FACTORIES, LOOKING FOR HIS MOTHER. WHEN HE FOUND HER, AN *INCENDIARY BOMB* BURST INTO THE FACTORY!

FIRE!

OUTSIDE, *CHARLEY'S DAD* - A SPECIAL CONSTABLE - WAS AMONG THE POLICE TRYING TO RESTORE ORDER.

HOLD ON! HAVE YOU SEEN MY MISSUS, GLADYS?

SHE'S STILL *INSIDE*, MISTER BOURNE! YOUR LAD, CHARLEY, HAS GONE IN TO GET HER! LET ME GO - WE'LL ALL BE *KILLED*!

THAT PLACE IS LIKE A *TINDERBOX*! I'VE GOT TO GO IN!

DON'T BE A FOOL, BOURNE! THERE'S NOTHING YOU CAN DO FOR THEM! WE'VE GOT TO GET THE REST OF THESE WORKERS CLEAR!

WE CAN'T GO PAST THOSE BOXES OF *T.N.T.* CHARLEY!

WE'VE *GOT* TO, MA... IT'S THE ONLY WAY OUT!

FULMINAT... DAN...

HIGH EXPLOSI...

T.N.T.

DAN...

HERE, MA... YOU DON'T HALF LOOK A SIGHT IN THAT MASK! IF THE ZEPPELINS SAW YOU NOW, THEY'D RUN A MILE!

WHY, YOU *CHEEKY MONKEY*!

LESS OF YOUR *LIP*! YOU'RE NOT TOO OLD TO GET THE BACK OF MY HAND, YOU KNOW!

FULMINATE OF MER... DANGER

HIGH EXPLOSIVE

WRITER P MILLS

ARTIST J COLQUHOUN

LETTERER M PETERS

BY KEEPING HIS MOTHER'S MIND OFF THE DANGER, CHARLEY EASED HER PAST THE T.N.T.

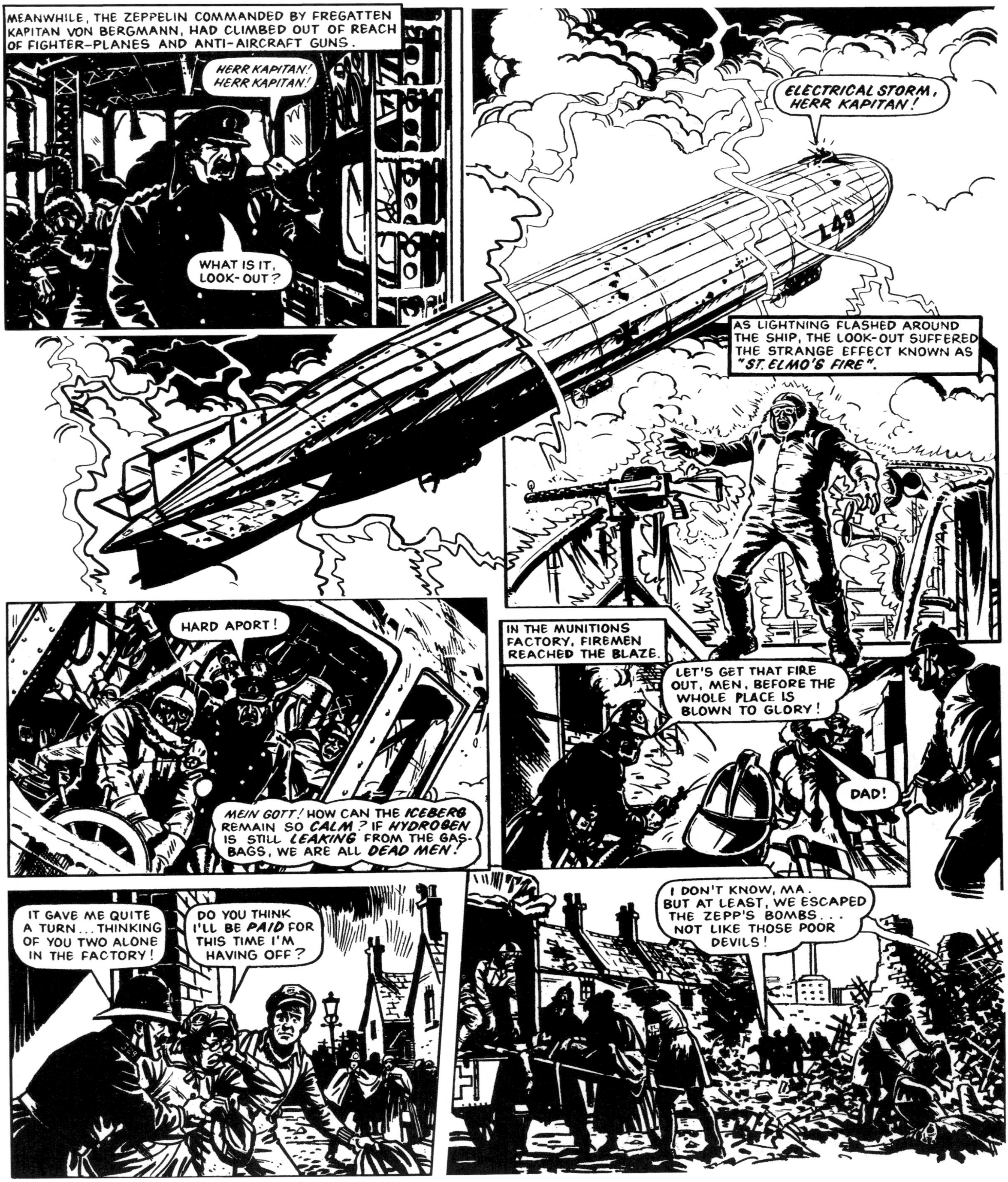
MEANWHILE, THE ZEPPELIN COMMANDED BY FREGATTEN KAPITAN VON BERGMANN, HAD CLIMBED OUT OF REACH OF FIGHTER-PLANES AND ANTI-AIRCRAFT GUNS.
HERR KAPITAN! HERR KAPITAN!
WHAT IS IT, LOOK-OUT?
ELECTRICAL STORM, HERR KAPITAN!
L49
AS LIGHTNING FLASHED AROUND THE SHIP, THE LOOK-OUT SUFFERED THE STRANGE EFFECT KNOWN AS "ST. ELMO'S FIRE".
HARD APORT!
MEIN GOTT! HOW CAN THE ICEBERG REMAIN SO CALM? IF HYDROGEN IS STILL LEAKING FROM THE GAS-BAGS, WE ARE ALL DEAD MEN!
IN THE MUNITIONS FACTORY, FIREMEN REACHED THE BLAZE.
LET'S GET THAT FIRE OUT, MEN, BEFORE THE WHOLE PLACE IS BLOWN TO GLORY!
DAD!
IT GAVE ME QUITE A TURN... THINKING OF YOU TWO ALONE IN THE FACTORY!
DO YOU THINK I'LL BE PAID FOR THIS TIME I'M HAVING OFF?
I DON'T KNOW, MA. BUT AT LEAST, WE ESCAPED THE ZEPP'S BOMBS... NOT LIKE THOSE POOR DEVILS!

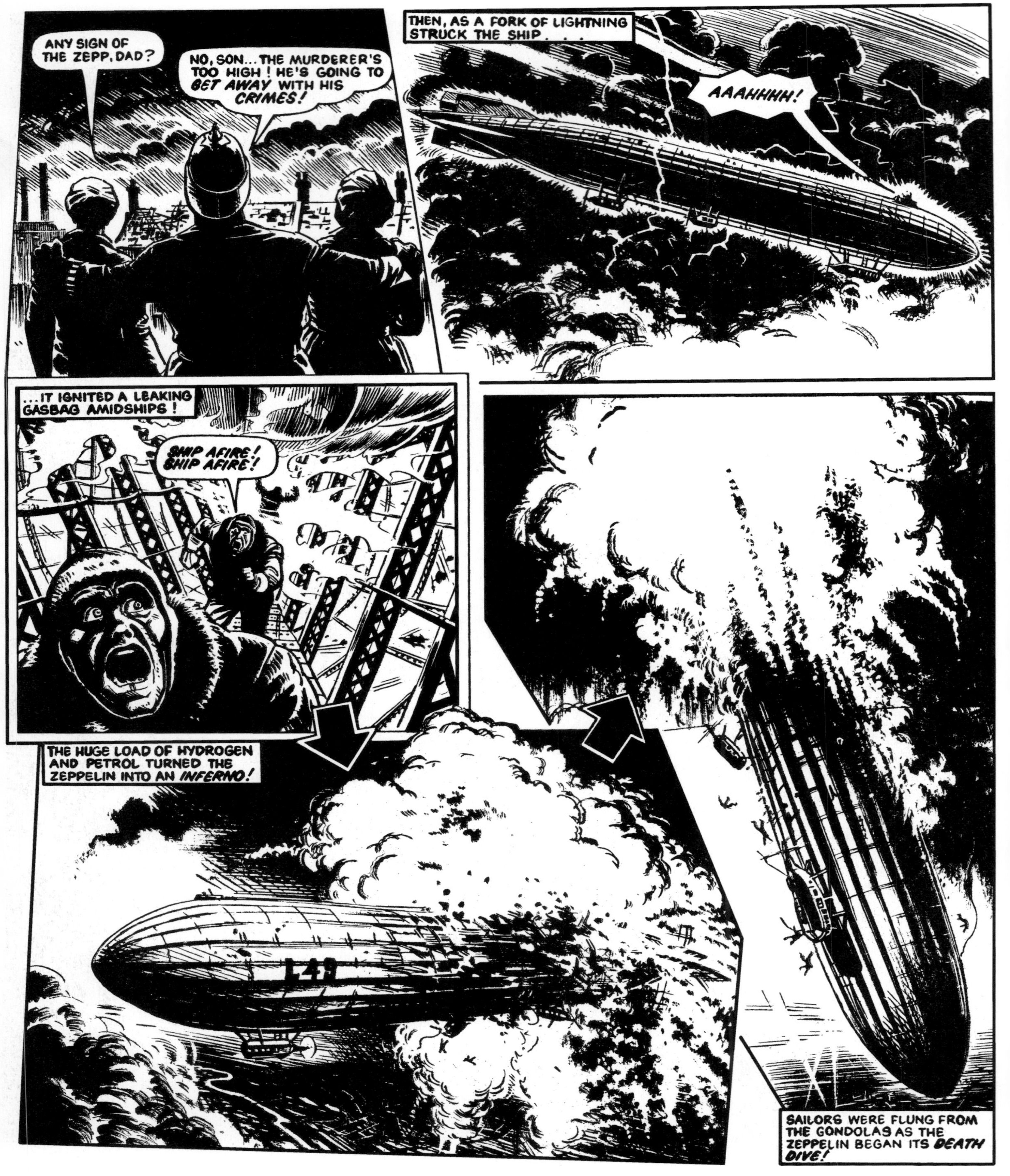
ANY SIGN OF THE ZEPP, DAD?
NO, SON... THE MURDERER'S TOO HIGH! HE'S GOING TO GET AWAY WITH HIS CRIMES!
THEN, AS A FORK OF LIGHTNING STRUCK THE SHIP . . .
AAAHHHH!
...IT IGNITED A LEAKING GASBAG AMIDSHIPS!
SHIP AFIRE! SHIP AFIRE!
THE HUGE LOAD OF HYDROGEN AND PETROL TURNED THE ZEPPELIN INTO AN INFERNO!
L49
SAILORS WERE FLUNG FROM THE GONDOLAS AS THE ZEPPELIN BEGAN ITS DEATH DIVE!

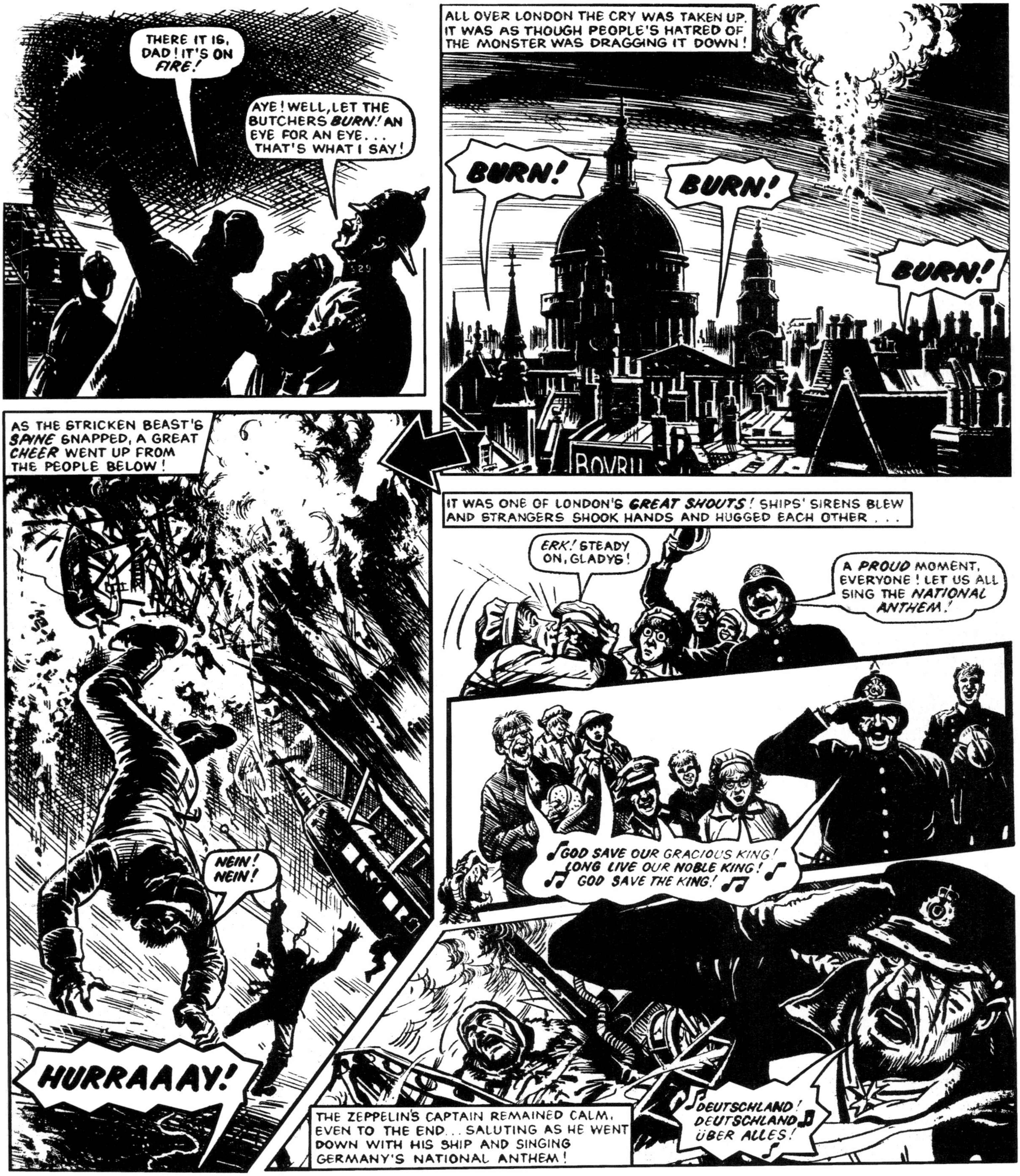
THERE IT IS, DAD! IT'S ON FIRE!
AYE! WELL, LET THE BUTCHERS BURN! AN EYE FOR AN EYE... THAT'S WHAT I SAY!
ALL OVER LONDON THE CRY WAS TAKEN UP. IT WAS AS THOUGH PEOPLE'S HATRED OF THE MONSTER WAS DRAGGING IT DOWN!
BURN!
BURN!
BURN!
AS THE STRICKEN BEAST'S SPINE SNAPPED, A GREAT CHEER WENT UP FROM THE PEOPLE BELOW!
NEIN! NEIN!
HURRAAAY!
IT WAS ONE OF LONDON'S GREAT SHOUTS! SHIPS' SIRENS BLEW AND STRANGERS SHOOK HANDS AND HUGGED EACH OTHER...
ERK! STEADY ON, GLADYS!
A PROUD MOMENT, EVERYONE! LET US ALL SING THE NATIONAL ANTHEM!
GOD SAVE OUR GRACIOUS KING! LONG LIVE OUR NOBLE KING! GOD SAVE THE KING!
THE ZEPPELIN'S CAPTAIN REMAINED CALM, EVEN TO THE END... SALUTING AS HE WENT DOWN WITH HIS SHIP AND SINGING GERMANY'S NATIONAL ANTHEM!
DEUTSCHLAND! DEUTSCHLAND ÜBER ALLES!

CHARLEY'S WAR

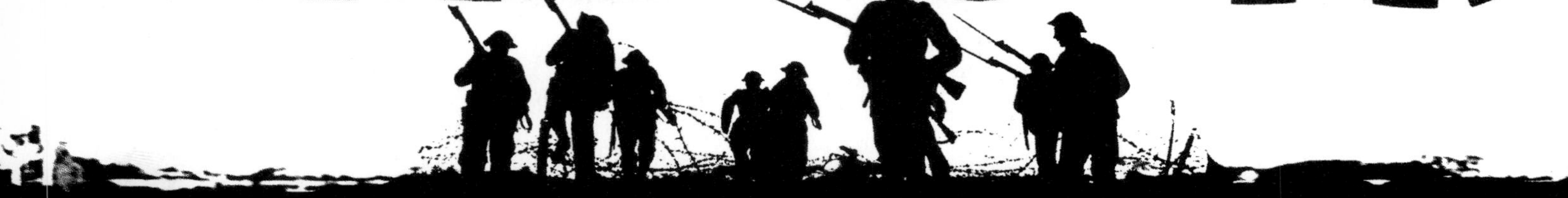

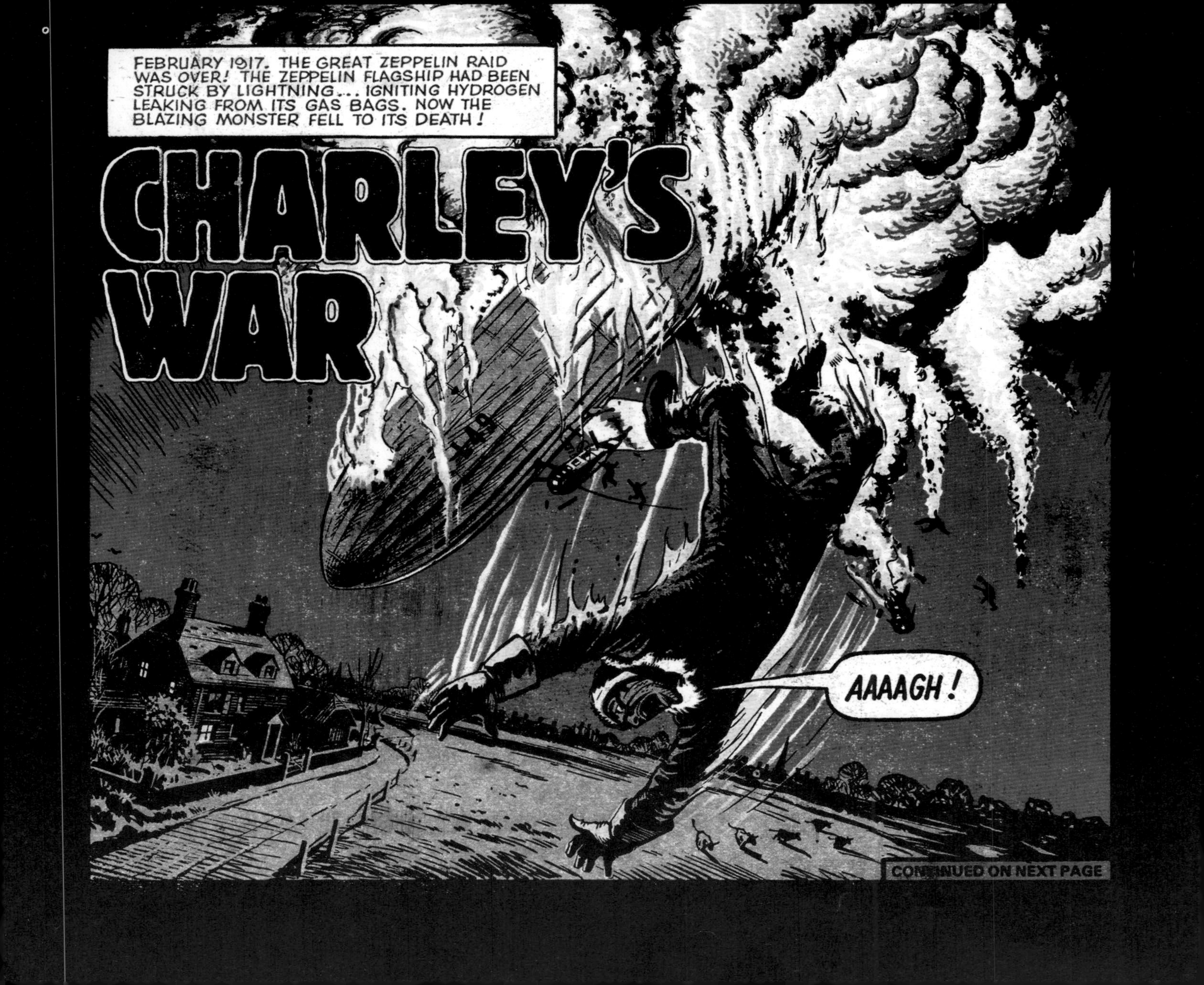

FEBRUARY 1917. THE GREAT ZEPPELIN RAID WAS OVER! THE ZEPPELIN FLAGSHIP HAD BEEN STRUCK BY LIGHTNING... IGNITING HYDROGEN LEAKING FROM ITS GAS BAGS. NOW THE BLAZING MONSTER FELL TO ITS DEATH!
CHARLEY'S WAR
AAAAGH!

CONTINUED ON NEXT PAGE

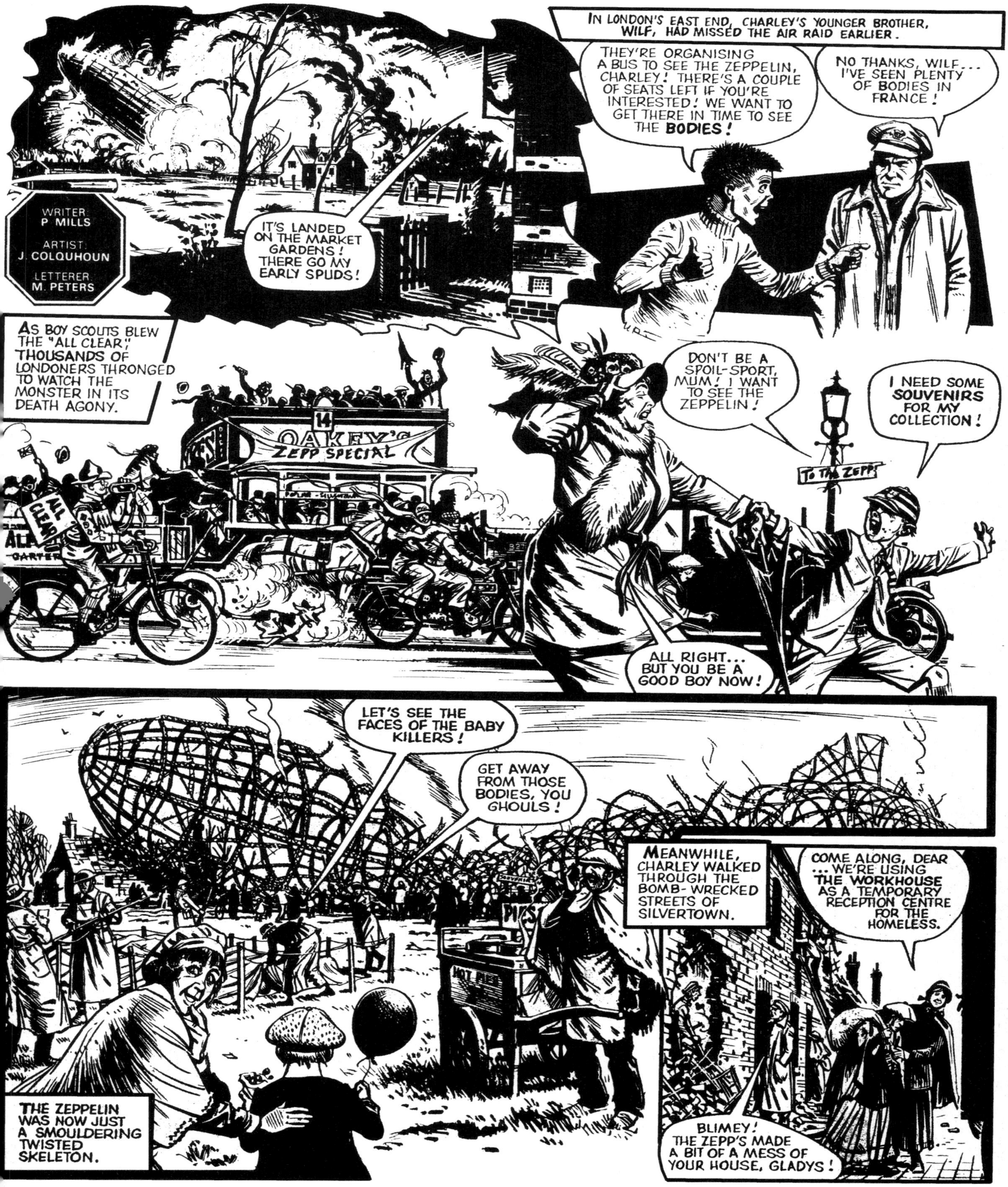
WRITER: P MILLS
ARTIST: J. COLQUHOUN
LETTERER: M. PETERS
IT'S LANDED ON THE MARKET GARDENS! THERE GO MY EARLY SPUDS!
IN LONDON'S EAST END, CHARLEY'S YOUNGER BROTHER, WILF, HAD MISSED THE AIR RAID EARLIER.
THEY'RE ORGANISING A BUS TO SEE THE ZEPPELIN, CHARLEY! THERE'S A COUPLE OF SEATS LEFT IF YOU'RE INTERESTED! WE WANT TO GET THERE IN TIME TO SEE THE BODIES!
NO THANKS, WILF... I'VE SEEN PLENTY OF BODIES IN FRANCE!
AS BOY SCOUTS BLEW THE "ALL CLEAR," THOUSANDS OF LONDONERS THRONGED TO WATCH THE MONSTER IN ITS DEATH AGONY.
14
OAKEY'S
ZEPP SPECIAL
ALL CLEAR
DON'T BE A SPOIL-SPORT, MUM! I WANT TO SEE THE ZEPPELIN!
I NEED SOME SOUVENIRS FOR MY COLLECTION!
TO THE ZEPP
ALL RIGHT... BUT YOU BE A GOOD BOY NOW!
LET'S SEE THE FACES OF THE BABY KILLERS!
GET AWAY FROM THOSE BODIES, YOU GHOULS!
THE ZEPPELIN WAS NOW JUST A SMOULDERING TWISTED SKELETON.
MEANWHILE, CHARLEY WALKED THROUGH THE BOMB-WRECKED STREETS OF SILVERTOWN.
COME ALONG, DEAR ... WE'RE USING THE WORKHOUSE AS A TEMPORARY RECEPTION CENTRE FOR THE HOMELESS.
BLIMEY! THE ZEPP'S MADE A BIT OF A MESS OF YOUR HOUSE, GLADYS!

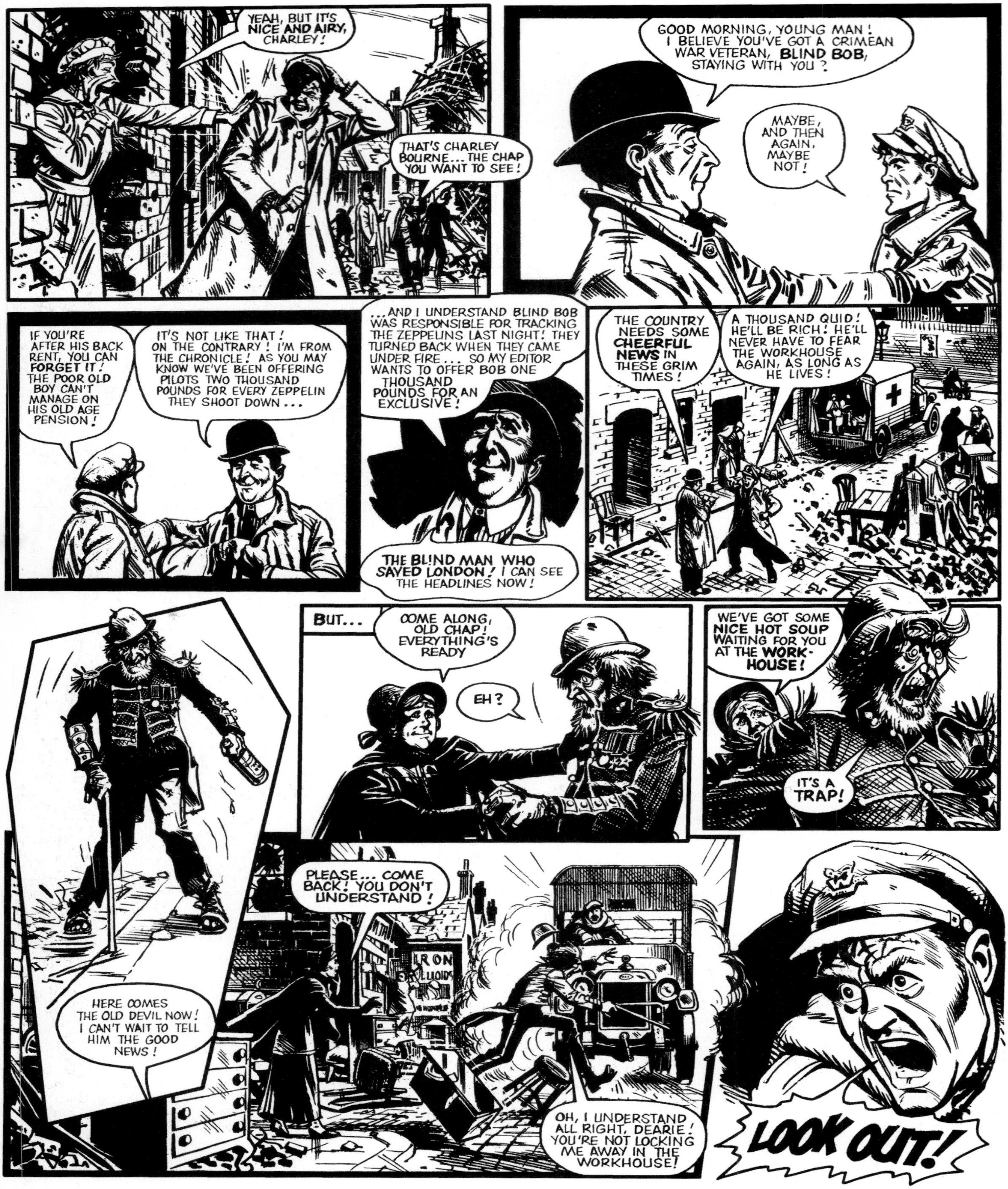
YEAH, BUT IT'S NICE AND AIRY, CHARLEY!
THAT'S CHARLEY BOURNE... THE CHAP YOU WANT TO SEE!
GOOD MORNING, YOUNG MAN! I BELIEVE YOU'VE GOT A CRIMEAN WAR VETERAN, BLIND BOB, STAYING WITH YOU?
MAYBE, AND THEN AGAIN, MAYBE NOT!
IF YOU'RE AFTER HIS BACK RENT, YOU CAN FORGET IT! THE POOR OLD BOY CAN'T MANAGE ON HIS OLD AGE PENSION!
IT'S NOT LIKE THAT! ON THE CONTRARY! I'M FROM THE CHRONICLE! AS YOU MAY KNOW WE'VE BEEN OFFERING PILOTS TWO THOUSAND POUNDS FOR EVERY ZEPPELIN THEY SHOOT DOWN...
...AND I UNDERSTAND BLIND BOB WAS RESPONSIBLE FOR TRACKING THE ZEPPELINS LAST NIGHT! THEY TURNED BACK WHEN THEY CAME UNDER FIRE... SO MY EDITOR WANTS TO OFFER BOB ONE THOUSAND POUNDS FOR AN EXCLUSIVE!
THE BLIND MAN WHO SAVED LONDON! I CAN SEE THE HEADLINES NOW!
THE COUNTRY NEEDS SOME CHEERFUL NEWS IN THESE GRIM TIMES!
A THOUSAND QUID! HE'LL BE RICH! HE'LL NEVER HAVE TO FEAR THE WORKHOUSE AGAIN, AS LONG AS HE LIVES!
HERE COMES THE OLD DEVIL NOW! I CAN'T WAIT TO TELL HIM THE GOOD NEWS!
BUT...
COME ALONG, OLD CHAP! EVERYTHING'S READY
EH?
WE'VE GOT SOME NICE HOT SOUP WAITING FOR YOU AT THE WORK-HOUSE!
IT'S A TRAP!
PLEASE... COME BACK! YOU DON'T UNDERSTAND!
IRON
OH, I UNDERSTAND ALL RIGHT, DEARIE! YOU'RE NOT LOCKING ME AWAY IN THE WORKHOUSE!
LOOK OUT!

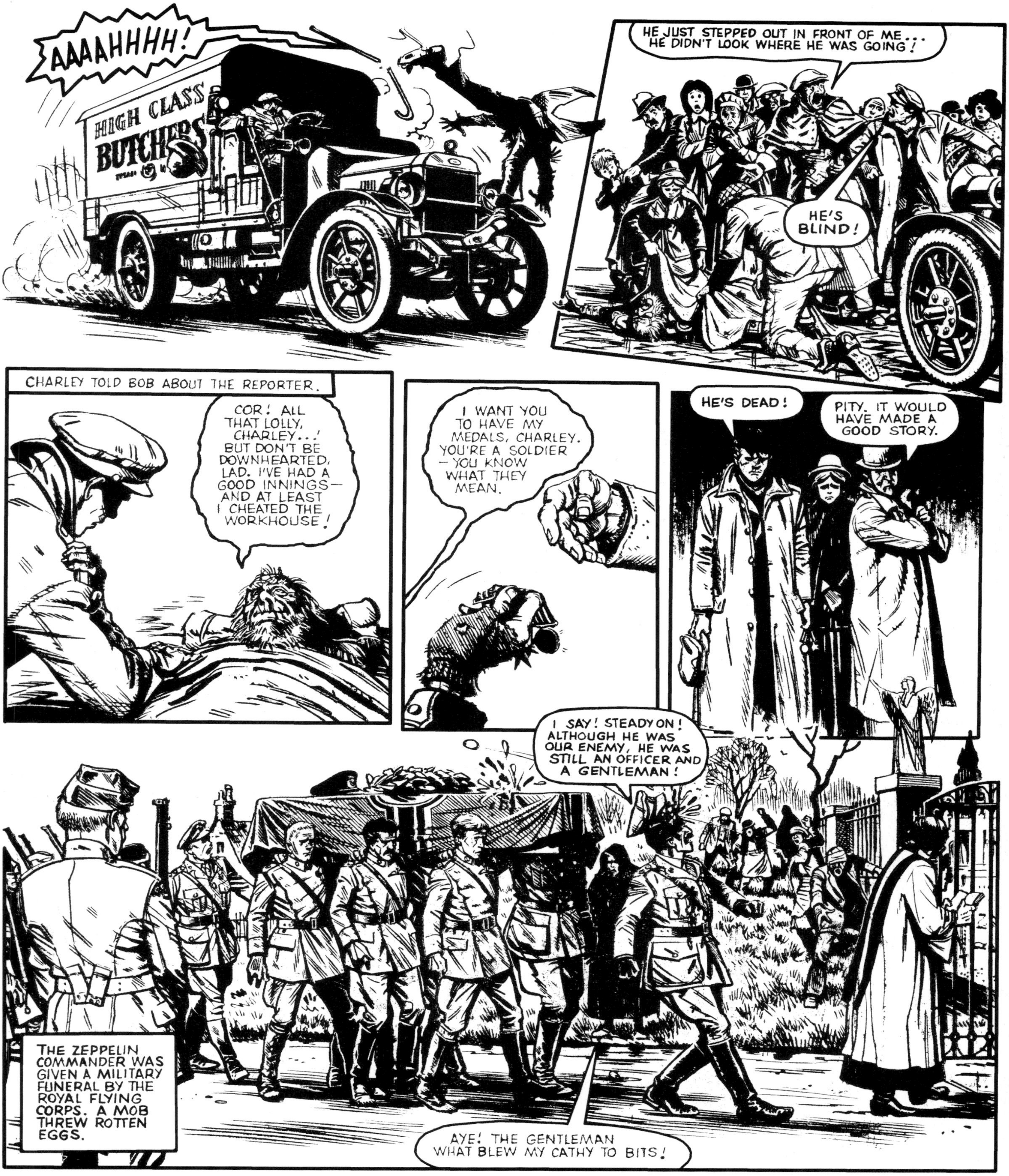
AAAAHHHH!
HIGH CLASS BUTCHERS
HE JUST STEPPED OUT IN FRONT OF ME... HE DIDN'T LOOK WHERE HE WAS GOING!
HE'S BLIND!
CHARLEY TOLD BOB ABOUT THE REPORTER.
COR! ALL THAT LOLLY, CHARLEY...! BUT DON'T BE DOWNHEARTED, LAD. I'VE HAD A GOOD INNINGS— AND AT LEAST I CHEATED THE WORKHOUSE!
I WANT YOU TO HAVE MY MEDALS, CHARLEY. YOU'RE A SOLDIER —YOU KNOW WHAT THEY MEAN.
HE'S DEAD!
PITY. IT WOULD HAVE MADE A GOOD STORY.
I SAY! STEADY ON! ALTHOUGH HE WAS OUR ENEMY, HE WAS STILL AN OFFICER AND A GENTLEMAN!
THE ZEPPELIN COMMANDER WAS GIVEN A MILITARY FUNERAL BY THE ROYAL FLYING CORPS. A MOB THREW ROTTEN EGGS.
AYE! THE GENTLEMAN WHAT BLEW MY CATHY TO BITS!

CHARLEY'S WAR

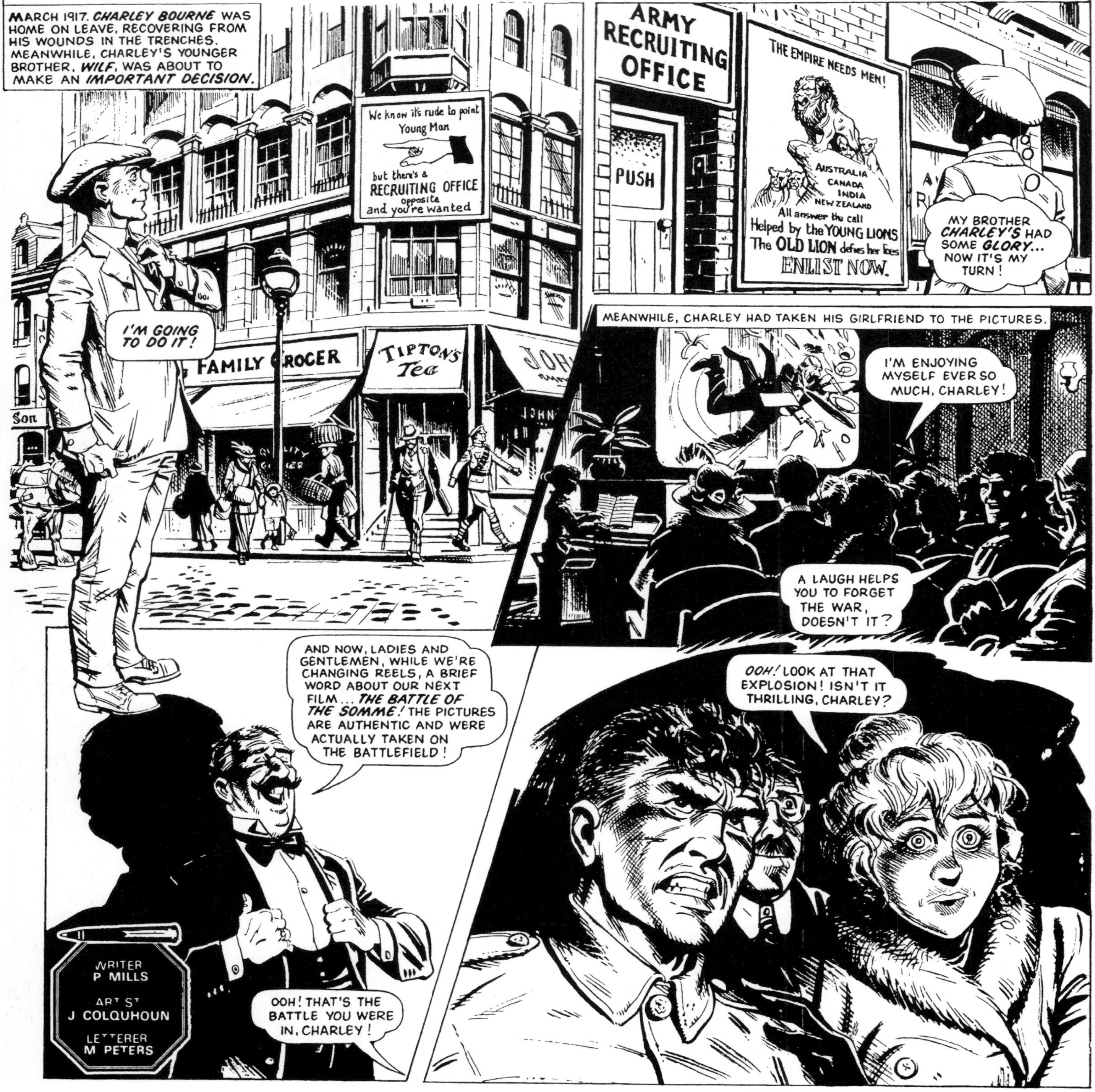

MARCH 1917. CHARLEY BOURNE WAS HOME ON LEAVE, RECOVERING FROM HIS WOUNDS IN THE TRENCHES. MEANWHILE, CHARLEY'S YOUNGER BROTHER, WILF, WAS ABOUT TO MAKE AN IMPORTANT DECISION.
We know it's rude to point Young Man but there's a RECRUITING OFFICE opposite and you're wanted
ARMY RECRUITING OFFICE
PUSH
THE EMPIRE NEEDS MEN!
AUSTRALIA CANADA INDIA NEW ZEALAND
All answer the call! Helped by the YOUNG LIONS The OLD LION defies her foes ENLIST NOW.
MY BROTHER CHARLEY'S HAD SOME GLORY... NOW IT'S MY TURN!
I'M GOING TO DO IT!
FAMILY GROCER
TIPTON'S Tea
MEANWHILE, CHARLEY HAD TAKEN HIS GIRLFRIEND TO THE PICTURES.
I'M ENJOYING MYSELF EVER SO MUCH, CHARLEY!
A LAUGH HELPS YOU TO FORGET THE WAR, DOESN'T IT?
AND NOW, LADIES AND GENTLEMEN, WHILE WE'RE CHANGING REELS, A BRIEF WORD ABOUT OUR NEXT FILM... THE BATTLE OF THE SOMME! THE PICTURES ARE AUTHENTIC AND WERE ACTUALLY TAKEN ON THE BATTLEFIELD!
OOH! THAT'S THE BATTLE YOU WERE IN, CHARLEY!
OOH! LOOK AT THAT EXPLOSION! ISN'T IT THRILLING, CHARLEY?
WRITER P MILLS
ARTIST J COLQUHOUN
LETTERER M PETERS

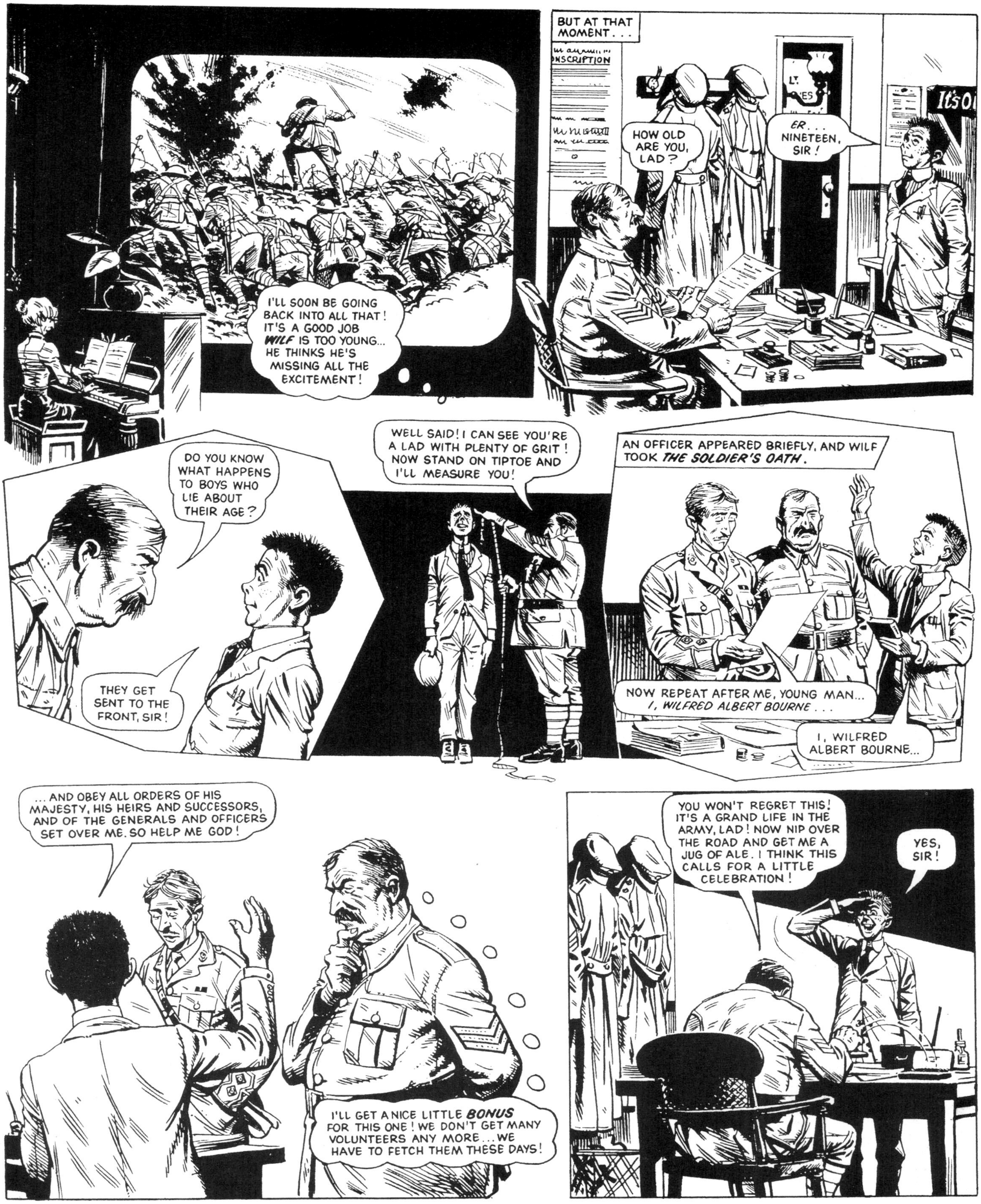
I'LL SOON BE GOING BACK INTO ALL THAT! IT'S A GOOD JOB WILF IS TOO YOUNG... HE THINKS HE'S MISSING ALL THE EXCITEMENT!
BUT AT THAT MOMENT...
HOW OLD ARE YOU, LAD?
ER... NINETEEN, SIR!
DO YOU KNOW WHAT HAPPENS TO BOYS WHO LIE ABOUT THEIR AGE?
THEY GET SENT TO THE FRONT, SIR!
WELL SAID! I CAN SEE YOU'RE A LAD WITH PLENTY OF GRIT! NOW STAND ON TIPTOE AND I'LL MEASURE YOU!
AN OFFICER APPEARED BRIEFLY, AND WILF TOOK THE SOLDIER'S OATH.
NOW REPEAT AFTER ME, YOUNG MAN... I, WILFRED ALBERT BOURNE...
I, WILFRED ALBERT BOURNE...
...AND OBEY ALL ORDERS OF HIS MAJESTY, HIS HEIRS AND SUCCESSORS, AND OF THE GENERALS AND OFFICERS SET OVER ME. SO HELP ME GOD!
I'LL GET A NICE LITTLE BONUS FOR THIS ONE! WE DON'T GET MANY VOLUNTEERS ANY MORE... WE HAVE TO FETCH THEM THESE DAYS!
YOU WON'T REGRET THIS! IT'S A GRAND LIFE IN THE ARMY, LAD! NOW NIP OVER THE ROAD AND GET ME A JUG OF ALE. I THINK THIS CALLS FOR A LITTLE CELEBRATION!
YES, SIR!

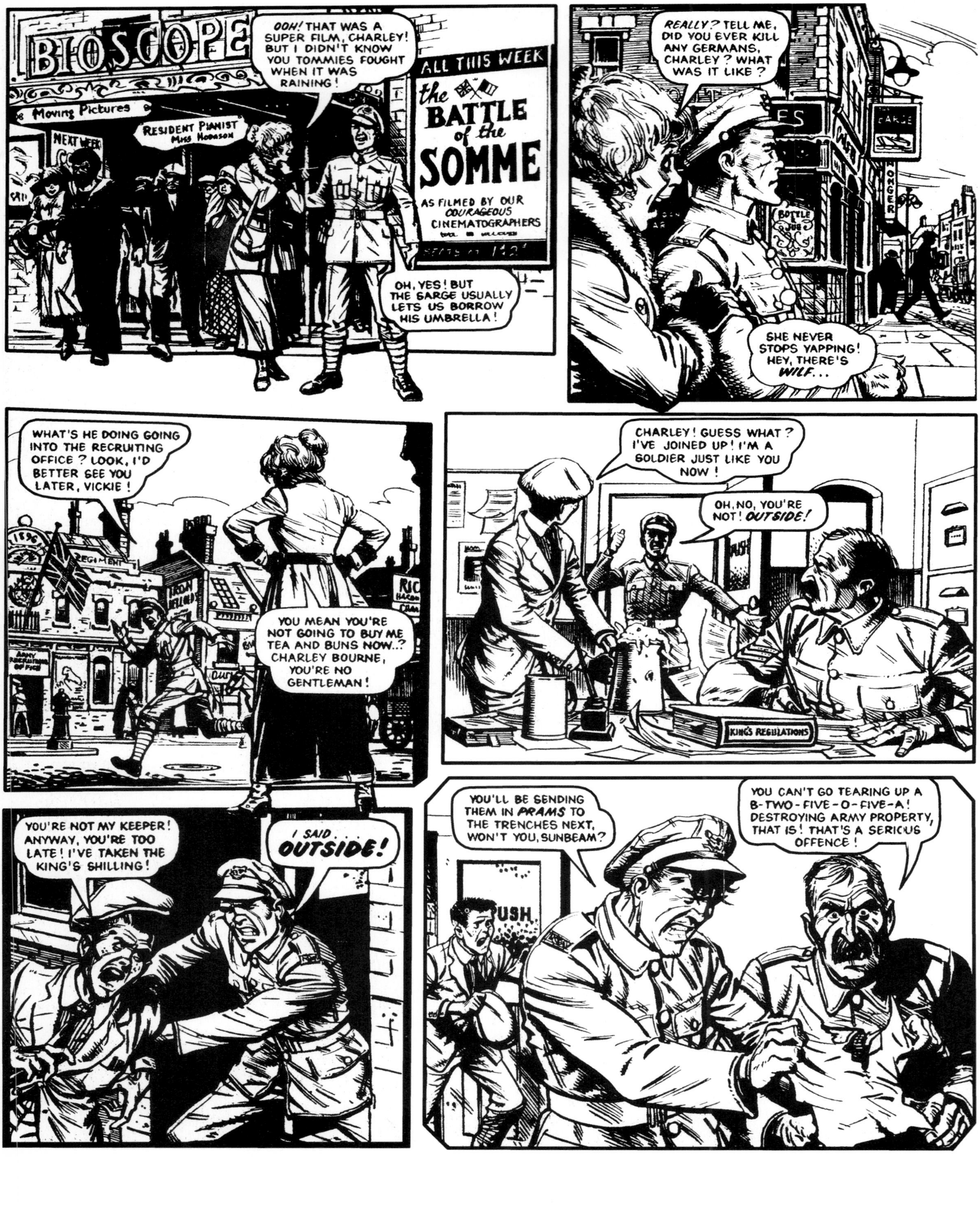
BIOSCOPE
Moving Pictures
RESIDENT PIANIST Miss Hodgson
NEXT WEEK
OOH! THAT WAS A SUPER FILM, CHARLEY! BUT I DIDN'T KNOW YOU TOMMIES FOUGHT WHEN IT WAS RAINING!
ALL THIS WEEK
the BATTLE of the SOMME
AS FILMED BY OUR COURAGEOUS CINEMATOGRAPHERS
OH, YES! BUT THE SARGE USUALLY LETS US BORROW HIS UMBRELLA!
REALLY? TELL ME, DID YOU EVER KILL ANY GERMANS, CHARLEY? WHAT WAS IT LIKE?
SHE NEVER STOPS YAPPING! HEY, THERE'S WILF...
WHAT'S HE DOING GOING INTO THE RECRUITING OFFICE? LOOK, I'D BETTER SEE YOU LATER, VICKIE!
YOU MEAN YOU'RE NOT GOING TO BUY ME TEA AND BUNS NOW..? CHARLEY BOURNE, YOU'RE NO GENTLEMAN!
CHARLEY! GUESS WHAT? I'VE JOINED UP! I'M A SOLDIER JUST LIKE YOU NOW!
OH, NO, YOU'RE NOT! OUTSIDE!
KING'S REGULATIONS
YOU'RE NOT MY KEEPER! ANYWAY, YOU'RE TOO LATE! I'VE TAKEN THE KING'S SHILLING!
I SAID... OUTSIDE!
YOU'LL BE SENDING THEM IN PRAMS TO THE TRENCHES NEXT, WON'T YOU, SUNBEAM?
YOU CAN'T GO TEARING UP A B-TWO-FIVE-O-FIVE-A! DESTROYING ARMY PROPERTY, THAT IS! THAT'S A SERIOUS OFFENCE!

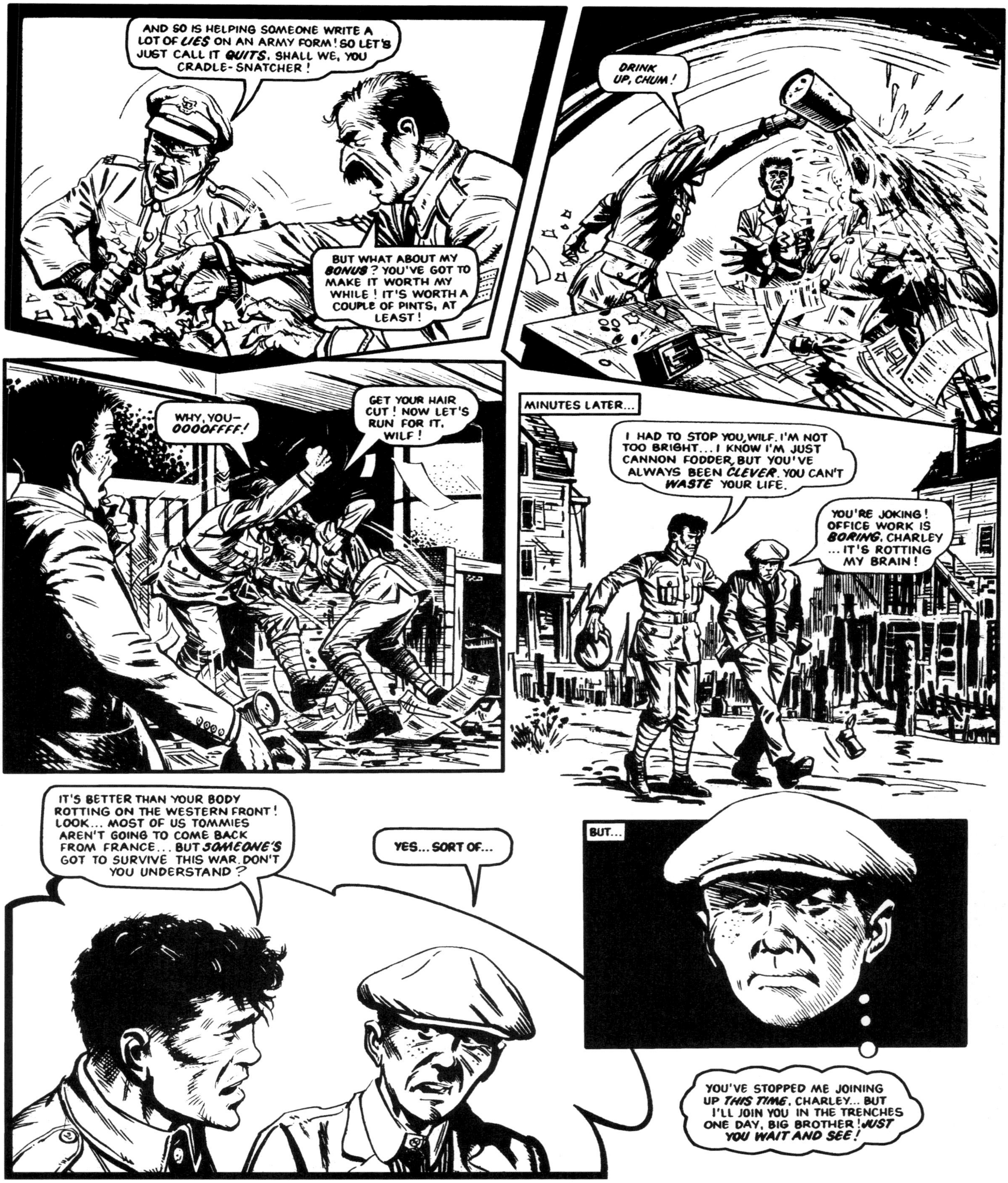
AND SO IS HELPING SOMEONE WRITE A LOT OF LIES ON AN ARMY FORM! SO LET'S JUST CALL IT QUITS, SHALL WE, YOU CRADLE-SNATCHER!
BUT WHAT ABOUT MY BONUS? YOU'VE GOT TO MAKE IT WORTH MY WHILE! IT'S WORTH A COUPLE OF PINTS, AT LEAST!
DRINK UP, CHUM!
WHY, YOU- OOOOFFFF!
GET YOUR HAIR CUT! NOW LET'S RUN FOR IT, WILF!
MINUTES LATER...
I HAD TO STOP YOU, WILF. I'M NOT TOO BRIGHT... I KNOW I'M JUST CANNON FODDER, BUT YOU'VE ALWAYS BEEN CLEVER. YOU CAN'T WASTE YOUR LIFE.
YOU'RE JOKING! OFFICE WORK IS BORING, CHARLEY ... IT'S ROTTING MY BRAIN!
IT'S BETTER THAN YOUR BODY ROTTING ON THE WESTERN FRONT! LOOK... MOST OF US TOMMIES AREN'T GOING TO COME BACK FROM FRANCE... BUT SOMEONE'S GOT TO SURVIVE THIS WAR. DON'T YOU UNDERSTAND?
YES... SORT OF...
BUT...
YOU'VE STOPPED ME JOINING UP THIS TIME, CHARLEY... BUT I'LL JOIN YOU IN THE TRENCHES ONE DAY, BIG BROTHER! JUST YOU WAIT AND SEE!

CHARLEY'S WAR

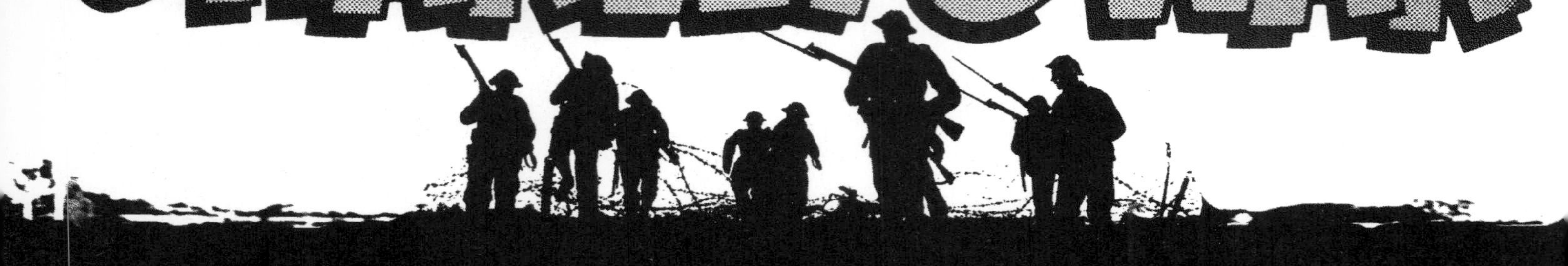

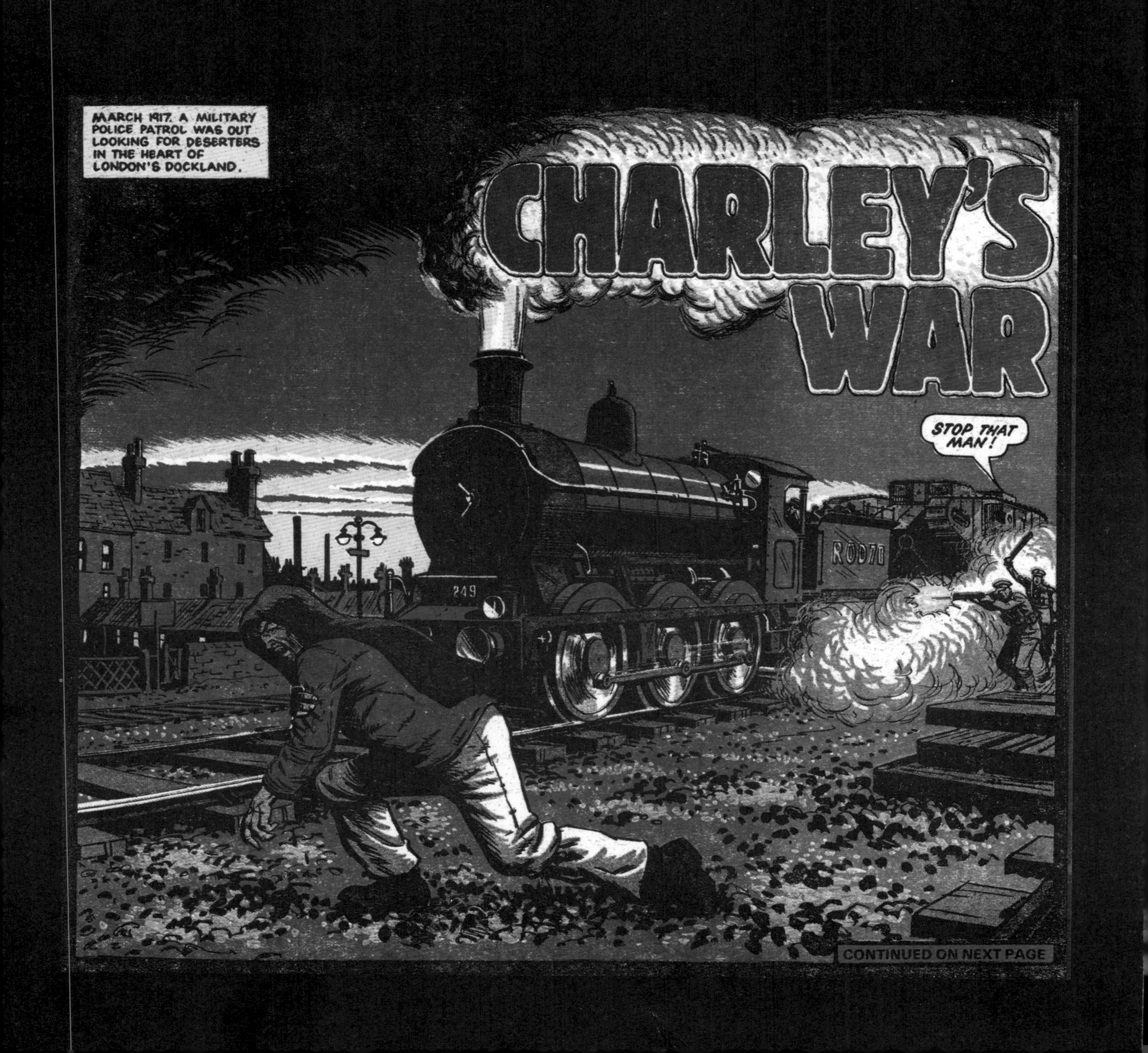
MARCH 1917. A MILITARY POLICE PATROL WAS OUT LOOKING FOR DESERTERS IN THE HEART OF LONDON'S DOCKLAND.
CHARLEY'S WAR
STOP THAT MAN!
ROD70
249
CONTINUED ON NEXT PAGE

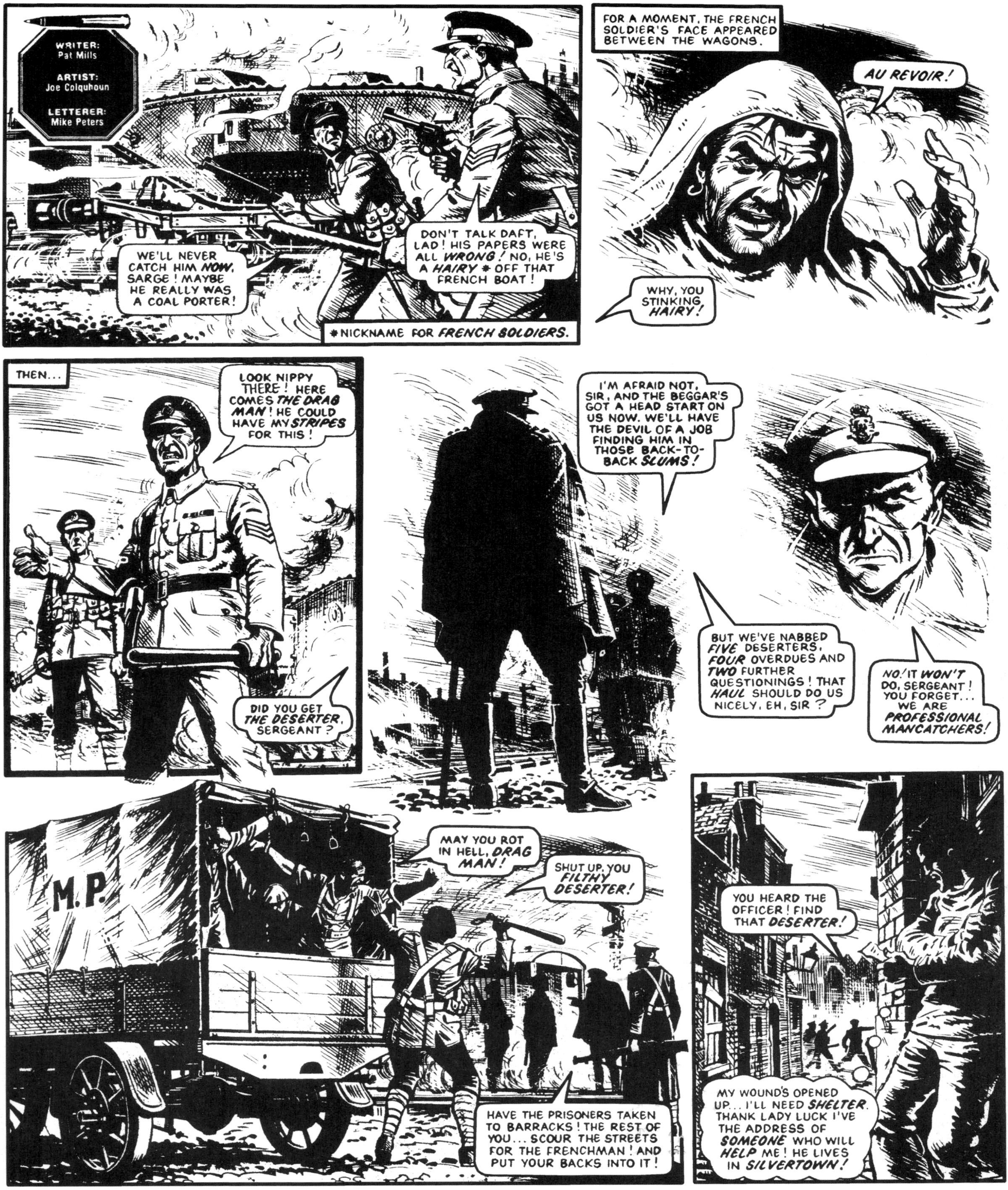

WRITER: Pat Mills
ARTIST: Joe Colquhoun
LETTERER: Mike Peters
WE'LL NEVER CATCH HIM NOW, SARGE! MAYBE HE REALLY WAS A COAL PORTER!
DON'T TALK DAFT, LAD! HIS PAPERS WERE ALL WRONG! NO, HE'S A HAIRY * OFF THAT FRENCH BOAT!
*NICKNAME FOR FRENCH SOLDIERS.
FOR A MOMENT, THE FRENCH SOLDIER'S FACE APPEARED BETWEEN THE WAGONS.
AU REVOIR!
WHY, YOU STINKING HAIRY!
THEN...
LOOK NIPPY THERE! HERE COMES THE DRAG MAN! HE COULD HAVE MY STRIPES FOR THIS!
DID YOU GET THE DESERTER, SERGEANT?
I'M AFRAID NOT, SIR, AND THE BEGGAR'S GOT A HEAD START ON US NOW. WE'LL HAVE THE DEVIL OF A JOB FINDING HIM IN THOSE BACK-TO-BACK SLUMS!
BUT WE'VE NABBED FIVE DESERTERS, FOUR OVERDUES AND TWO FURTHER QUESTIONINGS! THAT HAUL SHOULD DO US NICELY, EH, SIR?
NO! IT WON'T DO, SERGEANT! YOU FORGET... WE ARE PROFESSIONAL MANCATCHERS!
M.P.
MAY YOU ROT IN HELL, DRAG MAN!
SHUT UP, YOU FILTHY DESERTER!
HAVE THE PRISONERS TAKEN TO BARRACKS! THE REST OF YOU... SCOUR THE STREETS FOR THE FRENCHMAN! AND PUT YOUR BACKS INTO IT!
YOU HEARD THE OFFICER! FIND THAT DESERTER!
MY WOUND'S OPENED UP... I'LL NEED SHELTER. THANK LADY LUCK I'VE THE ADDRESS OF SOMEONE WHO WILL HELP ME! HE LIVES IN SILVERTOWN!

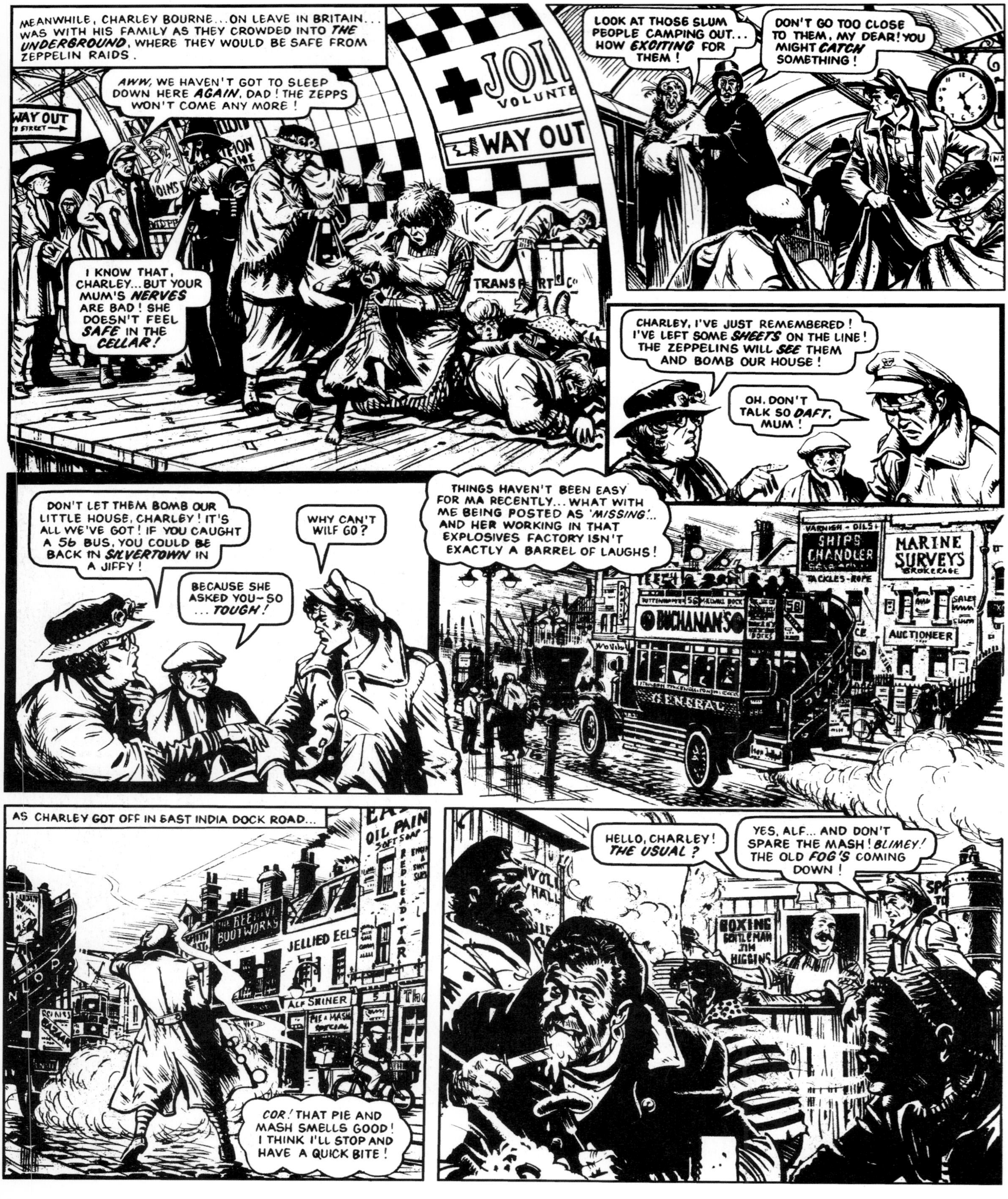

MEANWHILE, CHARLEY BOURNE... ON LEAVE IN BRITAIN... WAS WITH HIS FAMILY AS THEY CROWDED INTO THE UNDERGROUND, WHERE THEY WOULD BE SAFE FROM ZEPPELIN RAIDS.
AWW, WE HAVEN'T GOT TO SLEEP DOWN HERE AGAIN, DAD! THE ZEPPS WON'T COME ANY MORE!
I KNOW THAT, CHARLEY... BUT YOUR MUM'S NERVES ARE BAD! SHE DOESN'T FEEL SAFE IN THE CELLAR!
WAY OUT
WAY OUT
LOOK AT THOSE SLUM PEOPLE CAMPING OUT... HOW EXCITING FOR THEM!
DON'T GO TOO CLOSE TO THEM, MY DEAR! YOU MIGHT CATCH SOMETHING!
CHARLEY, I'VE JUST REMEMBERED! I'VE LEFT SOME SHEETS ON THE LINE! THE ZEPPELINS WILL SEE THEM AND BOMB OUR HOUSE!
OH, DON'T TALK SO DAFT, MUM!
DON'T LET THEM BOMB OUR LITTLE HOUSE, CHARLEY! IT'S ALL WE'VE GOT! IF YOU CAUGHT A 56 BUS, YOU COULD BE BACK IN SILVERTOWN IN A JIFFY!
WHY CAN'T WILF GO?
BECAUSE SHE ASKED YOU—SO ... TOUGH!
THINGS HAVEN'T BEEN EASY FOR MA RECENTLY... WHAT WITH ME BEING POSTED AS 'MISSING'... AND HER WORKING IN THAT EXPLOSIVES FACTORY ISN'T EXACTLY A BARREL OF LAUGHS!
SHIPS CHANDLER
MARINE SURVEYS
AUCTIONEER
BUCHANAN'S
AS CHARLEY GOT OFF IN EAST INDIA DOCK ROAD...
JELLIED EELS
ALF SHINER
RED LEAD TAR
COR! THAT PIE AND MASH SMELLS GOOD! I THINK I'LL STOP AND HAVE A QUICK BITE!
HELLO, CHARLEY! THE USUAL?
YES, ALF... AND DON'T SPARE THE MASH! BLIMEY! THE OLD FOG'S COMING DOWN!
BOXING GENTLEMAN JIM HIGGINS

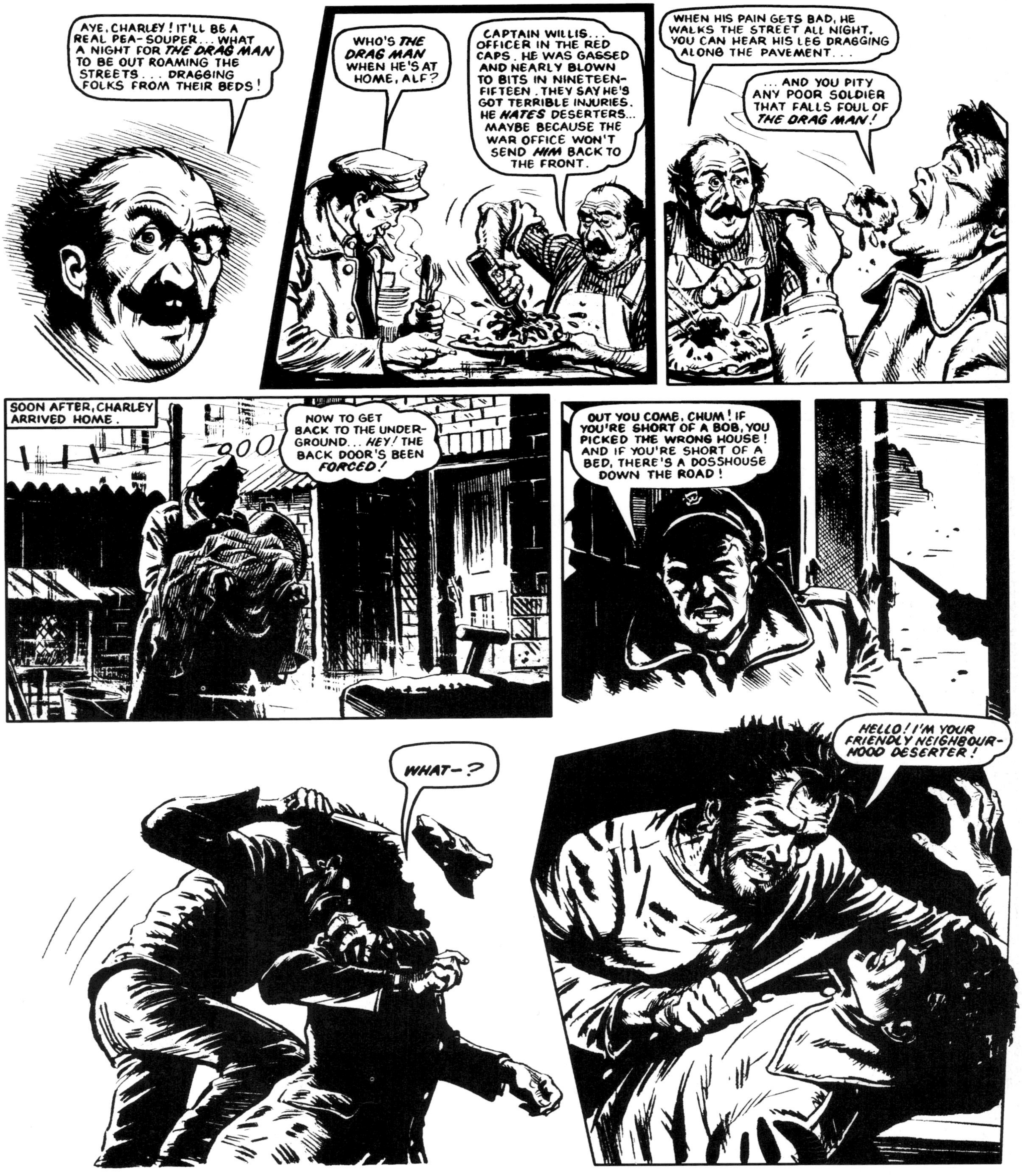
AYE, CHARLEY! IT'LL BE A REAL PEA-SOUPER... WHAT A NIGHT FOR THE DRAG MAN TO BE OUT ROAMING THE STREETS... DRAGGING FOLKS FROM THEIR BEDS!
WHO'S THE DRAG MAN WHEN HE'S AT HOME, ALF?
CAPTAIN WILLIS... OFFICER IN THE RED CAPS. HE WAS GASSED AND NEARLY BLOWN TO BITS IN NINETEEN-FIFTEEN. THEY SAY HE'S GOT TERRIBLE INJURIES. HE HATES DESERTERS... MAYBE BECAUSE THE WAR OFFICE WON'T SEND HIM BACK TO THE FRONT.
WHEN HIS PAIN GETS BAD, HE WALKS THE STREET ALL NIGHT. YOU CAN HEAR HIS LEG DRAGGING ALONG THE PAVEMENT...
... AND YOU PITY ANY POOR SOLDIER THAT FALLS FOUL OF THE DRAG MAN!
SOON AFTER, CHARLEY ARRIVED HOME.
OOO
NOW TO GET BACK TO THE UNDER-GROUND... HEY! THE BACK DOOR'S BEEN FORCED!
OUT YOU COME, CHUM! IF YOU'RE SHORT OF A BOB, YOU PICKED THE WRONG HOUSE! AND IF YOU'RE SHORT OF A BED, THERE'S A DOSSHOUSE DOWN THE ROAD!
WHAT-?
HELLO! I'M YOUR FRIENDLY NEIGHBOUR-HOOD DESERTER!

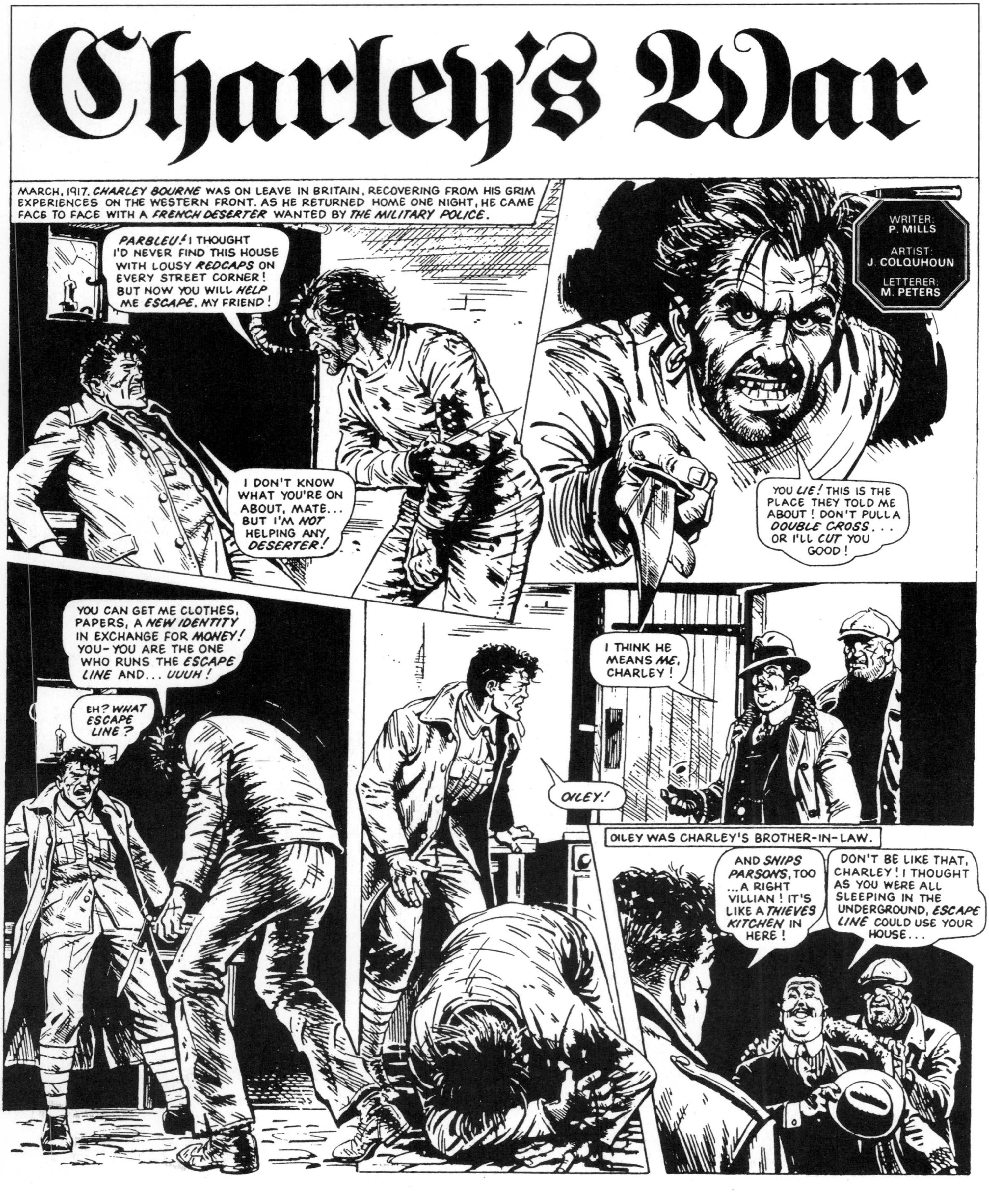
Charley's War
MARCH, 1917. CHARLEY BOURNE WAS ON LEAVE IN BRITAIN, RECOVERING FROM HIS GRIM EXPERIENCES ON THE WESTERN FRONT. AS HE RETURNED HOME ONE NIGHT, HE CAME FACE TO FACE WITH A FRENCH DESERTER WANTED BY THE MILITARY POLICE.
PARBLEU! I THOUGHT I'D NEVER FIND THIS HOUSE WITH LOUSY REDCAPS ON EVERY STREET CORNER! BUT NOW YOU WILL HELP ME ESCAPE, MY FRIEND!
I DON'T KNOW WHAT YOU'RE ON ABOUT, MATE... BUT I'M NOT HELPING ANY DESERTER!
WRITER: P. MILLS
ARTIST: J. COLQUHOUN
LETTERER: M. PETERS
YOU LIE! THIS IS THE PLACE THEY TOLD ME ABOUT! DON'T PULL A DOUBLE CROSS... OR I'LL CUT YOU GOOD!
YOU CAN GET ME CLOTHES, PAPERS, A NEW IDENTITY IN EXCHANGE FOR MONEY! YOU- YOU ARE THE ONE WHO RUNS THE ESCAPE LINE AND... UUUH!
EH? WHAT ESCAPE LINE?
I THINK HE MEANS ME, CHARLEY!
OILEY!
OILEY WAS CHARLEY'S BROTHER-IN-LAW.
AND SNIPS PARSONS, TOO ...A RIGHT VILLIAN! IT'S LIKE A THIEVES KITCHEN IN HERE!
DON'T BE LIKE THAT, CHARLEY! I THOUGHT AS YOU WERE ALL SLEEPING IN THE UNDERGROUND, ESCAPE LINE COULD USE YOUR HOUSE...

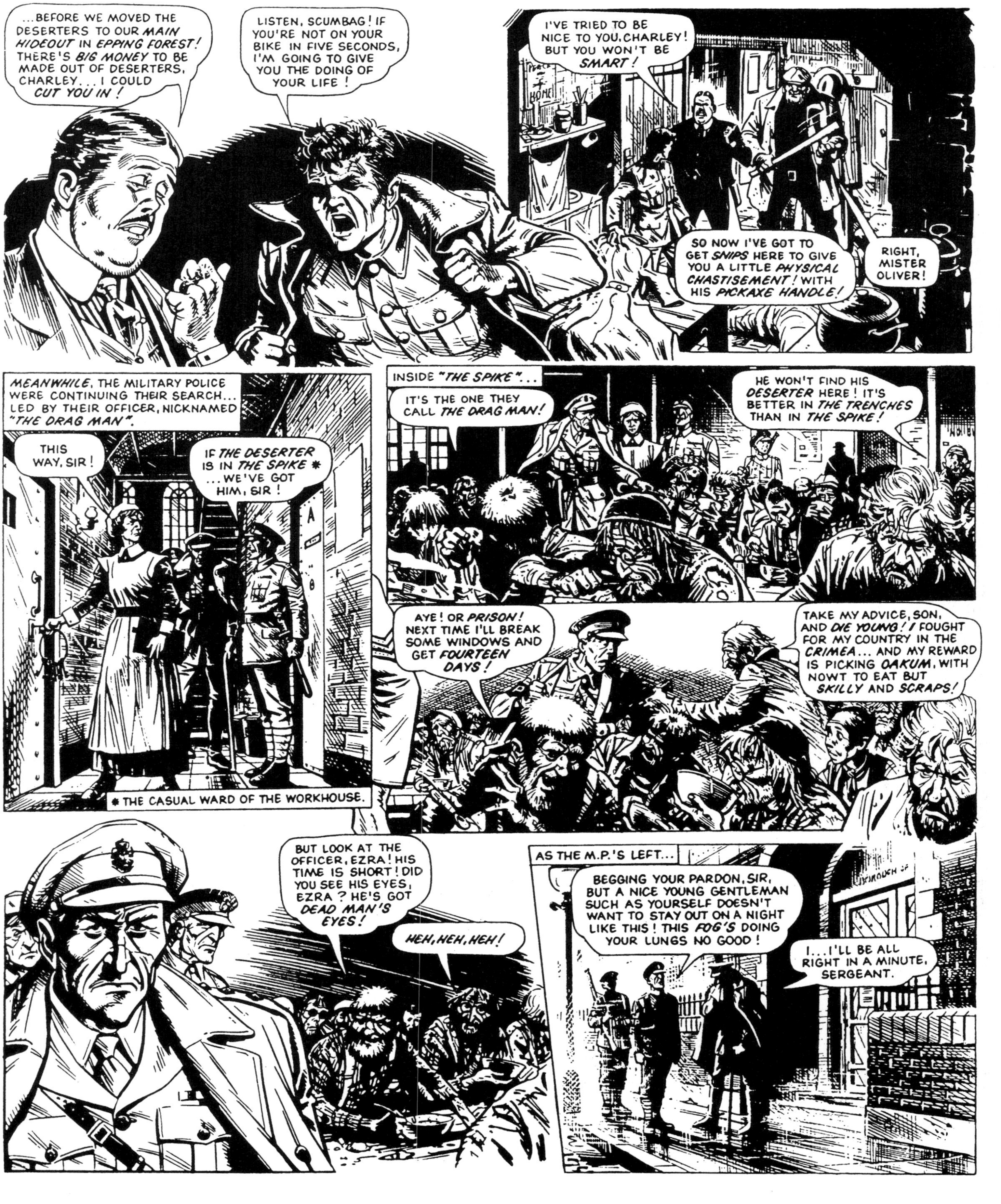
...BEFORE WE MOVED THE DESERTERS TO OUR MAIN HIDEOUT IN EPPING FOREST! THERE'S BIG MONEY TO BE MADE OUT OF DESERTERS, CHARLEY... I COULD CUT YOU IN!
LISTEN, SCUMBAG! IF YOU'RE NOT ON YOUR BIKE IN FIVE SECONDS, I'M GOING TO GIVE YOU THE DOING OF YOUR LIFE!
I'VE TRIED TO BE NICE TO YOU, CHARLEY! BUT YOU WON'T BE SMART!
SO NOW I'VE GOT TO GET SNIPS HERE TO GIVE YOU A LITTLE PHYSICAL CHASTISEMENT! WITH HIS PICKAXE HANDLE!
RIGHT, MISTER OLIVER!
MEANWHILE, THE MILITARY POLICE WERE CONTINUING THEIR SEARCH... LED BY THEIR OFFICER, NICKNAMED "THE DRAG MAN".
THIS WAY, SIR!
IF THE DESERTER IS IN THE SPIKE * ...WE'VE GOT HIM, SIR!
* THE CASUAL WARD OF THE WORKHOUSE.
INSIDE "THE SPIKE"...
IT'S THE ONE THEY CALL THE DRAG MAN!
HE WON'T FIND HIS DESERTER HERE! IT'S BETTER IN THE TRENCHES THAN IN THE SPIKE!
AYE! OR PRISON! NEXT TIME I'LL BREAK SOME WINDOWS AND GET FOURTEEN DAYS!
TAKE MY ADVICE, SON, AND DIE YOUNG! I FOUGHT FOR MY COUNTRY IN THE CRIMEA... AND MY REWARD IS PICKING OAKUM, WITH NOWT TO EAT BUT SKILLY AND SCRAPS!
BUT LOOK AT THE OFFICER, EZRA! HIS TIME IS SHORT! DID YOU SEE HIS EYES, EZRA? HE'S GOT DEAD MAN'S EYES!
HEH, HEH, HEH!
AS THE M.P.'S LEFT...
BEGGING YOUR PARDON, SIR, BUT A NICE YOUNG GENTLEMAN SUCH AS YOURSELF DOESN'T WANT TO STAY OUT ON A NIGHT LIKE THIS! THIS FOG'S DOING YOUR LUNGS NO GOOD!
I...I'LL BE ALL RIGHT IN A MINUTE, SERGEANT.

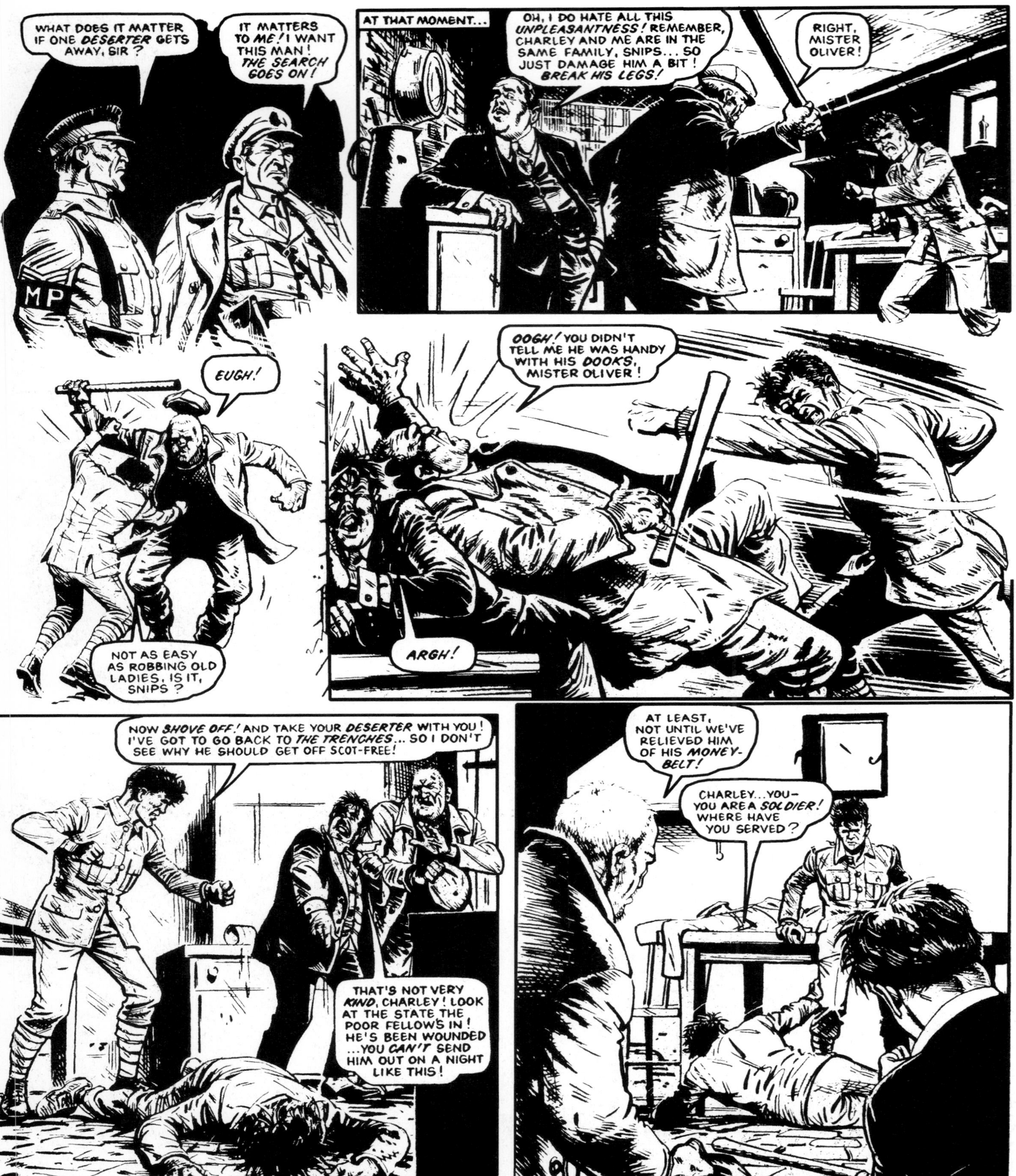
WHAT DOES IT MATTER IF ONE DESERTER GETS AWAY, SIR?
IT MATTERS TO ME! I WANT THIS MAN! THE SEARCH GOES ON!
MP
AT THAT MOMENT...
OH, I DO HATE ALL THIS UNPLEASANTNESS! REMEMBER, CHARLEY AND ME ARE IN THE SAME FAMILY, SNIPS... SO JUST DAMAGE HIM A BIT! BREAK HIS LEGS!
RIGHT, MISTER OLIVER!
EUGH!
NOT AS EASY AS ROBBING OLD LADIES, IS IT, SNIPS?
OOGH! YOU DIDN'T TELL ME HE WAS HANDY WITH HIS DOOKS, MISTER OLIVER!
ARGH!
NOW SHOVE OFF! AND TAKE YOUR DESERTER WITH YOU! I'VE GOT TO GO BACK TO THE TRENCHES... SO I DON'T SEE WHY HE SHOULD GET OFF SCOT-FREE!
THAT'S NOT VERY KIND, CHARLEY! LOOK AT THE STATE THE POOR FELLOW'S IN! HE'S BEEN WOUNDED ...YOU CAN'T SEND HIM OUT ON A NIGHT LIKE THIS!
AT LEAST, NOT UNTIL WE'VE RELIEVED HIM OF HIS MONEY-BELT!
CHARLEY... YOU- YOU ARE A SOLDIER! WHERE HAVE YOU SERVED?

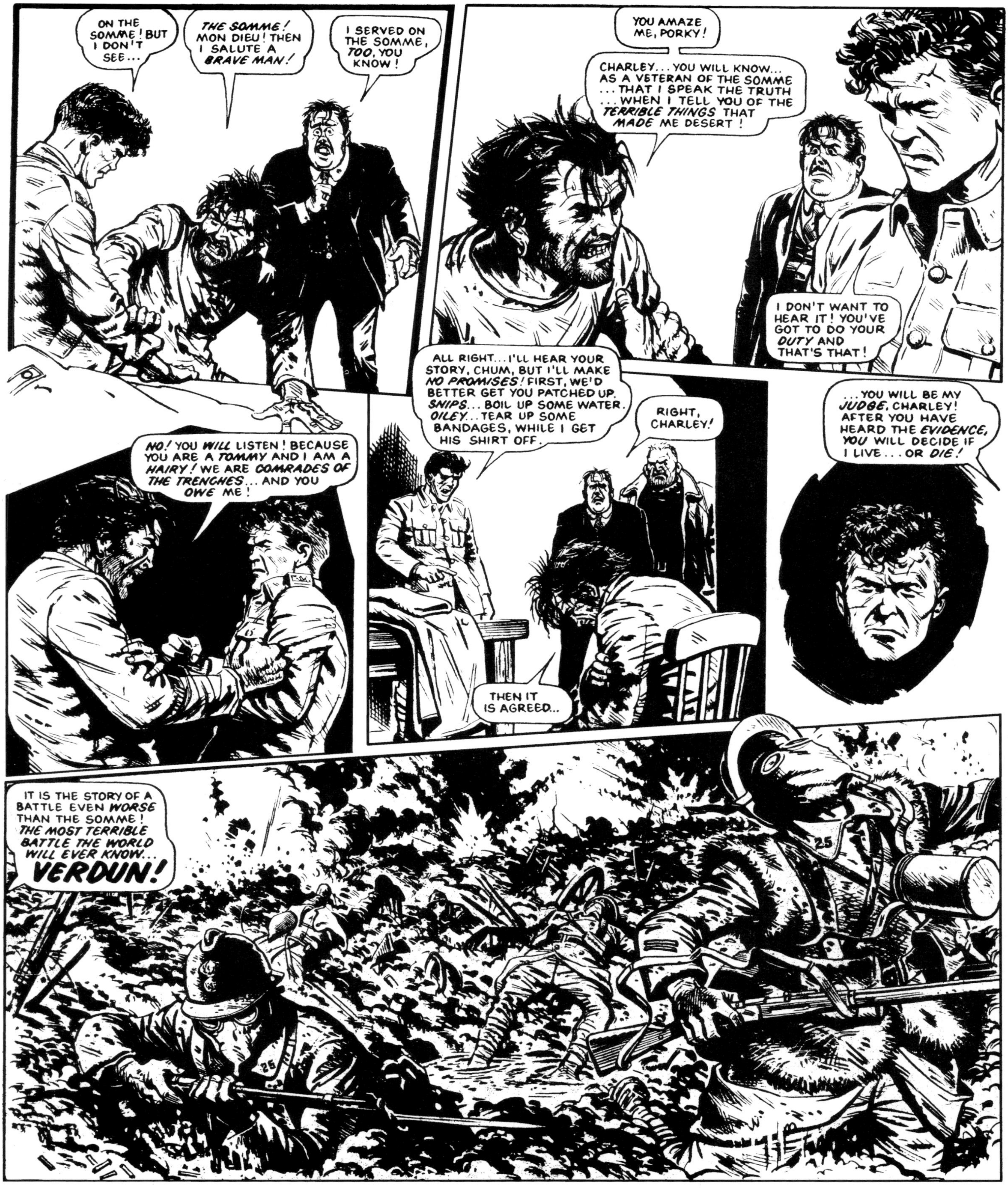
ON THE SOMME! BUT I DON'T SEE...
THE SOMME! MON DIEU! THEN I SALUTE A BRAVE MAN!
I SERVED ON THE SOMME, TOO, YOU KNOW!
YOU AMAZE ME, PORKY!
CHARLEY... YOU WILL KNOW... AS A VETERAN OF THE SOMME ... THAT I SPEAK THE TRUTH ... WHEN I TELL YOU OF THE TERRIBLE THINGS THAT MADE ME DESERT!
I DON'T WANT TO HEAR IT! YOU'VE GOT TO DO YOUR DUTY AND THAT'S THAT!
NO! YOU WILL LISTEN! BECAUSE YOU ARE A TOMMY AND I AM A HAIRY! WE ARE COMRADES OF THE TRENCHES... AND YOU OWE ME!
ALL RIGHT... I'LL HEAR YOUR STORY, CHUM, BUT I'LL MAKE NO PROMISES! FIRST, WE'D BETTER GET YOU PATCHED UP. SNIPS... BOIL UP SOME WATER. OILEY... TEAR UP SOME BANDAGES, WHILE I GET HIS SHIRT OFF.
RIGHT, CHARLEY!
THEN IT IS AGREED...
...YOU WILL BE MY JUDGE, CHARLEY! AFTER YOU HAVE HEARD THE EVIDENCE, YOU WILL DECIDE IF I LIVE... OR DIE!
IT IS THE STORY OF A BATTLE EVEN WORSE THAN THE SOMME! THE MOST TERRIBLE BATTLE THE WORLD WILL EVER KNOW... VERDUN!

CHARLEY'S WAR

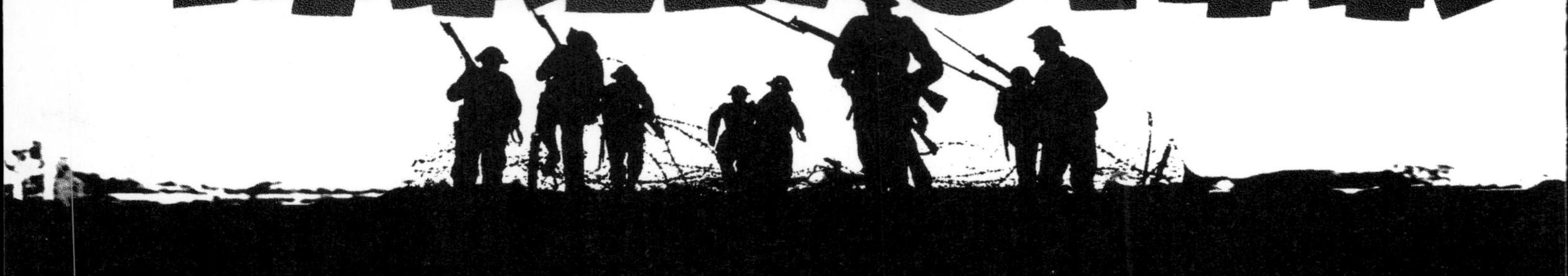

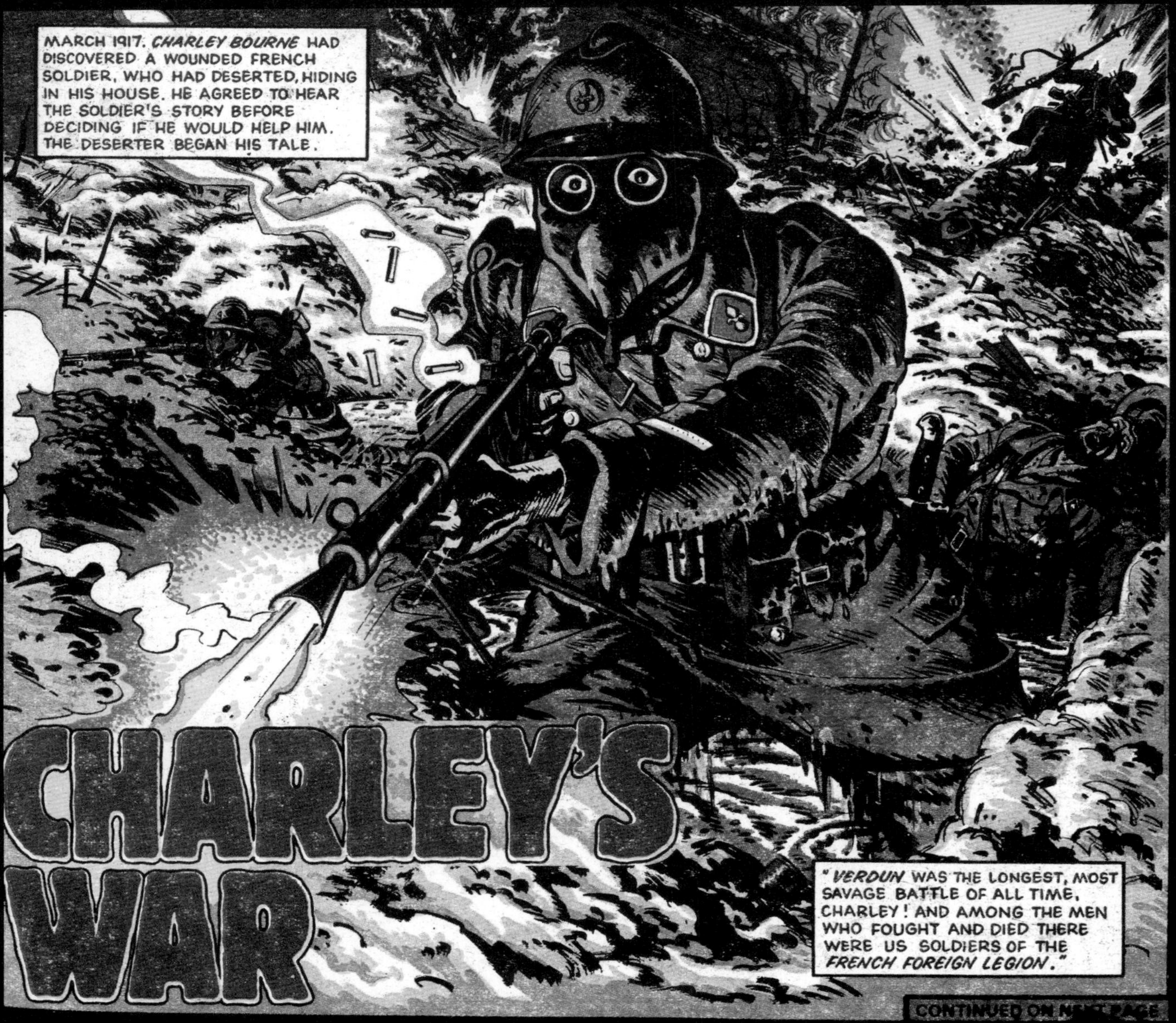
MARCH 1917. CHARLEY BOURNE HAD DISCOVERED A WOUNDED FRENCH SOLDIER, WHO HAD DESERTED, HIDING IN HIS HOUSE. HE AGREED TO HEAR THE SOLDIER'S STORY BEFORE DECIDING IF HE WOULD HELP HIM. THE DESERTER BEGAN HIS TALE.
CHARLEY'S WAR
"VERDUN WAS THE LONGEST, MOST SAVAGE BATTLE OF ALL TIME, CHARLEY! AND AMONG THE MEN WHO FOUGHT AND DIED THERE WERE US SOLDIERS OF THE FRENCH FOREIGN LEGION."

CONTINUED ON NEXT PAGE

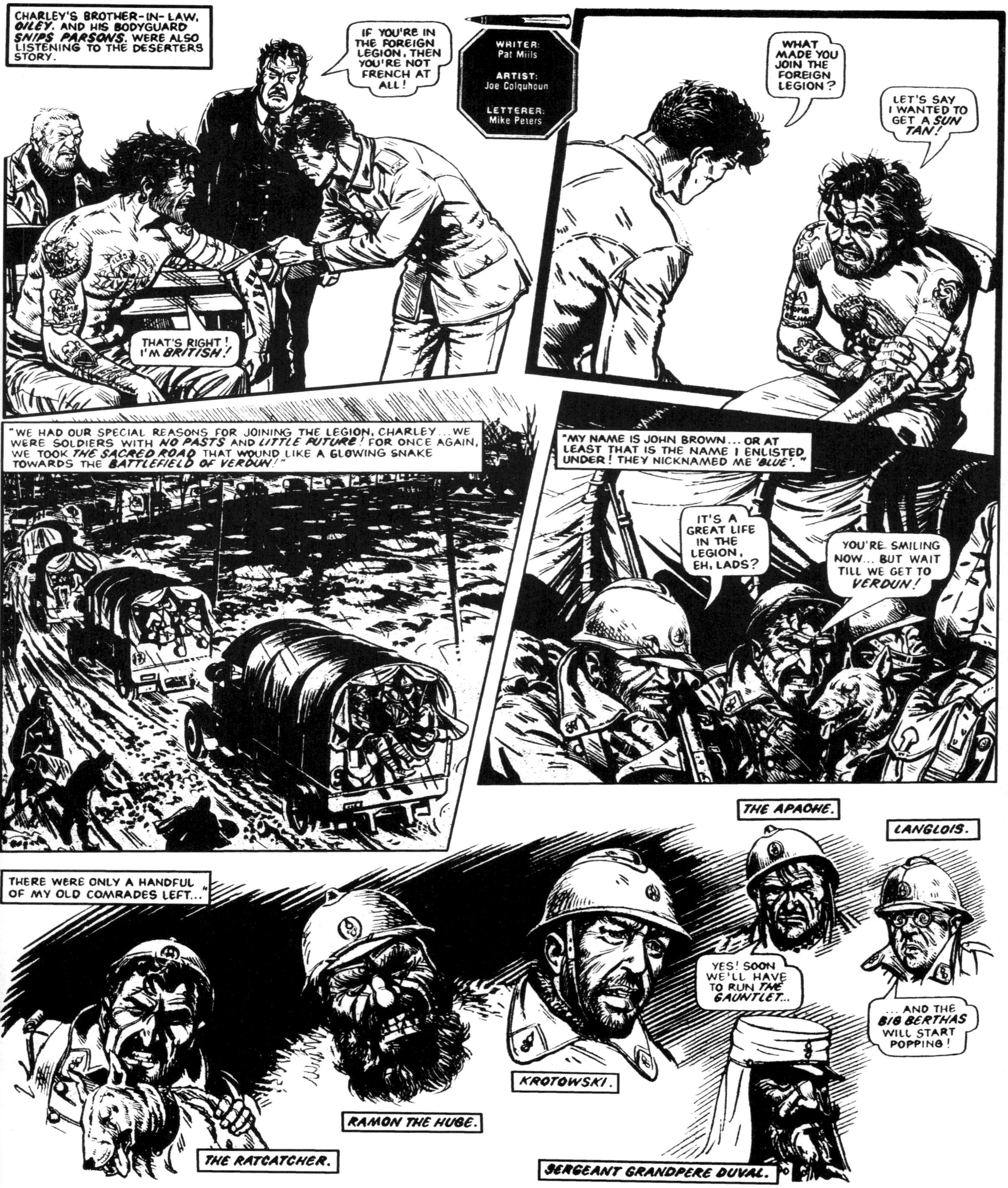
CHARLEY'S BROTHER-IN-LAW, OILEY, AND HIS BODYGUARD SNIPS PARSONS, WERE ALSO LISTENING TO THE DESERTERS STORY.
IF YOU'RE IN THE FOREIGN LEGION, THEN YOU'RE NOT FRENCH AT ALL!
THAT'S RIGHT! I'M BRITISH!
WRITER: Pat Mills
ARTIST: Joe Colquhoun
LETTERER: Mike Peters
WHAT MADE YOU JOIN THE FOREIGN LEGION?
LET'S SAY I WANTED TO GET A SUN TAN!
"WE HAD OUR SPECIAL REASONS FOR JOINING THE LEGION, CHARLEY... WE WERE SOLDIERS WITH NO PASTS AND LITTLE FUTURE! FOR ONCE AGAIN, WE TOOK THE SACRED ROAD THAT WOUND LIKE A GLOWING SNAKE TOWARDS THE BATTLEFIELD OF VERDUN!"
"MY NAME IS JOHN BROWN... OR AT LEAST THAT IS THE NAME I ENLISTED UNDER! THEY NICKNAMED ME 'BLUE'."
IT'S A GREAT LIFE IN THE LEGION, EH, LADS?
YOU'RE SMILING NOW... BUT WAIT TILL WE GET TO VERDUN!
THERE WERE ONLY A HANDFUL OF MY OLD COMRADES LEFT..."
THE RATCATCHER.
RAMON THE HUGE.
KROTOWSKI.
THE APACHE.
LANGLOIS.
YES! SOON WE'LL HAVE TO RUN THE GAUNTLET...
... AND THE BIG BERTHAS WILL START POPPING!
SERGEANT GRANDPERE DUVAL.

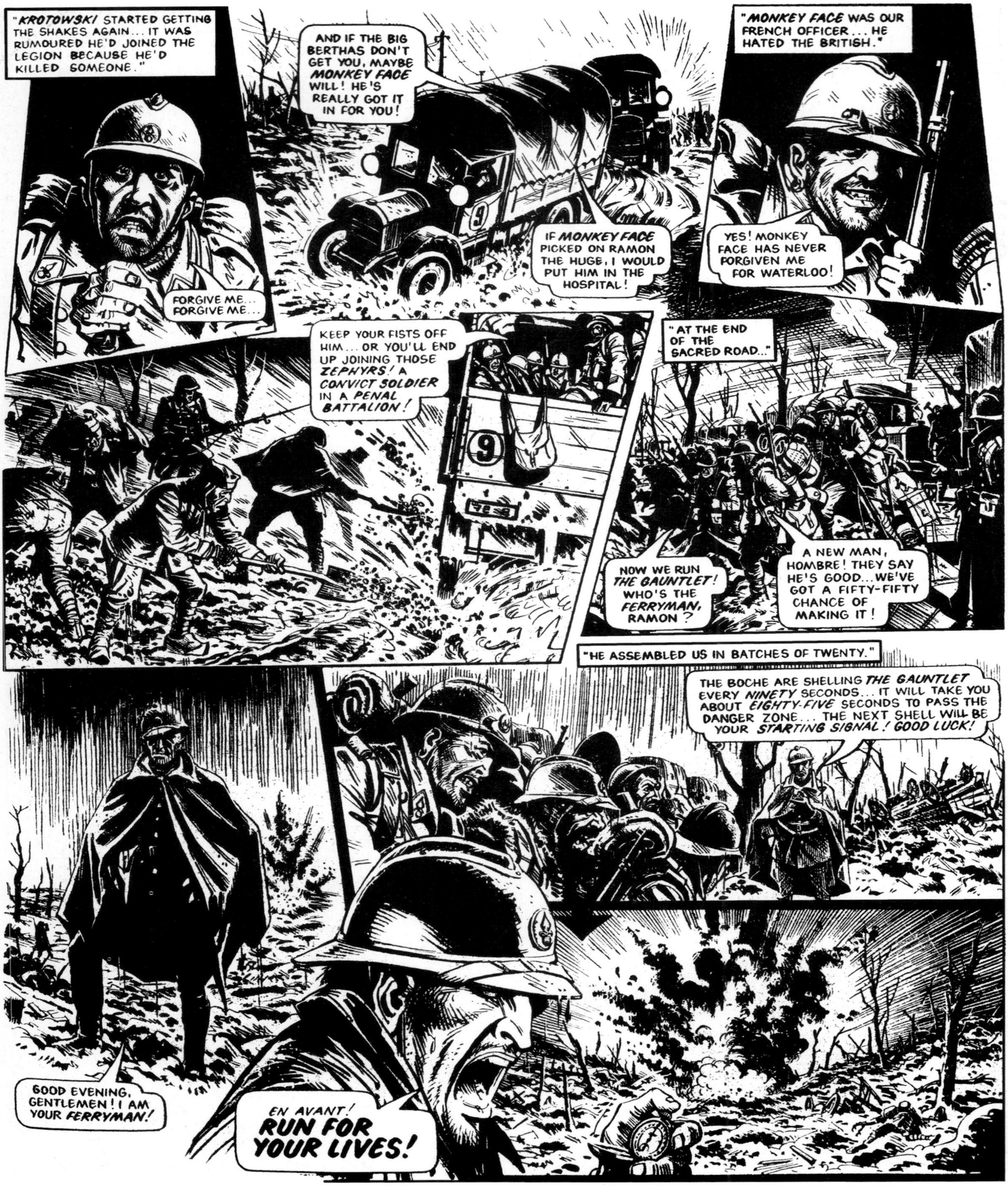
"KROTOWSKI STARTED GETTING THE SHAKES AGAIN... IT WAS RUMOURED HE'D JOINED THE LEGION BECAUSE HE'D KILLED SOMEONE."
FORGIVE ME... FORGIVE ME...
AND IF THE BIG BERTHAS DON'T GET YOU, MAYBE MONKEY FACE WILL! HE'S REALLY GOT IT IN FOR YOU!
IF MONKEY FACE PICKED ON RAMON THE HUGE, I WOULD PUT HIM IN THE HOSPITAL!
"MONKEY FACE WAS OUR FRENCH OFFICER... HE HATED THE BRITISH."
YES! MONKEY FACE HAS NEVER FORGIVEN ME FOR WATERLOO!
KEEP YOUR FISTS OFF HIM... OR YOU'LL END UP JOINING THOSE ZEPHYRS! A CONVICT SOLDIER IN A PENAL BATTALION!
"AT THE END OF THE SACRED ROAD..."
NOW WE RUN THE GAUNTLET! WHO'S THE FERRYMAN, RAMON?
A NEW MAN, HOMBRE! THEY SAY HE'S GOOD... WE'VE GOT A FIFTY-FIFTY CHANCE OF MAKING IT!
"HE ASSEMBLED US IN BATCHES OF TWENTY."
GOOD EVENING, GENTLEMEN! I AM YOUR FERRYMAN!
THE BOCHE ARE SHELLING THE GAUNTLET EVERY NINETY SECONDS... IT WILL TAKE YOU ABOUT EIGHTY-FIVE SECONDS TO PASS THE DANGER ZONE... THE NEXT SHELL WILL BE YOUR STARTING SIGNAL! GOOD LUCK!
EN AVANT! RUN FOR YOUR LIVES!

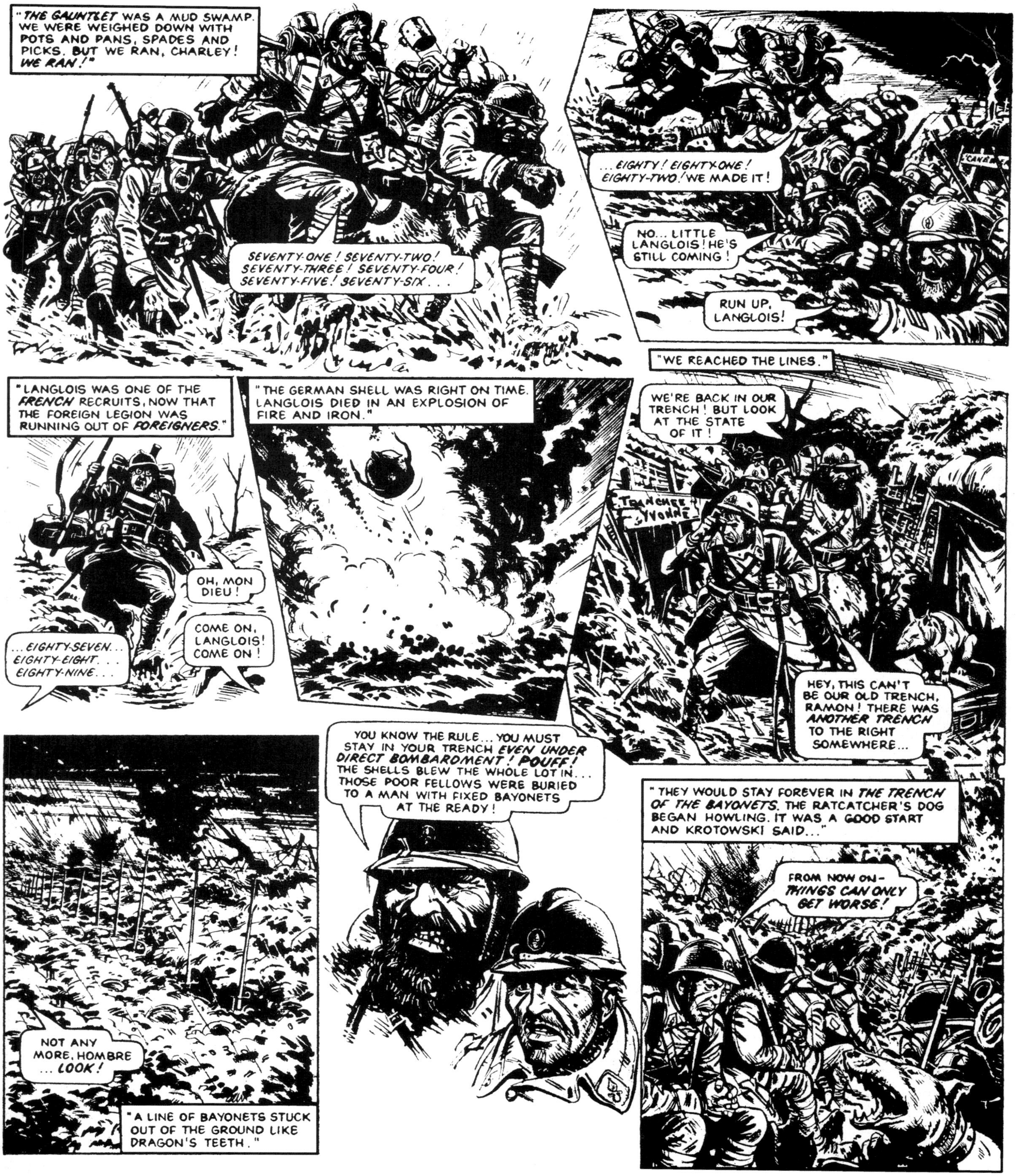
"THE GAUNTLET WAS A MUD SWAMP. WE WERE WEIGHED DOWN WITH POTS AND PANS, SPADES AND PICKS. BUT WE RAN, CHARLEY! WE RAN!"
SEVENTY-ONE! SEVENTY-TWO! SEVENTY-THREE! SEVENTY-FOUR! SEVENTY-FIVE! SEVENTY-SIX...
...EIGHTY! EIGHTY-ONE! EIGHTY-TWO! WE MADE IT!
NO... LITTLE LANGLOIS! HE'S STILL COMING!
RUN UP, LANGLOIS!
"LANGLOIS WAS ONE OF THE FRENCH RECRUITS, NOW THAT THE FOREIGN LEGION WAS RUNNING OUT OF FOREIGNERS."
OH, MON DIEU!
COME ON, LANGLOIS! COME ON!
...EIGHTY-SEVEN... EIGHTY-EIGHT... EIGHTY-NINE...
"THE GERMAN SHELL WAS RIGHT ON TIME. LANGLOIS DIED IN AN EXPLOSION OF FIRE AND IRON."
"WE REACHED THE LINES."
WE'RE BACK IN OUR TRENCH! BUT LOOK AT THE STATE OF IT!
HEY, THIS CAN'T BE OUR OLD TRENCH, RAMON! THERE WAS ANOTHER TRENCH TO THE RIGHT SOMEWHERE...
NOT ANY MORE, HOMBRE ...LOOK!
"A LINE OF BAYONETS STUCK OUT OF THE GROUND LIKE DRAGON'S TEETH."
YOU KNOW THE RULE... YOU MUST STAY IN YOUR TRENCH EVEN UNDER DIRECT BOMBARDMENT! POUFF! THE SHELLS BLEW THE WHOLE LOT IN... THOSE POOR FELLOWS WERE BURIED TO A MAN WITH FIXED BAYONETS AT THE READY!
"THEY WOULD STAY FOREVER IN THE TRENCH OF THE BAYONETS. THE RATCATCHER'S DOG BEGAN HOWLING. IT WAS A GOOD START AND KROTOWSKI SAID..."
FROM NOW ON - THINGS CAN ONLY GET WORSE!

EVEN IN THE HELL OF VERDUN, THERE WERE CERTAIN IRON RULES A LEGIONNAIRE HAD TO OBEY!

Charley's War

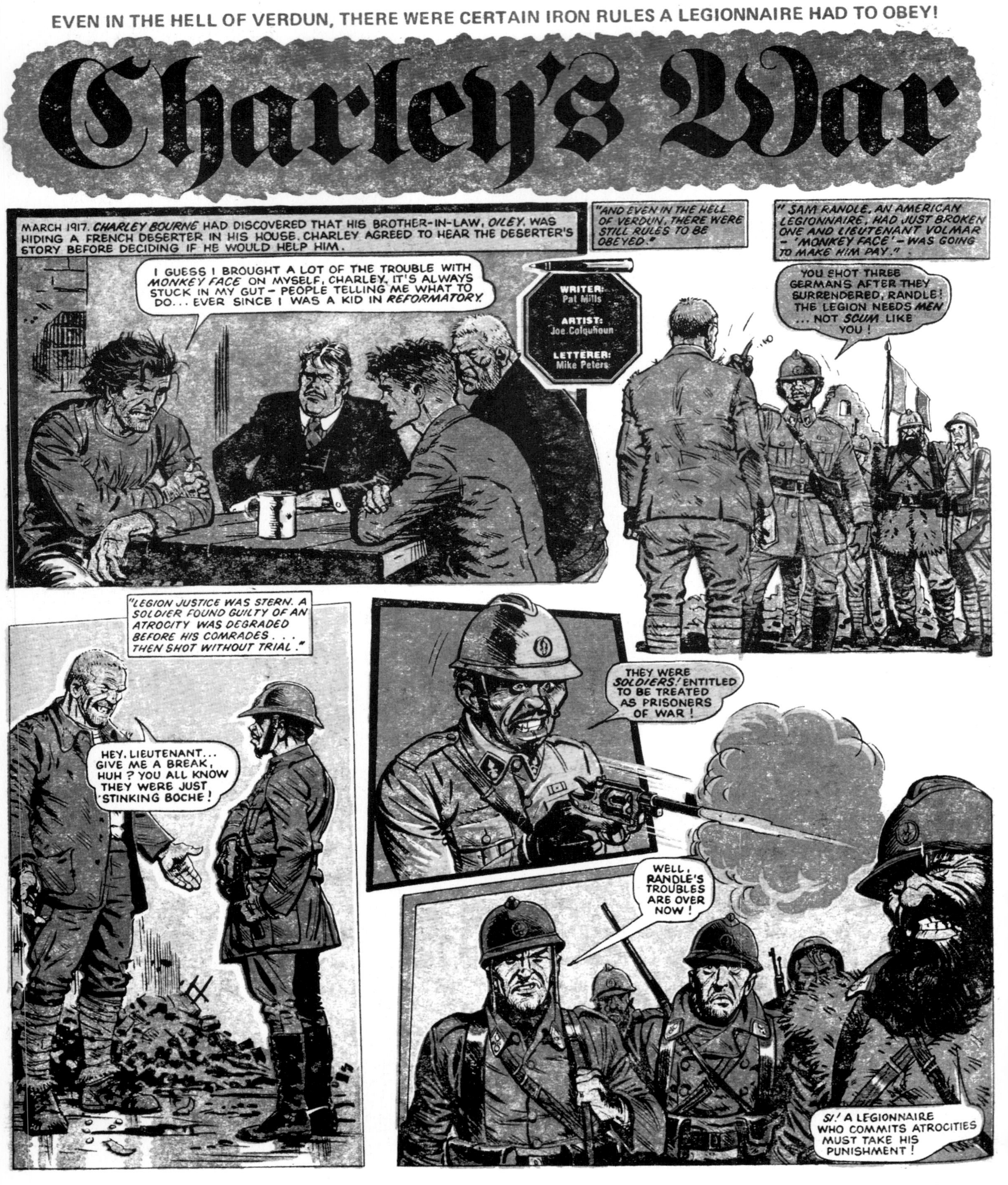

MARCH 1917. CHARLEY BOURNE HAD DISCOVERED THAT HIS BROTHER-IN-LAW, OILEY, WAS HIDING A FRENCH DESERTER IN HIS HOUSE. CHARLEY AGREED TO HEAR THE DESERTER'S STORY BEFORE DECIDING IF HE WOULD HELP HIM.
I GUESS I BROUGHT A LOT OF THE TROUBLE WITH MONKEY FACE ON MYSELF, CHARLEY. IT'S ALWAYS STUCK IN MY GUT – PEOPLE TELLING ME WHAT TO DO... EVER SINCE I WAS A KID IN REFORMATORY.
WRITER: Pat Mills
ARTIST: Joe Colquhoun
LETTERER: Mike Peters
"AND EVEN IN THE HELL OF VERDUN, THERE WERE STILL RULES TO BE OBEYED."
"SAM RANDLE, AN AMERICAN LEGIONNAIRE, HAD JUST BROKEN ONE AND LIEUTENANT VOLMAR – 'MONKEY FACE' – WAS GOING TO MAKE HIM PAY."
YOU SHOT THREE GERMANS AFTER THEY SURRENDERED, RANDLE! THE LEGION NEEDS MEN ... NOT SCUM LIKE YOU!
"LEGION JUSTICE WAS STERN. A SOLDIER FOUND GUILTY OF AN ATROCITY WAS DEGRADED BEFORE HIS COMRADES . . . THEN SHOT WITHOUT TRIAL."
HEY, LIEUTENANT... GIVE ME A BREAK, HUH? YOU ALL KNOW THEY WERE JUST STINKING BOCHE!
THEY WERE SOLDIERS! ENTITLED TO BE TREATED AS PRISONERS OF WAR!
WELL, RANDLE'S TROUBLES ARE OVER NOW!
SI! A LEGIONNAIRE WHO COMMITS ATROCITIES MUST TAKE HIS PUNISHMENT!

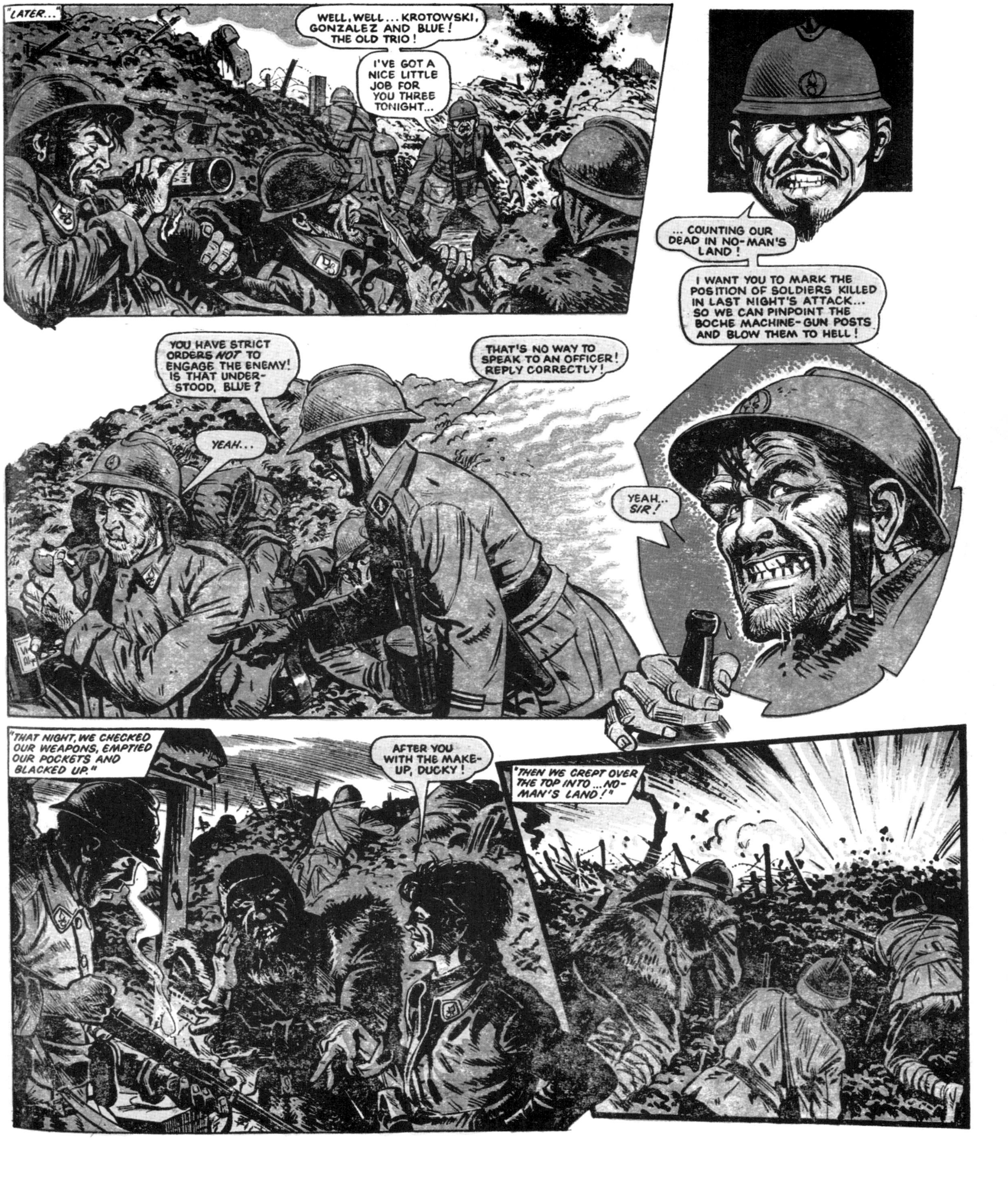
"LATER..."
WELL, WELL... KROTOWSKI, GONZALEZ AND BLUE! THE OLD TRIO!
I'VE GOT A NICE LITTLE JOB FOR YOU THREE TONIGHT...
... COUNTING OUR DEAD IN NO-MAN'S LAND!
I WANT YOU TO MARK THE POSITION OF SOLDIERS KILLED IN LAST NIGHT'S ATTACK... SO WE CAN PINPOINT THE BOCHE MACHINE-GUN POSTS AND BLOW THEM TO HELL!
YOU HAVE STRICT ORDERS NOT TO ENGAGE THE ENEMY! IS THAT UNDERSTOOD, BLUE?
YEAH...
THAT'S NO WAY TO SPEAK TO AN OFFICER! REPLY CORRECTLY!
YEAH... SIR!
"THAT NIGHT, WE CHECKED OUR WEAPONS, EMPTIED OUR POCKETS AND BLACKED UP."
AFTER YOU WITH THE MAKE-UP, DUCKY!
"THEN WE CREPT OVER THE TOP INTO... NO-MAN'S LAND!"

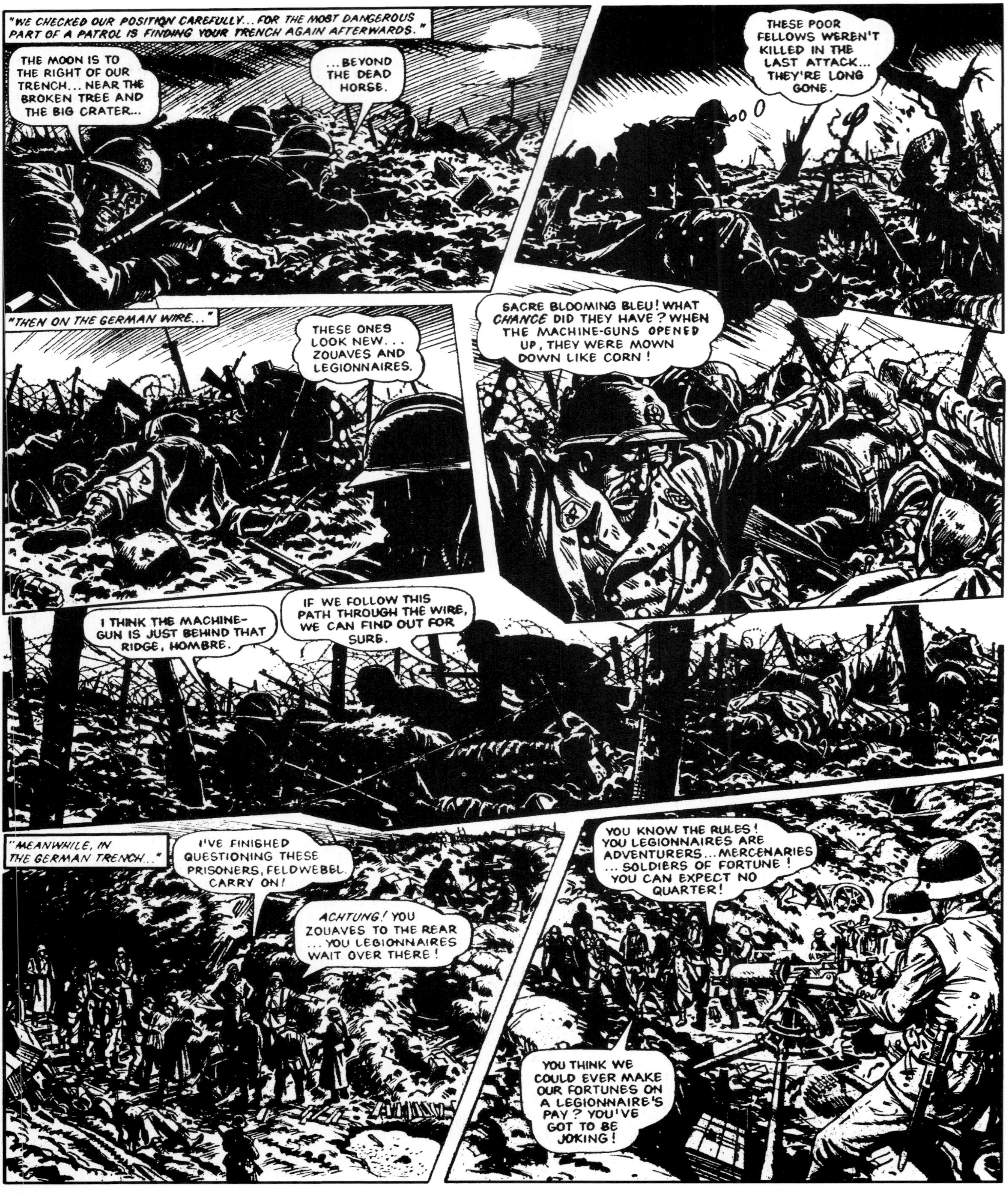
"WE CHECKED OUR POSITION CAREFULLY... FOR THE MOST DANGEROUS PART OF A PATROL IS FINDING YOUR TRENCH AGAIN AFTERWARDS."
THE MOON IS TO THE RIGHT OF OUR TRENCH... NEAR THE BROKEN TREE AND THE BIG CRATER...
...BEYOND THE DEAD HORSE.
THESE POOR FELLOWS WEREN'T KILLED IN THE LAST ATTACK... THEY'RE LONG GONE.
"THEN ON THE GERMAN WIRE..."
THESE ONES LOOK NEW... ZOUAVES AND LEGIONNAIRES.
SACRE BLOOMING BLEU! WHAT CHANCE DID THEY HAVE? WHEN THE MACHINE-GUNS OPENED UP, THEY WERE MOWN DOWN LIKE CORN!
I THINK THE MACHINE-GUN IS JUST BEHIND THAT RIDGE, HOMBRE.
IF WE FOLLOW THIS PATH THROUGH THE WIRE, WE CAN FIND OUT FOR SURE.
"MEANWHILE, IN THE GERMAN TRENCH..."
I'VE FINISHED QUESTIONING THESE PRISONERS, FELDWEBEL. CARRY ON!
ACHTUNG! YOU ZOUAVES TO THE REAR ...YOU LEGIONNAIRES WAIT OVER THERE!
YOU KNOW THE RULES! YOU LEGIONNAIRES ARE ADVENTURERS... MERCENARIES ... SOLDIERS OF FORTUNE! YOU CAN EXPECT NO QUARTER!
YOU THINK WE COULD EVER MAKE OUR FORTUNES ON A LEGIONNAIRE'S PAY? YOU'VE GOT TO BE JOKING!

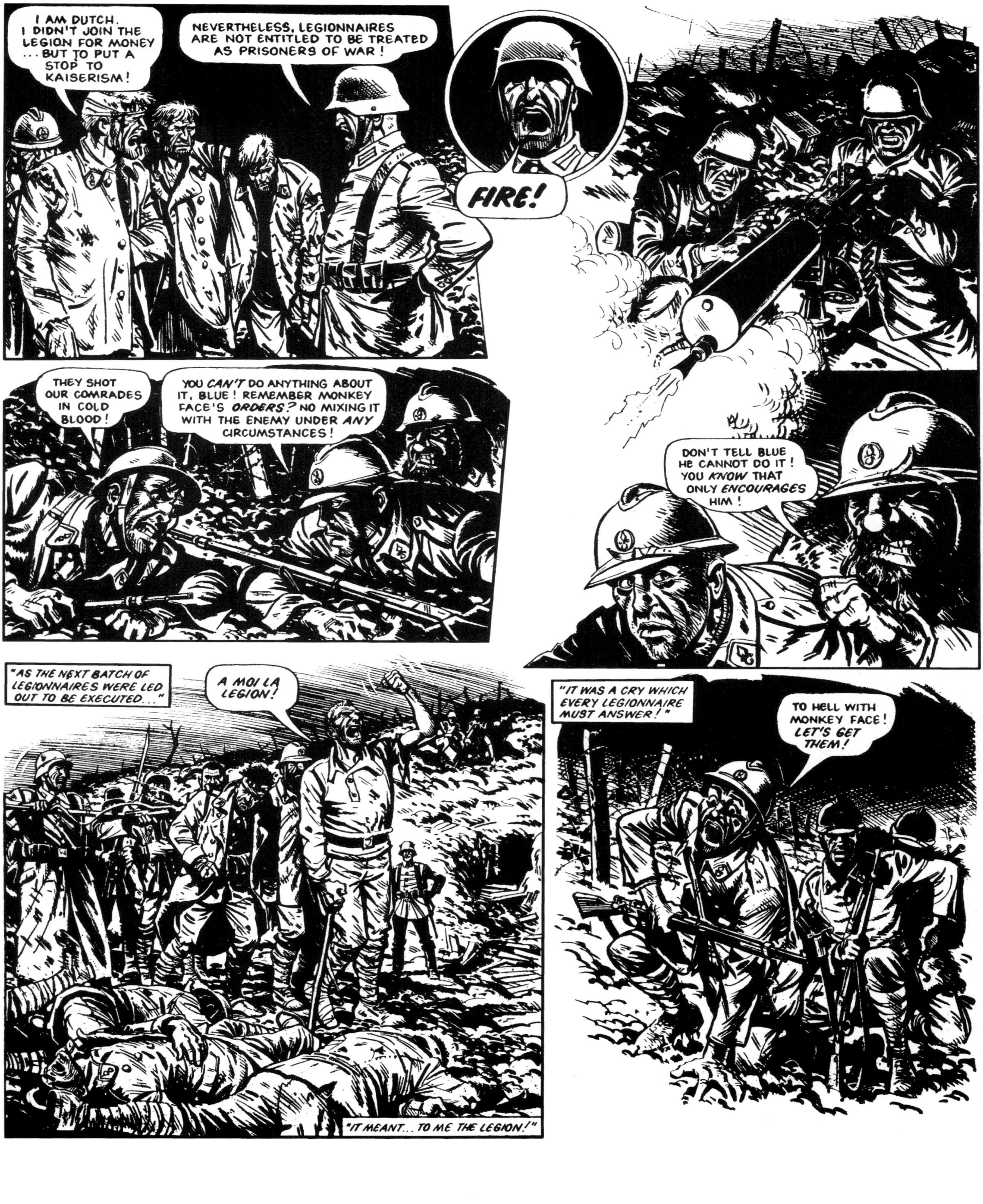
I AM DUTCH. I DIDN'T JOIN THE LEGION FOR MONEY ... BUT TO PUT A STOP TO KAISERISM!
NEVERTHELESS, LEGIONNAIRES ARE NOT ENTITLED TO BE TREATED AS PRISONERS OF WAR!
FIRE!
THEY SHOT OUR COMRADES IN COLD BLOOD!
YOU CAN'T DO ANYTHING ABOUT IT, BLUE! REMEMBER MONKEY FACE'S ORDERS? NO MIXING IT WITH THE ENEMY UNDER ANY CIRCUMSTANCES!
DON'T TELL BLUE HE CANNOT DO IT! YOU KNOW THAT ONLY ENCOURAGES HIM!
"AS THE NEXT BATCH OF LEGIONNAIRES WERE LED OUT TO BE EXECUTED..."
A MOI LA LEGION!
"IT MEANT... TO ME THE LEGION!"
"IT WAS A CRY WHICH EVERY LEGIONNAIRE MUST ANSWER!"
TO HELL WITH MONKEY FACE! LET'S GET THEM!

CHARLEY'S WAR

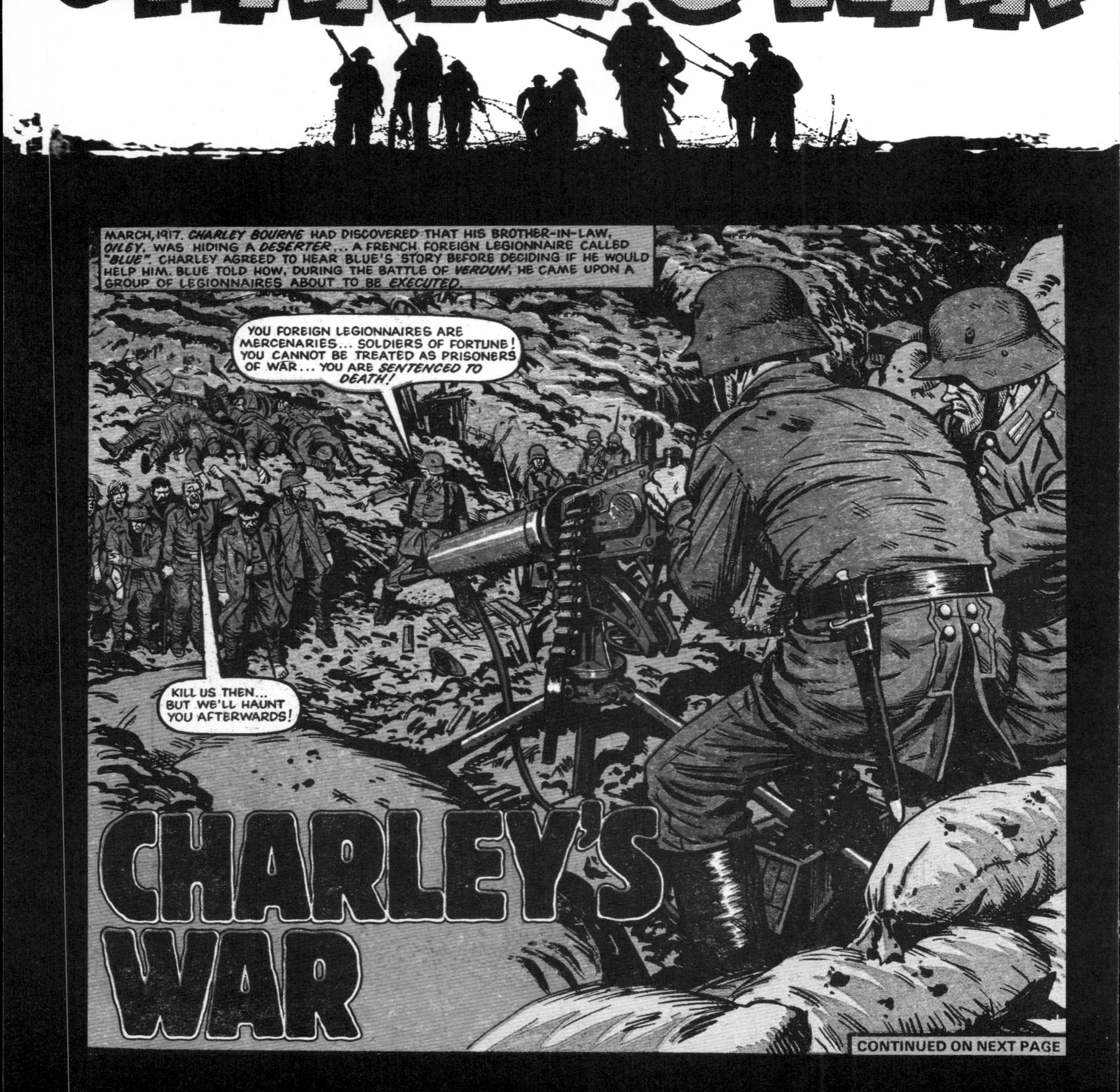

CONTINUED ON NEXT PAGE

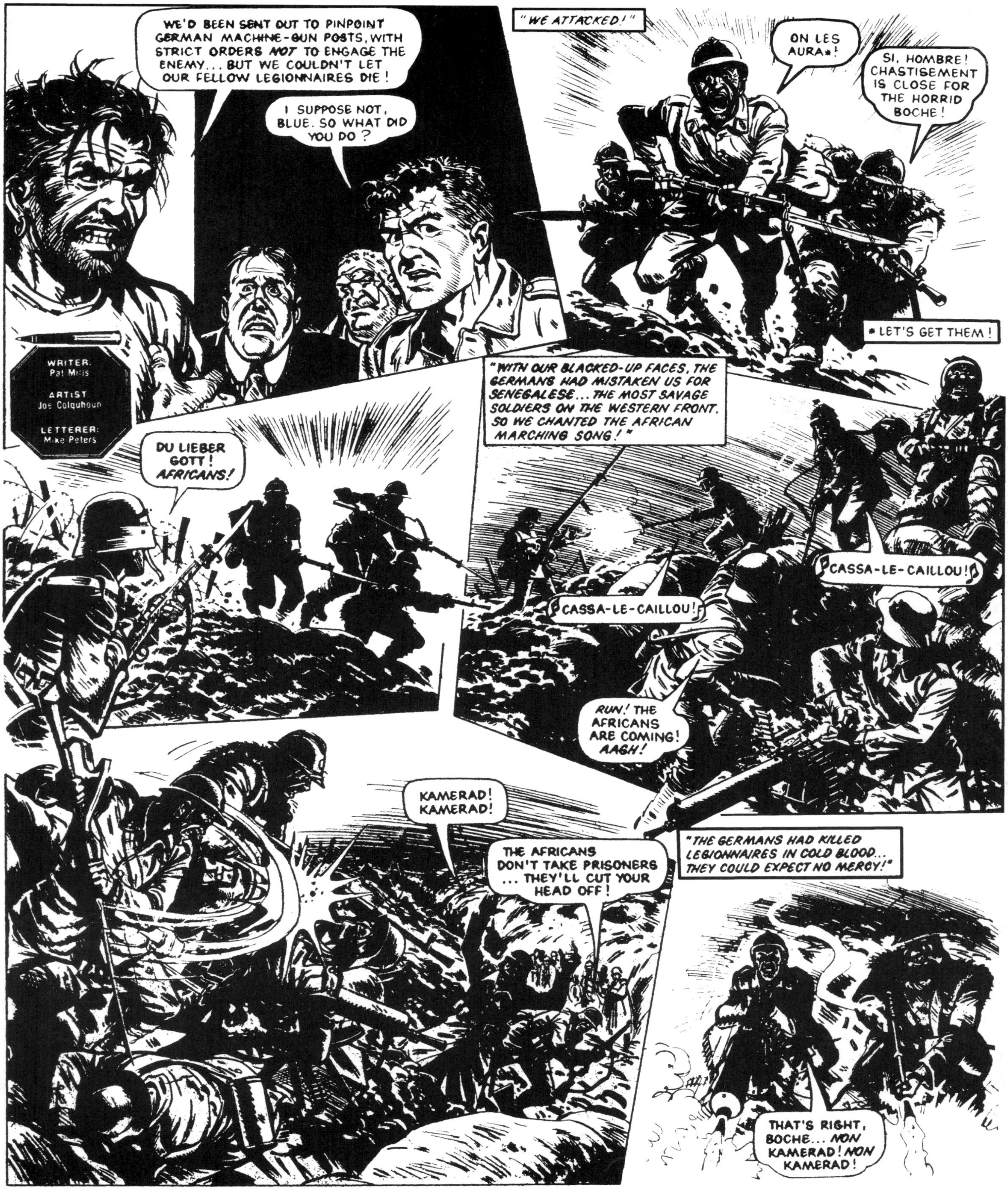
WE'D BEEN SENT OUT TO PINPOINT GERMAN MACHINE-GUN POSTS, WITH STRICT ORDERS NOT TO ENGAGE THE ENEMY... BUT WE COULDN'T LET OUR FELLOW LEGIONNAIRES DIE!
I SUPPOSE NOT, BLUE. SO WHAT DID YOU DO?
WRITER: Pat Mills
ARTIST Joe Colquhoun
LETTERER: Mike Peters
"WE ATTACKED!"
ON LES AURA*!
SI, HOMBRE! CHASTISEMENT IS CLOSE FOR THE HORRID BOCHE!
* LET'S GET THEM!
DU LIEBER GOTT! AFRICANS!
"WITH OUR BLACKED-UP FACES, THE GERMANS HAD MISTAKEN US FOR SENEGALESE... THE MOST SAVAGE SOLDIERS ON THE WESTERN FRONT. SO WE CHANTED THE AFRICAN MARCHING SONG!"
CASSA-LE-CAILLOU!
CASSA-LE-CAILLOU!
RUN! THE AFRICANS ARE COMING! AAGH!
KAMERAD! KAMERAD!
THE AFRICANS DON'T TAKE PRISONERS ... THEY'LL CUT YOUR HEAD OFF!
"THE GERMANS HAD KILLED LEGIONNAIRES IN COLD BLOOD... THEY COULD EXPECT NO MERCY!"
THAT'S RIGHT, BOCHE... NON KAMERAD! NON KAMERAD!

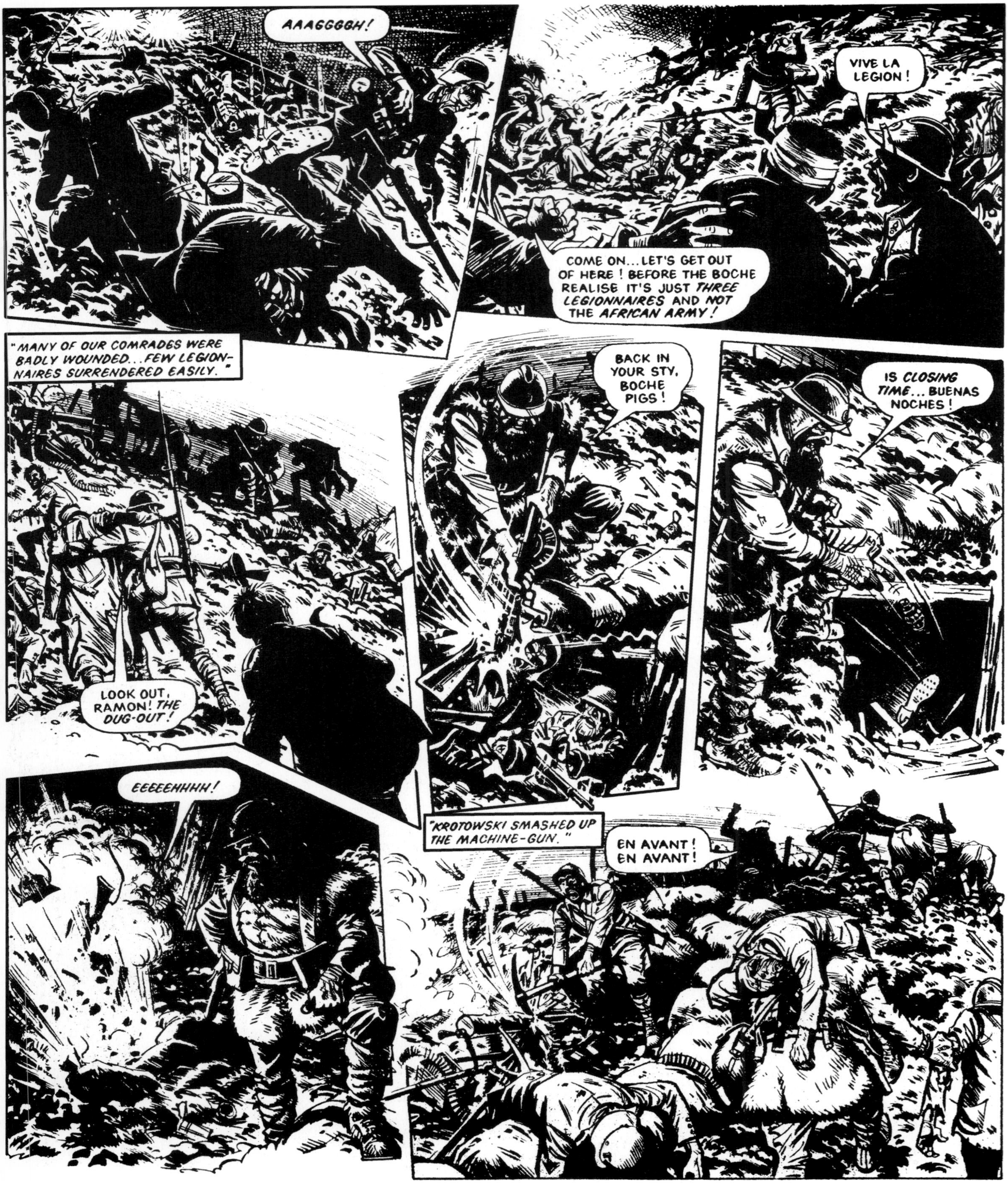

AAAGGGGH!
VIVE LA LEGION!
COME ON... LET'S GET OUT OF HERE! BEFORE THE BOCHE REALISE IT'S JUST THREE LEGIONNAIRES AND NOT THE AFRICAN ARMY!
"MANY OF OUR COMRADES WERE BADLY WOUNDED... FEW LEGIONNAIRES SURRENDERED EASILY."
LOOK OUT, RAMON! THE DUG-OUT!
BACK IN YOUR STY, BOCHE PIGS!
IS CLOSING TIME... BUENAS NOCHES!
EEEEEHHHH!
"KROTOWSKI SMASHED UP THE MACHINE-GUN."
EN AVANT! EN AVANT!

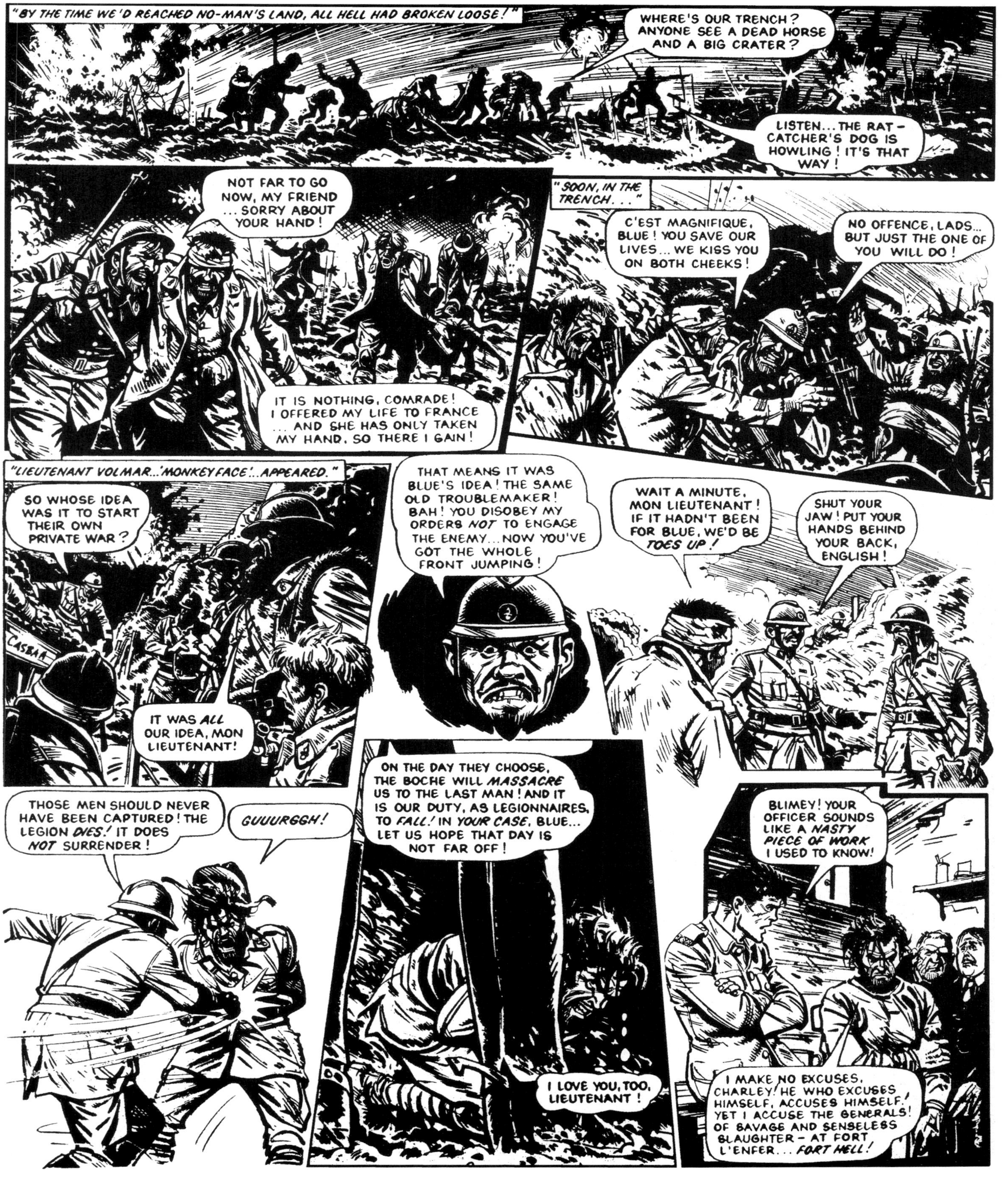
"BY THE TIME WE'D REACHED NO-MAN'S LAND, ALL HELL HAD BROKEN LOOSE!"
WHERE'S OUR TRENCH? ANYONE SEE A DEAD HORSE AND A BIG CRATER?
LISTEN... THE RAT-CATCHER'S DOG IS HOWLING! IT'S THAT WAY!
NOT FAR TO GO NOW, MY FRIEND ...SORRY ABOUT YOUR HAND!
IT IS NOTHING, COMRADE! I OFFERED MY LIFE TO FRANCE ... AND SHE HAS ONLY TAKEN MY HAND. SO THERE I GAIN!
"SOON, IN THE TRENCH..."
C'EST MAGNIFIQUE, BLUE! YOU SAVE OUR LIVES... WE KISS YOU ON BOTH CHEEKS!
NO OFFENCE, LADS... BUT JUST THE ONE OF YOU WILL DO!
"LIEUTENANT VOLMAR...'MONKEY FACE'...APPEARED."
SO WHOSE IDEA WAS IT TO START THEIR OWN PRIVATE WAR?
CASBAA
IT WAS ALL OUR IDEA, MON LIEUTENANT!
THAT MEANS IT WAS BLUE'S IDEA! THE SAME OLD TROUBLEMAKER! BAH! YOU DISOBEY MY ORDERS NOT TO ENGAGE THE ENEMY... NOW YOU'VE GOT THE WHOLE FRONT JUMPING!
WAIT A MINUTE, MON LIEUTENANT! IF IT HADN'T BEEN FOR BLUE, WE'D BE TOES UP!
SHUT YOUR JAW! PUT YOUR HANDS BEHIND YOUR BACK, ENGLISH!
THOSE MEN SHOULD NEVER HAVE BEEN CAPTURED! THE LEGION DIES! IT DOES NOT SURRENDER!
GUUURGGH!
ON THE DAY THEY CHOOSE, THE BOCHE WILL MASSACRE US TO THE LAST MAN! AND IT IS OUR DUTY, AS LEGIONNAIRES, TO FALL! IN YOUR CASE, BLUE... LET US HOPE THAT DAY IS NOT FAR OFF!
I LOVE YOU, TOO, LIEUTENANT!
BLIMEY! YOUR OFFICER SOUNDS LIKE A NASTY PIECE OF WORK I USED TO KNOW!
I MAKE NO EXCUSES, CHARLEY! HE WHO EXCUSES HIMSELF, ACCUSES HIMSELF! YET I ACCUSE THE GENERALS! OF SAVAGE AND SENSELESS SLAUGHTER - AT FORT L'ENFER... FORT HELL!

CHARLEY'S WAR

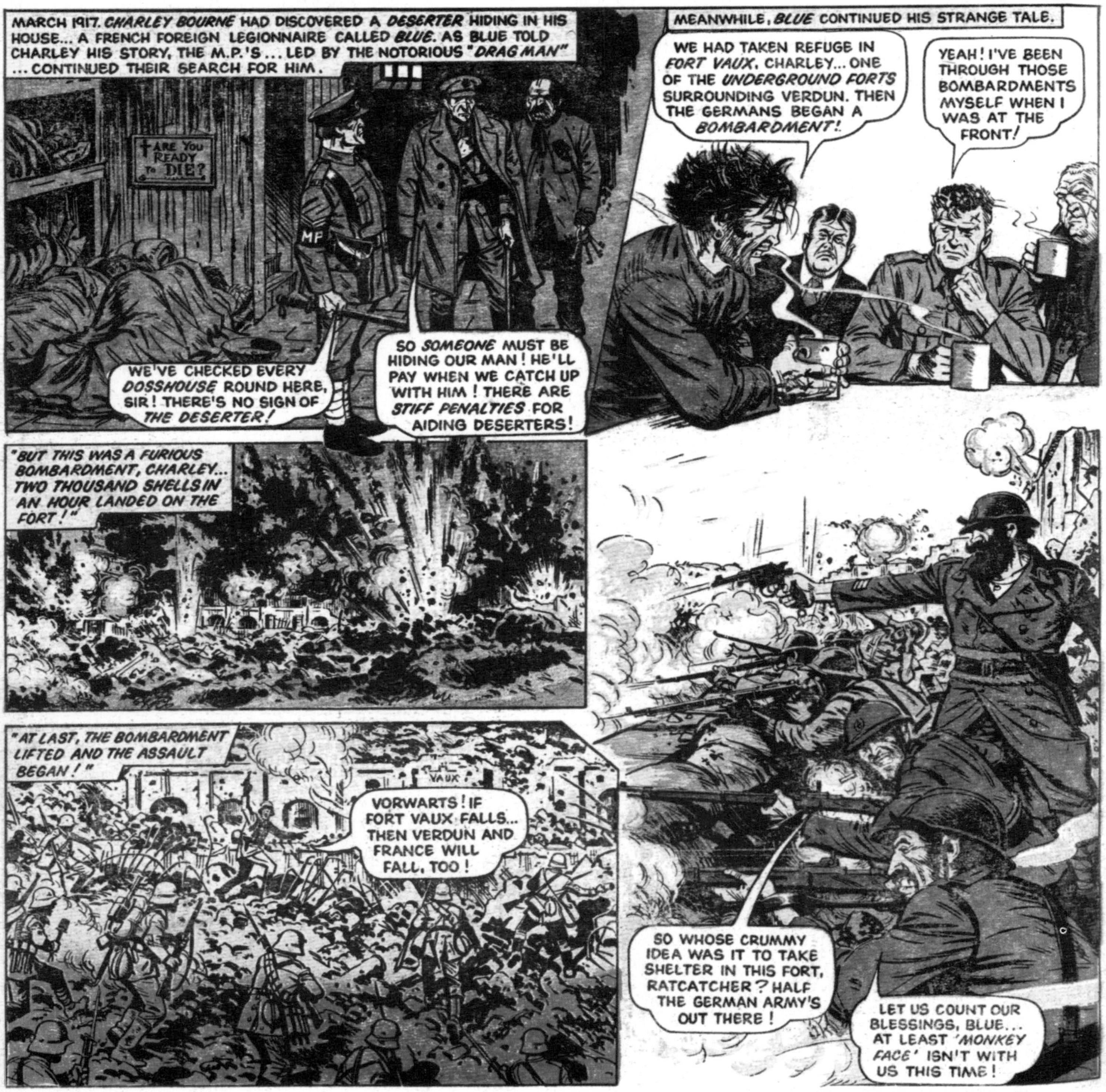

MARCH 1917. CHARLEY BOURNE HAD DISCOVERED A DESERTER HIDING IN HIS HOUSE... A FRENCH FOREIGN LEGIONNAIRE CALLED BLUE. AS BLUE TOLD CHARLEY HIS STORY, THE M.P.'S ... LED BY THE NOTORIOUS "DRAG MAN" ... CONTINUED THEIR SEARCH FOR HIM.
ARE YOU READY TO DIE?
MP
WE'VE CHECKED EVERY DOSSHOUSE ROUND HERE, SIR! THERE'S NO SIGN OF THE DESERTER!
SO SOMEONE MUST BE HIDING OUR MAN! HE'LL PAY WHEN WE CATCH UP WITH HIM! THERE ARE STIFF PENALTIES FOR AIDING DESERTERS!
MEANWHILE, BLUE CONTINUED HIS STRANGE TALE.
WE HAD TAKEN REFUGE IN FORT VAUX, CHARLEY... ONE OF THE UNDERGROUND FORTS SURROUNDING VERDUN. THEN THE GERMANS BEGAN A BOMBARDMENT!
YEAH! I'VE BEEN THROUGH THOSE BOMBARDMENTS MYSELF WHEN I WAS AT THE FRONT!
"BUT THIS WAS A FURIOUS BOMBARDMENT, CHARLEY... TWO THOUSAND SHELLS IN AN HOUR LANDED ON THE FORT!"
"AT LAST, THE BOMBARDMENT LIFTED AND THE ASSAULT BEGAN!"
VAUX
VORWARTS! IF FORT VAUX FALLS... THEN VERDUN AND FRANCE WILL FALL, TOO!
SO WHOSE CRUMMY IDEA WAS IT TO TAKE SHELTER IN THIS FORT, RATCATCHER? HALF THE GERMAN ARMY'S OUT THERE!
LET US COUNT OUR BLESSINGS, BLUE... AT LEAST 'MONKEY FACE' ISN'T WITH US THIS TIME!

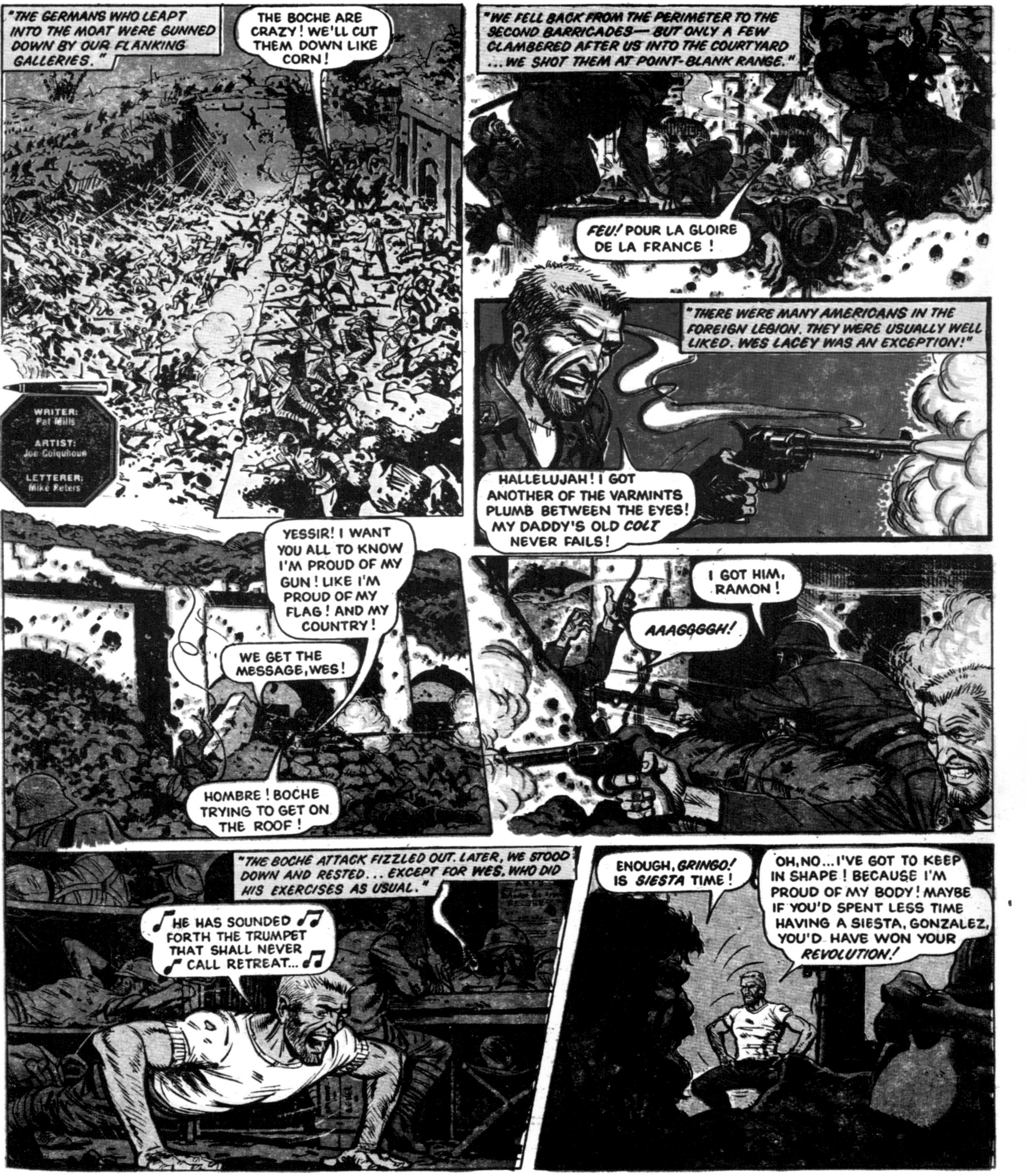
"THE GERMANS WHO LEAPT INTO THE MOAT WERE GUNNED DOWN BY OUR FLANKING GALLERIES."
THE BOCHE ARE CRAZY! WE'LL CUT THEM DOWN LIKE CORN!
WRITER: Pat Mills
ARTIST: Joe Colquhoun
LETTERER: Mike Peters
"WE FELL BACK FROM THE PERIMETER TO THE SECOND BARRICADES— BUT ONLY A FEW CLAMBERED AFTER US INTO THE COURTYARD ... WE SHOT THEM AT POINT-BLANK RANGE."
FEU! POUR LA GLOIRE DE LA FRANCE!
"THERE WERE MANY AMERICANS IN THE FOREIGN LEGION. THEY WERE USUALLY WELL LIKED. WES LACEY WAS AN EXCEPTION!"
HALLELUJAH! I GOT ANOTHER OF THE VARMINTS PLUMB BETWEEN THE EYES! MY DADDY'S OLD COLT NEVER FAILS!
YESSIR! I WANT YOU ALL TO KNOW I'M PROUD OF MY GUN! LIKE I'M PROUD OF MY FLAG! AND MY COUNTRY!
WE GET THE MESSAGE, WES!
HOMBRE! BOCHE TRYING TO GET ON THE ROOF!
I GOT HIM, RAMON!
AAAGGGGH!
"THE BOCHE ATTACK FIZZLED OUT. LATER, WE STOOD DOWN AND RESTED... EXCEPT FOR WES, WHO DID HIS EXERCISES AS USUAL."
♪ HE HAS SOUNDED ♫ FORTH THE TRUMPET THAT SHALL NEVER ♪ CALL RETREAT... ♫
ENOUGH, GRINGO! IS SIESTA TIME!
OH, NO... I'VE GOT TO KEEP IN SHAPE! BECAUSE I'M PROUD OF MY BODY! MAYBE IF YOU'D SPENT LESS TIME HAVING A SIESTA, GONZALEZ, YOU'D HAVE WON YOUR REVOLUTION!

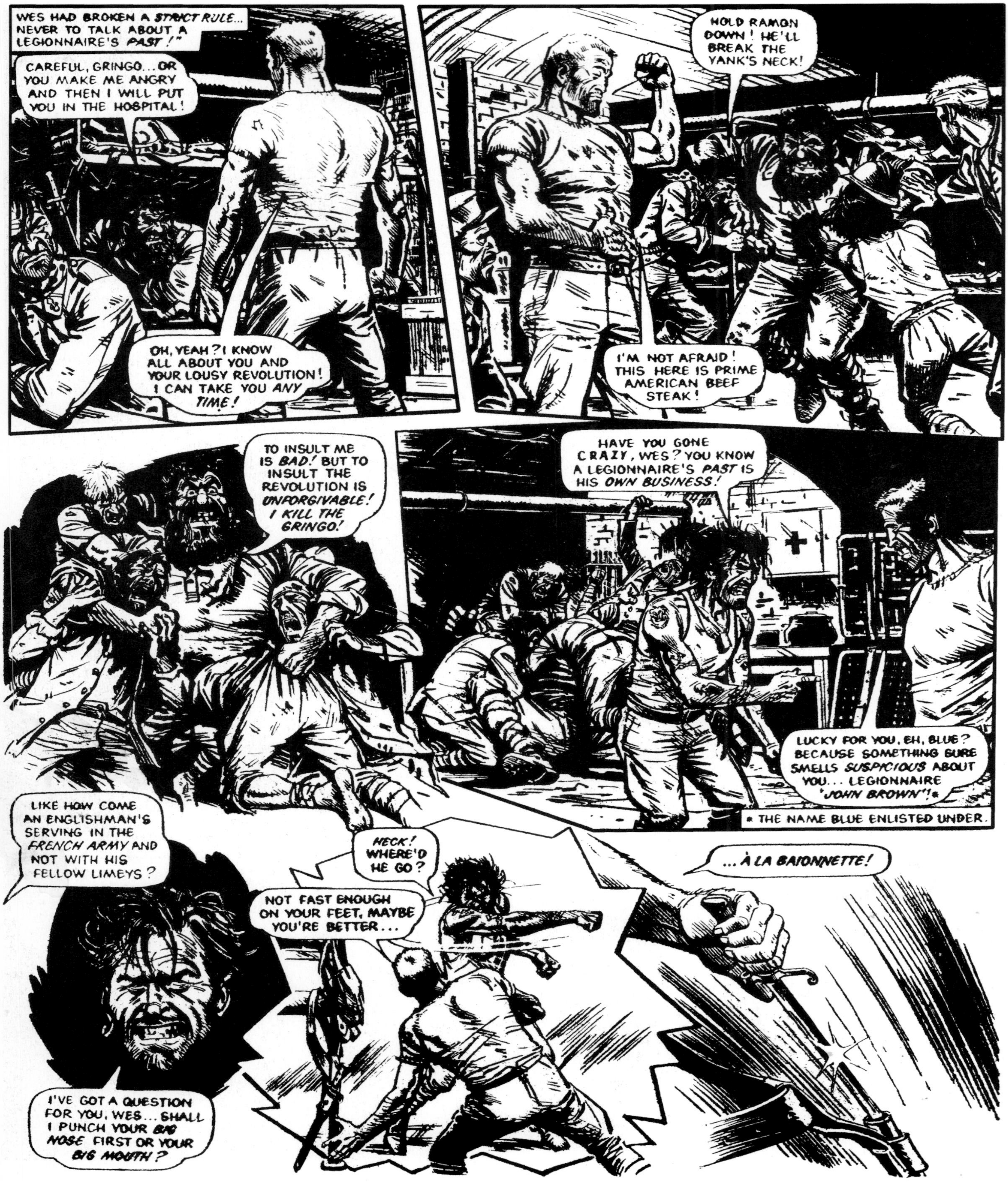
WES HAD BROKEN A STRICT RULE... NEVER TO TALK ABOUT A LEGIONNAIRE'S PAST!"
CAREFUL, GRINGO... OR YOU MAKE ME ANGRY AND THEN I WILL PUT YOU IN THE HOSPITAL!
OH, YEAH? I KNOW ALL ABOUT YOU AND YOUR LOUSY REVOLUTION! I CAN TAKE YOU ANY TIME!
HOLD RAMON DOWN! HE'LL BREAK THE YANK'S NECK!
I'M NOT AFRAID! THIS HERE IS PRIME AMERICAN BEEF STEAK!
TO INSULT ME IS BAD! BUT TO INSULT THE REVOLUTION IS UNFORGIVABLE! I KILL THE GRINGO!
HAVE YOU GONE CRAZY, WES? YOU KNOW A LEGIONNAIRE'S PAST IS HIS OWN BUSINESS!
LUCKY FOR YOU, EH, BLUE? BECAUSE SOMETHING SURE SMELLS SUSPICIOUS ABOUT YOU... LEGIONNAIRE "JOHN BROWN"!*
* THE NAME BLUE ENLISTED UNDER.
LIKE HOW COME AN ENGLISHMAN'S SERVING IN THE FRENCH ARMY AND NOT WITH HIS FELLOW LIMEYS?
I'VE GOT A QUESTION FOR YOU, WES... SHALL I PUNCH YOUR BIG NOSE FIRST OR YOUR BIG MOUTH?
HECK! WHERE'D HE GO?
NOT FAST ENOUGH ON YOUR FEET, MAYBE YOU'RE BETTER...
... À LA BAIONNETTE!

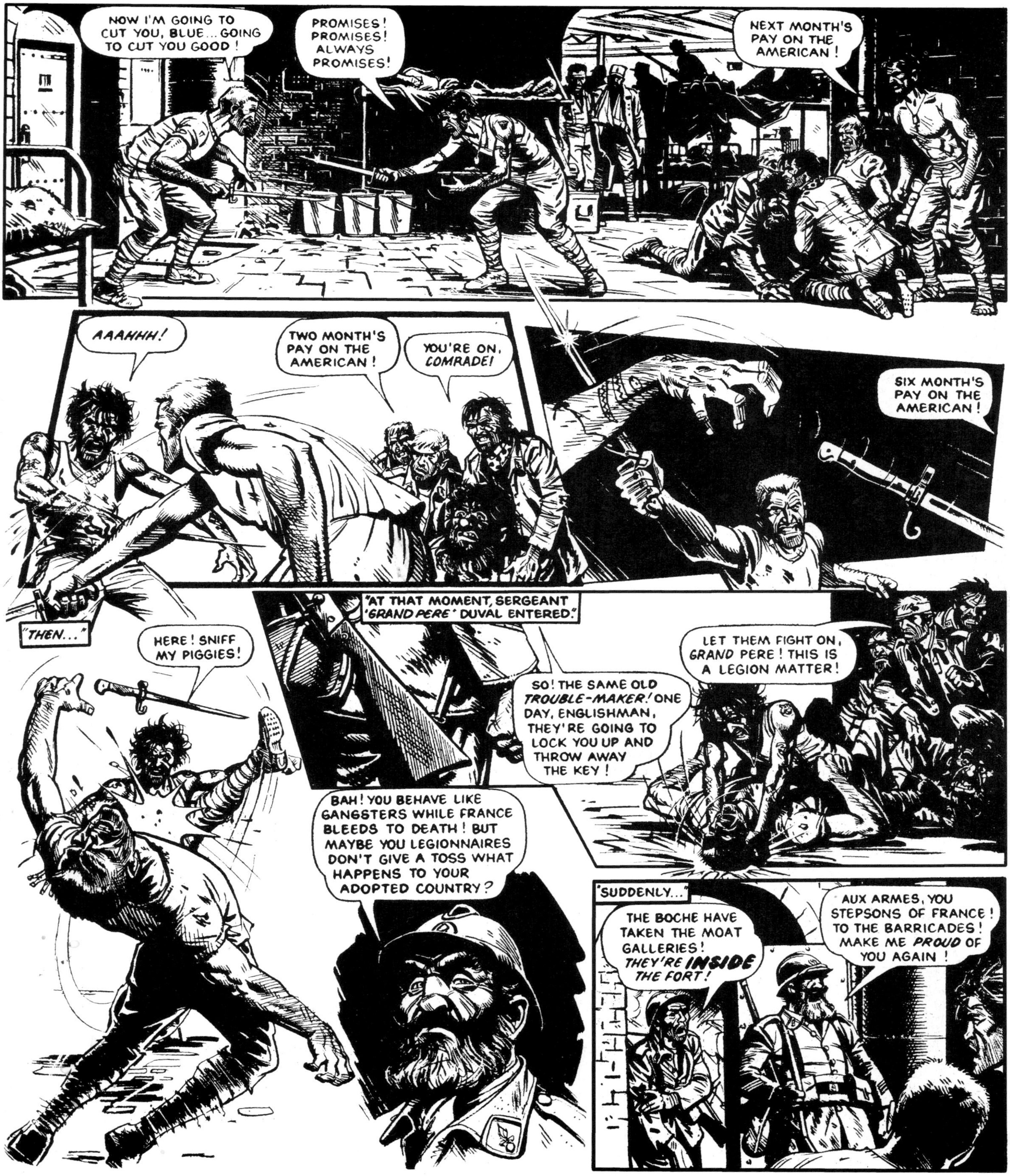
NOW I'M GOING TO CUT YOU, BLUE... GOING TO CUT YOU GOOD!
PROMISES! PROMISES! ALWAYS PROMISES!
NEXT MONTH'S PAY ON THE AMERICAN!
AAAHHH!
TWO MONTH'S PAY ON THE AMERICAN!
YOU'RE ON, COMRADE!
SIX MONTH'S PAY ON THE AMERICAN!
"THEN..."
HERE! SNIFF MY PIGGIES!
"AT THAT MOMENT, SERGEANT 'GRAND PERE' DUVAL ENTERED."
SO! THE SAME OLD TROUBLE-MAKER! ONE DAY, ENGLISHMAN, THEY'RE GOING TO LOCK YOU UP AND THROW AWAY THE KEY!
LET THEM FIGHT ON, GRAND PERE! THIS IS A LEGION MATTER!
BAH! YOU BEHAVE LIKE GANGSTERS WHILE FRANCE BLEEDS TO DEATH! BUT MAYBE YOU LEGIONNAIRES DON'T GIVE A TOSS WHAT HAPPENS TO YOUR ADOPTED COUNTRY?
"SUDDENLY..."
THE BOCHE HAVE TAKEN THE MOAT GALLERIES! THEY'RE INSIDE THE FORT!
AUX ARMES, YOU STEPSONS OF FRANCE! TO THE BARRICADES! MAKE ME PROUD OF YOU AGAIN!

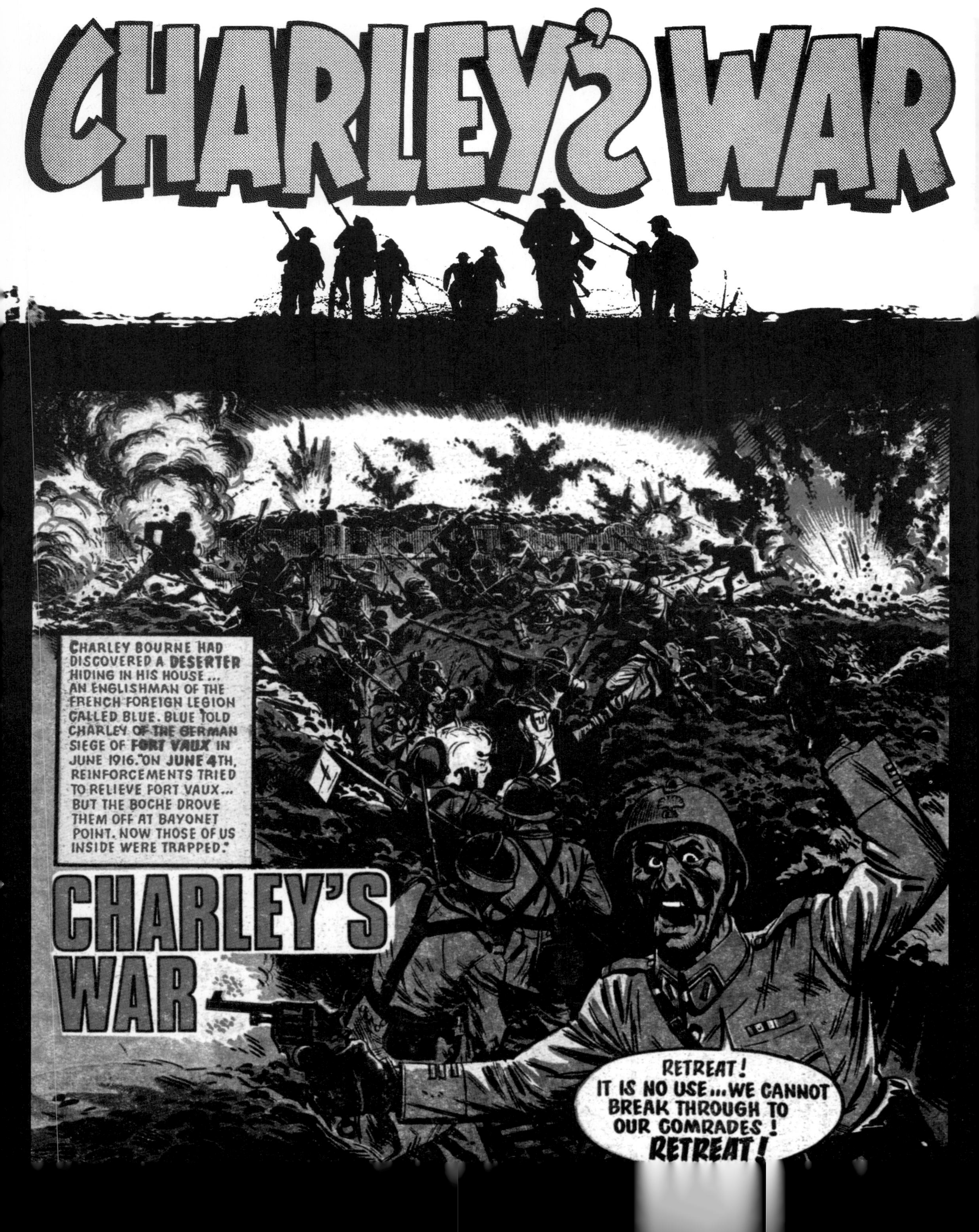
CHARLEY'S WAR
CHARLEY BOURNE HAD DISCOVERED A DESERTER HIDING IN HIS HOUSE... AN ENGLISHMAN OF THE FRENCH FOREIGN LEGION CALLED BLUE. BLUE TOLD CHARLEY OF THE GERMAN SIEGE OF FORT VAUX IN JUNE 1916. "ON JUNE 4TH, REINFORCEMENTS TRIED TO RELIEVE FORT VAUX... BUT THE BOCHE DROVE THEM OFF AT BAYONET POINT. NOW THOSE OF US INSIDE WERE TRAPPED."
CHARLEY'S WAR
RETREAT! IT IS NO USE... WE CANNOT BREAK THROUGH TO OUR COMRADES! RETREAT!

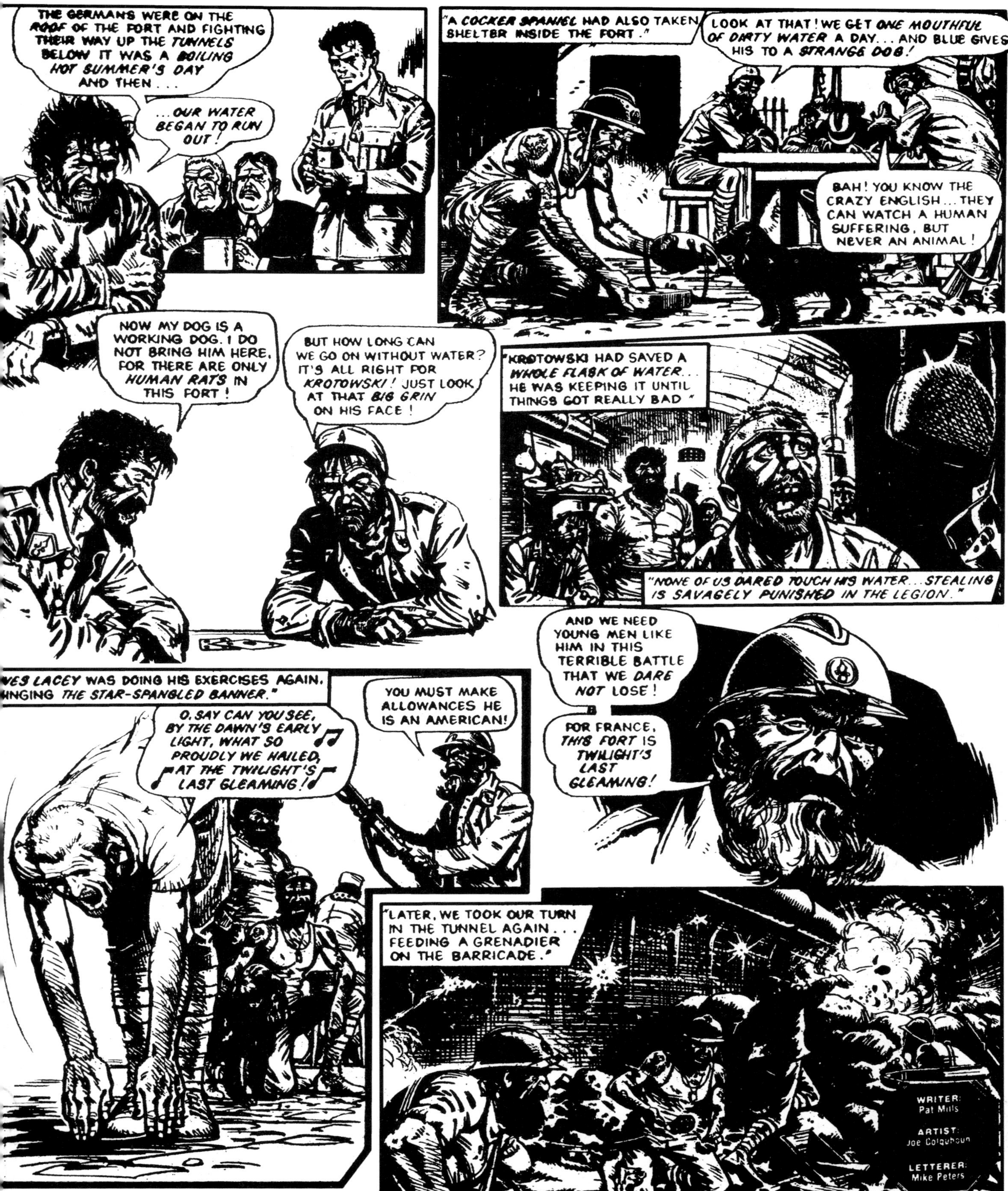
THE GERMANS WERE ON THE ROOF OF THE FORT AND FIGHTING THEIR WAY UP THE TUNNELS BELOW IT WAS A BOILING HOT SUMMER'S DAY AND THEN . . .
. . . OUR WATER BEGAN TO RUN OUT!
"A COCKER SPANIEL HAD ALSO TAKEN SHELTER INSIDE THE FORT."
LOOK AT THAT! WE GET ONE MOUTHFUL OF DIRTY WATER A DAY. . . AND BLUE GIVES HIS TO A STRANGE DOG!
BAH! YOU KNOW THE CRAZY ENGLISH. . . THEY CAN WATCH A HUMAN SUFFERING, BUT NEVER AN ANIMAL!
NOW MY DOG IS A WORKING DOG. I DO NOT BRING HIM HERE, FOR THERE ARE ONLY HUMAN RATS IN THIS FORT!
BUT HOW LONG CAN WE GO ON WITHOUT WATER? IT'S ALL RIGHT FOR KROTOWSKI! JUST LOOK AT THAT BIG GRIN ON HIS FACE!
"KROTOWSKI HAD SAVED A WHOLE FLASK OF WATER. . . HE WAS KEEPING IT UNTIL THINGS GOT REALLY BAD."
"NONE OF US DARED TOUCH HIS WATER. . . STEALING IS SAVAGELY PUNISHED IN THE LEGION."
VES LACEY WAS DOING HIS EXERCISES AGAIN. NGING THE STAR-SPANGLED BANNER."
O, SAY CAN YOU SEE, BY THE DAWN'S EARLY LIGHT, WHAT SO PROUDLY WE HAILED, AT THE TWILIGHT'S LAST GLEAMING!
YOU MUST MAKE ALLOWANCES HE IS AN AMERICAN!
AND WE NEED YOUNG MEN LIKE HIM IN THIS TERRIBLE BATTLE THAT WE DARE NOT LOSE!
FOR FRANCE, THIS FORT IS TWILIGHT'S LAST GLEAMING!
"LATER, WE TOOK OUR TURN IN THE TUNNEL AGAIN. . . FEEDING A GRENADIER ON THE BARRICADE."
WRITER: Pat Mills
ARTIST: Joe Colquhoun
LETTERER: Mike Peters

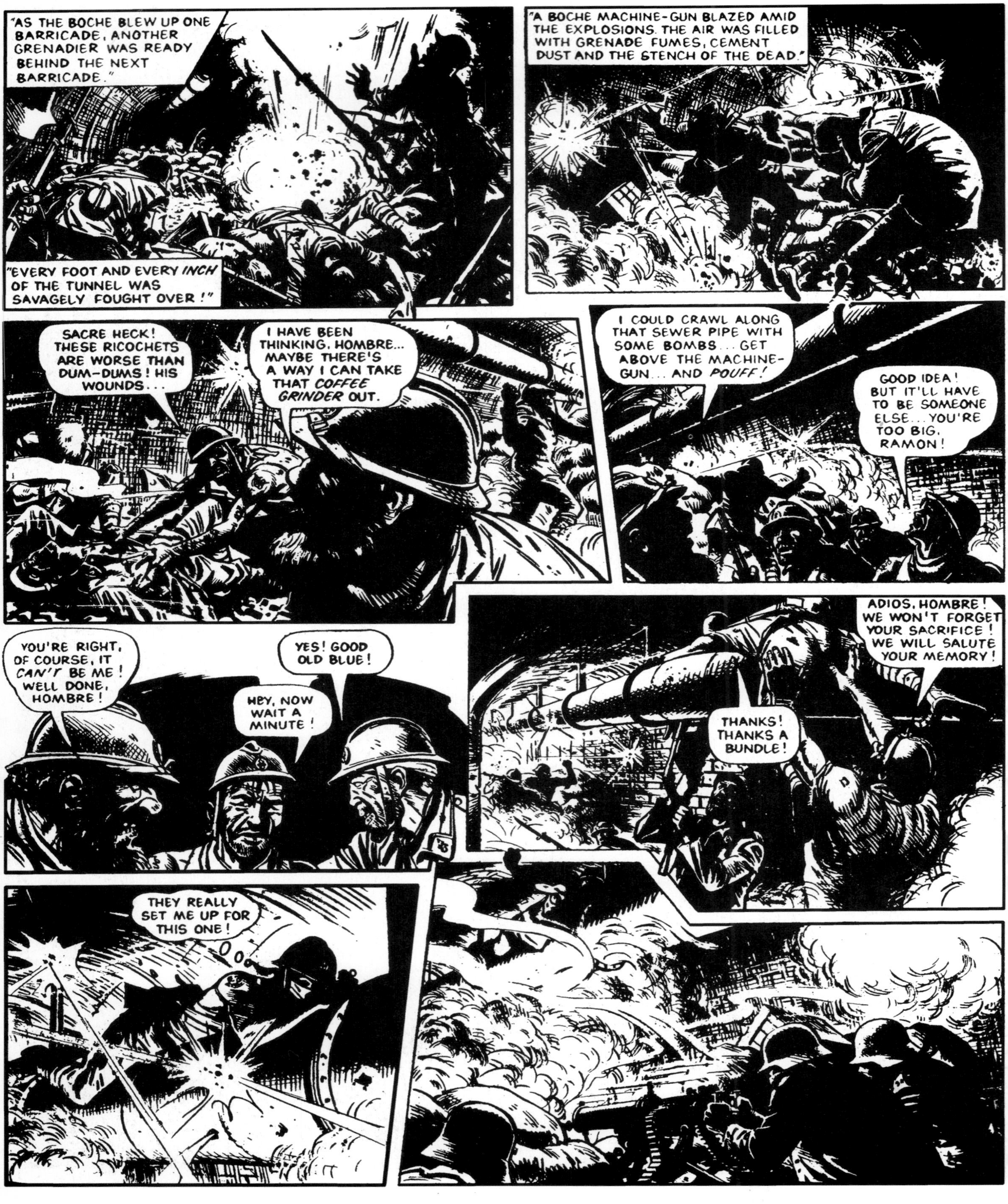
"AS THE BOCHE BLEW UP ONE BARRICADE, ANOTHER GRENADIER WAS READY BEHIND THE NEXT BARRICADE."
"EVERY FOOT AND EVERY *INCH* OF THE TUNNEL WAS SAVAGELY FOUGHT OVER!"
"A BOCHE MACHINE-GUN BLAZED AMID THE EXPLOSIONS. THE AIR WAS FILLED WITH GRENADE FUMES, CEMENT DUST AND THE STENCH OF THE DEAD."
SACRE HECK! THESE RICOCHETS ARE WORSE THAN DUM-DUMS! HIS WOUNDS...
I HAVE BEEN THINKING, HOMBRE... MAYBE THERE'S A WAY I CAN TAKE THAT *COFFEE GRINDER* OUT.
I COULD CRAWL ALONG THAT SEWER PIPE WITH SOME BOMBS... GET ABOVE THE MACHINE-GUN... AND *POUFF!*
GOOD IDEA! BUT IT'LL HAVE TO BE SOMEONE ELSE... YOU'RE TOO BIG, RAMON!
YOU'RE RIGHT, OF COURSE, IT *CAN'T* BE ME! WELL DONE, HOMBRE!
HEY, NOW WAIT A MINUTE!
YES! GOOD OLD BLUE!
ADIOS, HOMBRE! WE WON'T FORGET YOUR SACRIFICE! WE WILL SALUTE YOUR MEMORY!
THANKS! THANKS A BUNDLE!
THEY REALLY SET ME UP FOR THIS ONE!

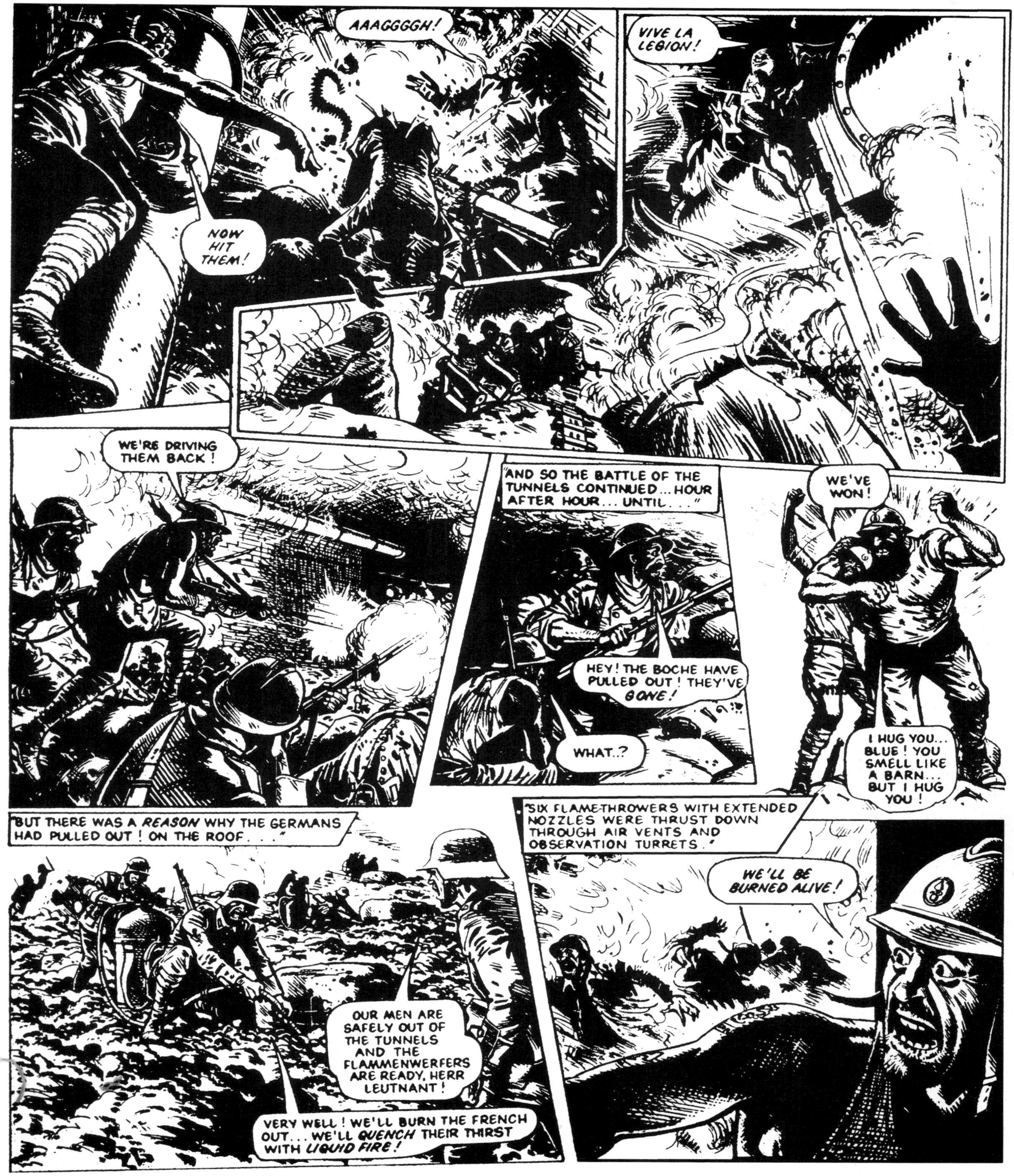
NOW HIT THEM!
AAAGGGGH!
VIVE LA LEGION!
WE'RE DRIVING THEM BACK!
"AND SO THE BATTLE OF THE TUNNELS CONTINUED... HOUR AFTER HOUR... UNTIL..."
HEY! THE BOCHE HAVE PULLED OUT! THEY'VE GONE!
WHAT..?
WE'VE WON!
I HUG YOU... BLUE! YOU SMELL LIKE A BARN... BUT I HUG YOU!
"BUT THERE WAS A REASON WHY THE GERMANS HAD PULLED OUT! ON THE ROOF..."
OUR MEN ARE SAFELY OUT OF THE TUNNELS AND THE FLAMMENWERFERS ARE READY, HERR LEUTNANT!
VERY WELL! WE'LL BURN THE FRENCH OUT... WE'LL QUENCH THEIR THIRST WITH LIQUID FIRE!
"SIX FLAMETHROWERS WITH EXTENDED NOZZLES WERE THRUST DOWN THROUGH AIR VENTS AND OBSERVATION TURRETS."
WE'LL BE BURNED ALIVE!

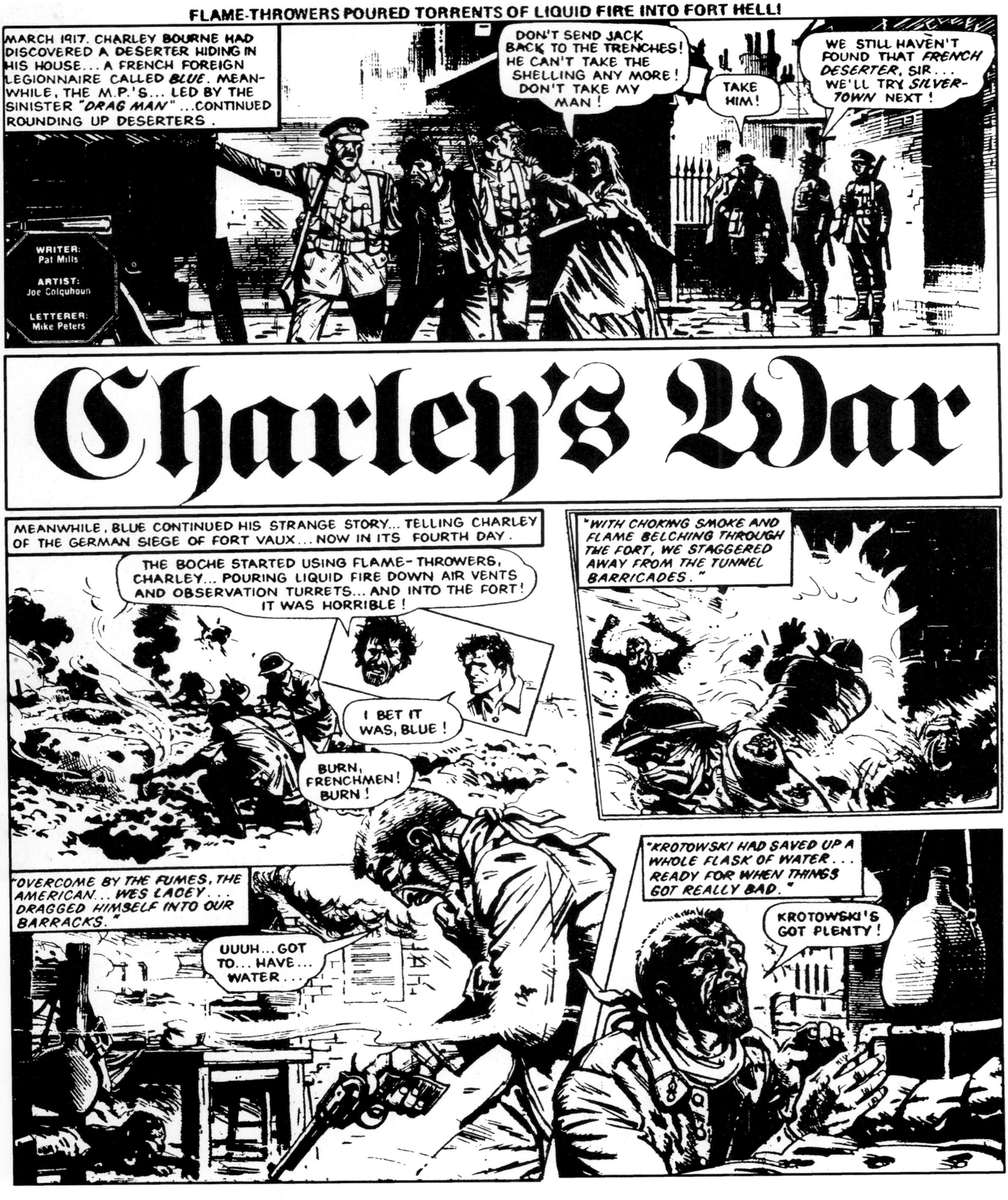
FLAME-THROWERS POURED TORRENTS OF LIQUID FIRE INTO FORT HELL!
MARCH 1917. CHARLEY BOURNE HAD DISCOVERED A DESERTER HIDING IN HIS HOUSE... A FRENCH FOREIGN LEGIONNAIRE CALLED BLUE. MEANWHILE, THE M.P.'S... LED BY THE SINISTER "DRAG MAN"...CONTINUED ROUNDING UP DESERTERS.
DON'T SEND JACK BACK TO THE TRENCHES! HE CAN'T TAKE THE SHELLING ANY MORE! DON'T TAKE MY MAN!
TAKE HIM!
WE STILL HAVEN'T FOUND THAT FRENCH DESERTER, SIR... WE'LL TRY SILVERTOWN NEXT!
WRITER: Pat Mills
ARTIST: Joe Colquhoun
LETTERER: Mike Peters
Charley's War
MEANWHILE, BLUE CONTINUED HIS STRANGE STORY... TELLING CHARLEY OF THE GERMAN SIEGE OF FORT VAUX... NOW IN ITS FOURTH DAY.
THE BOCHE STARTED USING FLAME-THROWERS, CHARLEY... POURING LIQUID FIRE DOWN AIR VENTS AND OBSERVATION TURRETS... AND INTO THE FORT! IT WAS HORRIBLE!
I BET IT WAS, BLUE!
BURN, FRENCHMEN! BURN!
"WITH CHOKING SMOKE AND FLAME BELCHING THROUGH THE FORT, WE STAGGERED AWAY FROM THE TUNNEL BARRICADES."
"OVERCOME BY THE FUMES, THE AMERICAN... WES LACEY... DRAGGED HIMSELF INTO OUR BARRACKS."
UUUH... GOT TO... HAVE... WATER...
"KROTOWSKI HAD SAVED UP A WHOLE FLASK OF WATER... READY FOR WHEN THINGS GOT REALLY BAD."
KROTOWSKI'S GOT PLENTY!

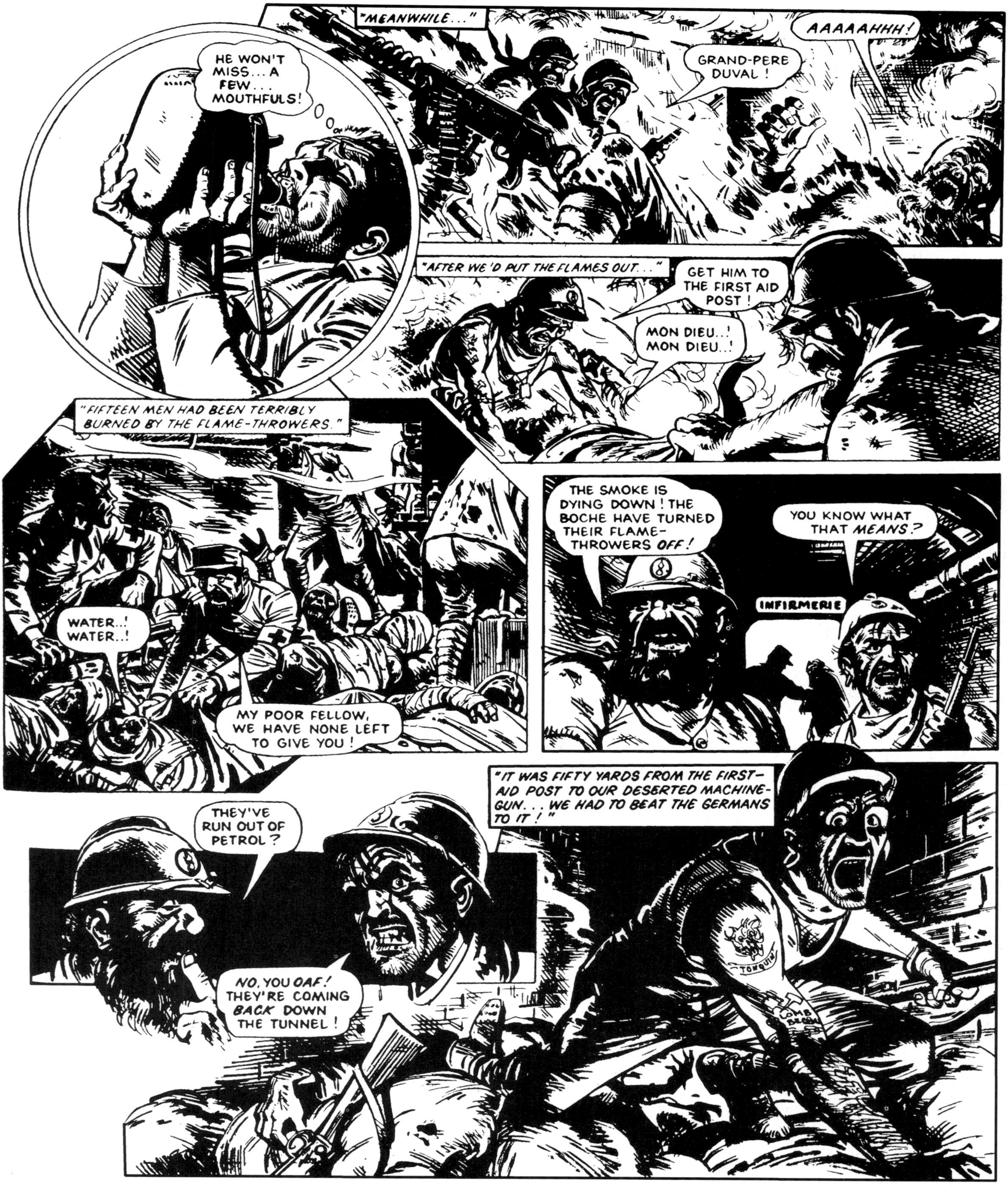
HE WON'T MISS... A FEW... MOUTHFULS!
"MEANWHILE..."
GRAND-PERE DUVAL!
AAAAAHHH!
"AFTER WE'D PUT THE FLAMES OUT..."
GET HIM TO THE FIRST AID POST!
MON DIEU..! MON DIEU..!
"FIFTEEN MEN HAD BEEN TERRIBLY BURNED BY THE FLAME-THROWERS."
WATER..! WATER..!
MY POOR FELLOW, WE HAVE NONE LEFT TO GIVE YOU!
THE SMOKE IS DYING DOWN! THE BOCHE HAVE TURNED THEIR FLAME-THROWERS OFF!
YOU KNOW WHAT THAT MEANS?
INFIRMERIE
THEY'VE RUN OUT OF PETROL?
NO, YOU OAF! THEY'RE COMING BACK DOWN THE TUNNEL!
"IT WAS FIFTY YARDS FROM THE FIRST-AID POST TO OUR DESERTED MACHINE-GUN... WE HAD TO BEAT THE GERMANS TO IT!"

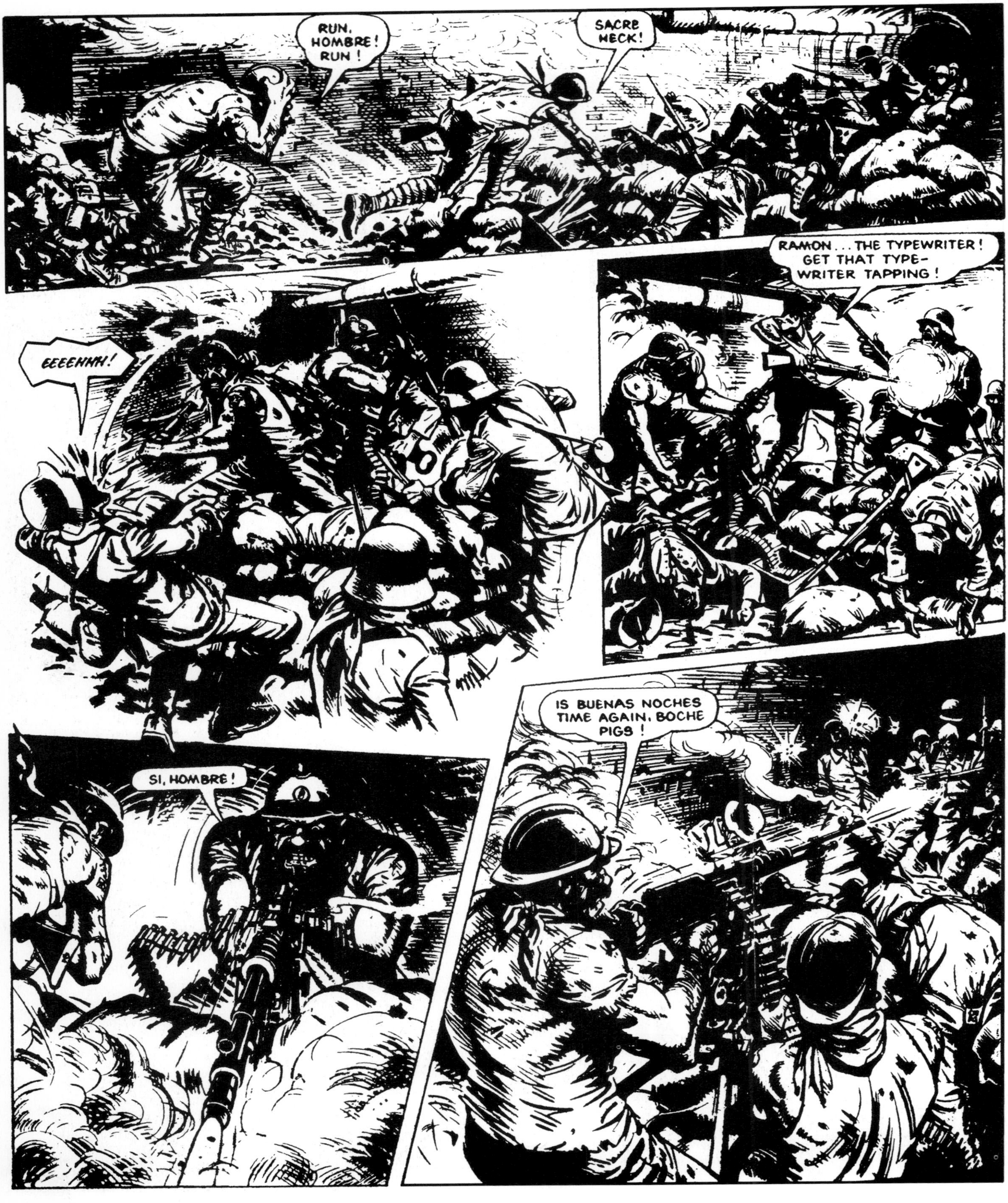
RUN, HOMBRE! RUN!
SACRE HECK!
EEEEHHH!
RAMON... THE TYPEWRITER! GET THAT TYPE-WRITER TAPPING!
SI, HOMBRE!
IS BUENAS NOCHES TIME AGAIN, BOCHE PIGS!

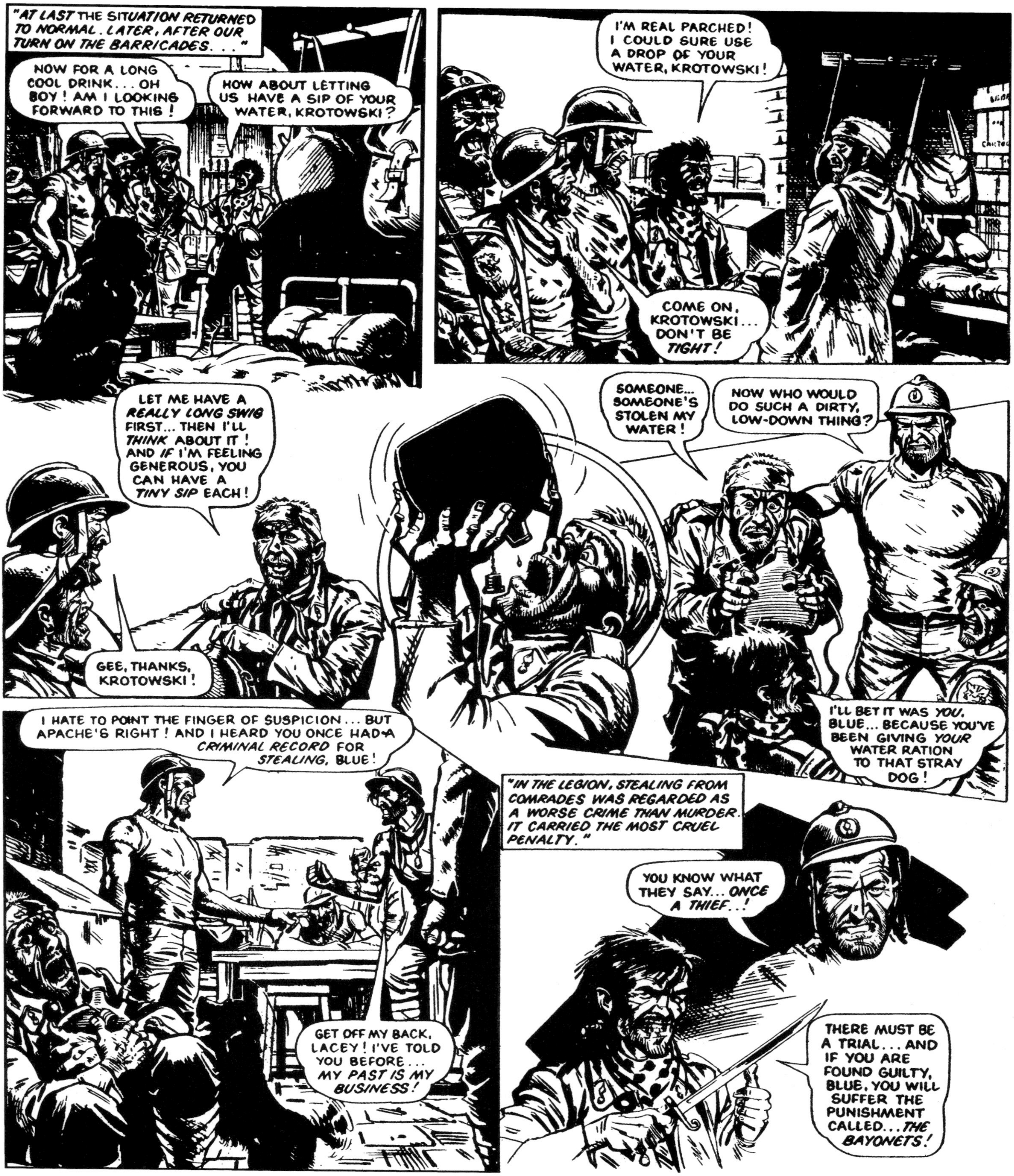
"AT LAST THE SITUATION RETURNED TO NORMAL. LATER, AFTER OUR TURN ON THE BARRICADES..."
NOW FOR A LONG COOL DRINK... OH BOY! AM I LOOKING FORWARD TO THIS!
HOW ABOUT LETTING US HAVE A SIP OF YOUR WATER, KROTOWSKI?
I'M REAL PARCHED! I COULD SURE USE A DROP OF YOUR WATER, KROTOWSKI!
COME ON, KROTOWSKI... DON'T BE TIGHT!
LET ME HAVE A REALLY LONG SWIG FIRST... THEN I'LL THINK ABOUT IT! AND IF I'M FEELING GENEROUS, YOU CAN HAVE A TINY SIP EACH!
GEE, THANKS, KROTOWSKI!
SOMEONE... SOMEONE'S STOLEN MY WATER!
NOW WHO WOULD DO SUCH A DIRTY, LOW-DOWN THING?
I'LL BET IT WAS YOU, BLUE... BECAUSE YOU'VE BEEN GIVING YOUR WATER RATION TO THAT STRAY DOG!
I HATE TO POINT THE FINGER OF SUSPICION... BUT APACHE'S RIGHT! AND I HEARD YOU ONCE HAD A CRIMINAL RECORD FOR STEALING, BLUE!
GET OFF MY BACK, LACEY! I'VE TOLD YOU BEFORE... MY PAST IS MY BUSINESS!
"IN THE LEGION, STEALING FROM COMRADES WAS REGARDED AS A WORSE CRIME THAN MURDER. IT CARRIED THE MOST CRUEL PENALTY."
YOU KNOW WHAT THEY SAY... ONCE A THIEF..!
THERE MUST BE A TRIAL... AND IF YOU ARE FOUND GUILTY, BLUE, YOU WILL SUFFER THE PUNISHMENT CALLED... THE BAYONETS!

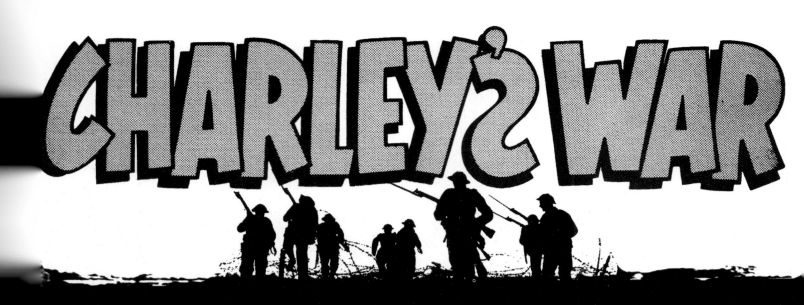

CHARLEY'S WAR

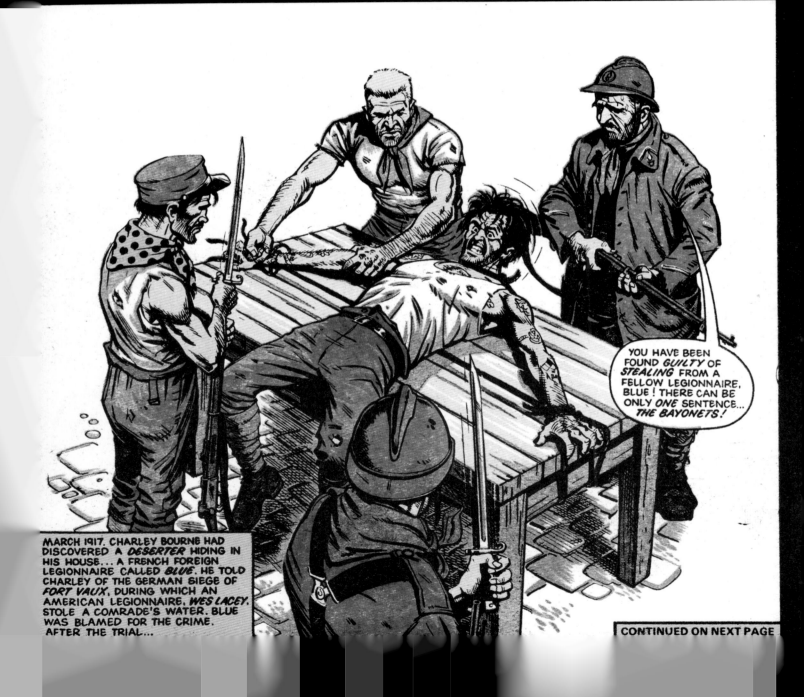

MARCH 1917. CHARLEY BOURNE HAD DISCOVERED A *DESERTER* HIDING IN HIS HOUSE... A FRENCH FOREIGN LEGIONNAIRE CALLED *BLUE*. HE TOLD CHARLEY OF THE GERMAN SIEGE OF *FORT VAUX*, DURING WHICH AN AMERICAN LEGIONNAIRE, *WES LACEY*, STOLE A COMRADE'S WATER. BLUE WAS BLAMED FOR THE CRIME. AFTER THE TRIAL...

YOU HAVE BEEN FOUND *GUILTY* OF *STEALING* FROM A FELLOW LEGIONNAIRE, BLUE! THERE CAN BE ONLY *ONE* SENTENCE... *THE BAYONETS!*

CONTINUED ON NEXT PAGE

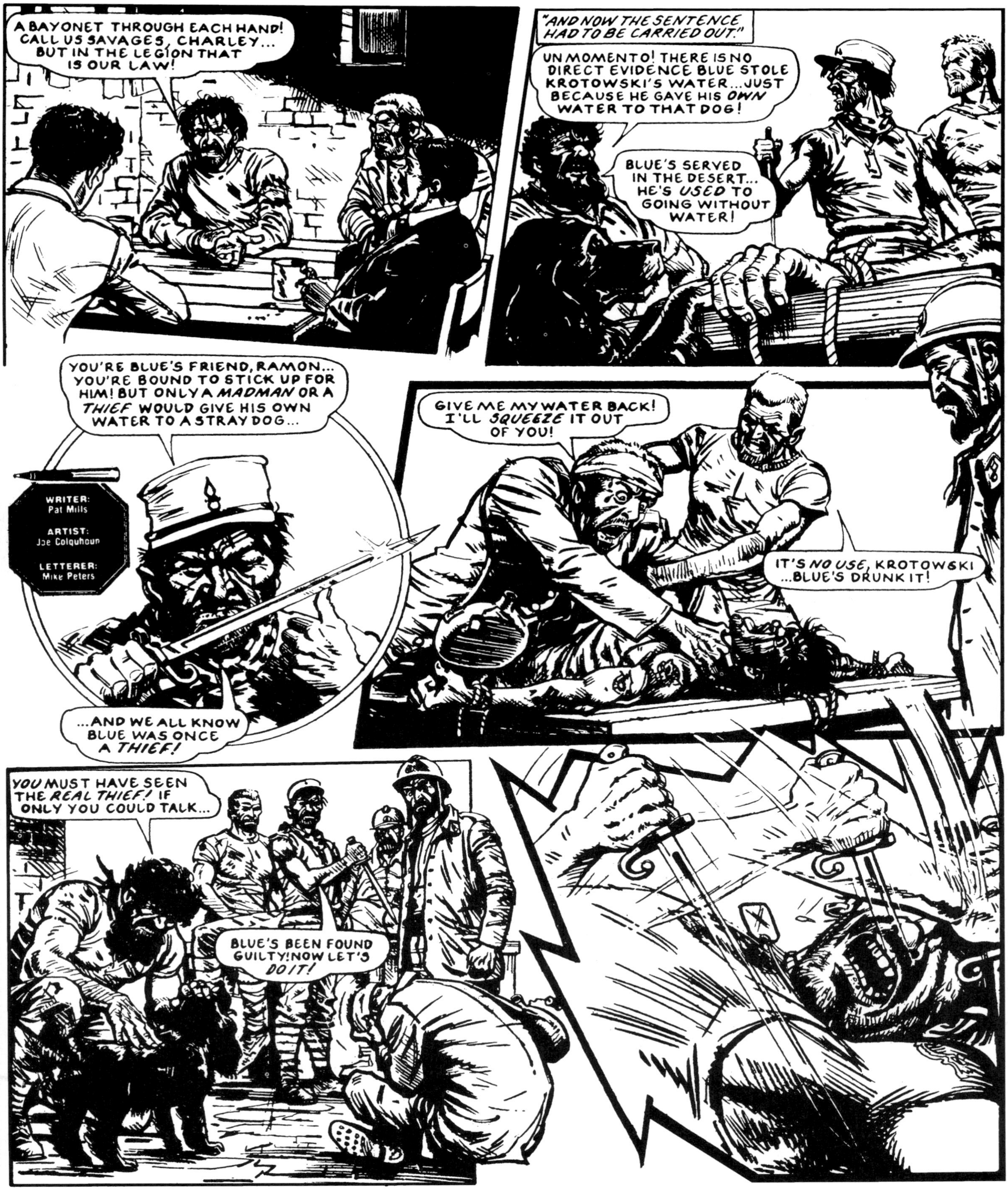
A BAYONET THROUGH EACH HAND! CALL US SAVAGES, CHARLEY... BUT IN THE LEGION THAT IS OUR LAW!
"AND NOW THE SENTENCE HAD TO BE CARRIED OUT."
UN MOMENTO! THERE IS NO DIRECT EVIDENCE BLUE STOLE KROTOWSKI'S WATER... JUST BECAUSE HE GAVE HIS OWN WATER TO THAT DOG!
BLUE'S SERVED IN THE DESERT... HE'S USED TO GOING WITHOUT WATER!
YOU'RE BLUE'S FRIEND, RAMON... YOU'RE BOUND TO STICK UP FOR HIM! BUT ONLY A MADMAN OR A THIEF WOULD GIVE HIS OWN WATER TO A STRAY DOG...
WRITER: Pat Mills
ARTIST: Joe Colquhoun
LETTERER: Mike Peters
...AND WE ALL KNOW BLUE WAS ONCE A THIEF!
GIVE ME MY WATER BACK! I'LL SQUEEZE IT OUT OF YOU!
IT'S NO USE, KROTOWSKI ...BLUE'S DRUNK IT!
YOU MUST HAVE SEEN THE REAL THIEF! IF ONLY YOU COULD TALK...
BLUE'S BEEN FOUND GUILTY! NOW LET'S DO IT!

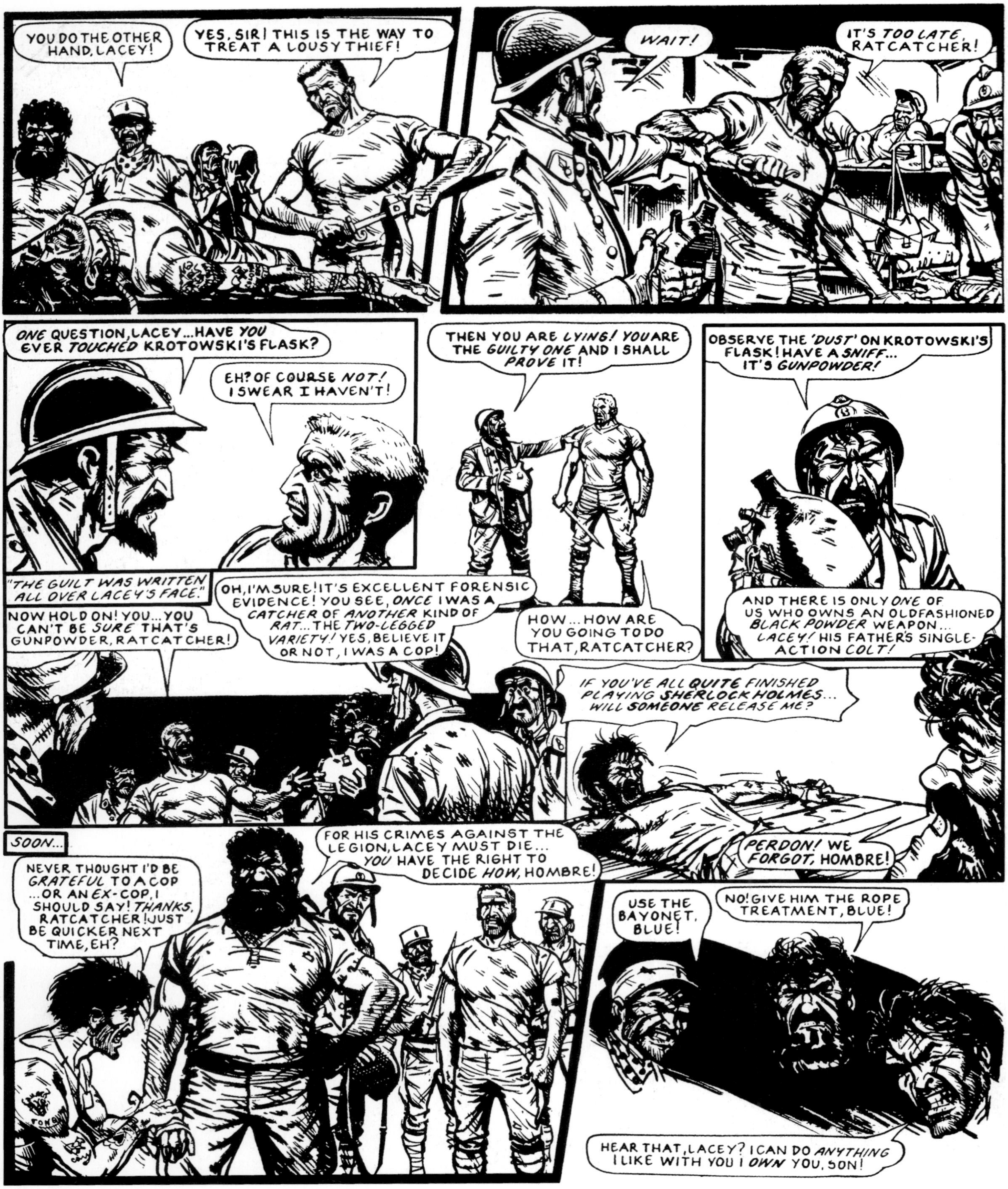
YOU DO THE OTHER HAND, LACEY!
YES, SIR! THIS IS THE WAY TO TREAT A LOUSY THIEF!
WAIT!
IT'S TOO LATE, RATCATCHER!
ONE QUESTION, LACEY... HAVE YOU EVER TOUCHED KROTOWSKI'S FLASK?
EH? OF COURSE NOT! I SWEAR I HAVEN'T!
THEN YOU ARE LYING! YOU ARE THE GUILTY ONE AND I SHALL PROVE IT!
HOW... HOW ARE YOU GOING TO DO THAT, RATCATCHER?
OBSERVE THE 'DUST' ON KROTOWSKI'S FLASK! HAVE A SNIFF... IT'S GUNPOWDER!
AND THERE IS ONLY ONE OF US WHO OWNS AN OLDFASHIONED BLACK POWDER WEAPON... LACEY! HIS FATHER'S SINGLE-ACTION COLT!
"THE GUILT WAS WRITTEN ALL OVER LACEY'S FACE."
NOW HOLD ON! YOU... YOU CAN'T BE SURE THAT'S GUNPOWDER, RATCATCHER!
OH, I'M SURE! IT'S EXCELLENT FORENSIC EVIDENCE! YOU SEE, ONCE I WAS A CATCHER OF ANOTHER KIND OF RAT... THE TWO-LEGGED VARIETY! YES, BELIEVE IT OR NOT, I WAS A COP!
IF YOU'VE ALL QUITE FINISHED PLAYING SHERLOCK HOLMES... WILL SOMEONE RELEASE ME?
PERDON! WE FORGOT, HOMBRE!
SOON...
NEVER THOUGHT I'D BE GRATEFUL TO A COP ...OR AN EX-COP, I SHOULD SAY! THANKS, RATCATCHER! JUST BE QUICKER NEXT TIME, EH?
FOR HIS CRIMES AGAINST THE LEGION, LACEY MUST DIE... YOU HAVE THE RIGHT TO DECIDE HOW, HOMBRE!
USE THE BAYONET, BLUE!
NO! GIVE HIM THE ROPE TREATMENT, BLUE!
HEAR THAT, LACEY? I CAN DO ANYTHING I LIKE WITH YOU I OWN YOU, SON!

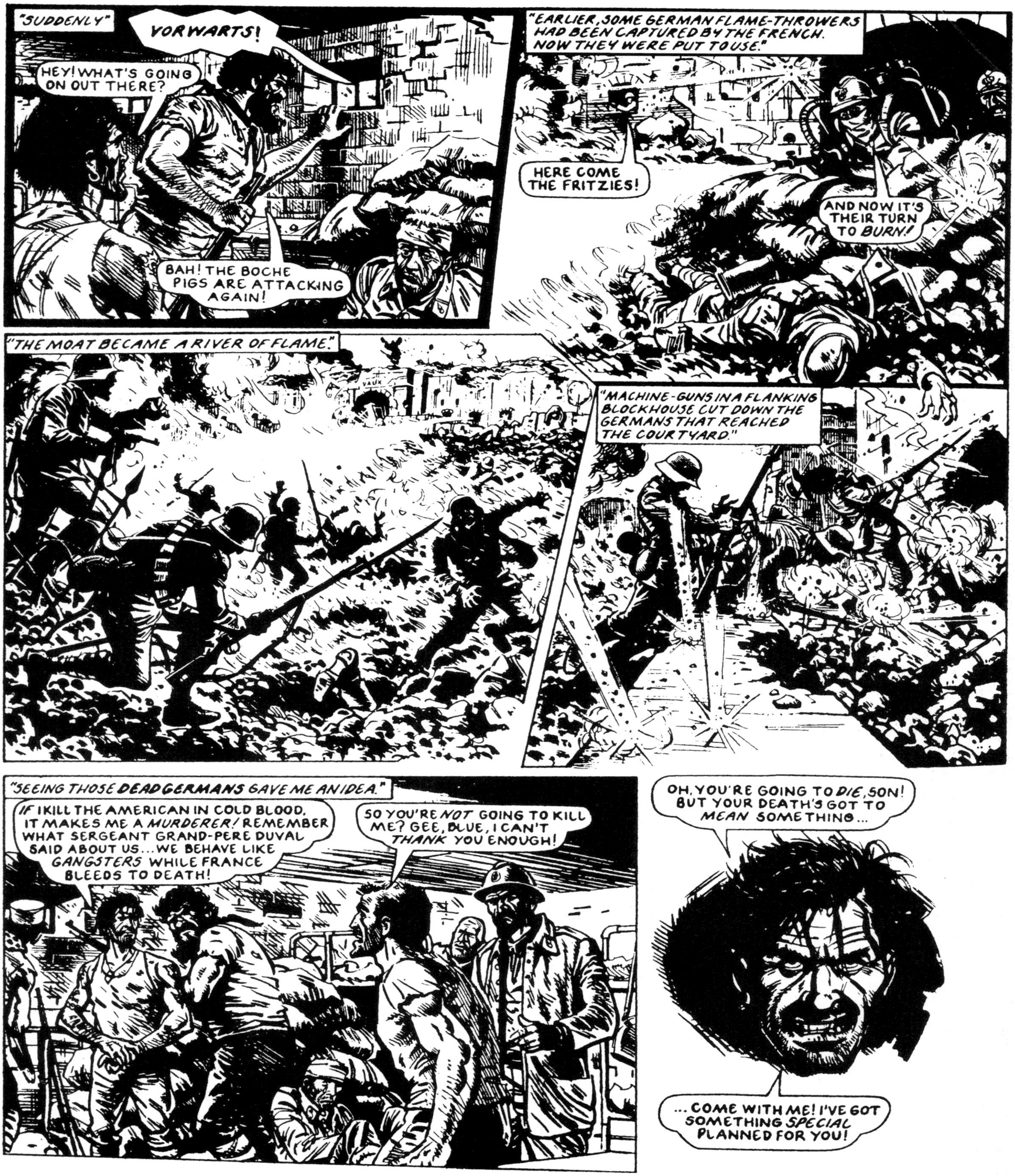

"SUDDENLY"
VORWARTS!
HEY! WHAT'S GOING ON OUT THERE?
BAH! THE BOCHE PIGS ARE ATTACKING AGAIN!
"EARLIER, SOME GERMAN FLAME-THROWERS HAD BEEN CAPTURED BY THE FRENCH. NOW THEY WERE PUT TO USE."
HERE COME THE FRITZIES!
AND NOW IT'S THEIR TURN TO BURN!
"THE MOAT BECAME A RIVER OF FLAME."
VAUX
"MACHINE-GUNS IN A FLANKING BLOCKHOUSE CUT DOWN THE GERMANS THAT REACHED THE COURTYARD."
"SEEING THOSE DEAD GERMANS GAVE ME AN IDEA."
IF I KILL THE AMERICAN IN COLD BLOOD, IT MAKES ME A MURDERER! REMEMBER WHAT SERGEANT GRAND-PERE DUVAL SAID ABOUT US... WE BEHAVE LIKE GANGSTERS WHILE FRANCE BLEEDS TO DEATH!
SO YOU'RE NOT GOING TO KILL ME? GEE, BLUE, I CAN'T THANK YOU ENOUGH!
OH, YOU'RE GOING TO DIE, SON! BUT YOUR DEATH'S GOT TO MEAN SOMETHING...
...COME WITH ME! I'VE GOT SOMETHING SPECIAL PLANNED FOR YOU!

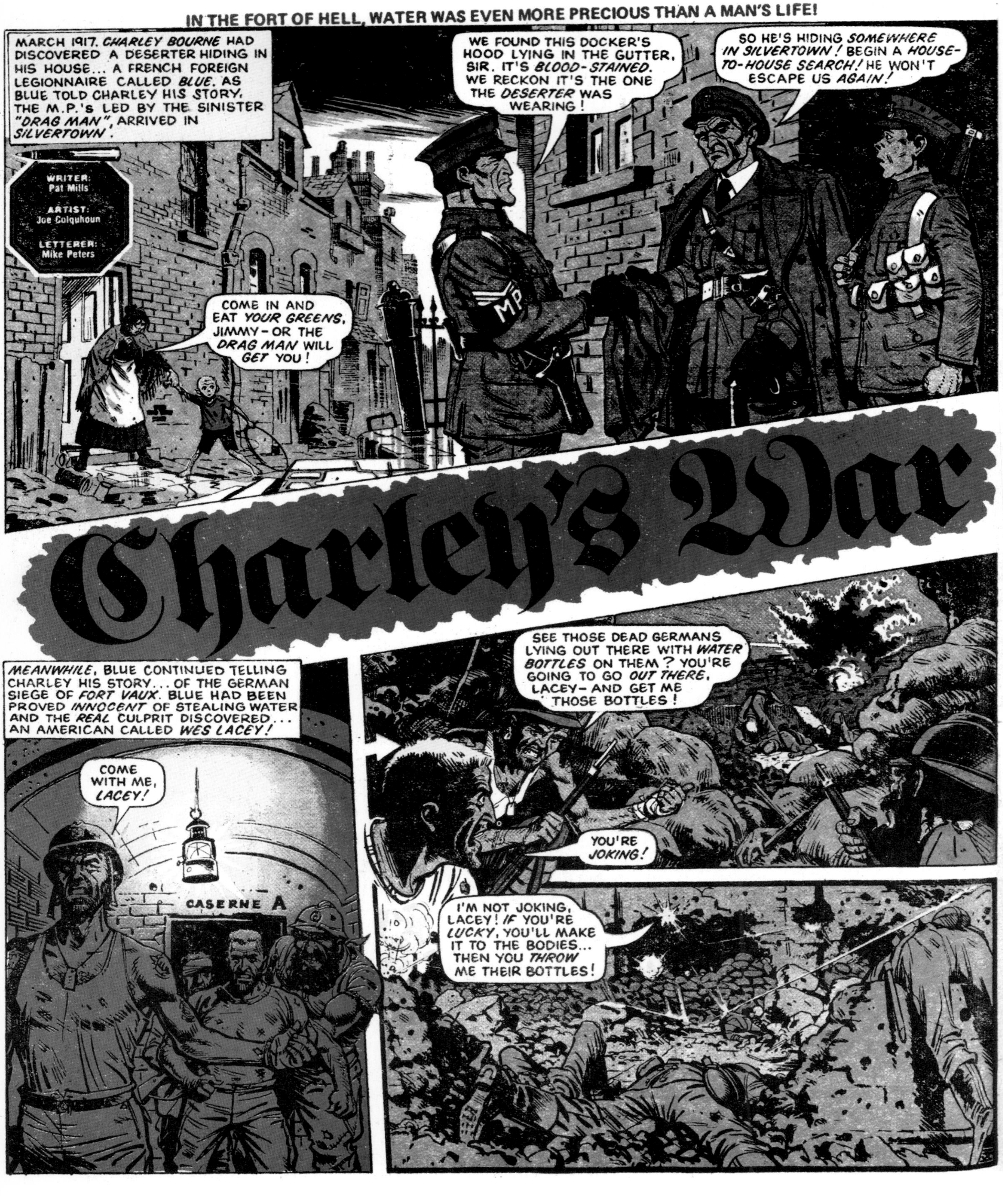

IN THE FORT OF HELL, WATER WAS EVEN MORE PRECIOUS THAN A MAN'S LIFE!
MARCH 1917. CHARLEY BOURNE HAD DISCOVERED A DESERTER HIDING IN HIS HOUSE... A FRENCH FOREIGN LEGIONNAIRE CALLED BLUE. AS BLUE TOLD CHARLEY HIS STORY, THE M.P.'s LED BY THE SINISTER "DRAG MAN", ARRIVED IN SILVERTOWN.
WRITER: Pat Mills
ARTIST: Joe Colquhoun
LETTERER: Mike Peters
COME IN AND EAT YOUR GREENS, JIMMY - OR THE DRAG MAN WILL GET YOU!
WE FOUND THIS DOCKER'S HOOD LYING IN THE GUTTER, SIR. IT'S BLOOD-STAINED. WE RECKON IT'S THE ONE THE DESERTER WAS WEARING!
SO HE'S HIDING SOMEWHERE IN SILVERTOWN! BEGIN A HOUSE-TO-HOUSE SEARCH! HE WON'T ESCAPE US AGAIN!
MP
Charley's War
MEANWHILE, BLUE CONTINUED TELLING CHARLEY HIS STORY... OF THE GERMAN SIEGE OF FORT VAUX. BLUE HAD BEEN PROVED INNOCENT OF STEALING WATER AND THE REAL CULPRIT DISCOVERED... AN AMERICAN CALLED WES LACEY!
COME WITH ME, LACEY!
CASERNE A
SEE THOSE DEAD GERMANS LYING OUT THERE WITH WATER BOTTLES ON THEM? YOU'RE GOING TO GO OUT THERE, LACEY - AND GET ME THOSE BOTTLES!
YOU'RE JOKING!
I'M NOT JOKING, LACEY! IF YOU'RE LUCKY, YOU'LL MAKE IT TO THE BODIES... THEN YOU THROW ME THEIR BOTTLES!

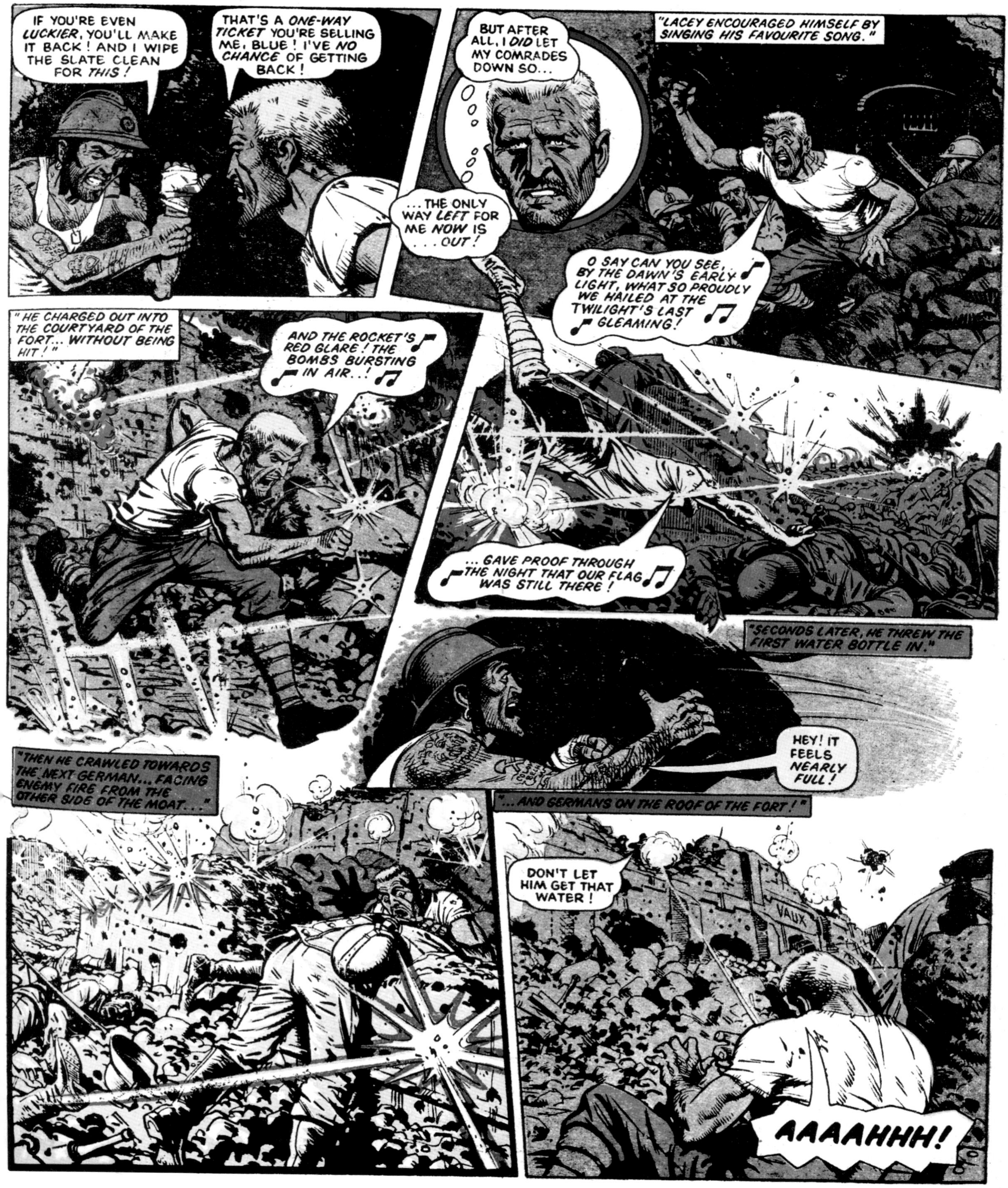

IF YOU'RE EVEN LUCKIER, YOU'LL MAKE IT BACK! AND I WIPE THE SLATE CLEAN FOR THIS!
THAT'S A ONE-WAY TICKET YOU'RE SELLING ME, BLUE! I'VE NO CHANCE OF GETTING BACK!
BUT AFTER ALL, I DID LET MY COMRADES DOWN SO...
...THE ONLY WAY LEFT FOR ME NOW IS . . . OUT!
"LACEY ENCOURAGED HIMSELF BY SINGING HIS FAVOURITE SONG."
O SAY CAN YOU SEE, BY THE DAWN'S EARLY LIGHT, WHAT SO PROUDLY WE HAILED AT THE TWILIGHT'S LAST GLEAMING!
"HE CHARGED OUT INTO THE COURTYARD OF THE FORT... WITHOUT BEING HIT!"
AND THE ROCKET'S RED GLARE! THE BOMBS BURSTING IN AIR..!
...GAVE PROOF THROUGH THE NIGHT THAT OUR FLAG WAS STILL THERE!
"SECONDS LATER, HE THREW THE FIRST WATER BOTTLE IN."
HEY! IT FEELS NEARLY FULL!
"THEN HE CRAWLED TOWARDS THE NEXT GERMAN... FACING ENEMY FIRE FROM THE OTHER SIDE OF THE MOAT..."
"...AND GERMANS ON THE ROOF OF THE FORT!"
DON'T LET HIM GET THAT WATER!
VAUX
AAAAHHH!

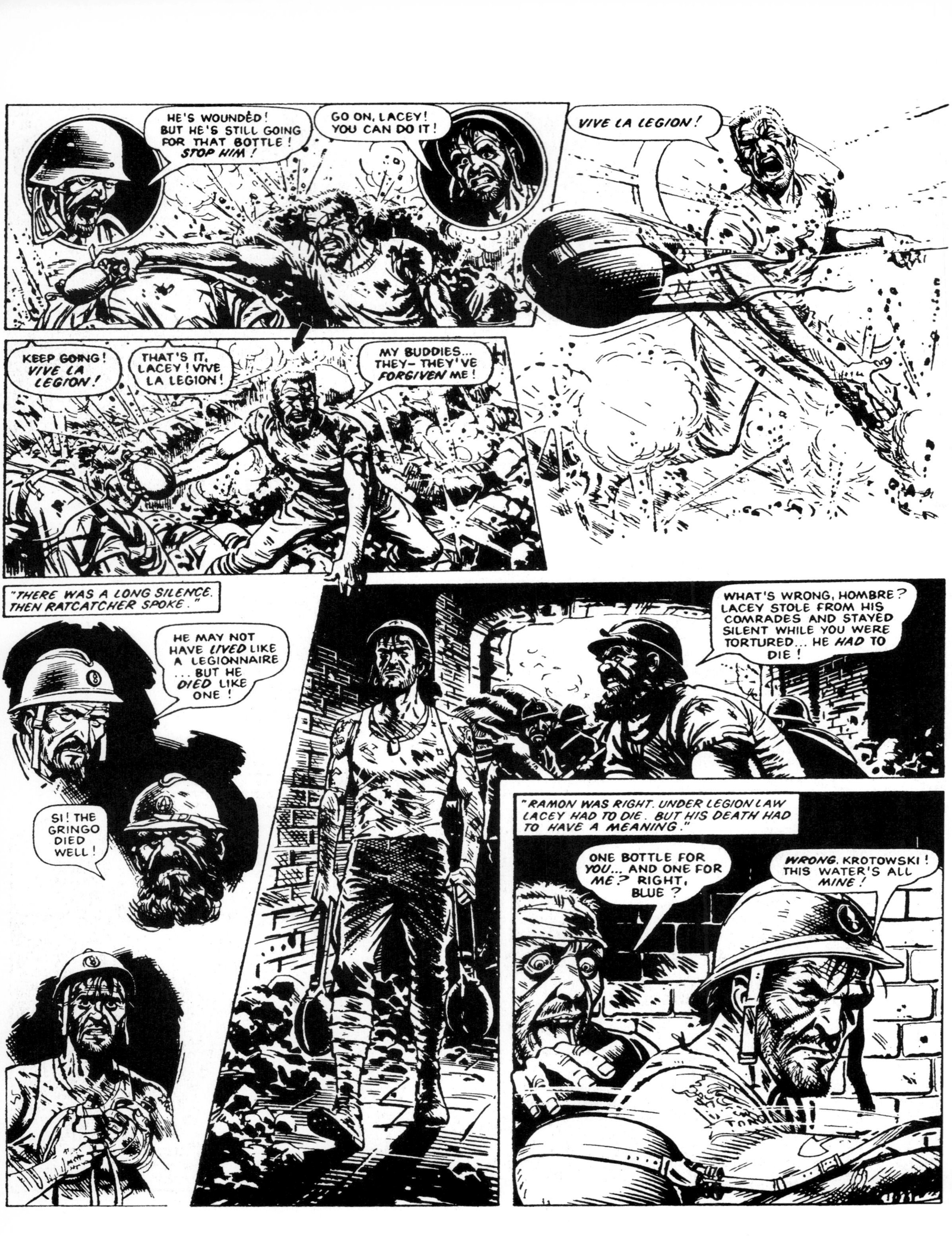

HE'S WOUNDED! BUT HE'S STILL GOING FOR THAT BOTTLE! STOP HIM!
GO ON, LACEY! YOU CAN DO IT!
VIVE LA LEGION!
KEEP GOING! VIVE LA LEGION!
THAT'S IT, LACEY! VIVE LA LEGION!
MY BUDDIES... THEY- THEY'VE FORGIVEN ME!
"THERE WAS A LONG SILENCE. THEN RATCATCHER SPOKE."
HE MAY NOT HAVE LIVED LIKE A LEGIONNAIRE ... BUT HE DIED LIKE ONE!
SI! THE GRINGO DIED WELL!
WHAT'S WRONG, HOMBRE? LACEY STOLE FROM HIS COMRADES AND STAYED SILENT WHILE YOU WERE TORTURED... HE HAD TO DIE!
"RAMON WAS RIGHT. UNDER LEGION LAW LACEY HAD TO DIE. BUT HIS DEATH HAD TO HAVE A MEANING."
ONE BOTTLE FOR YOU... AND ONE FOR ME? RIGHT, BLUE?
WRONG, KROTOWSKI! THIS WATER'S ALL MINE!

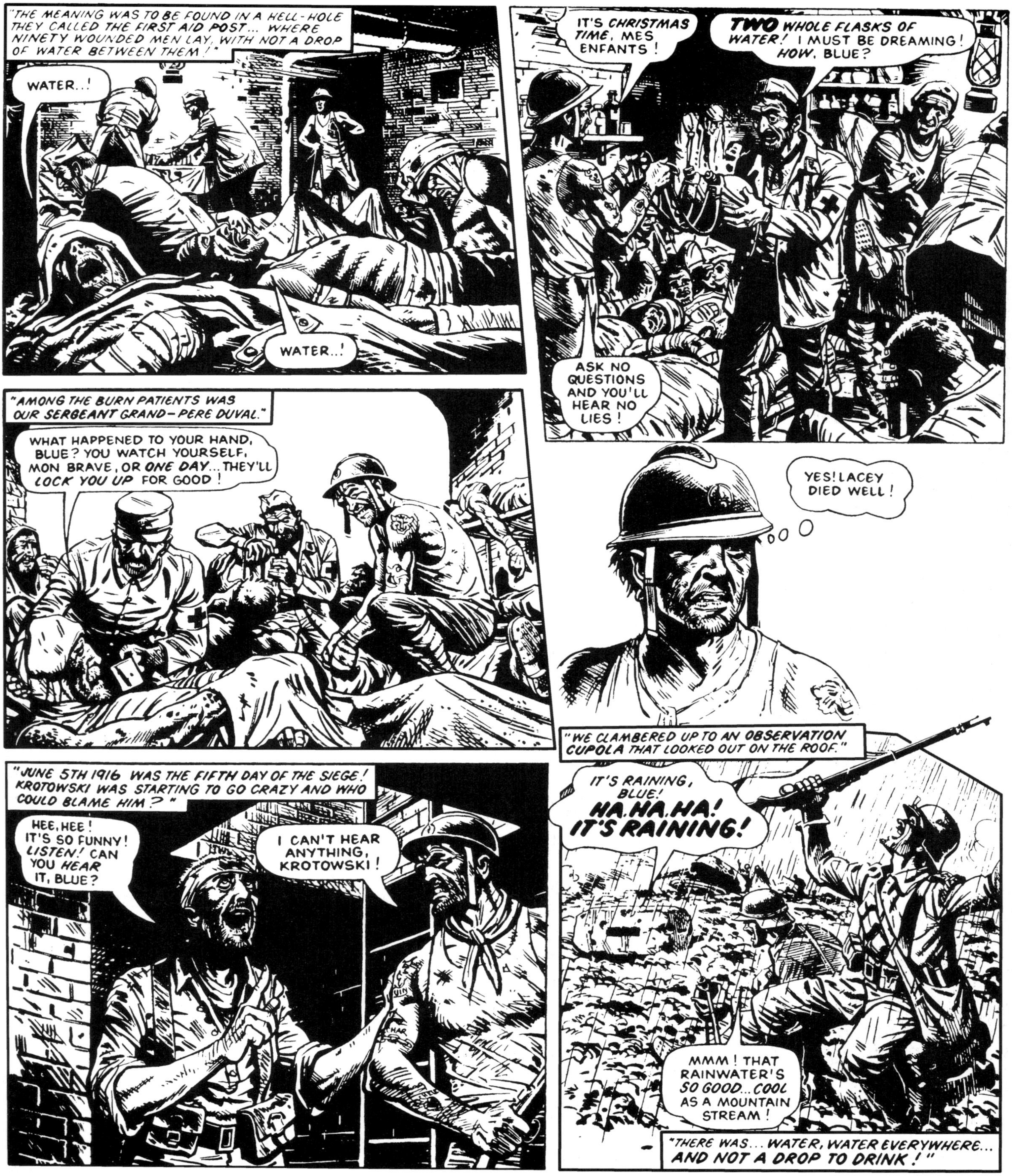
"THE MEANING WAS TO BE FOUND IN A HELL-HOLE THEY CALLED THE FIRST AID POST... WHERE NINETY WOUNDED MEN LAY, WITH NOT A DROP OF WATER BETWEEN THEM!"
WATER..!
WATER..!
IT'S CHRISTMAS TIME, MES ENFANTS!
TWO WHOLE FLASKS OF WATER! I MUST BE DREAMING! HOW, BLUE?
ASK NO QUESTIONS AND YOU'LL HEAR NO LIES!
"AMONG THE BURN PATIENTS WAS OUR SERGEANT GRAND-PERE DUVAL."
WHAT HAPPENED TO YOUR HAND, BLUE? YOU WATCH YOURSELF, MON BRAVE, OR ONE DAY... THEY'LL LOCK YOU UP FOR GOOD!
YES! LACEY DIED WELL!
"JUNE 5TH 1916 WAS THE FIFTH DAY OF THE SIEGE! KROTOWSKI WAS STARTING TO GO CRAZY AND WHO COULD BLAME HIM?"
HEE, HEE! IT'S SO FUNNY! LISTEN! CAN YOU HEAR IT, BLUE?
I CAN'T HEAR ANYTHING, KROTOWSKI!
"WE CLAMBERED UP TO AN OBSERVATION CUPOLA THAT LOOKED OUT ON THE ROOF."
IT'S RAINING, BLUE! HA.HA.HA! IT'S RAINING!
MMM! THAT RAINWATER'S SO GOOD... COOL AS A MOUNTAIN STREAM!
"THERE WAS... WATER, WATER EVERYWHERE... AND NOT A DROP TO DRINK!"

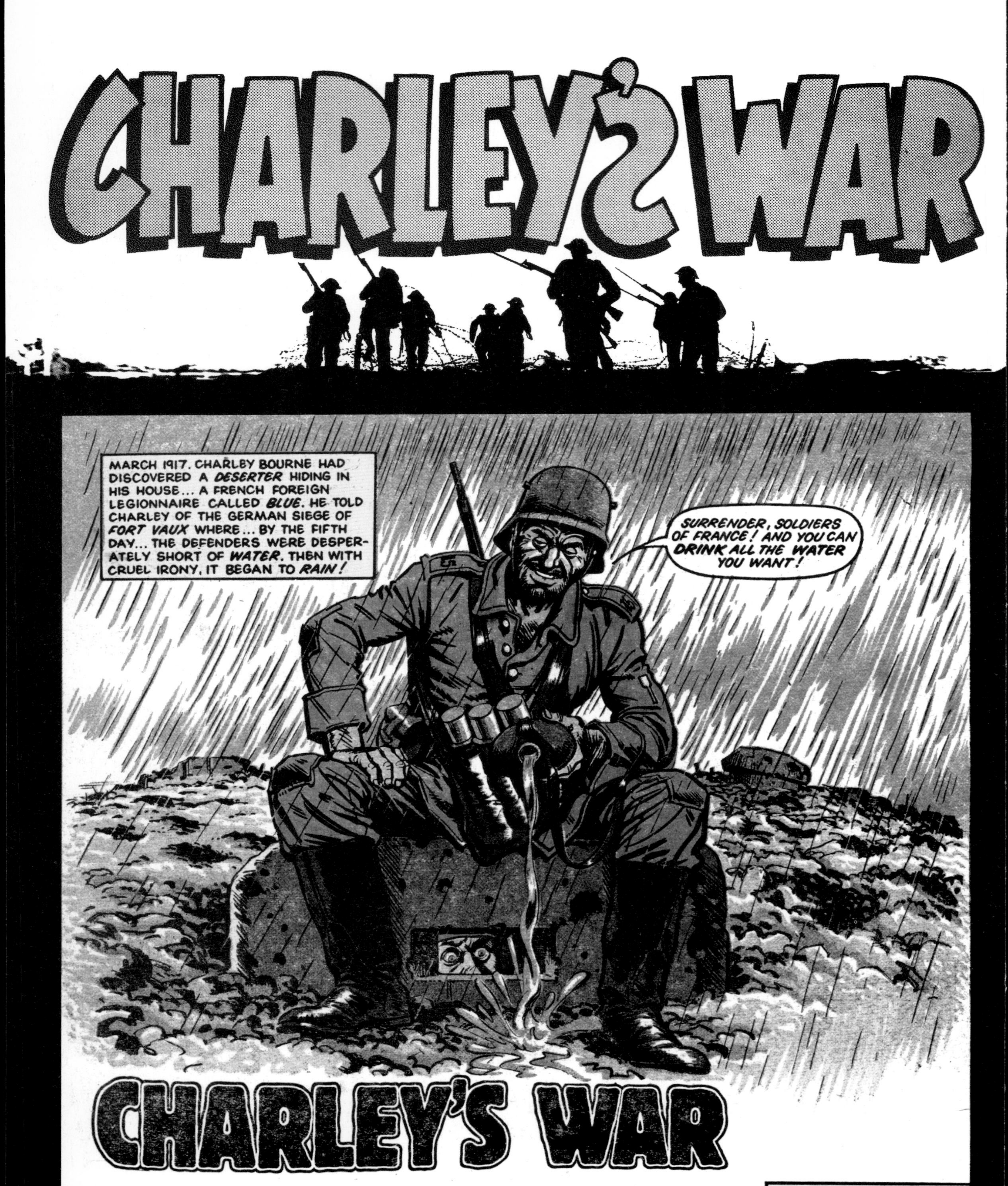
CHARLEY'S WAR
MARCH 1917. CHARLBY BOURNE HAD DISCOVERED A DESERTER HIDING IN HIS HOUSE... A FRENCH FOREIGN LEGIONNAIRE CALLED BLUE. HE TOLD CHARLEY OF THE GERMAN SIEGE OF FORT VAUX WHERE... BY THE FIFTH DAY... THE DEFENDERS WERE DESPERATELY SHORT OF WATER. THEN WITH CRUEL IRONY, IT BEGAN TO RAIN!
SURRENDER, SOLDIERS OF FRANCE! AND YOU CAN DRINK ALL THE WATER YOU WANT!
CHARLEY'S WAR

CONTINUED ON NEXT PAGE

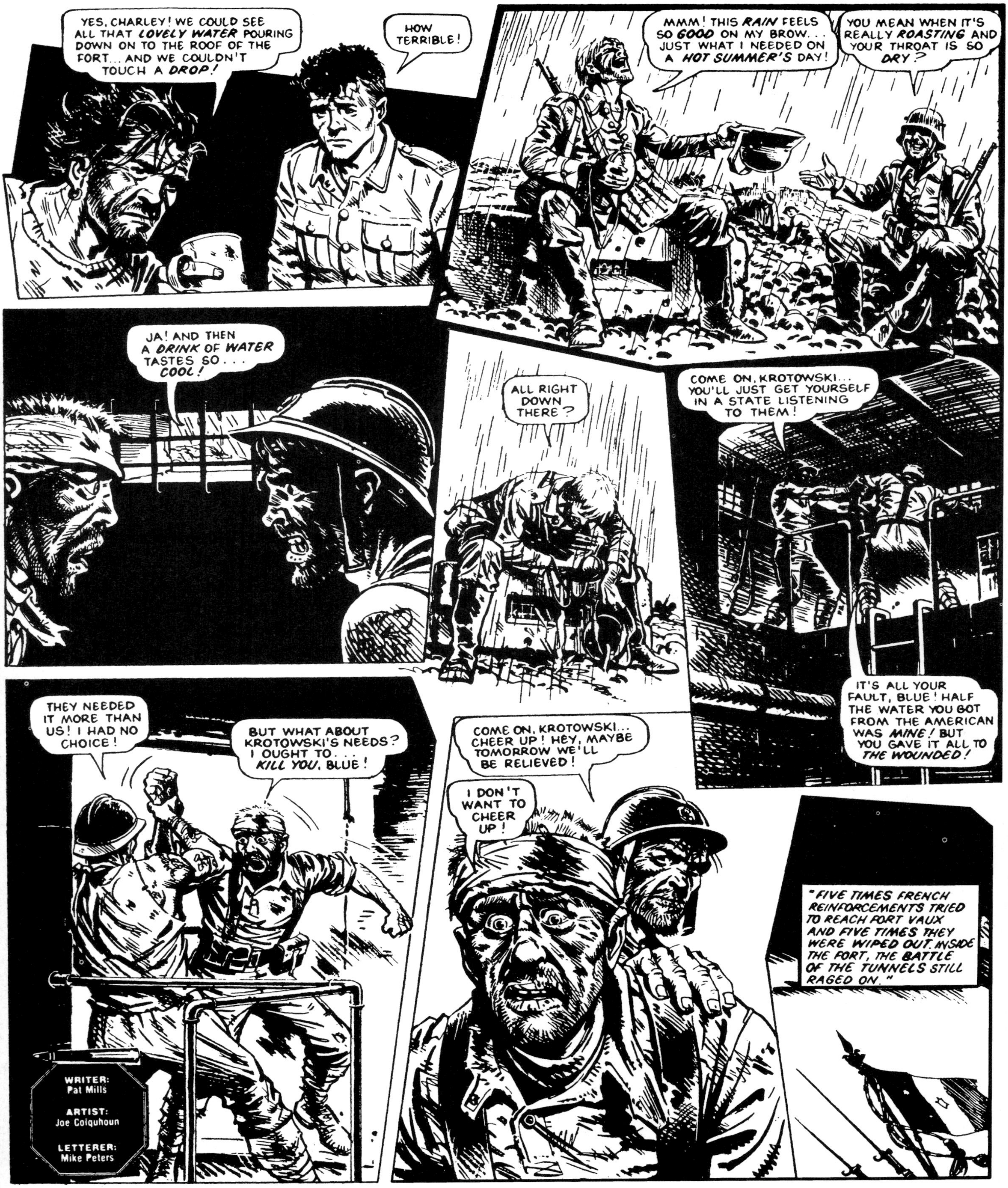
YES, CHARLEY! WE COULD SEE ALL THAT LOVELY WATER POURING DOWN ON TO THE ROOF OF THE FORT... AND WE COULDN'T TOUCH A DROP!
HOW TERRIBLE!
MMM! THIS RAIN FEELS SO GOOD ON MY BROW... JUST WHAT I NEEDED ON A HOT SUMMER'S DAY!
YOU MEAN WHEN IT'S REALLY ROASTING AND YOUR THROAT IS SO DRY?
JA! AND THEN A DRINK OF WATER TASTES SO... COOL!
ALL RIGHT DOWN THERE?
COME ON, KROTOWSKI... YOU'LL JUST GET YOURSELF IN A STATE LISTENING TO THEM!
IT'S ALL YOUR FAULT, BLUE! HALF THE WATER YOU GOT FROM THE AMERICAN WAS MINE! BUT YOU GAVE IT ALL TO THE WOUNDED!
THEY NEEDED IT MORE THAN US! I HAD NO CHOICE!
BUT WHAT ABOUT KROTOWSKI'S NEEDS? I OUGHT TO... KILL YOU, BLUE!
COME ON, KROTOWSKI... CHEER UP! HEY, MAYBE TOMORROW WE'LL BE RELIEVED!
I DON'T WANT TO CHEER UP!
"FIVE TIMES FRENCH REINFORCEMENTS TRIED TO REACH FORT VAUX AND FIVE TIMES THEY WERE WIPED OUT. INSIDE THE FORT, THE BATTLE OF THE TUNNELS STILL RAGED ON."
WRITER: Pat Mills
ARTIST: Joe Colquhoun
LETTERER: Mike Peters

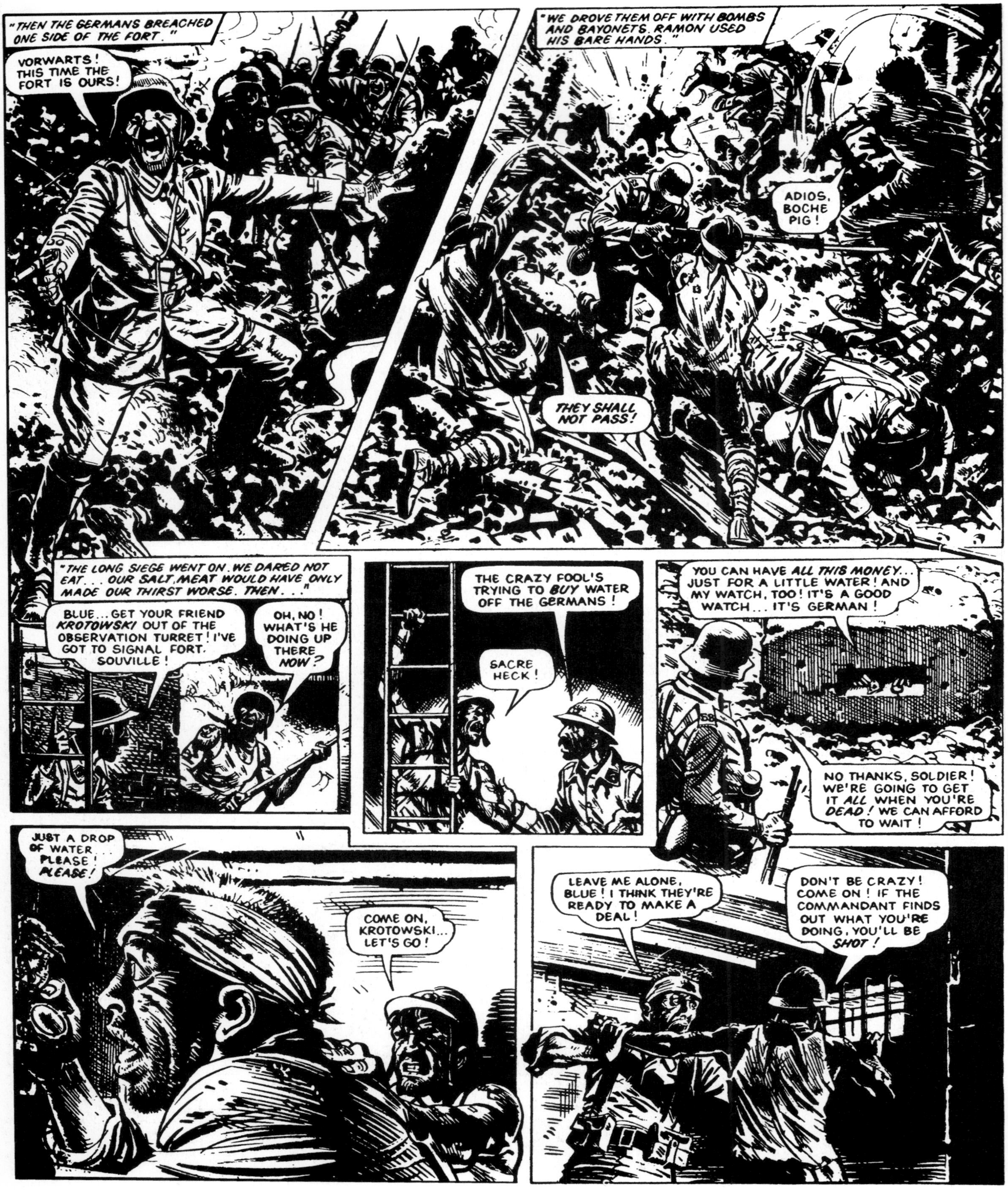

"THEN THE GERMANS BREACHED ONE SIDE OF THE FORT."
VORWARTS! THIS TIME THE FORT IS OURS!
"WE DROVE THEM OFF WITH BOMBS AND BAYONETS. RAMON USED HIS BARE HANDS."
ADIOS, BOCHE PIG!
THEY SHALL NOT PASS!
"THE LONG SIEGE WENT ON. WE DARED NOT EAT... OUR SALT MEAT WOULD HAVE ONLY MADE OUR THIRST WORSE. THEN..."
BLUE... GET YOUR FRIEND KROTOWSKI OUT OF THE OBSERVATION TURRET! I'VE GOT TO SIGNAL FORT SOUVILLE!
OH, NO! WHAT'S HE DOING UP THERE NOW?
THE CRAZY FOOL'S TRYING TO BUY WATER OFF THE GERMANS!
SACRE HECK!
YOU CAN HAVE ALL THIS MONEY... JUST FOR A LITTLE WATER! AND MY WATCH, TOO! IT'S A GOOD WATCH... IT'S GERMAN!
NO THANKS, SOLDIER! WE'RE GOING TO GET IT ALL WHEN YOU'RE DEAD! WE CAN AFFORD TO WAIT!
JUST A DROP OF WATER... PLEASE! PLEASE!
COME ON, KROTOWSKI... LET'S GO!
LEAVE ME ALONE, BLUE! I THINK THEY'RE READY TO MAKE A DEAL!
DON'T BE CRAZY! COME ON! IF THE COMMANDANT FINDS OUT WHAT YOU'RE DOING, YOU'LL BE SHOT!

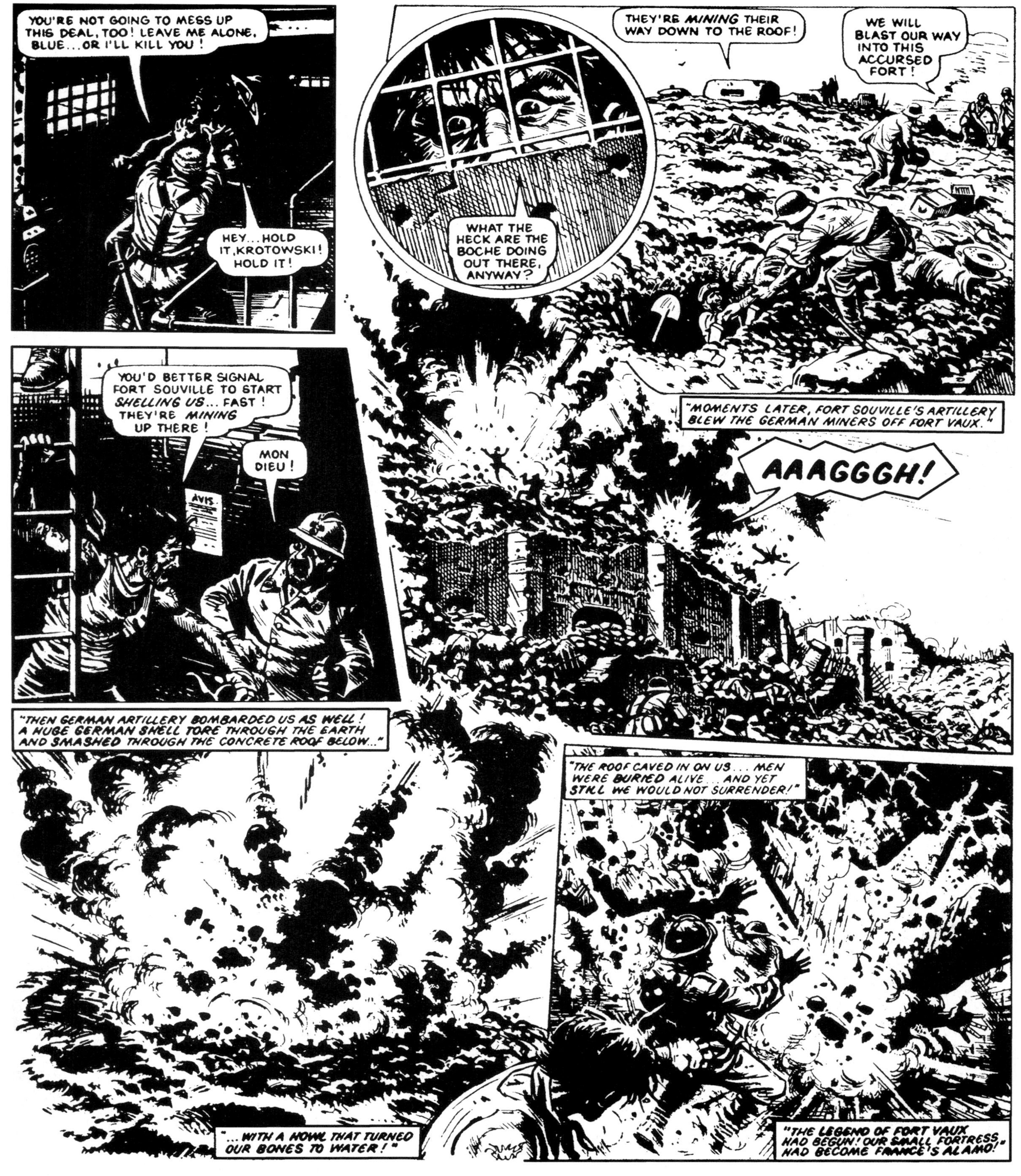

YOU'RE NOT GOING TO MESS UP THIS DEAL, TOO! LEAVE ME ALONE, BLUE...OR I'LL KILL YOU!
HEY...HOLD IT, KROTOWSKI! HOLD IT!
WHAT THE HECK ARE THE BOCHE DOING OUT THERE, ANYWAY?
THEY'RE MINING THEIR WAY DOWN TO THE ROOF!
WE WILL BLAST OUR WAY INTO THIS ACCURSED FORT!
YOU'D BETTER SIGNAL FORT SOUVILLE TO START SHELLING US... FAST! THEY'RE MINING UP THERE!
MON DIEU!
AVIS.
"MOMENTS LATER, FORT SOUVILLE'S ARTILLERY BLEW THE GERMAN MINERS OFF FORT VAUX."
AAAGGGH!
"THEN GERMAN ARTILLERY BOMBARDED US AS WELL! A HUGE GERMAN SHELL TORE THROUGH THE EARTH AND SMASHED THROUGH THE CONCRETE ROOF BELOW..."
"...WITH A HOWL THAT TURNED OUR BONES TO WATER!"
"THE ROOF CAVED IN ON US... MEN WERE BURIED ALIVE... AND YET STILL WE WOULD NOT SURRENDER!"
"THE LEGEND OF FORT VAUX HAD BEGUN! OUR SMALL FORTRESS HAD BECOME FRANCE'S ALAMO!"

THREE MEN FORMED A HUMAN PYRAMID TO ESCAPE FROM THE CLUTCHES OF FORT HELL!

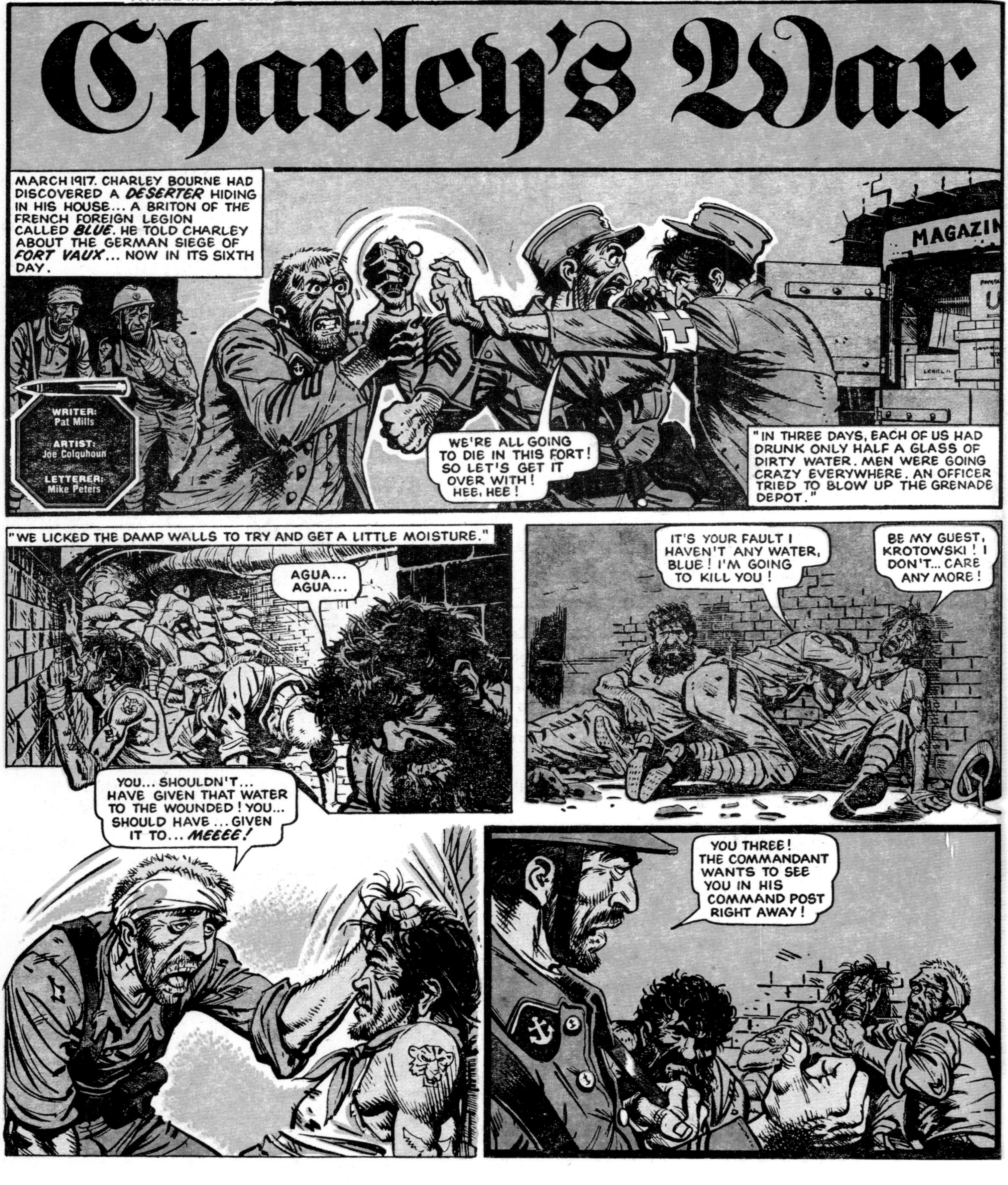
Charley's War
MARCH 1917. CHARLEY BOURNE HAD DISCOVERED A DESERTER HIDING IN HIS HOUSE... A BRITON OF THE FRENCH FOREIGN LEGION CALLED BLUE. HE TOLD CHARLEY ABOUT THE GERMAN SIEGE OF FORT VAUX... NOW IN ITS SIXTH DAY.
MAGAZIN
WRITER: Pat Mills
ARTIST: Joe Colquhoun
LETTERER: Mike Peters
WE'RE ALL GOING TO DIE IN THIS FORT! SO LET'S GET IT OVER WITH! HEE, HEE!
"IN THREE DAYS, EACH OF US HAD DRUNK ONLY HALF A GLASS OF DIRTY WATER. MEN WERE GOING CRAZY EVERYWHERE. AN OFFICER TRIED TO BLOW UP THE GRENADE DEPOT."
"WE LICKED THE DAMP WALLS TO TRY AND GET A LITTLE MOISTURE."
AGUA... AGUA...
IT'S YOUR FAULT I HAVEN'T ANY WATER, BLUE! I'M GOING TO KILL YOU!
BE MY GUEST, KROTOWSKI! I DON'T... CARE ANY MORE!
YOU... SHOULDN'T... HAVE GIVEN THAT WATER TO THE WOUNDED! YOU... SHOULD HAVE ... GIVEN IT TO... MEEEE!
YOU THREE! THE COMMANDANT WANTS TO SEE YOU IN HIS COMMAND POST RIGHT AWAY!

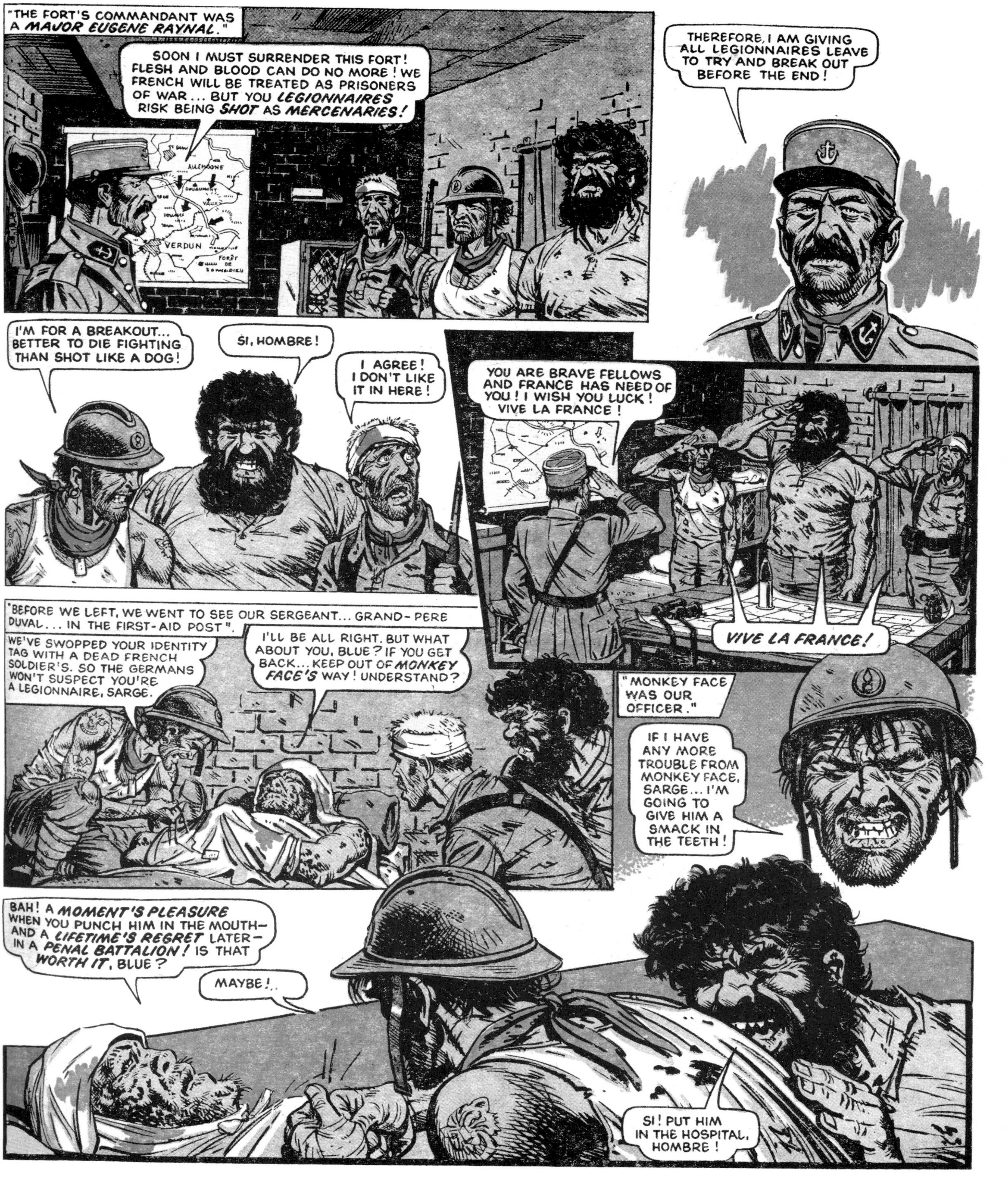
"THE FORT'S COMMANDANT WAS A MAJOR EUGENE RAYNAL."
SOON I MUST SURRENDER THIS FORT! FLESH AND BLOOD CAN DO NO MORE! WE FRENCH WILL BE TREATED AS PRISONERS OF WAR... BUT YOU LEGIONNAIRES RISK BEING SHOT AS MERCENARIES!
VERDUN
THEREFORE, I AM GIVING ALL LEGIONNAIRES LEAVE TO TRY AND BREAK OUT BEFORE THE END!
I'M FOR A BREAKOUT... BETTER TO DIE FIGHTING THAN SHOT LIKE A DOG!
SI, HOMBRE!
I AGREE! I DON'T LIKE IT IN HERE!
YOU ARE BRAVE FELLOWS AND FRANCE HAS NEED OF YOU! I WISH YOU LUCK! VIVE LA FRANCE!
VIVE LA FRANCE!
"BEFORE WE LEFT, WE WENT TO SEE OUR SERGEANT... GRAND-PERE DUVAL... IN THE FIRST-AID POST".
WE'VE SWOPPED YOUR IDENTITY TAG WITH A DEAD FRENCH SOLDIER'S. SO THE GERMANS WON'T SUSPECT YOU'RE A LEGIONNAIRE, SARGE.
I'LL BE ALL RIGHT. BUT WHAT ABOUT YOU, BLUE? IF YOU GET BACK... KEEP OUT OF MONKEY FACE'S WAY! UNDERSTAND?
"MONKEY FACE WAS OUR OFFICER."
IF I HAVE ANY MORE TROUBLE FROM MONKEY FACE, SARGE... I'M GOING TO GIVE HIM A SMACK IN THE TEETH!
BAH! A MOMENT'S PLEASURE WHEN YOU PUNCH HIM IN THE MOUTH— AND A LIFETIME'S REGRET LATER— IN A PENAL BATTALION! IS THAT WORTH IT, BLUE?
MAYBE!..
SI! PUT HIM IN THE HOSPITAL, HOMBRE!

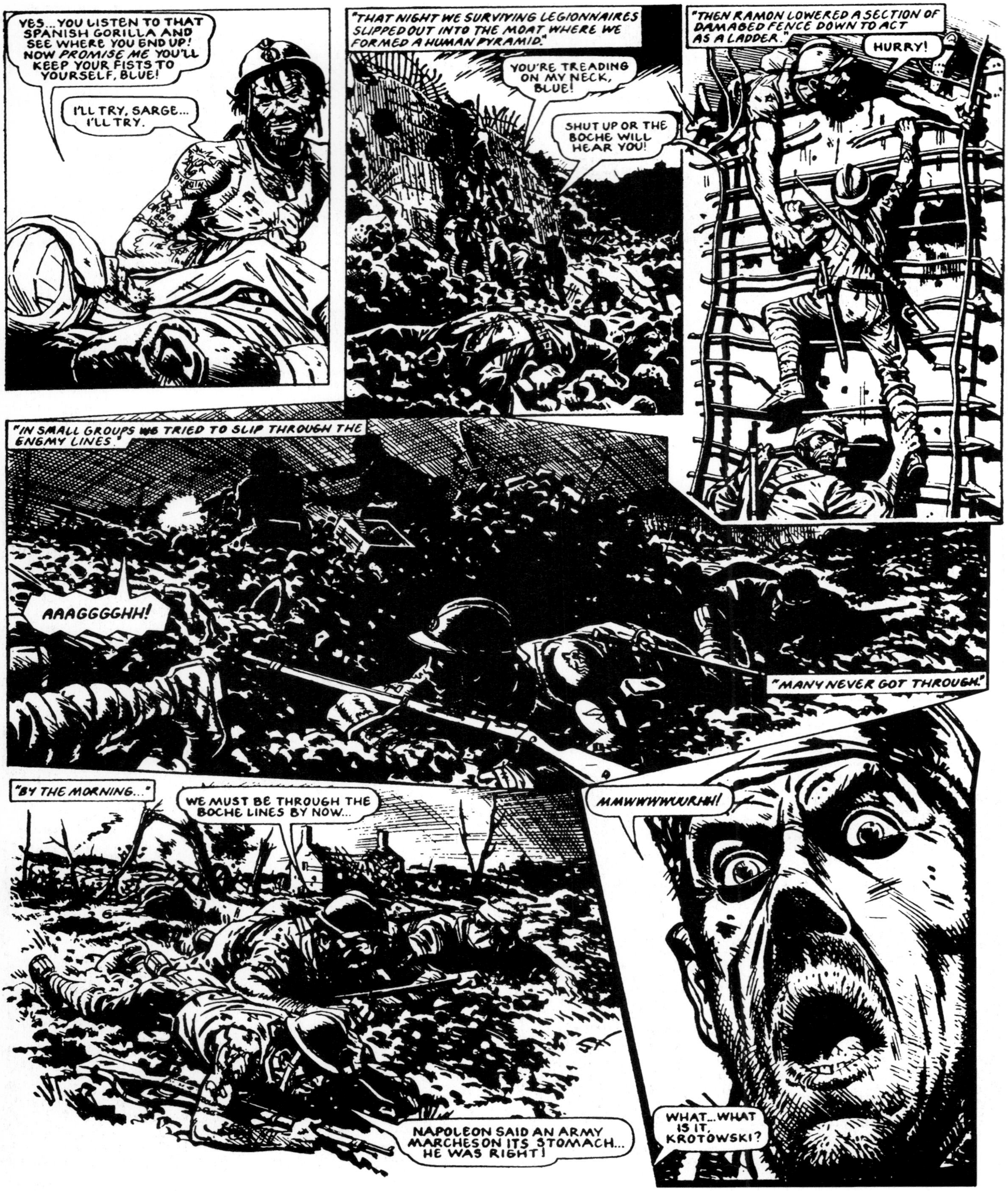
YES... YOU LISTEN TO THAT SPANISH GORILLA AND SEE WHERE YOU END UP! NOW PROMISE ME YOU'LL KEEP YOUR FISTS TO YOURSELF, BLUE!
I'LL TRY, SARGE... I'LL TRY.
"THAT NIGHT WE SURVIVING LEGIONNAIRES SLIPPED OUT INTO THE MOAT WHERE WE FORMED A HUMAN PYRAMID."
YOU'RE TREADING ON MY NECK, BLUE!
SHUT UP OR THE BOCHE WILL HEAR YOU!
"THEN RAMON LOWERED A SECTION OF DAMAGED FENCE DOWN TO ACT AS A LADDER."
HURRY!
"IN SMALL GROUPS WE TRIED TO SLIP THROUGH THE ENEMY LINES."
AAAGGGGHH!
"MANY NEVER GOT THROUGH."
"BY THE MORNING..."
WE MUST BE THROUGH THE BOCHE LINES BY NOW...
NAPOLEON SAID AN ARMY MARCHES ON ITS STOMACH... HE WAS RIGHT!
MMWWWWUURHH!
WHAT... WHAT IS IT, KROTOWSKI?

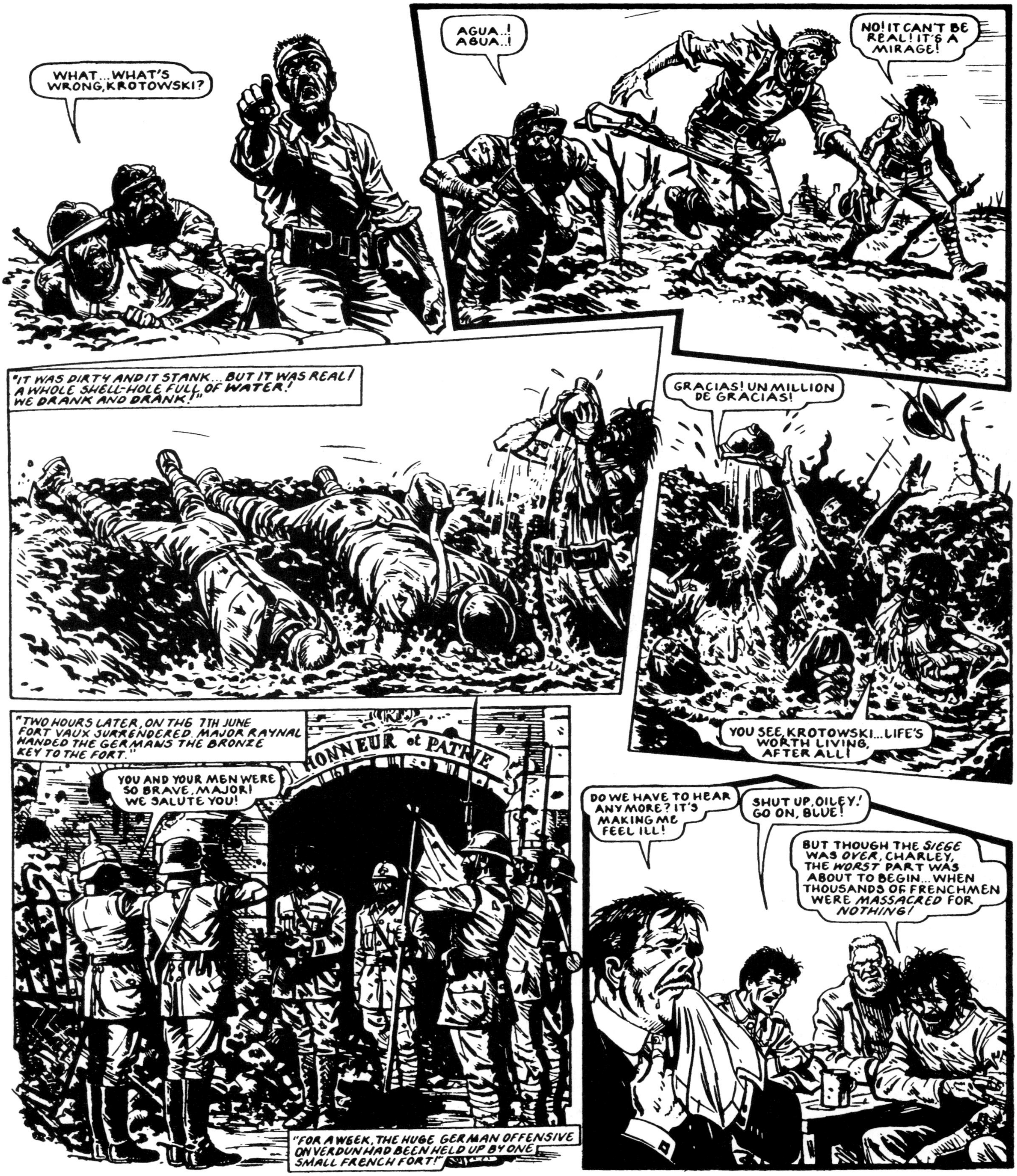
WHAT... WHAT'S WRONG, KROTOWSKI?
AGUA..! ABUA..!
NO! IT CAN'T BE REAL! IT'S A MIRAGE!
"IT WAS DIRTY AND IT STANK... BUT IT WAS REAL! A WHOLE SHELL-HOLE FULL OF WATER! WE DRANK AND DRANK!"
GRACIAS! UN MILLION DE GRACIAS!
YOU SEE, KROTOWSKI... LIFE'S WORTH LIVING, AFTER ALL!
"TWO HOURS LATER, ON THE 7TH JUNE FORT VAUX SURRENDERED. MAJOR RAYNAL HANDED THE GERMANS THE BRONZE KEY TO THE FORT."
HONNEUR et PATRIE
YOU AND YOUR MEN WERE SO BRAVE, MAJOR! WE SALUTE YOU!
"FOR A WEEK, THE HUGE GERMAN OFFENSIVE ON VERDUN HAD BEEN HELD UP BY ONE SMALL FRENCH FORT!"
DO WE HAVE TO HEAR ANY MORE? IT'S MAKING ME FEEL ILL!
SHUT UP, OILEY! GO ON, BLUE!
BUT THOUGH THE SIEGE WAS OVER, CHARLEY, THE WORST PART WAS ABOUT TO BEGIN... WHEN THOUSANDS OF FRENCHMEN WERE MASSACRED FOR NOTHING!

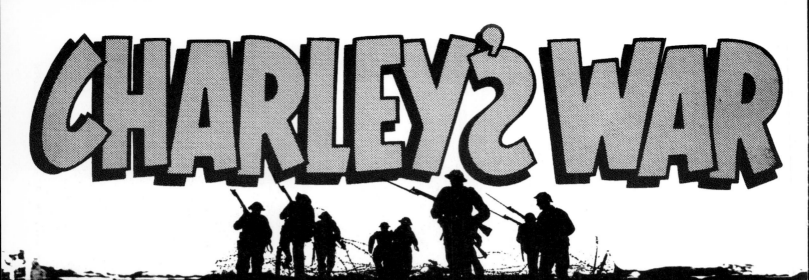

CHARLEY'S WAR

MARCH 1917. CHARLEY BOURNE HAD DISCOVERED A *DESERTER* HIDING IN HIS HOUSE... A BRITON OF THE FRENCH FOREIGN LEGION CALLED *BLUE*. BLUE TOLD CHARLEY OF THE GERMAN VICTORY AT FORT VAUX AND ITS *TRAGIC AFTERMATH*... ONE OF THE MOST SENSELESS AND BLOODY ACTIONS OF WORLD WAR ONE.

CONTINUED ON NEXT PAGE

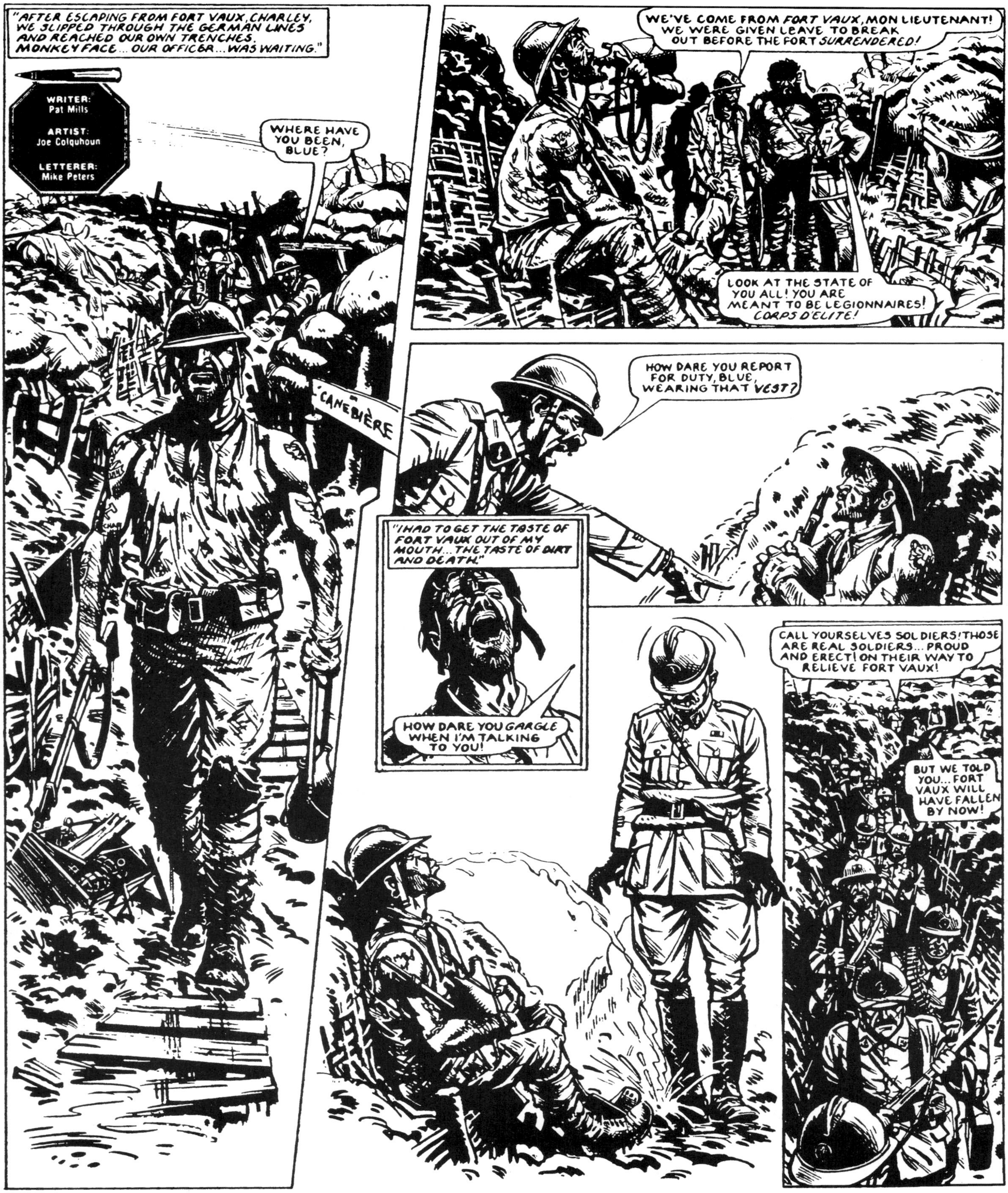

"AFTER ESCAPING FROM FORT VAUX, CHARLEY, WE SLIPPED THROUGH THE GERMAN LINES AND REACHED OUR OWN TRENCHES. MONKEY FACE... OUR OFFICER... WAS WAITING."
WRITER: Pat Mills
ARTIST: Joe Colquhoun
LETTERER: Mike Peters
WHERE HAVE YOU BEEN, BLUE?
CANEBIÈRE
WE'VE COME FROM FORT VAUX, MON LIEUTENANT! WE WERE GIVEN LEAVE TO BREAK OUT BEFORE THE FORT SURRENDERED!
LOOK AT THE STATE OF YOU ALL! YOU ARE MEANT TO BE LEGIONNAIRES! CORPS D'ELITE!
HOW DARE YOU REPORT FOR DUTY, BLUE, WEARING THAT VEST?
"I HAD TO GET THE TASTE OF FORT VAUX OUT OF MY MOUTH... THE TASTE OF DIRT AND DEATH."
HOW DARE YOU GARGLE WHEN I'M TALKING TO YOU!
CALL YOURSELVES SOLDIERS! THOSE ARE REAL SOLDIERS... PROUD AND ERECT! ON THEIR WAY TO RELIEVE FORT VAUX!
BUT WE TOLD YOU... FORT VAUX WILL HAVE FALLEN BY NOW!

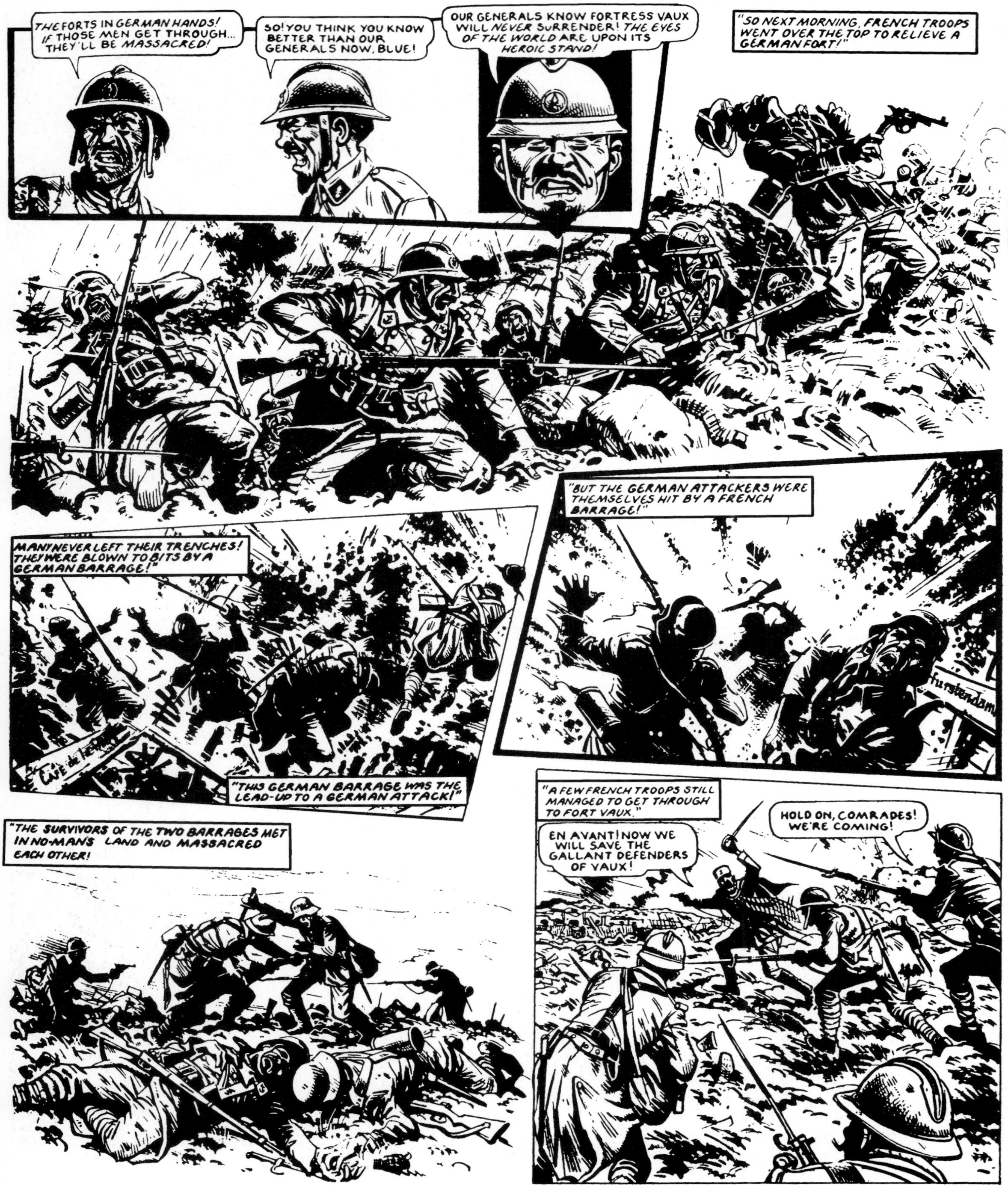
THE FORTS IN GERMAN HANDS! IF THOSE MEN GET THROUGH... THEY'LL BE MASSACRED!
SO! YOU THINK YOU KNOW BETTER THAN OUR GENERALS NOW, BLUE!
OUR GENERALS KNOW FORTRESS VAUX WILL NEVER SURRENDER! THE EYES OF THE WORLD ARE UPON ITS HEROIC STAND!
"SO NEXT MORNING, FRENCH TROOPS WENT OVER THE TOP TO RELIEVE A GERMAN FORT!"
MANY NEVER LEFT THEIR TRENCHES! THEY WERE BLOWN TO BITS BY A GERMAN BARRAGE!"
"THIS GERMAN BARRAGE WAS THE LEAD-UP TO A GERMAN ATTACK!"
"BUT THE GERMAN ATTACKERS WERE THEMSELVES HIT BY A FRENCH BARRAGE!"
"THE SURVIVORS OF THE TWO BARRAGES MET IN NO-MAN'S LAND AND MASSACRED EACH OTHER!
"A FEW FRENCH TROOPS STILL MANAGED TO GET THROUGH TO FORT VAUX."
EN AVANT! NOW WE WILL SAVE THE GALLANT DEFENDERS OF VAUX!
HOLD ON, COMRADES! WE'RE COMING!

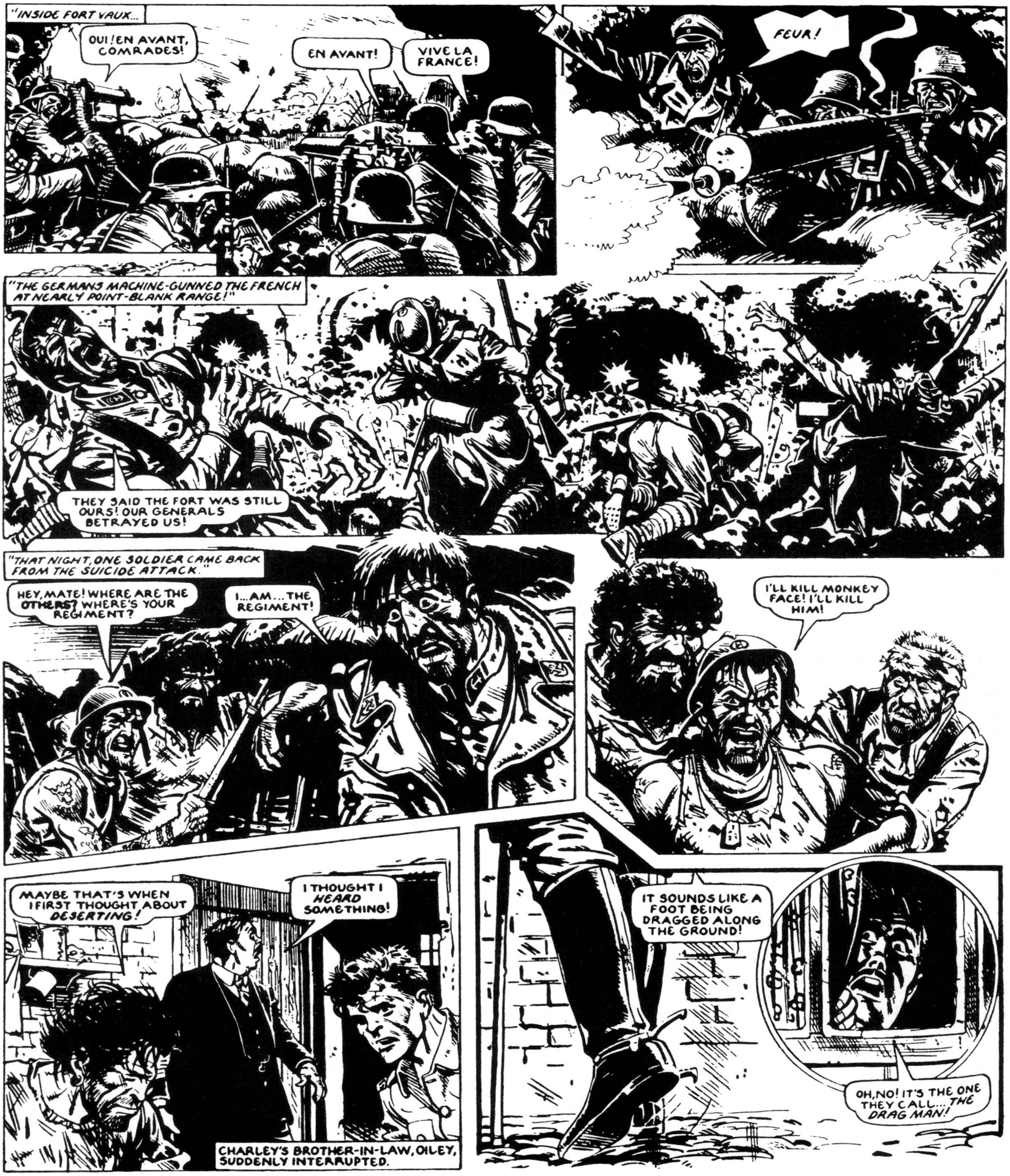
"INSIDE FORT VAUX...
OUI! EN AVANT, COMRADES!
EN AVANT!
VIVE LA FRANCE!
FEUR!
"THE GERMANS MACHINE-GUNNED THE FRENCH AT NEARLY POINT-BLANK RANGE!"
THEY SAID THE FORT WAS STILL OURS! OUR GENERALS BETRAYED US!
"THAT NIGHT, ONE SOLDIER CAME BACK FROM THE SUICIDE ATTACK."
HEY, MATE! WHERE ARE THE OTHERS? WHERE'S YOUR REGIMENT?
I...AM...THE REGIMENT!
I'LL KILL MONKEY FACE! I'LL KILL HIM!
MAYBE THAT'S WHEN I FIRST THOUGHT ABOUT DESERTING!
I THOUGHT I HEARD SOMETHING!
CHARLEY'S BROTHER-IN-LAW, OILEY, SUDDENLY INTERRUPTED.
IT SOUNDS LIKE A FOOT BEING DRAGGED ALONG THE GROUND!
OH, NO! IT'S THE ONE THEY CALL... THE DRAG MAN!

WHEN THE DRAG MAN STALKED THE STREETS, TERROR WALKED WITH HIM!

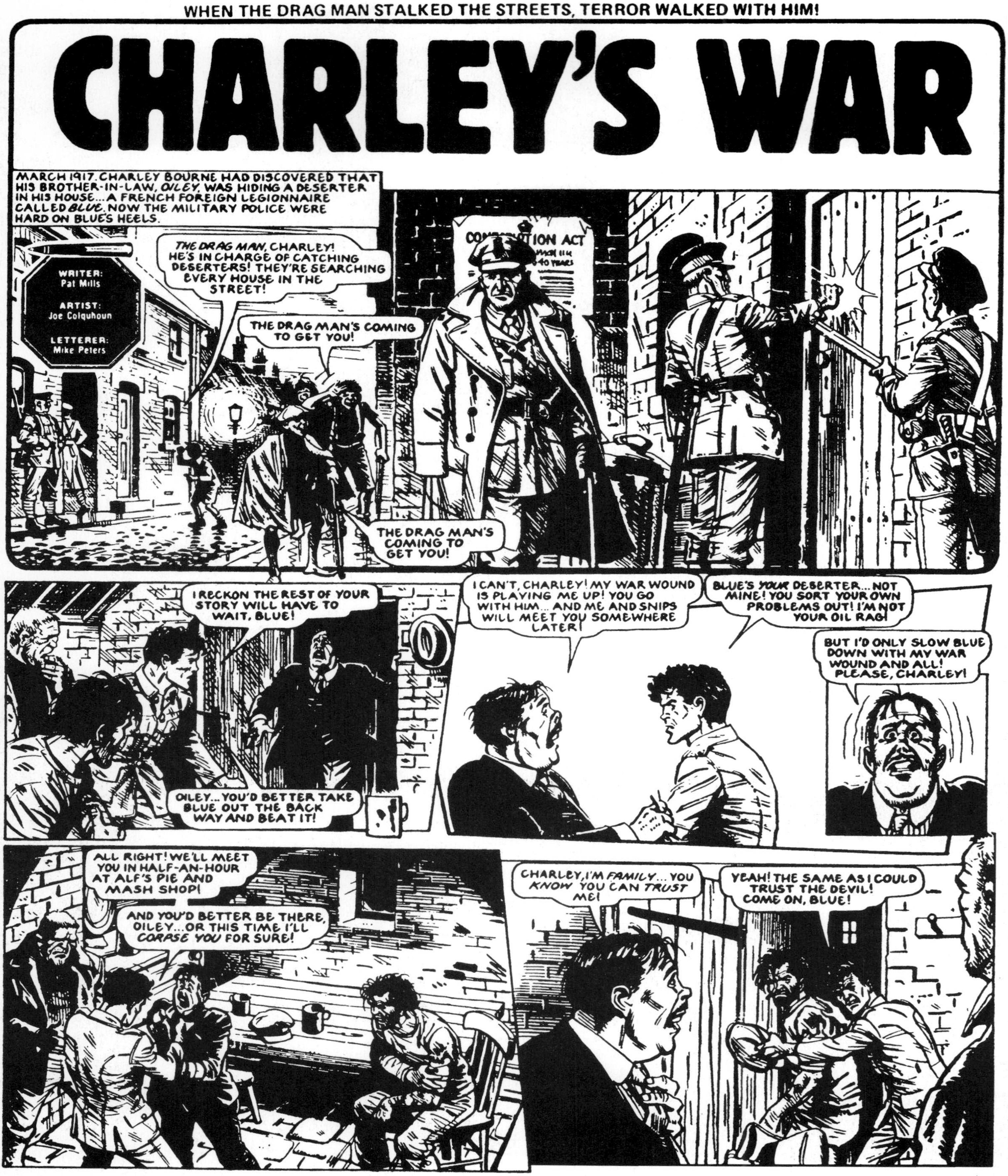

CHARLEY'S WAR
MARCH 1917. CHARLEY BOURNE HAD DISCOVERED THAT HIS BROTHER-IN-LAW, OILEY, WAS HIDING A DESERTER IN HIS HOUSE... A FRENCH FOREIGN LEGIONNAIRE CALLED BLUE. NOW THE MILITARY POLICE WERE HARD ON BLUE'S HEELS.
WRITER: Pat Mills
ARTIST: Joe Colquhoun
LETTERER: Mike Peters
THE DRAG MAN, CHARLEY! HE'S IN CHARGE OF CATCHING DESERTERS! THEY'RE SEARCHING EVERY HOUSE IN THE STREET!
THE DRAG MAN'S COMING TO GET YOU!
THE DRAG MAN'S COMING TO GET YOU!
I RECKON THE REST OF YOUR STORY WILL HAVE TO WAIT, BLUE!
OILEY... YOU'D BETTER TAKE BLUE OUT THE BACK WAY AND BEAT IT!
I CAN'T, CHARLEY! MY WAR WOUND IS PLAYING ME UP! YOU GO WITH HIM... AND ME AND SNIPS WILL MEET YOU SOMEWHERE LATER!
BLUE'S YOUR DESERTER... NOT MINE! YOU SORT YOUR OWN PROBLEMS OUT! I'M NOT YOUR OIL RAG!
BUT I'D ONLY SLOW BLUE DOWN WITH MY WAR WOUND AND ALL! PLEASE, CHARLEY!
ALL RIGHT! WE'LL MEET YOU IN HALF-AN-HOUR AT ALF'S PIE AND MASH SHOP!
AND YOU'D BETTER BE THERE, OILEY... OR THIS TIME I'LL CORPSE YOU FOR SURE!
CHARLEY, I'M FAMILY... YOU KNOW YOU CAN TRUST ME!
YEAH! THE SAME AS I COULD TRUST THE DEVIL! COME ON, BLUE!

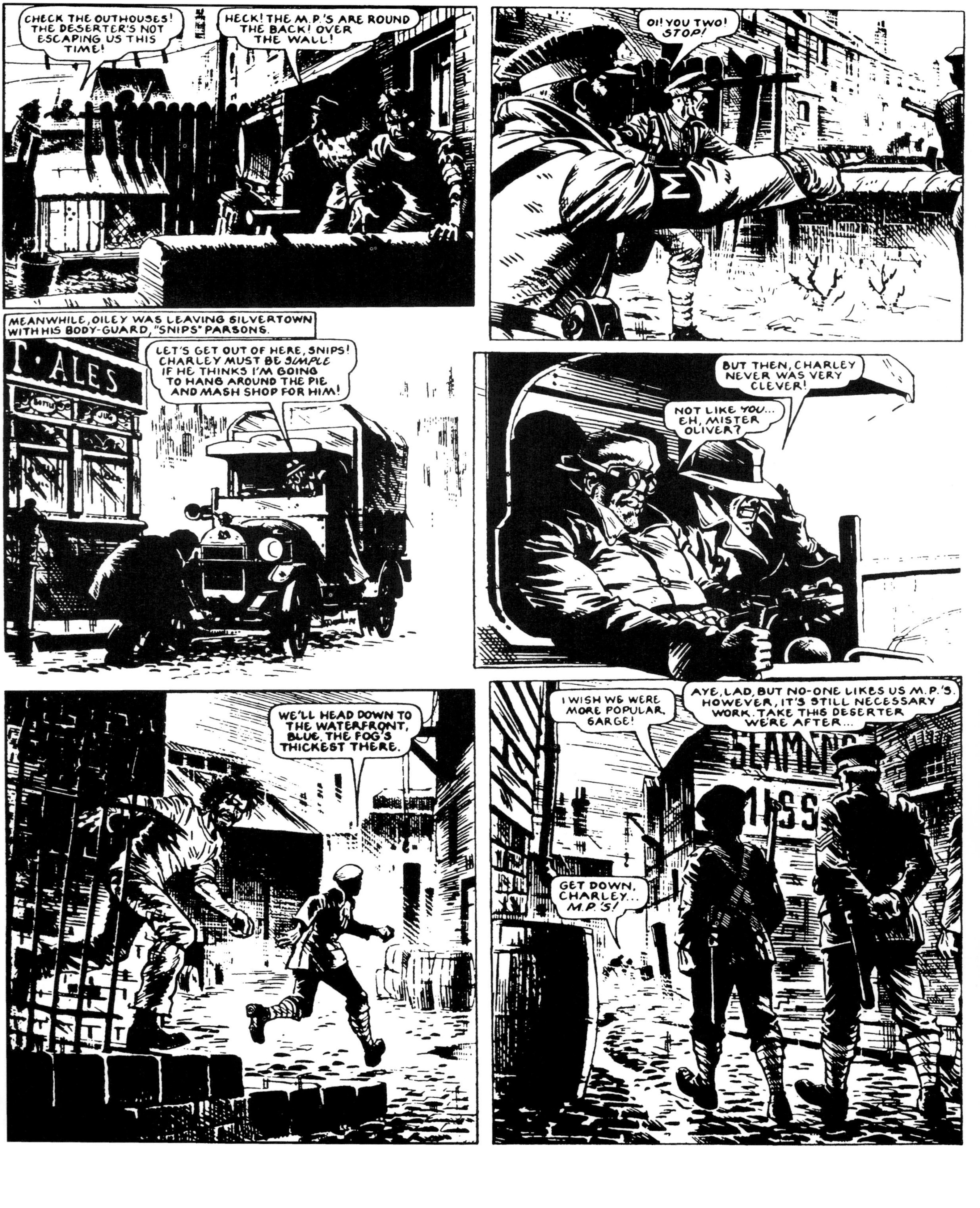
CHECK THE OUTHOUSES! THE DESERTER'S NOT ESCAPING US THIS TIME!
HECK! THE M.P.'S ARE ROUND THE BACK! OVER THE WALL!
OI! YOU TWO! STOP!
MEANWHILE, OILEY WAS LEAVING SILVERTOWN WITH HIS BODY-GUARD, "SNIPS" PARSONS.
LET'S GET OUT OF HERE, SNIPS! CHARLEY MUST BE SIMPLE IF HE THINKS I'M GOING TO HANG AROUND THE PIE AND MASH SHOP FOR HIM!
ALES
BUT THEN, CHARLEY NEVER WAS VERY CLEVER!
NOT LIKE YOU... EH, MISTER OLIVER?
WE'LL HEAD DOWN TO THE WATERFRONT, BLUE. THE FOG'S THICKEST THERE.
I WISH WE WERE MORE POPULAR, SARGE!
AYE, LAD, BUT NO-ONE LIKES US M.P.'S. HOWEVER, IT'S STILL NECESSARY WORK. TAKE THIS DESERTER WE'RE AFTER...
GET DOWN, CHARLEY... M.P.'S!

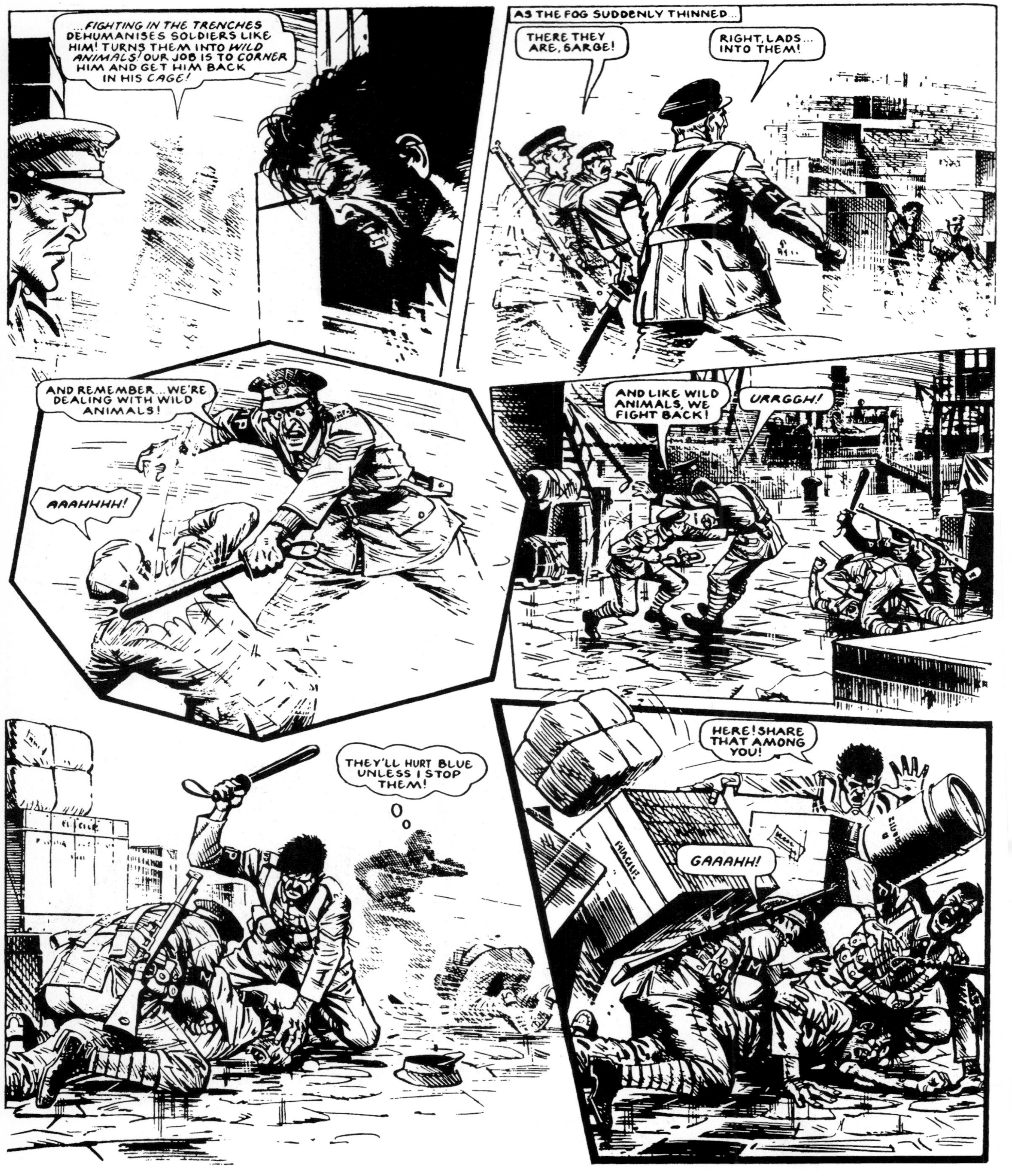
...FIGHTING IN THE TRENCHES DEHUMANISES SOLDIERS LIKE HIM! TURNS THEM INTO WILD ANIMALS! OUR JOB IS TO CORNER HIM AND GET HIM BACK IN HIS CAGE!
AS THE FOG SUDDENLY THINNED...
THERE THEY ARE, SARGE!
RIGHT, LADS... INTO THEM!
AND REMEMBER... WE'RE DEALING WITH WILD ANIMALS!
AAAHHHH!
AND LIKE WILD ANIMALS, WE FIGHT BACK!
URRGGH!
THEY'LL HURT BLUE UNLESS I STOP THEM!
HERE! SHARE THAT AMONG YOU!
GAAAHH!

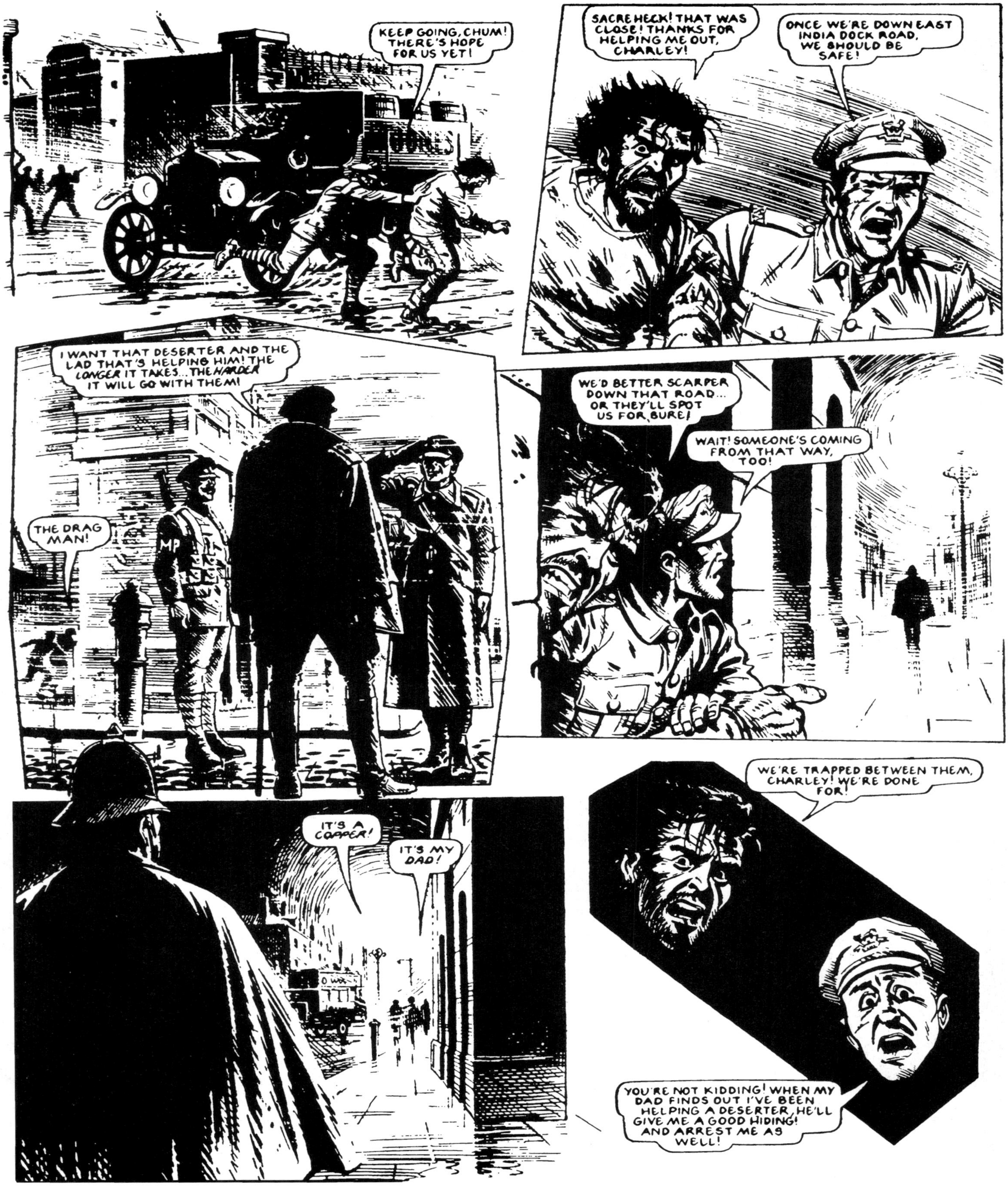

KEEP GOING, CHUM! THERE'S HOPE FOR US YET!
SACRE HECK! THAT WAS CLOSE! THANKS FOR HELPING ME OUT, CHARLEY!
ONCE WE'RE DOWN EAST INDIA DOCK ROAD, WE SHOULD BE SAFE!
I WANT THAT DESERTER AND THE LAD THAT'S HELPING HIM! THE LONGER IT TAKES... THE HARDER IT WILL GO WITH THEM!
THE DRAG MAN!
MP
WE'D BETTER SCARPER DOWN THAT ROAD... OR THEY'LL SPOT US FOR SURE!
WAIT! SOMEONE'S COMING FROM THAT WAY, TOO!
IT'S A COPPER!
IT'S MY DAD!
WE'RE TRAPPED BETWEEN THEM, CHARLEY! WE'RE DONE FOR!
YOU'RE NOT KIDDING! WHEN MY DAD FINDS OUT I'VE BEEN HELPING A DESERTER, HE'LL GIVE ME A GOOD HIDING! AND ARREST ME AS WELL!

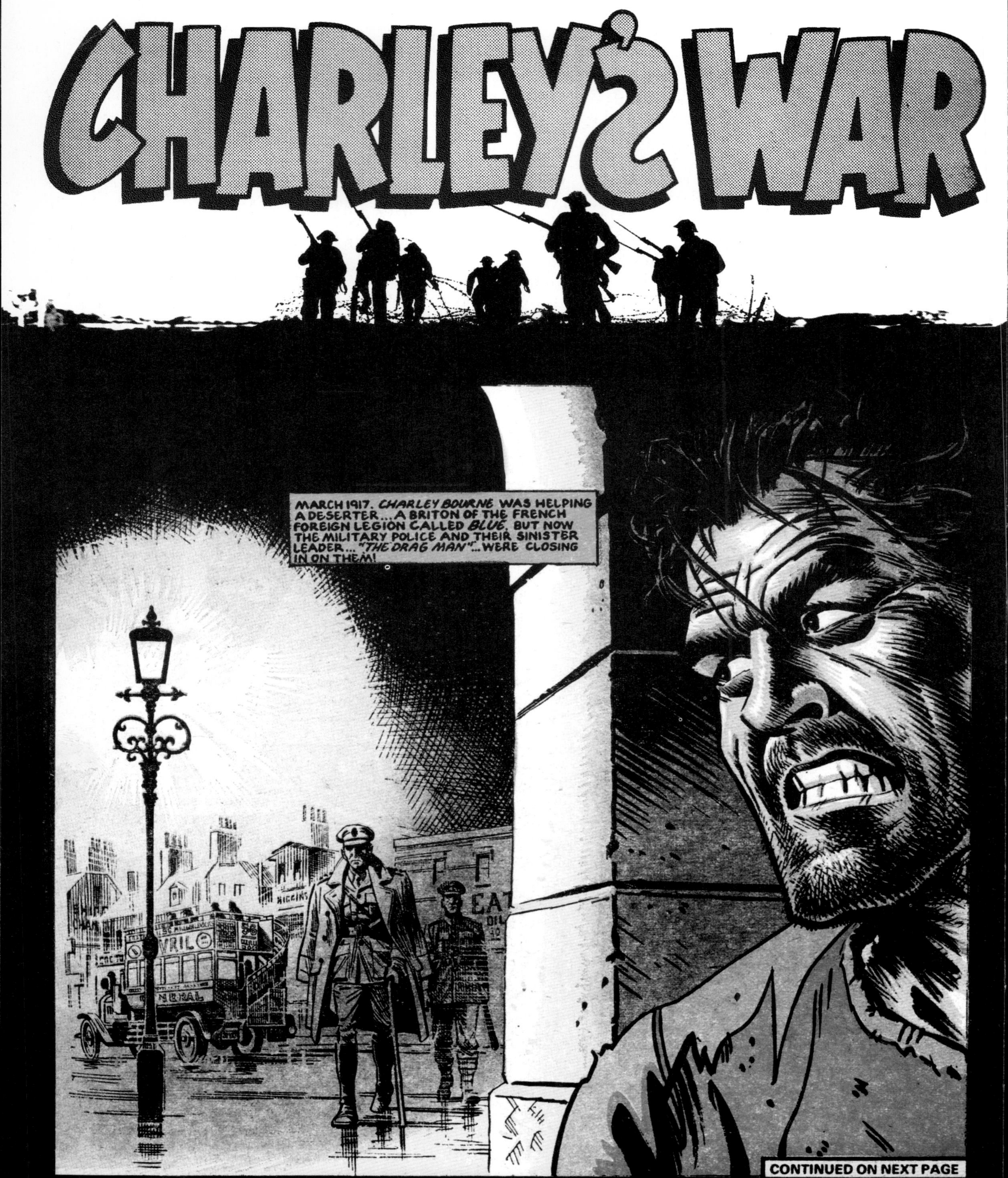
CHARLEY'S WAR
MARCH 1917. CHARLEY BOURNE WAS HELPING A DESERTER... A BRITON OF THE FRENCH FOREIGN LEGION CALLED BLUE. BUT NOW THE MILITARY POLICE AND THEIR SINISTER LEADER... "THE DRAG MAN"... WERE CLOSING IN ON THEM!
CONTINUED ON NEXT PAGE

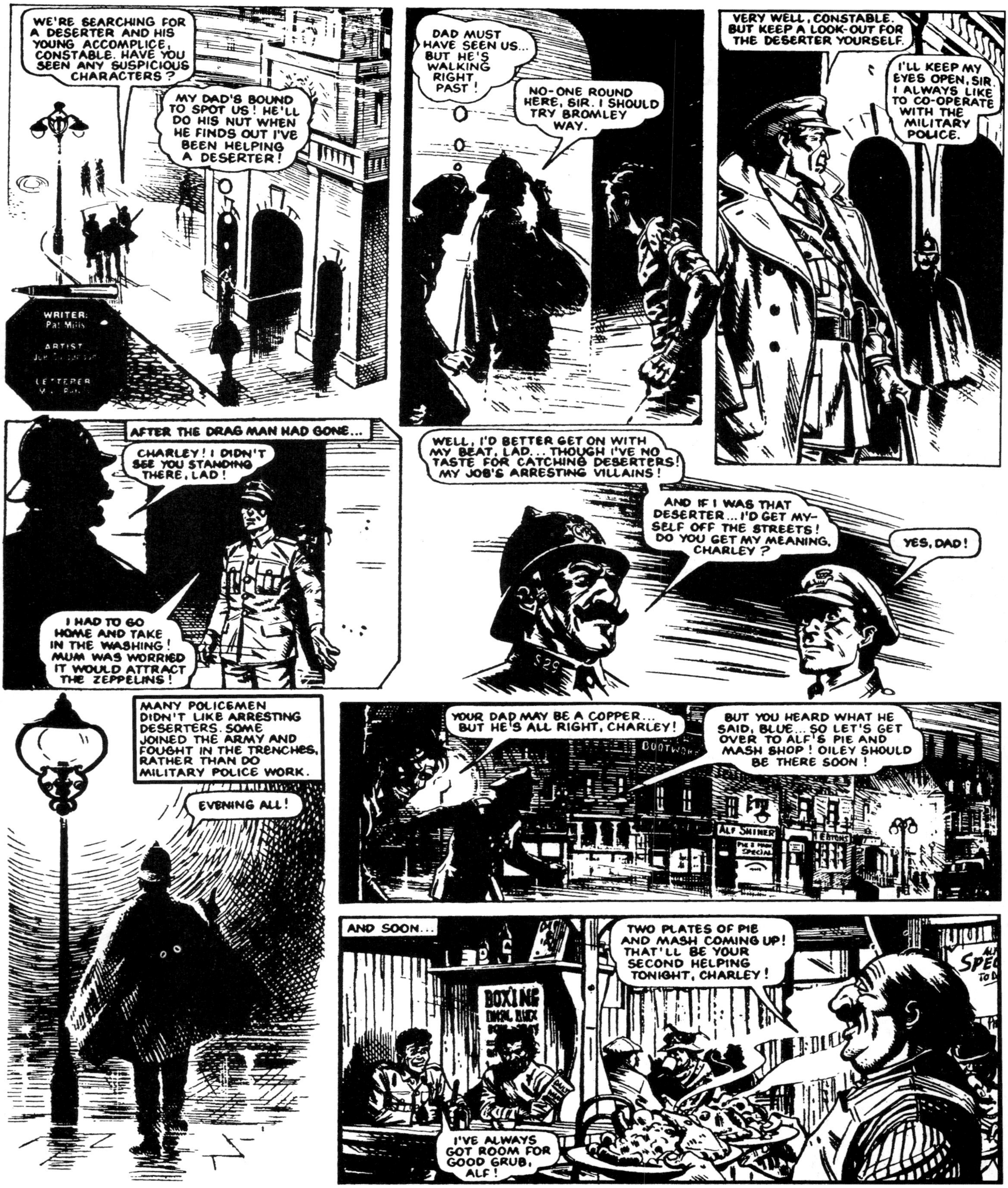
WE'RE SEARCHING FOR A DESERTER AND HIS YOUNG ACCOMPLICE, CONSTABLE. HAVE YOU SEEN ANY SUSPICIOUS CHARACTERS?
MY DAD'S BOUND TO SPOT US! HE'LL DO HIS NUT WHEN HE FINDS OUT I'VE BEEN HELPING A DESERTER!
WRITER:
Pat Mills
ARTIST
LETTERER
DAD MUST HAVE SEEN US... BUT HE'S WALKING RIGHT PAST!
NO-ONE ROUND HERE, SIR. I SHOULD TRY BROMLEY WAY.
VERY WELL, CONSTABLE. BUT KEEP A LOOK-OUT FOR THE DESERTER YOURSELF.
I'LL KEEP MY EYES OPEN, SIR. I ALWAYS LIKE TO CO-OPERATE WITH THE MILITARY POLICE.
AFTER THE DRAG MAN HAD GONE...
CHARLEY! I DIDN'T SEE YOU STANDING THERE, LAD!
I HAD TO GO HOME AND TAKE IN THE WASHING! MUM WAS WORRIED IT WOULD ATTRACT THE ZEPPELINS!
WELL, I'D BETTER GET ON WITH MY BEAT, LAD... THOUGH I'VE NO TASTE FOR CATCHING DESERTERS! MY JOB'S ARRESTING VILLAINS!
AND IF I WAS THAT DESERTER... I'D GET MYSELF OFF THE STREETS! DO YOU GET MY MEANING, CHARLEY?
YES, DAD!
MANY POLICEMEN DIDN'T LIKE ARRESTING DESERTERS. SOME JOINED THE ARMY AND FOUGHT IN THE TRENCHES, RATHER THAN DO MILITARY POLICE WORK.
EVENING ALL!
YOUR DAD MAY BE A COPPER... BUT HE'S ALL RIGHT, CHARLEY!
BUT YOU HEARD WHAT HE SAID, BLUE... SO LET'S GET OVER TO ALF'S PIE AND MASH SHOP! OILEY SHOULD BE THERE SOON!
ALF SHINER
AND SOON...
TWO PLATES OF PIE AND MASH COMING UP! THAT'LL BE YOUR SECOND HELPING TONIGHT, CHARLEY!
BOXING
I'VE ALWAYS GOT ROOM FOR GOOD GRUB, ALF!

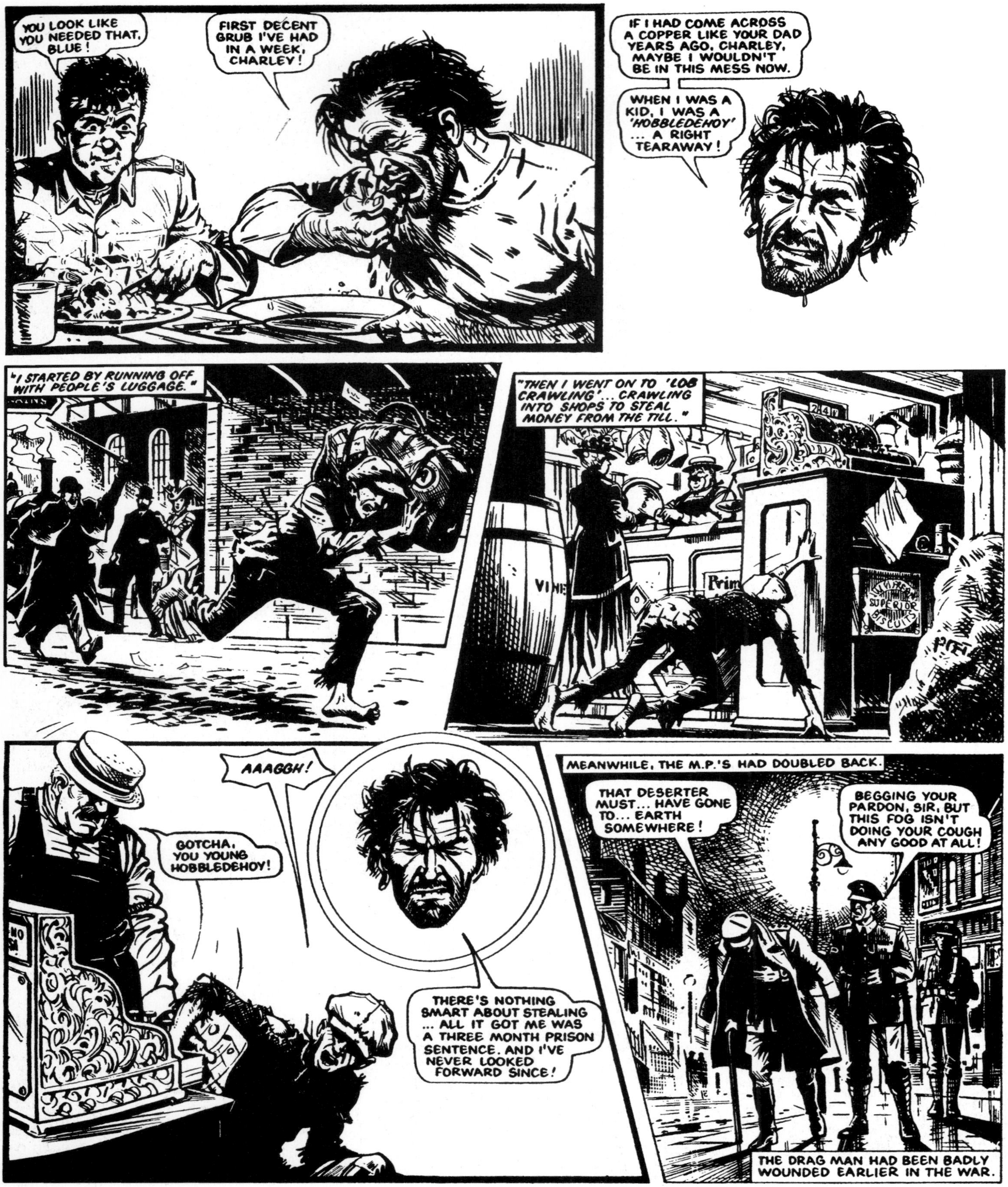
YOU LOOK LIKE YOU NEEDED THAT, BLUE!
FIRST DECENT GRUB I'VE HAD IN A WEEK, CHARLEY!
IF I HAD COME ACROSS A COPPER LIKE YOUR DAD YEARS AGO, CHARLEY, MAYBE I WOULDN'T BE IN THIS MESS NOW.
WHEN I WAS A KID, I WAS A 'HOBBLEDEHOY' ... A RIGHT TEARAWAY!
"I STARTED BY RUNNING OFF WITH PEOPLE'S LUGGAGE."
"THEN I WENT ON TO 'LOB CRAWLING'... CRAWLING INTO SHOPS TO STEAL MONEY FROM THE TILL."
SUPERIOR BISCUITS
GOTCHA, YOU YOUNG HOBBLEDEHOY!
AAAGGH!
THERE'S NOTHING SMART ABOUT STEALING ... ALL IT GOT ME WAS A THREE MONTH PRISON SENTENCE. AND I'VE NEVER LOOKED FORWARD SINCE!
MEANWHILE, THE M.P.'S HAD DOUBLED BACK.
THAT DESERTER MUST... HAVE GONE TO... EARTH SOMEWHERE!
BEGGING YOUR PARDON, SIR, BUT THIS FOG ISN'T DOING YOUR COUGH ANY GOOD AT ALL!
THE DRAG MAN HAD BEEN BADLY WOUNDED EARLIER IN THE WAR.

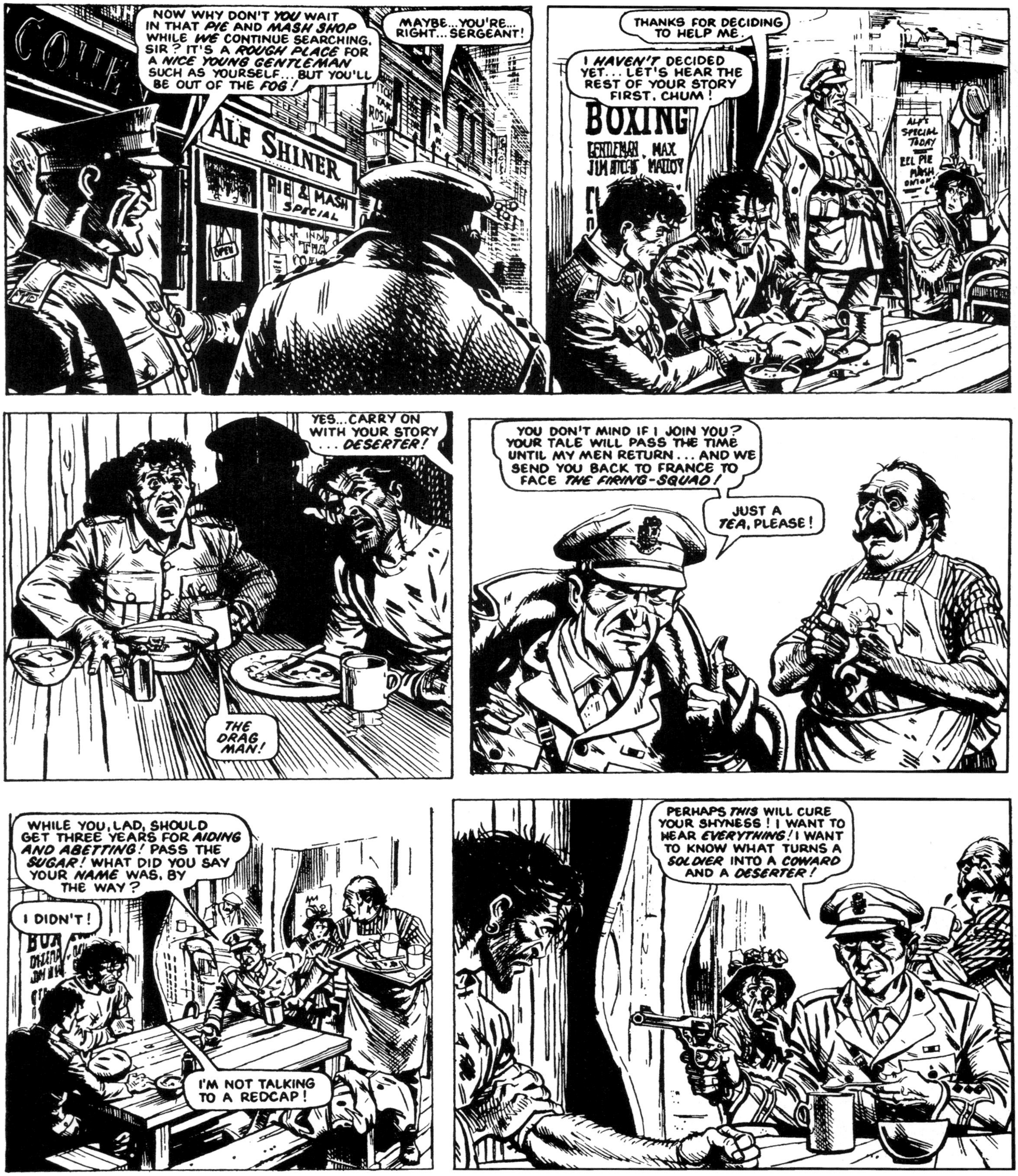

COWE
NOW WHY DON'T YOU WAIT IN THAT PIE AND MASH SHOP WHILE WE CONTINUE SEARCHING, SIR? IT'S A ROUGH PLACE FOR A NICE YOUNG GENTLEMAN SUCH AS YOURSELF... BUT YOU'LL BE OUT OF THE FOG!
MAYBE...YOU'RE... RIGHT...SERGEANT!
ALF SHINER
PIE & MASH SPECIAL
OPEN
THANKS FOR DECIDING TO HELP ME.
I HAVEN'T DECIDED YET... LET'S HEAR THE REST OF YOUR STORY FIRST, CHUM!
BOXING
GENTLEMAN JIM HITCHINS
MAX MALLOY
ALF'S SPECIAL TODAY
EEL PIE MASH
YES...CARRY ON WITH YOUR STORY ...DESERTER!
THE DRAG MAN!
YOU DON'T MIND IF I JOIN YOU? YOUR TALE WILL PASS THE TIME UNTIL MY MEN RETURN... AND WE SEND YOU BACK TO FRANCE TO FACE THE FIRING-SQUAD!
JUST A TEA, PLEASE!
WHILE YOU, LAD, SHOULD GET THREE YEARS FOR AIDING AND ABETTING! PASS THE SUGAR! WHAT DID YOU SAY YOUR NAME WAS, BY THE WAY?
I DIDN'T!
I'M NOT TALKING TO A REDCAP!
PERHAPS THIS WILL CURE YOUR SHYNESS! I WANT TO HEAR EVERYTHING! I WANT TO KNOW WHAT TURNS A SOLDIER INTO A COWARD AND A DESERTER!

"I'M WARNING YOU! ON YOUR FEET! OR I SHOOT YOU WHERE YOU LIE!"

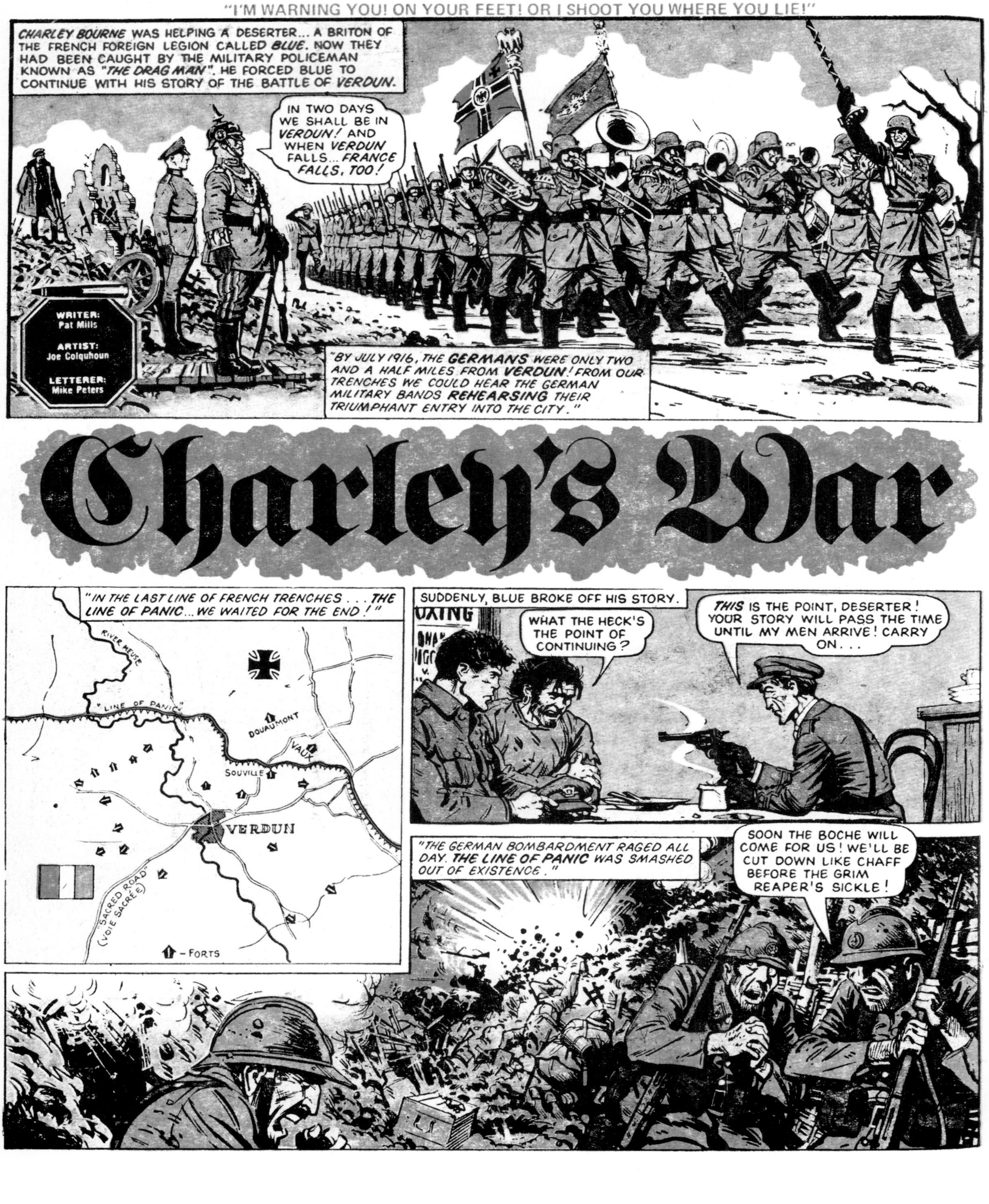

CHARLEY BOURNE WAS HELPING A DESERTER... A BRITON OF THE FRENCH FOREIGN LEGION CALLED BLUE. NOW THEY HAD BEEN CAUGHT BY THE MILITARY POLICEMAN KNOWN AS "THE DRAG MAN". HE FORCED BLUE TO CONTINUE WITH HIS STORY OF THE BATTLE OF VERDUN.
IN TWO DAYS WE SHALL BE IN VERDUN! AND WHEN VERDUN FALLS... FRANCE FALLS, TOO!
WRITER: Pat Mills
ARTIST: Joe Colquhoun
LETTERER: Mike Peters
"BY JULY 1916, THE GERMANS WERE ONLY TWO AND A HALF MILES FROM VERDUN! FROM OUR TRENCHES WE COULD HEAR THE GERMAN MILITARY BANDS REHEARSING THEIR TRIUMPHANT ENTRY INTO THE CITY."
Charley's War
"IN THE LAST LINE OF FRENCH TRENCHES . . . THE LINE OF PANIC... WE WAITED FOR THE END!"
RIVER MEUSE
"LINE OF PANIC"
DOUAUMONT
VAUX
SOUVILLE
VERDUN
"SACRED ROAD" (VOIE SACRÉE)
– FORTS
SUDDENLY, BLUE BROKE OFF HIS STORY.
WHAT THE HECK'S THE POINT OF CONTINUING?
THIS IS THE POINT, DESERTER! YOUR STORY WILL PASS THE TIME UNTIL MY MEN ARRIVE! CARRY ON . . .
"THE GERMAN BOMBARDMENT RAGED ALL DAY. THE LINE OF PANIC WAS SMASHED OUT OF EXISTENCE."
SOON THE BOCHE WILL COME FOR US! WE'LL BE CUT DOWN LIKE CHAFF BEFORE THE GRIM REAPER'S SICKLE!

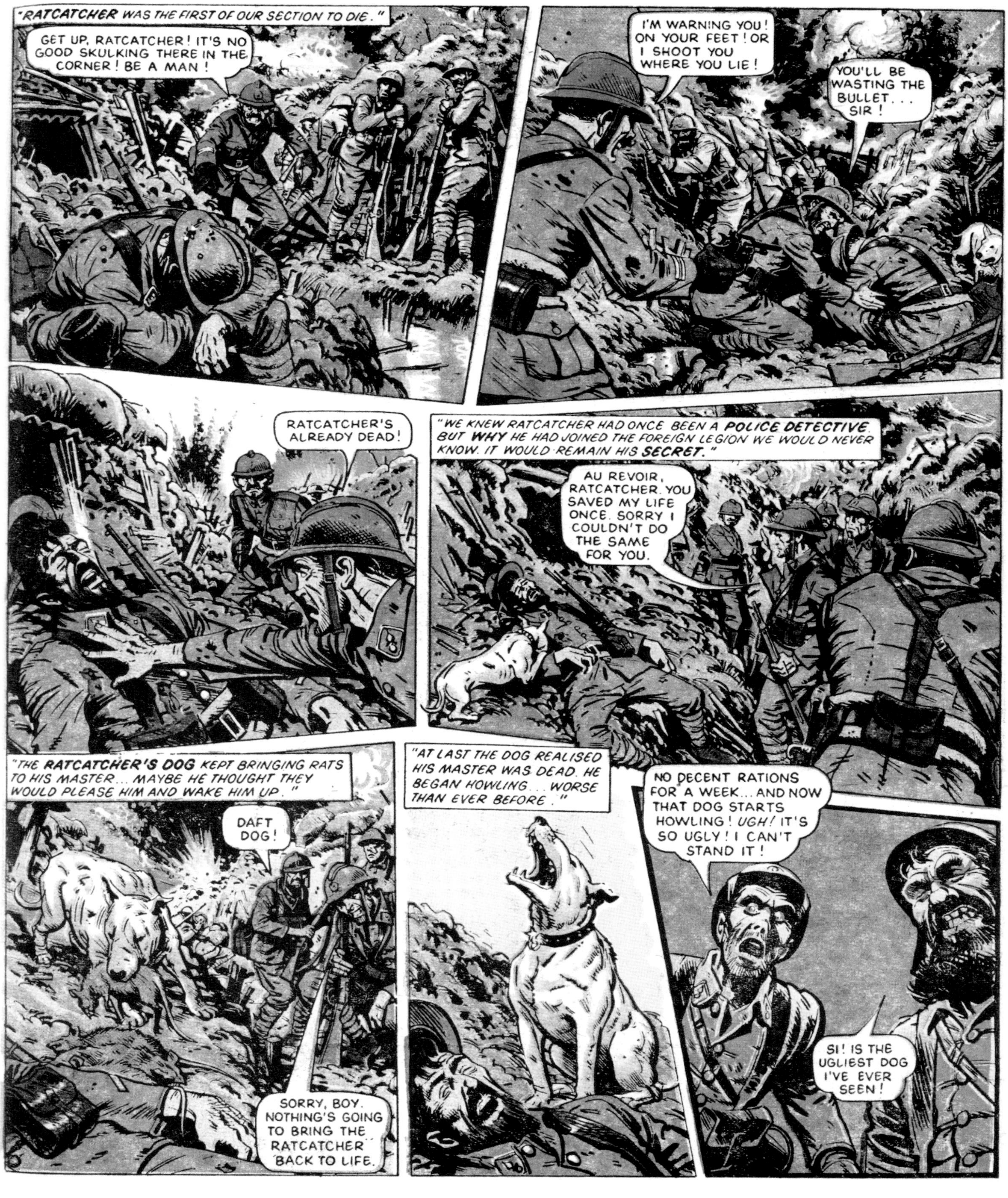
"RATCATCHER WAS THE FIRST OF OUR SECTION TO DIE."
GET UP, RATCATCHER! IT'S NO GOOD SKULKING THERE IN THE CORNER! BE A MAN!
I'M WARNING YOU! ON YOUR FEET! OR I SHOOT YOU WHERE YOU LIE!
YOU'LL BE WASTING THE BULLET... SIR!
RATCATCHER'S ALREADY DEAD!
"WE KNEW RATCATCHER HAD ONCE BEEN A POLICE DETECTIVE. BUT WHY HE HAD JOINED THE FOREIGN LEGION WE WOULD NEVER KNOW. IT WOULD REMAIN HIS SECRET."
AU REVOIR, RATCATCHER. YOU SAVED MY LIFE ONCE. SORRY I COULDN'T DO THE SAME FOR YOU.
"THE RATCATCHER'S DOG KEPT BRINGING RATS TO HIS MASTER... MAYBE HE THOUGHT THEY WOULD PLEASE HIM AND WAKE HIM UP."
DAFT DOG!
SORRY, BOY. NOTHING'S GOING TO BRING THE RATCATCHER BACK TO LIFE.
"AT LAST THE DOG REALISED HIS MASTER WAS DEAD. HE BEGAN HOWLING... WORSE THAN EVER BEFORE."
NO DECENT RATIONS FOR A WEEK... AND NOW THAT DOG STARTS HOWLING! UGH! IT'S SO UGLY! I CAN'T STAND IT!
SI! IS THE UGLIEST DOG I'VE EVER SEEN!

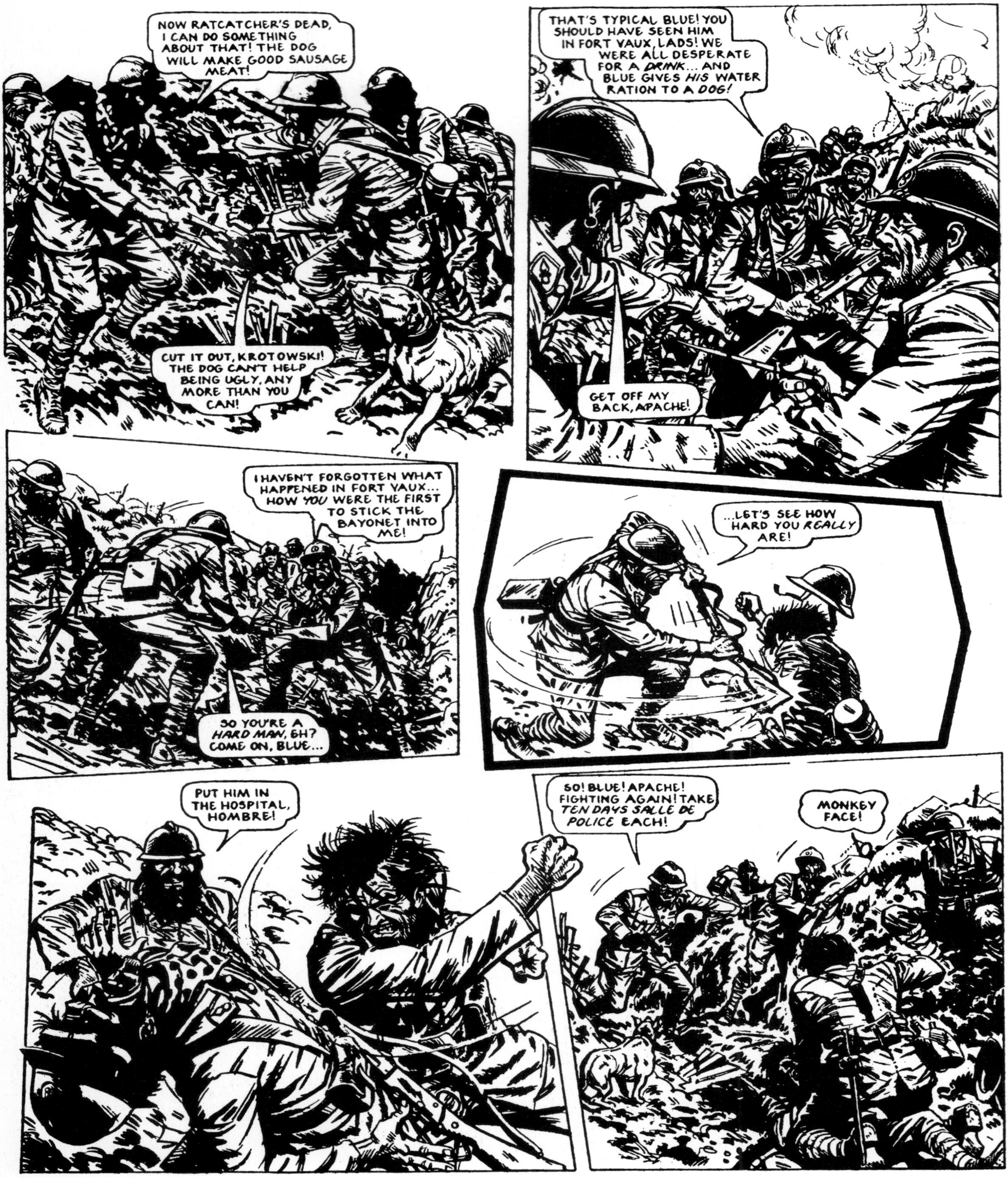
NOW RATCATCHER'S DEAD, I CAN DO SOMETHING ABOUT THAT! THE DOG WILL MAKE GOOD SAUSAGE MEAT!
CUT IT OUT, KROTOWSKI! THE DOG CAN'T HELP BEING UGLY, ANY MORE THAN YOU CAN!
THAT'S TYPICAL BLUE! YOU SHOULD HAVE SEEN HIM IN FORT VAUX, LADS! WE WERE ALL DESPERATE FOR A *DRINK*... AND BLUE GIVES *HIS* WATER RATION TO A *DOG*!
GET OFF MY BACK, APACHE!
I HAVEN'T FORGOTTEN WHAT HAPPENED IN FORT VAUX... HOW *YOU* WERE THE FIRST TO STICK THE BAYONET INTO ME!
SO YOU'RE A *HARD MAN*, EH? COME ON, BLUE...
...LET'S SEE HOW HARD YOU *REALLY* ARE!
PUT HIM IN THE HOSPITAL, HOMBRE!
SO! BLUE! APACHE! FIGHTING AGAIN! TAKE *TEN DAYS SALLE DE POLICE* EACH!
MONKEY FACE!

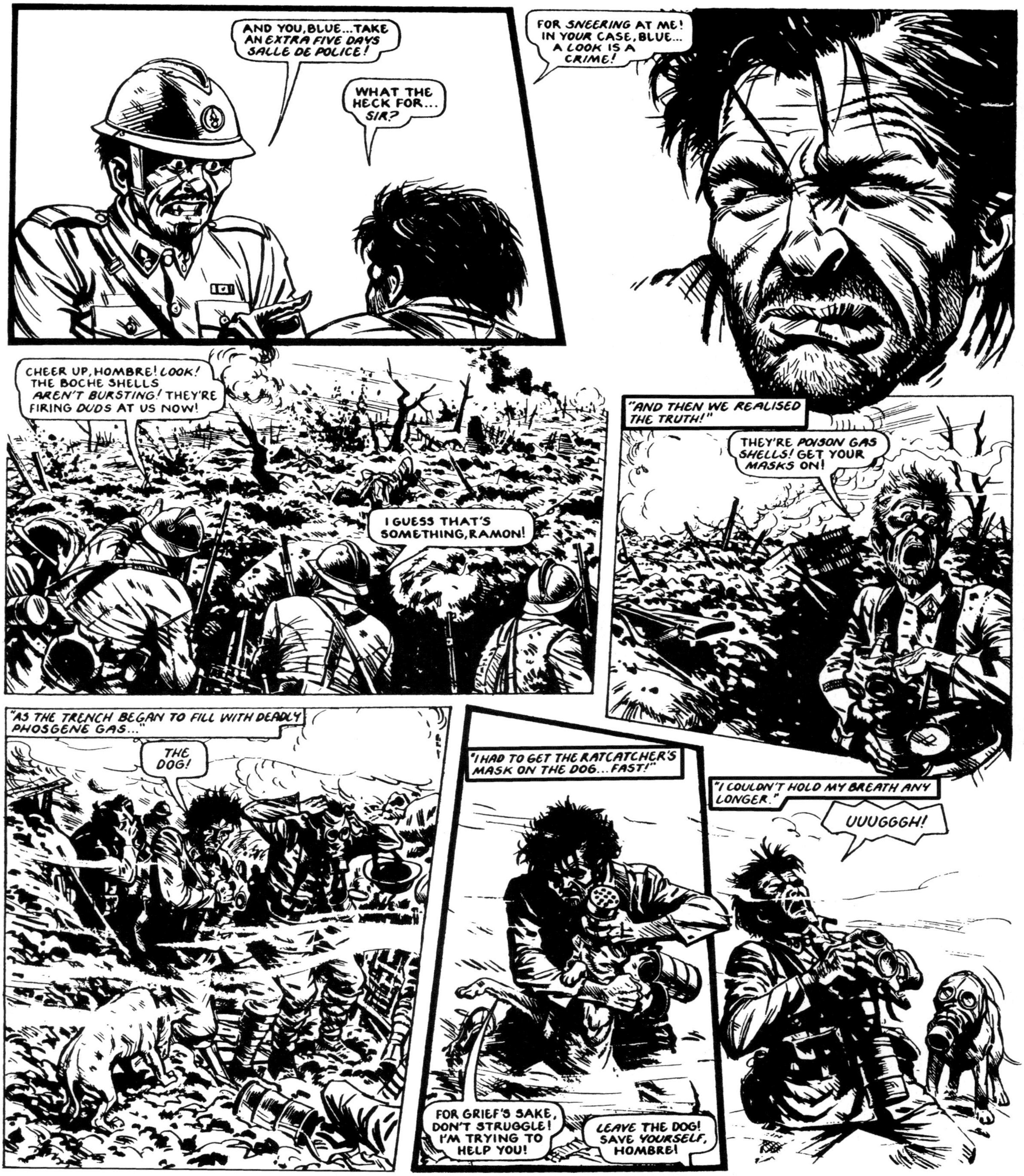
AND YOU, BLUE... TAKE AN EXTRA FIVE DAYS SALLE DE POLICE!
WHAT THE HECK FOR... SIR?
FOR SNEERING AT ME! IN YOUR CASE, BLUE... A LOOK IS A CRIME!
CHEER UP, HOMBRE! LOOK! THE BOCHE SHELLS AREN'T BURSTING! THEY'RE FIRING DUDS AT US NOW!
I GUESS THAT'S SOMETHING, RAMON!
"AND THEN WE REALISED THE TRUTH!"
THEY'RE POISON GAS SHELLS! GET YOUR MASKS ON!
"AS THE TRENCH BEGAN TO FILL WITH DEADLY PHOSGENE GAS..."
THE DOG!
"I HAD TO GET THE RATCATCHER'S MASK ON THE DOG... FAST!"
FOR GRIEF'S SAKE, DON'T STRUGGLE! I'M TRYING TO HELP YOU!
LEAVE THE DOG! SAVE YOURSELF, HOMBRE!
"I COULDN'T HOLD MY BREATH ANY LONGER."
UUUGGGH!

CHARLEY'S WAR

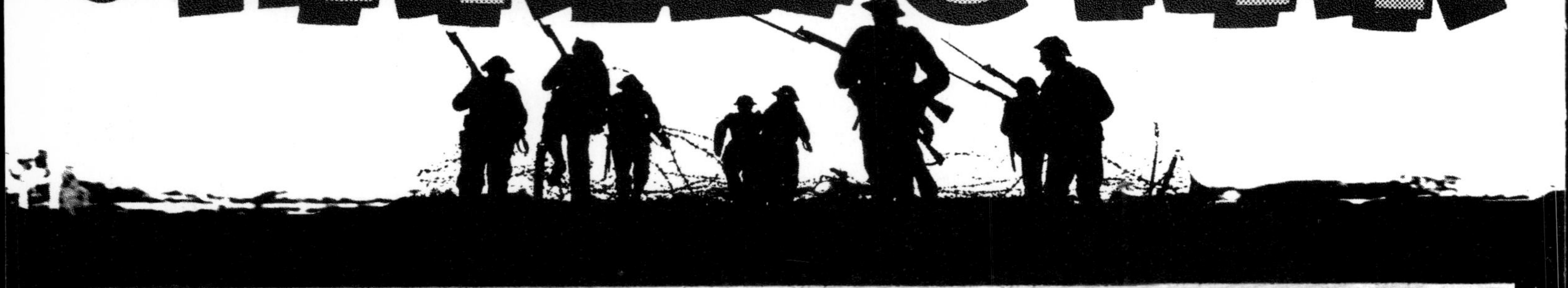

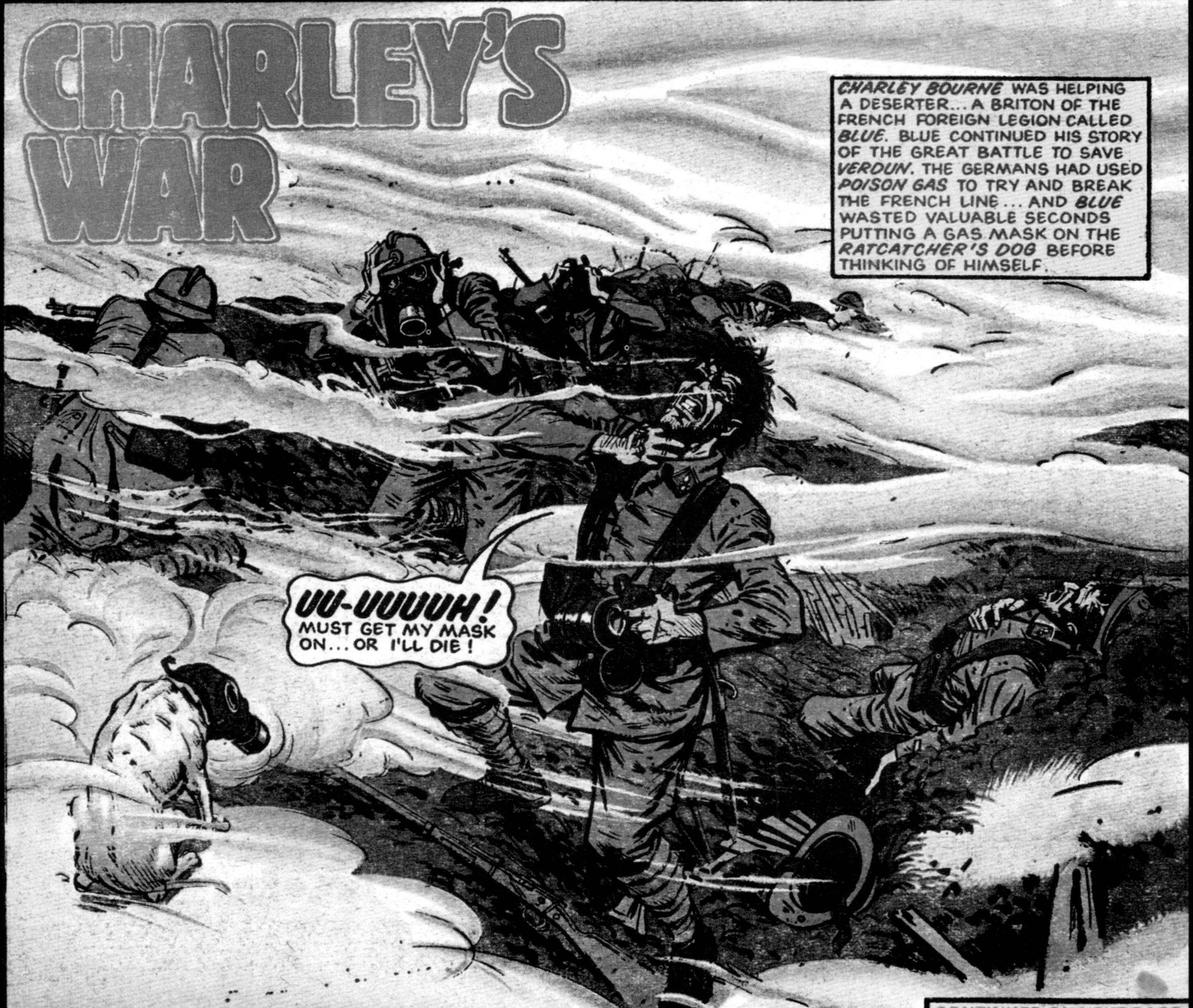
CHARLEY'S WAR
CHARLEY BOURNE WAS HELPING A DESERTER... A BRITON OF THE FRENCH FOREIGN LEGION CALLED BLUE. BLUE CONTINUED HIS STORY OF THE GREAT BATTLE TO SAVE VERDUN. THE GERMANS HAD USED POISON GAS TO TRY AND BREAK THE FRENCH LINE... AND BLUE WASTED VALUABLE SECONDS PUTTING A GAS MASK ON THE RATCATCHER'S DOG BEFORE THINKING OF HIMSELF.
UU-UUUUH! MUST GET MY MASK ON... OR I'LL DIE!

CONTINUED ON NEXT PAGE

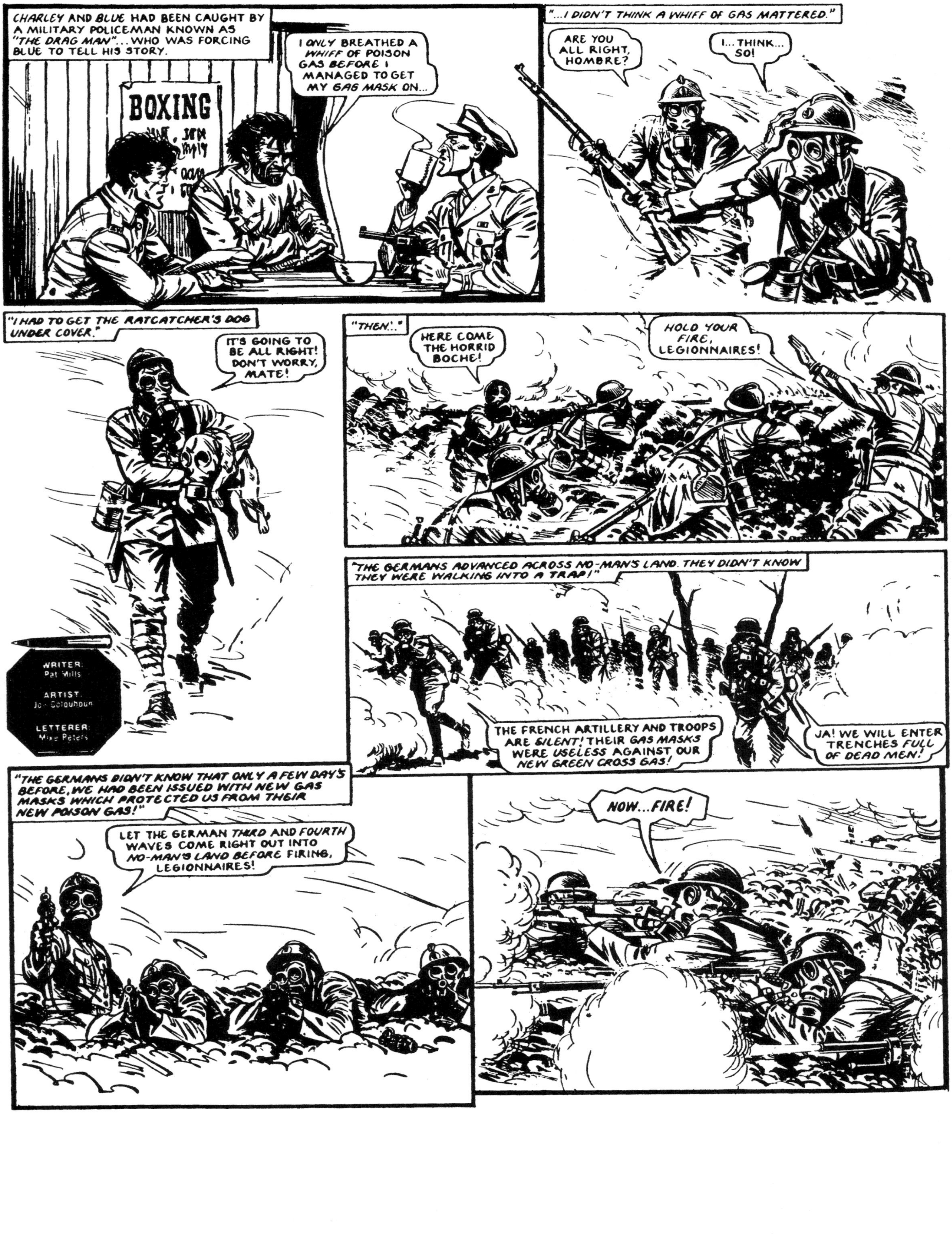
CHARLEY AND BLUE HAD BEEN CAUGHT BY A MILITARY POLICEMAN KNOWN AS "THE DRAG MAN"... WHO WAS FORCING BLUE TO TELL HIS STORY.
BOXING
I ONLY BREATHED A WHIFF OF POISON GAS BEFORE I MANAGED TO GET MY GAS MASK ON...
"...I DIDN'T THINK A WHIFF OF GAS MATTERED."
ARE YOU ALL RIGHT, HOMBRE?
I... THINK... SO!
"I HAD TO GET THE RATCATCHER'S DOG UNDER COVER."
IT'S GOING TO BE ALL RIGHT! DON'T WORRY, MATE!
WRITER: Pat Mills
ARTIST: Joe Colquhoun
LETTERER: Mike Peters
"THEN..."
HERE COME THE HORRID BOCHE!
HOLD YOUR FIRE, LEGIONNAIRES!
"THE GERMANS ADVANCED ACROSS NO-MAN'S LAND. THEY DIDN'T KNOW THEY WERE WALKING INTO A TRAP!"
THE FRENCH ARTILLERY AND TROOPS ARE SILENT! THEIR GAS MASKS WERE USELESS AGAINST OUR NEW GREEN CROSS GAS!
JA! WE WILL ENTER TRENCHES FULL OF DEAD MEN!
"THE GERMANS DIDN'T KNOW THAT ONLY A FEW DAYS BEFORE, WE HAD BEEN ISSUED WITH NEW GAS MASKS WHICH PROTECTED US FROM THEIR NEW POISON GAS!"
LET THE GERMAN THIRD AND FOURTH WAVES COME RIGHT OUT INTO NO-MAN'S LAND BEFORE FIRING, LEGIONNAIRES!
NOW... FIRE!

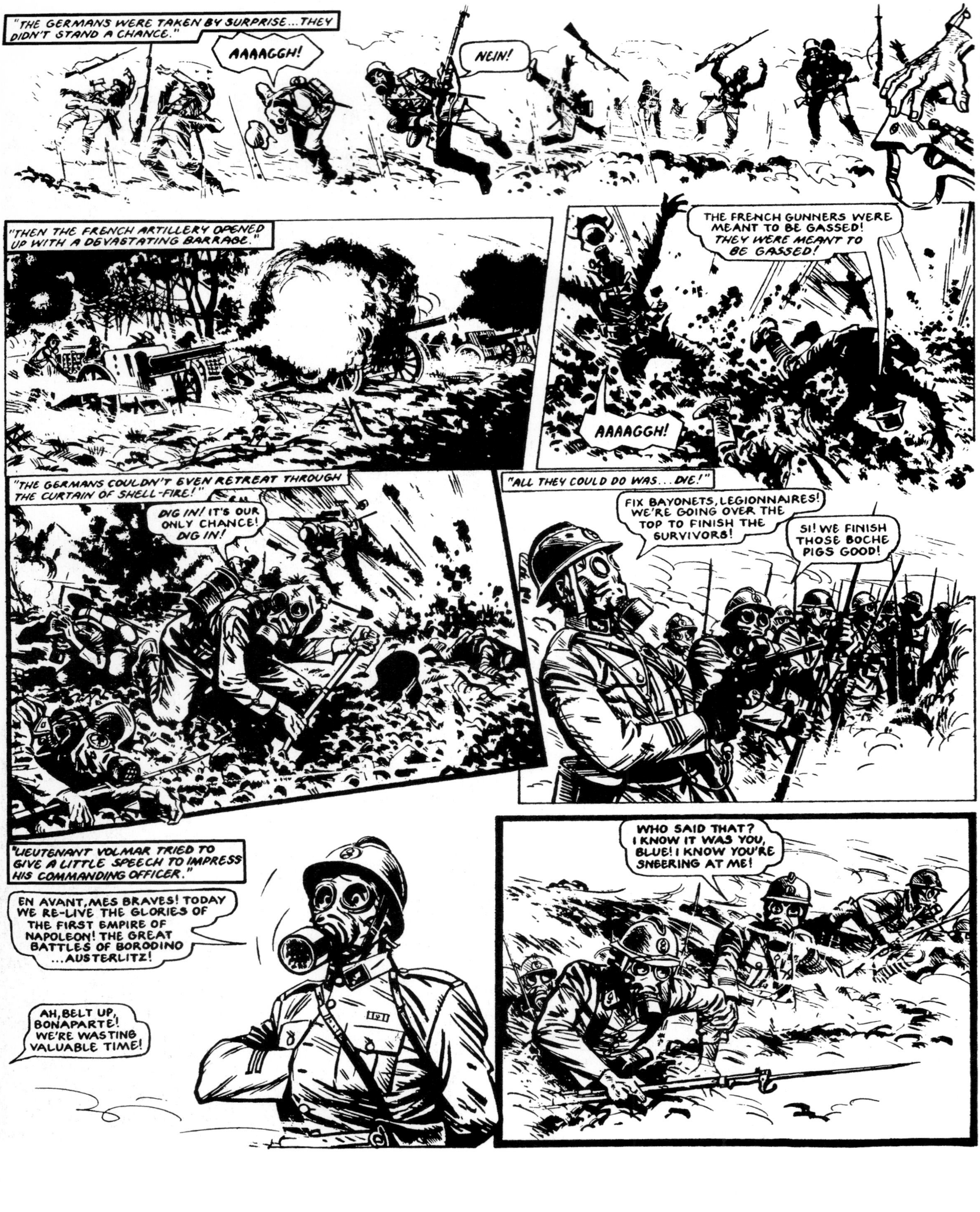

"THE GERMANS WERE TAKEN BY SURPRISE... THEY DIDN'T STAND A CHANCE."
AAAAGGH!
NEIN!
"THEN THE FRENCH ARTILLERY OPENED UP WITH A DEVASTATING BARRAGE."
THE FRENCH GUNNERS WERE MEANT TO BE GASSED! THEY WERE MEANT TO BE GASSED!
AAAAGGH!
"THE GERMANS COULDN'T EVEN RETREAT THROUGH THE CURTAIN OF SHELL-FIRE!"
DIG IN! IT'S OUR ONLY CHANCE! DIG IN!
"ALL THEY COULD DO WAS... DIE!"
FIX BAYONETS, LEGIONNAIRES! WE'RE GOING OVER THE TOP TO FINISH THE SURVIVORS!
SI! WE FINISH THOSE BOCHE PIGS GOOD!
"LIEUTENANT VOLMAR TRIED TO GIVE A LITTLE SPEECH TO IMPRESS HIS COMMANDING OFFICER."
EN AVANT, MES BRAVES! TODAY WE RE-LIVE THE GLORIES OF THE FIRST EMPIRE OF NAPOLEON! THE GREAT BATTLES OF BORODINO ...AUSTERLITZ!
AH, BELT UP, BONAPARTE! WE'RE WASTING VALUABLE TIME!
WHO SAID THAT? I KNOW IT WAS YOU, BLUE! I KNOW YOU'RE SNEERING AT ME!

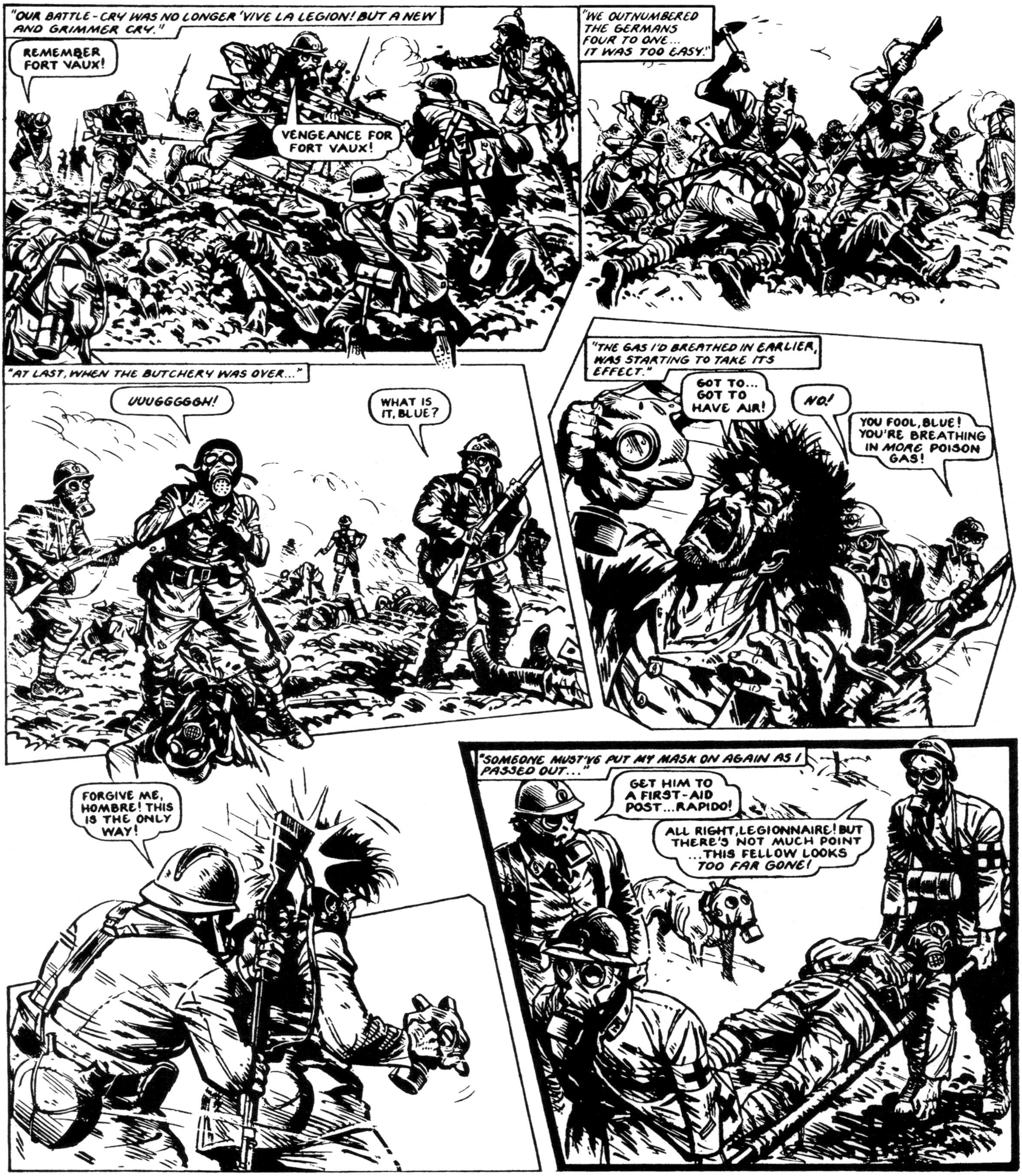
"OUR BATTLE-CRY WAS NO LONGER 'VIVE LA LEGION!' BUT A NEW AND GRIMMER CRY."
REMEMBER FORT VAUX!
VENGEANCE FOR FORT VAUX!
"WE OUTNUMBERED THE GERMANS FOUR TO ONE... IT WAS TOO EASY."
"AT LAST, WHEN THE BUTCHERY WAS OVER..."
UUUGGGGGH!
WHAT IS IT, BLUE?
"THE GAS I'D BREATHED IN EARLIER, WAS STARTING TO TAKE ITS EFFECT."
GOT TO... GOT TO HAVE AIR!
NO!
YOU FOOL, BLUE! YOU'RE BREATHING IN MORE POISON GAS!
FORGIVE ME, HOMBRE! THIS IS THE ONLY WAY!
"SOMEONE MUST'VE PUT MY MASK ON AGAIN AS I PASSED OUT..."
GET HIM TO A FIRST-AID POST...RAPIDO!
ALL RIGHT, LEGIONNAIRE! BUT THERE'S NOT MUCH POINT ...THIS FELLOW LOOKS TOO FAR GONE!

THE "DRAG MAN" TOLD HIS VERSION ABOUT . . . MEN SLICED IN HALF!

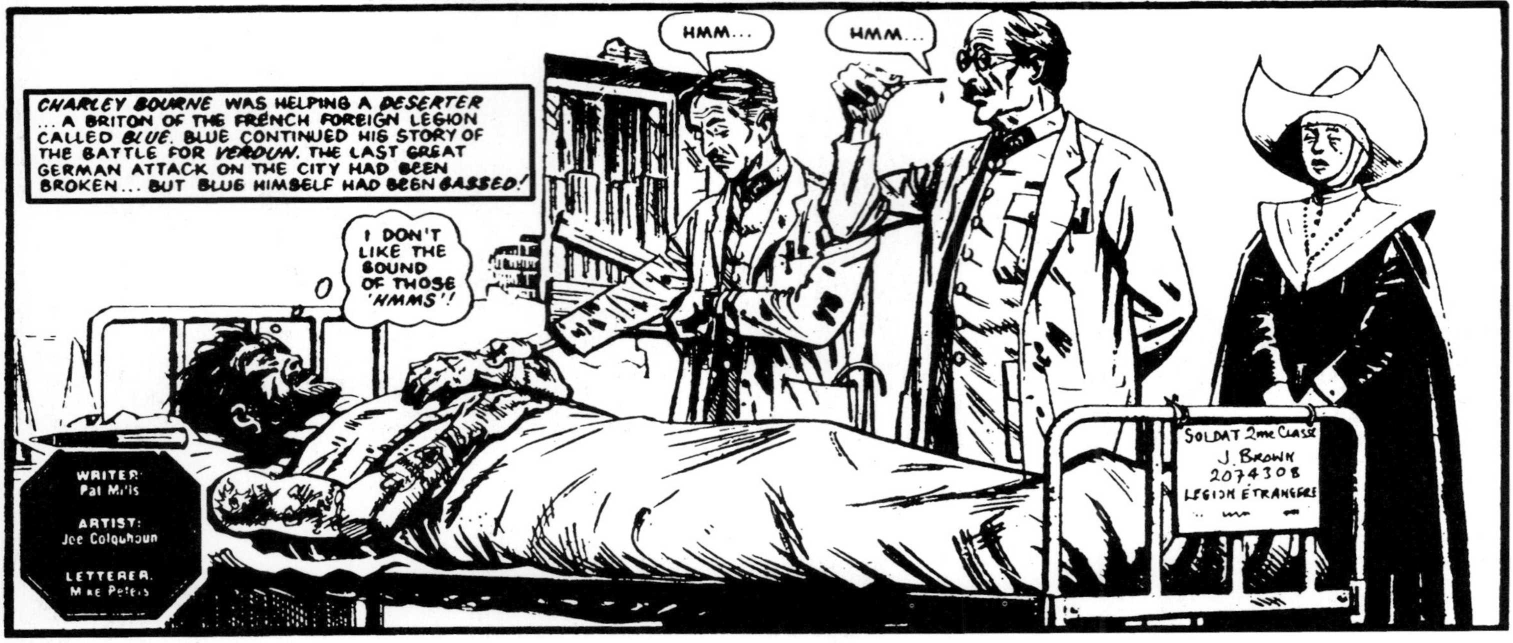

CHARLEY BOURNE WAS HELPING A DESERTER ... A BRITON OF THE FRENCH FOREIGN LEGION CALLED BLUE. BLUE CONTINUED HIS STORY OF THE BATTLE FOR VERDUN. THE LAST GREAT GERMAN ATTACK ON THE CITY HAD BEEN BROKEN ... BUT BLUE HIMSELF HAD BEEN GASSED!
HMM...
HMM...
I DON'T LIKE THE SOUND OF THOSE 'HMMS'!
WRITER: Pat Mills
ARTIST: Joe Colquhoun
LETTERER: Mike Peters
SOLDAT 2me CLASSE
J. BROWN
2074308
LEGION ETRANGERE

Charley's War

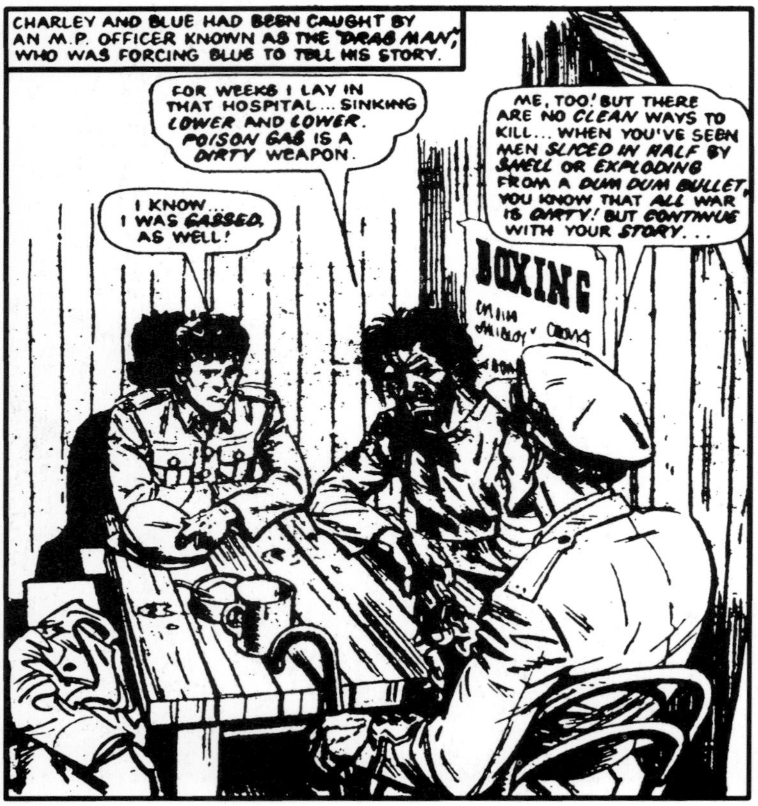

CHARLEY AND BLUE HAD BEEN CAUGHT BY AN M.P. OFFICER KNOWN AS THE "DRAG MAN", WHO WAS FORCING BLUE TO TELL HIS STORY.
FOR WEEKS I LAY IN THAT HOSPITAL ... SINKING LOWER AND LOWER. POISON GAS IS A DIRTY WEAPON.
I KNOW... I WAS GASSED, AS WELL!
ME, TOO! BUT THERE ARE NO CLEAN WAYS TO KILL... WHEN YOU'VE SEEN MEN SLICED IN HALF BY SHELL OR EXPLODING FROM A DUM DUM BULLET, YOU KNOW THAT ALL WAR IS DIRTY! BUT CONTINUE WITH YOUR STORY...
BOXING

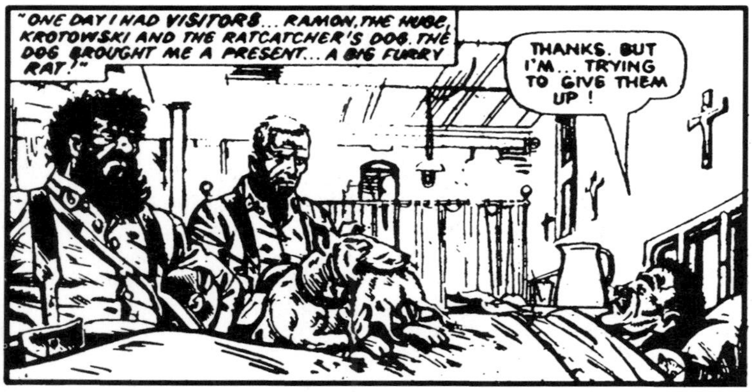

"ONE DAY I HAD VISITORS... RAMON, THE HUGE KROTOWSKI AND THE RATCATCHER'S DOG. THE DOG BROUGHT ME A PRESENT... A BIG FURRY RAT!"
THANKS. BUT I'M... TRYING TO GIVE THEM UP!

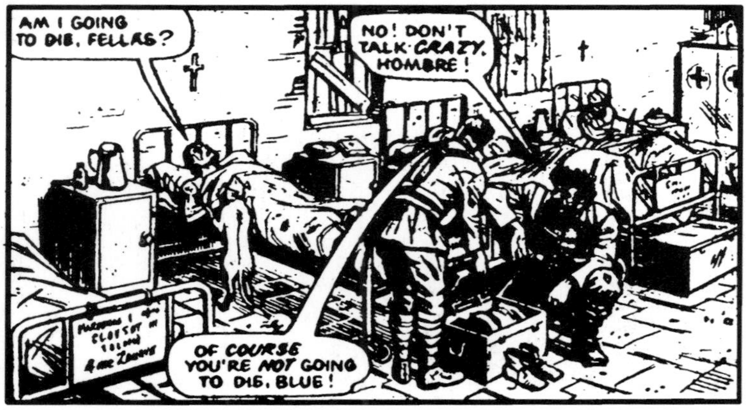

AM I GOING TO DIE, FELLAS?
NO! DON'T TALK CRAZY, HOMBRE!
OF COURSE YOU'RE NOT GOING TO DIE, BLUE!

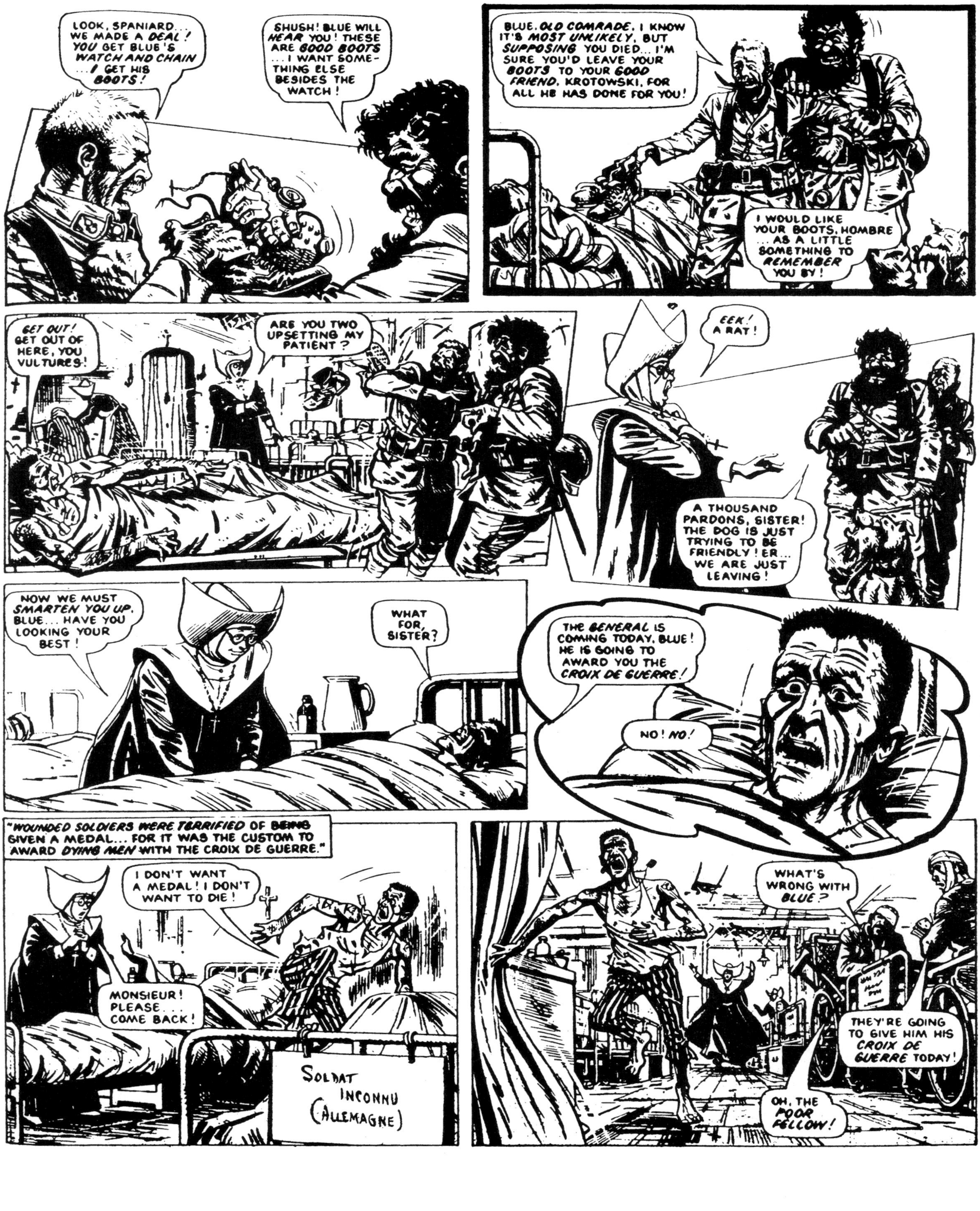
LOOK, SPANIARD... WE MADE A DEAL! YOU GET BLUE'S WATCH AND CHAIN ...I GET HIS BOOTS!
SHUSH! BLUE WILL HEAR YOU! THESE ARE GOOD BOOTS ...I WANT SOMETHING ELSE BESIDES THE WATCH!
BLUE, OLD COMRADE, I KNOW IT'S MOST UNLIKELY, BUT SUPPOSING YOU DIED... I'M SURE YOU'D LEAVE YOUR BOOTS TO YOUR GOOD FRIEND, KROTOWSKI, FOR ALL HE HAS DONE FOR YOU!
I WOULD LIKE YOUR BOOTS, HOMBRE ...AS A LITTLE SOMETHING TO REMEMBER YOU BY!
GET OUT! GET OUT OF HERE, YOU VULTURES!
ARE YOU TWO UPSETTING MY PATIENT?
EEK! A RAT!
A THOUSAND PARDONS, SISTER! THE DOG IS JUST TRYING TO BE FRIENDLY! ER... WE ARE JUST LEAVING!
NOW WE MUST SMARTEN YOU UP, BLUE... HAVE YOU LOOKING YOUR BEST!
WHAT FOR, SISTER?
THE GENERAL IS COMING TODAY, BLUE! HE IS GOING TO AWARD YOU THE CROIX DE GUERRE!
NO! NO!
"WOUNDED SOLDIERS WERE TERRIFIED OF BEING GIVEN A MEDAL... FOR IT WAS THE CUSTOM TO AWARD DYING MEN WITH THE CROIX DE GUERRE."
I DON'T WANT A MEDAL! I DON'T WANT TO DIE!
MONSIEUR! PLEASE... COME BACK!
SOLDAT INCONNU (ALLEMAGNE)
WHAT'S WRONG WITH BLUE?
THEY'RE GOING TO GIVE HIM HIS CROIX DE GUERRE TODAY!
OH, THE POOR FELLOW!

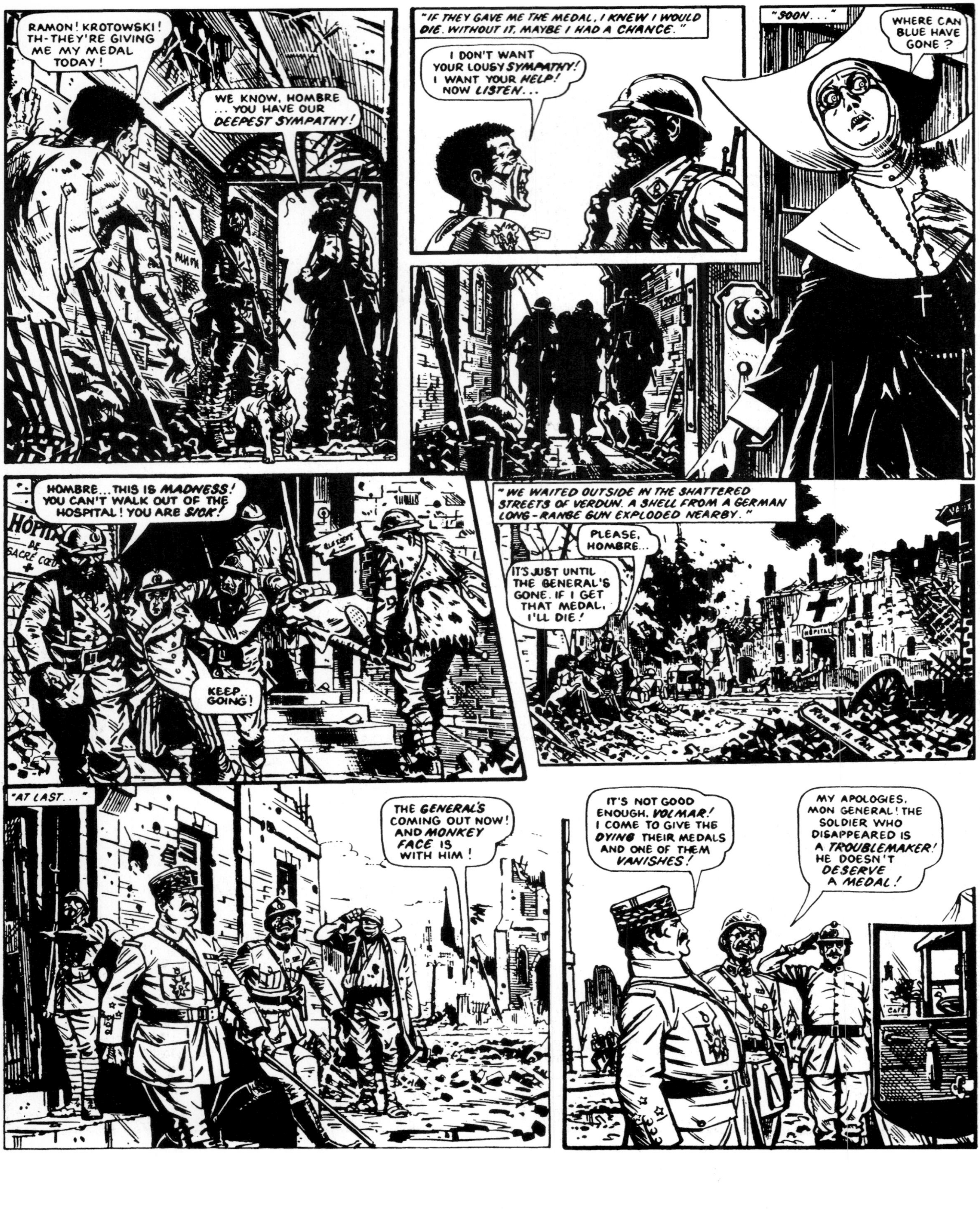
RAMON! KROTOWSKI! TH-THEY'RE GIVING ME MY MEDAL TODAY!
WE KNOW, HOMBRE ... YOU HAVE OUR DEEPEST SYMPATHY!
"IF THEY GAVE ME THE MEDAL, I KNEW I WOULD DIE. WITHOUT IT, MAYBE I HAD A CHANCE."
I DON'T WANT YOUR LOUSY SYMPATHY! I WANT YOUR HELP! NOW LISTEN...
"SOON..."
WHERE CAN BLUE HAVE GONE?
HOMBRE... THIS IS MADNESS! YOU CAN'T WALK OUT OF THE HOSPITAL! YOU ARE SICK!
KEEP GOING!
"WE WAITED OUTSIDE IN THE SHATTERED STREETS OF VERDUN. A SHELL FROM A GERMAN LONG-RANGE GUN EXPLODED NEARBY."
PLEASE, HOMBRE...
IT'S JUST UNTIL THE GENERAL'S GONE. IF I GET THAT MEDAL, I'LL DIE!
"AT LAST..."
THE GENERAL'S COMING OUT NOW! AND MONKEY FACE IS WITH HIM!
IT'S NOT GOOD ENOUGH, VOLMAR! I COME TO GIVE THE DYING THEIR MEDALS AND ONE OF THEM VANISHES!
MY APOLOGIES, MON GENERAL! THE SOLDIER WHO DISAPPEARED IS A TROUBLEMAKER! HE DOESN'T DESERVE A MEDAL!

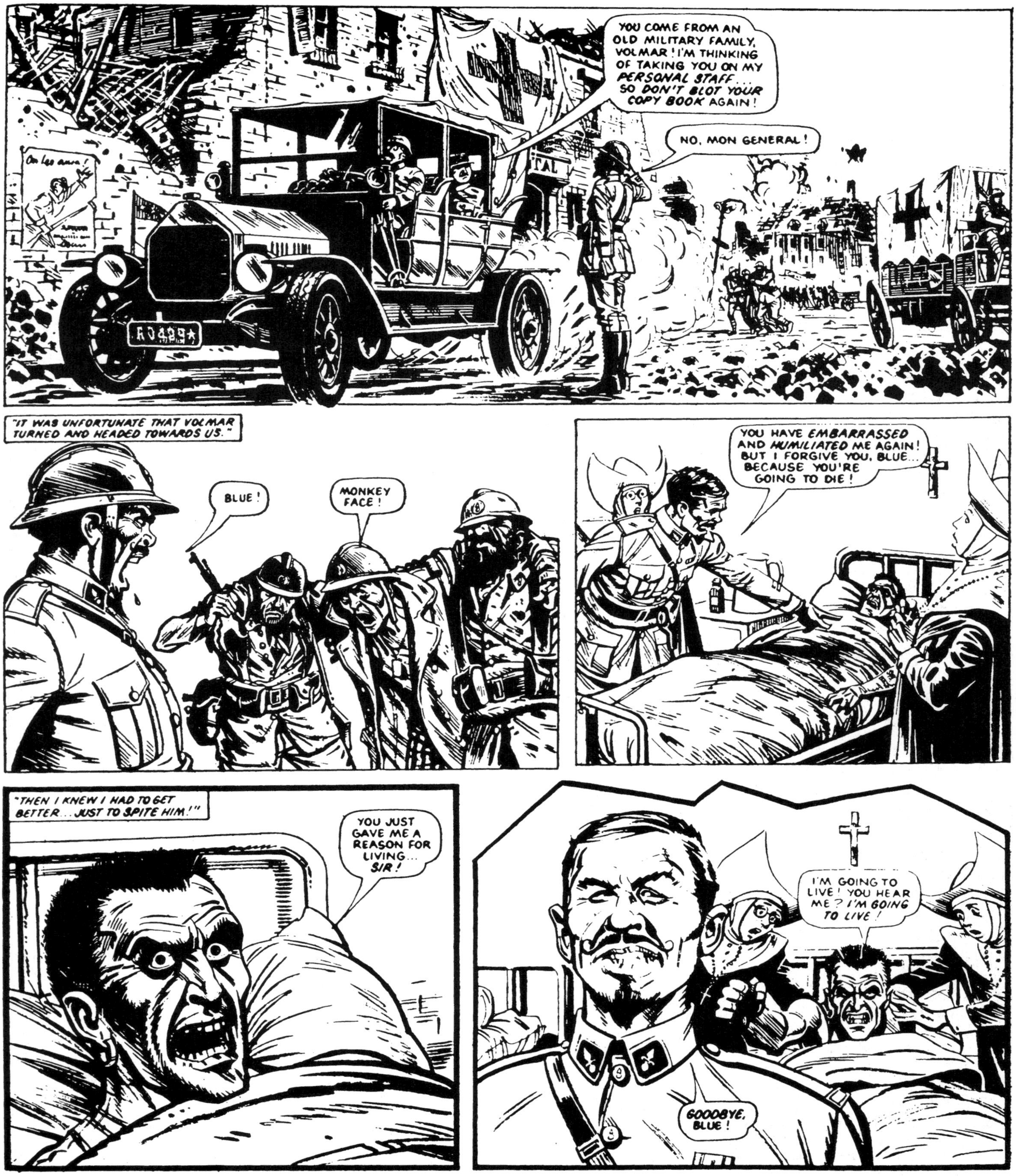
YOU COME FROM AN OLD MILITARY FAMILY, VOLMAR! I'M THINKING OF TAKING YOU ON MY PERSONAL STAFF... SO DON'T BLOT YOUR COPY BOOK AGAIN!
NO, MON GENERAL!
"IT WAS UNFORTUNATE THAT VOLMAR TURNED AND HEADED TOWARDS US."
BLUE!
MONKEY FACE!
YOU HAVE EMBARRASSED AND HUMILIATED ME AGAIN! BUT I FORGIVE YOU, BLUE... BECAUSE YOU'RE GOING TO DIE!
"THEN I KNEW I HAD TO GET BETTER... JUST TO SPITE HIM!"
YOU JUST GAVE ME A REASON FOR LIVING... SIR!
I'M GOING TO LIVE! YOU HEAR ME? I'M GOING TO LIVE!
GOODBYE, BLUE!

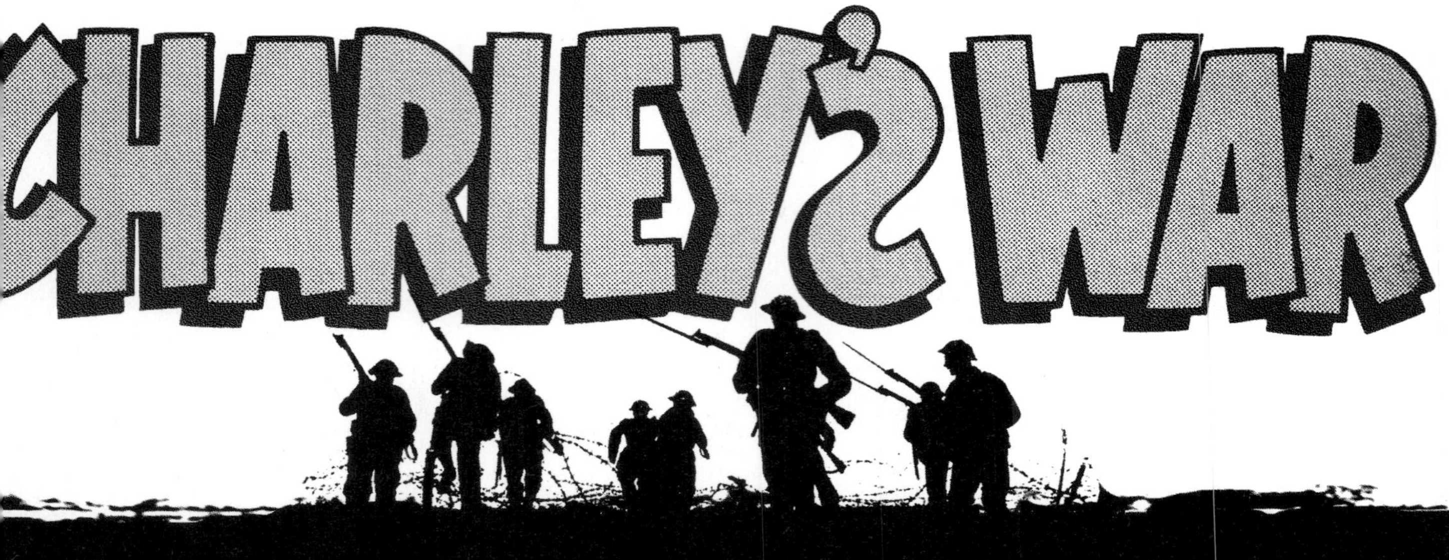
CHARLEY'S WAR

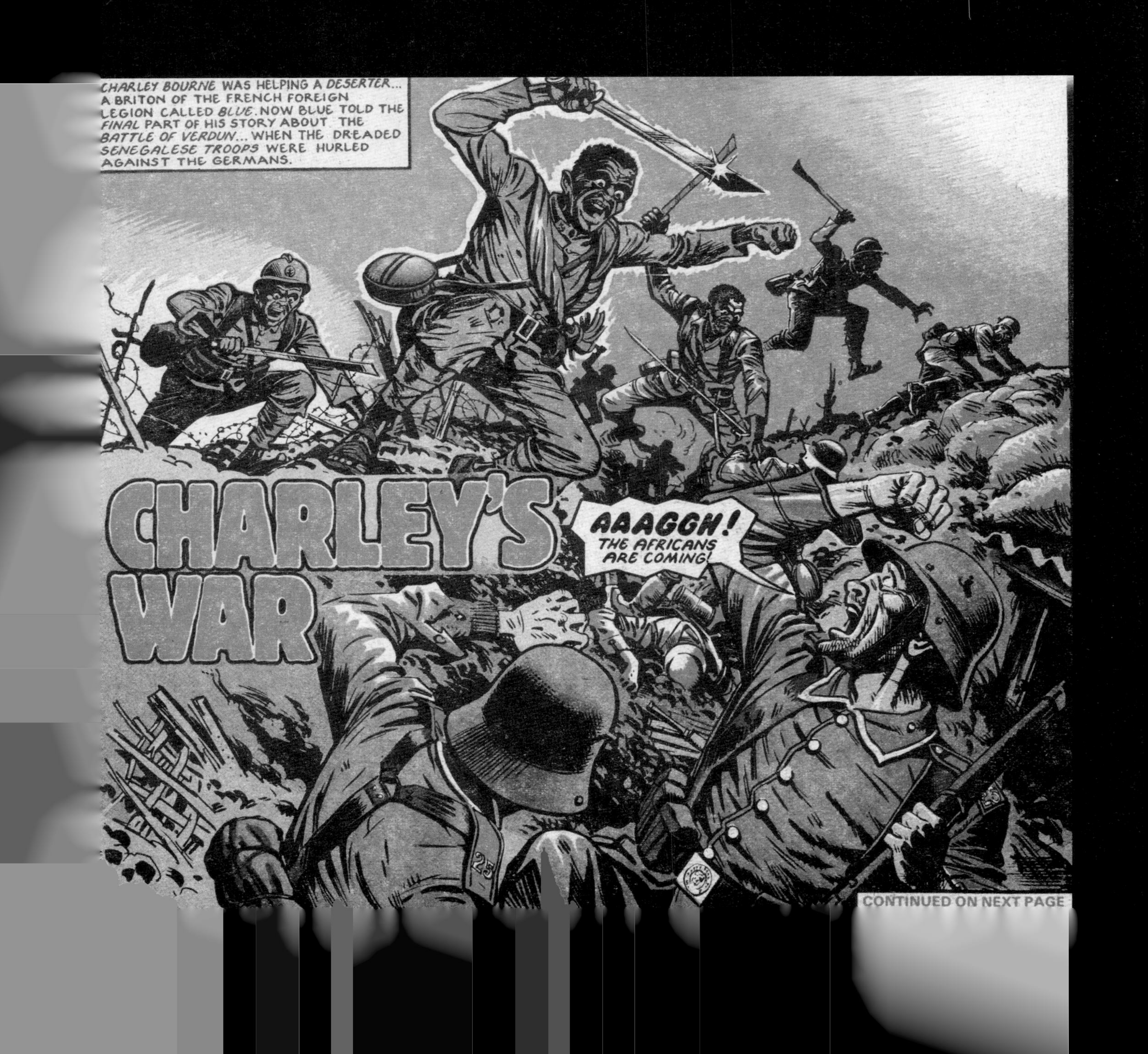
CHARLEY BOURNE WAS HELPING A DESERTER... A BRITON OF THE FRENCH FOREIGN LEGION CALLED BLUE. NOW BLUE TOLD THE FINAL PART OF HIS STORY ABOUT THE BATTLE OF VERDUN... WHEN THE DREADED SENEGALESE TROOPS WERE HURLED AGAINST THE GERMANS.
CHARLEY'S WAR
AAAGGH! THE AFRICANS ARE COMING!

CONTINUED ON NEXT PAGE

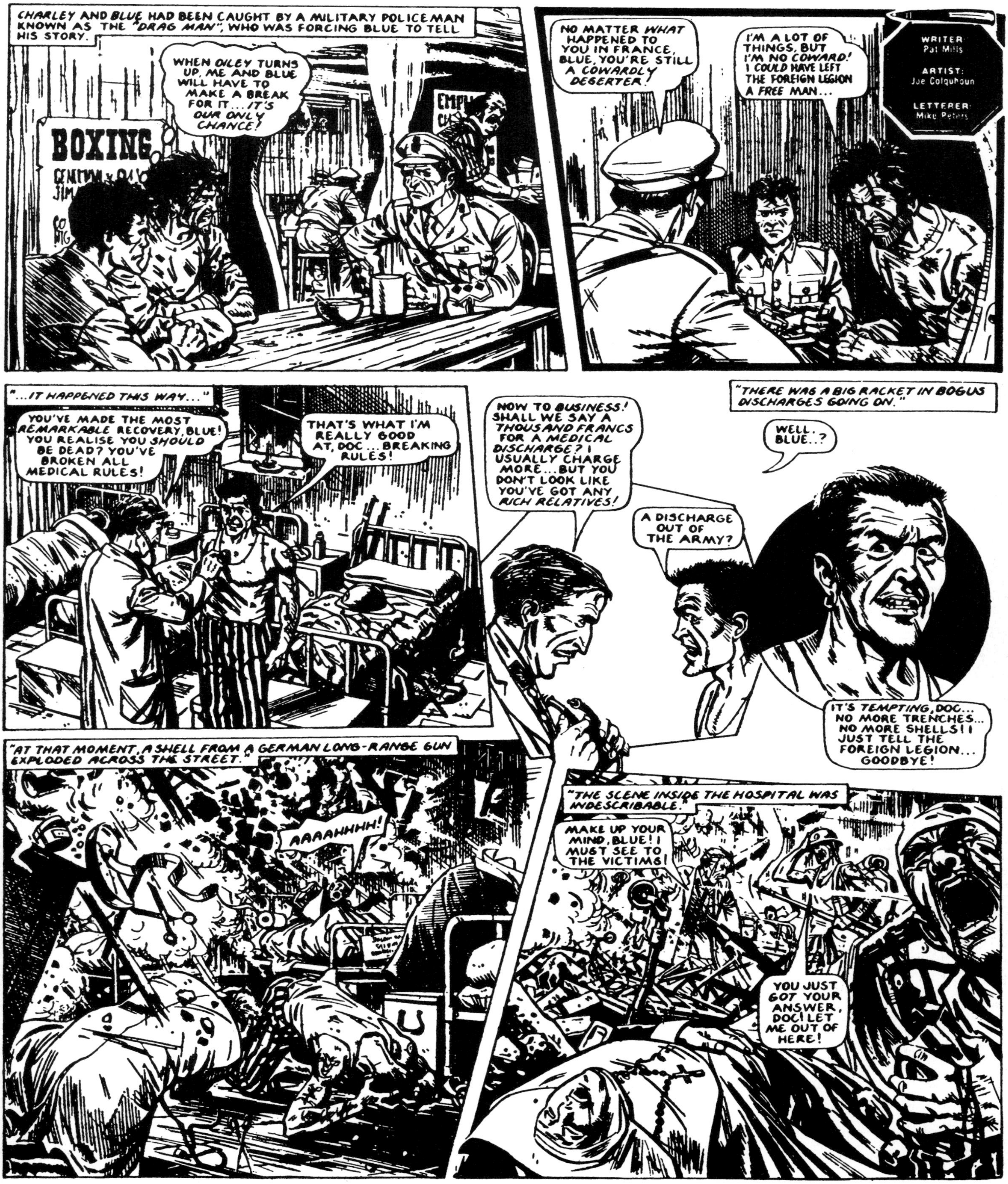
CHARLEY AND BLUE HAD BEEN CAUGHT BY A MILITARY POLICEMAN KNOWN AS THE "DRAG MAN", WHO WAS FORCING BLUE TO TELL HIS STORY.
WHEN OILEY TURNS UP, ME AND BLUE WILL HAVE TO MAKE A BREAK FOR IT... IT'S OUR ONLY CHANCE!
BOXING
NO MATTER WHAT HAPPENED TO YOU IN FRANCE, BLUE, YOU'RE STILL A COWARDLY DESERTER!
I'M A LOT OF THINGS, BUT I'M NO COWARD! I COULD HAVE LEFT THE FOREIGN LEGION A FREE MAN...
WRITER: Pat Mills
ARTIST: Joe Colquhoun
LETTERER: Mike Peters
"...IT HAPPENED THIS WAY..."
YOU'VE MADE THE MOST REMARKABLE RECOVERY, BLUE! YOU REALISE YOU SHOULD BE DEAD? YOU'VE BROKEN ALL MEDICAL RULES!
THAT'S WHAT I'M REALLY GOOD AT, DOC... BREAKING RULES!
NOW TO BUSINESS! SHALL WE SAY A THOUSAND FRANCS FOR A MEDICAL DISCHARGE? I USUALLY CHARGE MORE... BUT YOU DON'T LOOK LIKE YOU'VE GOT ANY RICH RELATIVES!
A DISCHARGE OUT OF THE ARMY?
"THERE WAS A BIG RACKET IN BOGUS DISCHARGES GOING ON."
WELL. BLUE..?
IT'S TEMPTING, DOC... NO MORE TRENCHES... NO MORE SHELLS!! I JUST TELL THE FOREIGN LEGION... GOODBYE!
"AT THAT MOMENT, A SHELL FROM A GERMAN LONG-RANGE GUN EXPLODED ACROSS THE STREET."
AAAAHHHH!
"THE SCENE INSIDE THE HOSPITAL WAS INDESCRIBABLE."
MAKE UP YOUR MIND, BLUE! I MUST SEE TO THE VICTIMS!
YOU JUST GOT YOUR ANSWER, DOC! LET ME OUT OF HERE!

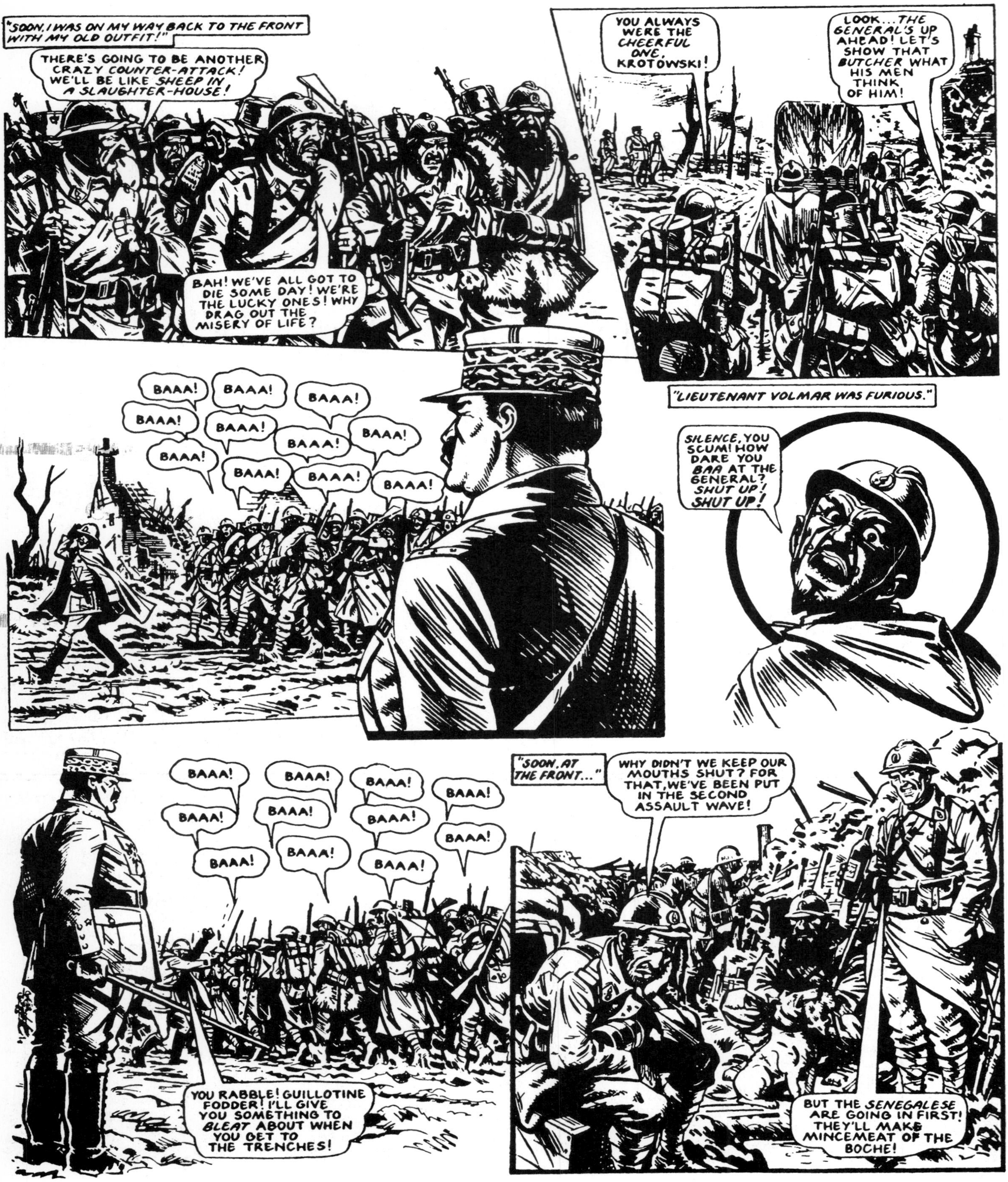
"SOON, I WAS ON MY WAY BACK TO THE FRONT WITH MY OLD OUTFIT!"
THERE'S GOING TO BE ANOTHER CRAZY COUNTER-ATTACK! WE'LL BE LIKE SHEEP IN A SLAUGHTER-HOUSE!
BAH! WE'VE ALL GOT TO DIE SOME DAY! WE'RE THE LUCKY ONES! WHY DRAG OUT THE MISERY OF LIFE?
YOU ALWAYS WERE THE CHEERFUL ONE, KROTOWSKI!
LOOK... THE GENERAL'S UP AHEAD! LET'S SHOW THAT BUTCHER WHAT HIS MEN THINK OF HIM!
BAAA! BAAA! BAAA! BAAA! BAAA! BAAA! BAAA! BAAA! BAAA! BAAA! BAAA!
"LIEUTENANT VOLMAR WAS FURIOUS."
SILENCE, YOU SCUM! HOW DARE YOU BAA AT THE GENERAL? SHUT UP! SHUT UP!
BAAA! BAAA! BAAA! BAAA! BAAA! BAAA! BAAA! BAAA! BAAA! BAAA! BAAA!
YOU RABBLE! GUILLOTINE FODDER! I'LL GIVE YOU SOMETHING TO BLEAT ABOUT WHEN YOU GET TO THE TRENCHES!
"SOON, AT THE FRONT..."
WHY DIDN'T WE KEEP OUR MOUTHS SHUT? FOR THAT, WE'VE BEEN PUT IN THE SECOND ASSAULT WAVE!
BUT THE SENEGALESE ARE GOING IN FIRST! THEY'LL MAKE MINCEMEAT OF THE BOCHE!

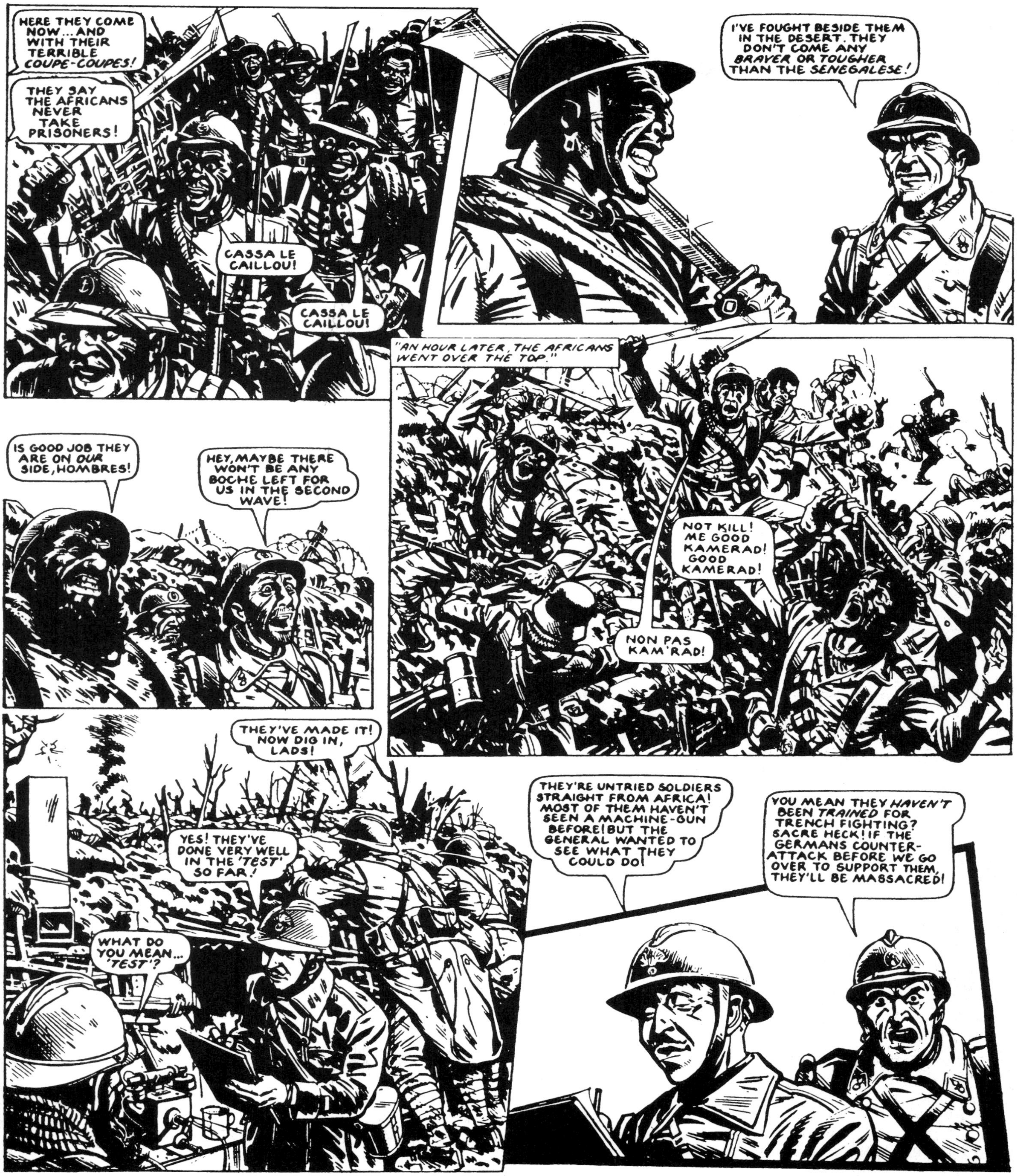
HERE THEY COME NOW... AND WITH THEIR TERRIBLE COUPE-COUPES!
THEY SAY THE AFRICANS NEVER TAKE PRISONERS!
CASSA LE CAILLOU!
CASSA LE CAILLOU!
I'VE FOUGHT BESIDE THEM IN THE DESERT. THEY DON'T COME ANY BRAVER OR TOUGHER THAN THE SENEGALESE!
IS GOOD JOB THEY ARE ON OUR SIDE, HOMBRES!
HEY, MAYBE THERE WON'T BE ANY BOCHE LEFT FOR US IN THE SECOND WAVE!
"AN HOUR LATER, THE AFRICANS WENT OVER THE TOP."
NOT KILL! ME GOOD KAMERAD! GOOD KAMERAD!
NON PAS KAM'RAD!
THEY'VE MADE IT! NOW DIG IN, LADS!
YES! THEY'VE DONE VERY WELL IN THE 'TEST' SO FAR!
WHAT DO YOU MEAN... 'TEST'?
THEY'RE UNTRIED SOLDIERS STRAIGHT FROM AFRICA! MOST OF THEM HAVEN'T SEEN A MACHINE-GUN BEFORE! BUT THE GENERAL WANTED TO SEE WHAT THEY COULD DO!
YOU MEAN THEY HAVEN'T BEEN TRAINED FOR TRENCH FIGHTING? SACRE HECK! IF THE GERMANS COUNTER-ATTACK BEFORE WE GO OVER TO SUPPORT THEM, THEY'LL BE MASSACRED!

THE SENEGAL TROOPS HAD NEVER SEEN A MACHINE-GUN BEFORE!

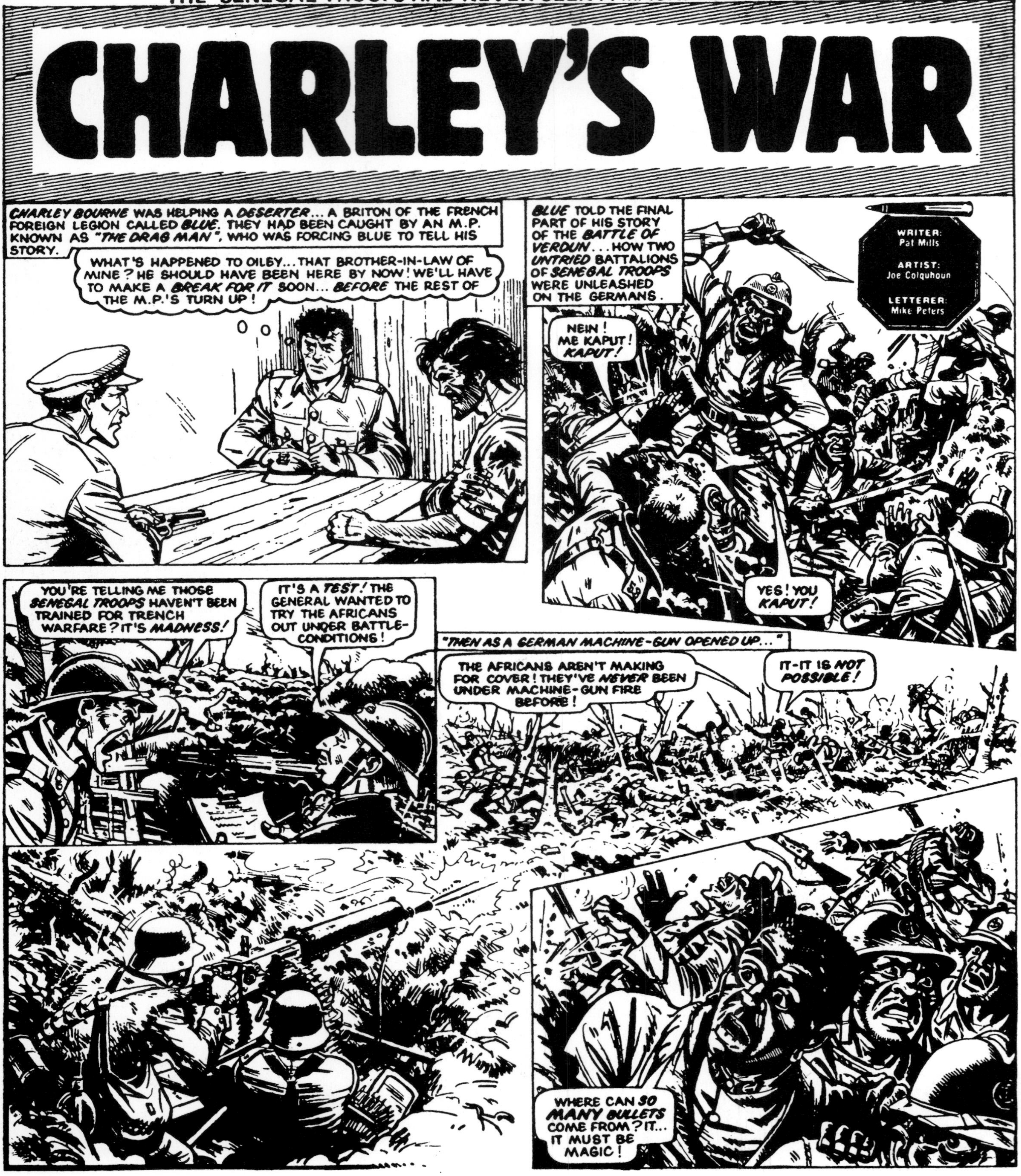
CHARLEY'S WAR
CHARLEY BOURNE WAS HELPING A DESERTER... A BRITON OF THE FRENCH FOREIGN LEGION CALLED BLUE. THEY HAD BEEN CAUGHT BY AN M.P. KNOWN AS "THE DRAG MAN", WHO WAS FORCING BLUE TO TELL HIS STORY.
WHAT'S HAPPENED TO OILEY... THAT BROTHER-IN-LAW OF MINE? HE SHOULD HAVE BEEN HERE BY NOW! WE'LL HAVE TO MAKE A BREAK FOR IT SOON... BEFORE THE REST OF THE M.P.'S TURN UP!
BLUE TOLD THE FINAL PART OF HIS STORY OF THE BATTLE OF VERDUN... HOW TWO UNTRIED BATTALIONS OF SENEGAL TROOPS WERE UNLEASHED ON THE GERMANS.
WRITER: Pat Mills
ARTIST: Joe Colquhoun
LETTERER: Mike Peters
NEIN! ME KAPUT! KAPUT!
YES! YOU KAPUT!
YOU'RE TELLING ME THOSE SENEGAL TROOPS HAVEN'T BEEN TRAINED FOR TRENCH WARFARE? IT'S MADNESS!
IT'S A TEST! THE GENERAL WANTED TO TRY THE AFRICANS OUT UNDER BATTLE-CONDITIONS!
"THEN AS A GERMAN MACHINE-GUN OPENED UP..."
THE AFRICANS AREN'T MAKING FOR COVER! THEY'VE NEVER BEEN UNDER MACHINE-GUN FIRE BEFORE!
IT-IT IS NOT POSSIBLE!
WHERE CAN SO MANY BULLETS COME FROM? IT... IT MUST BE MAGIC!

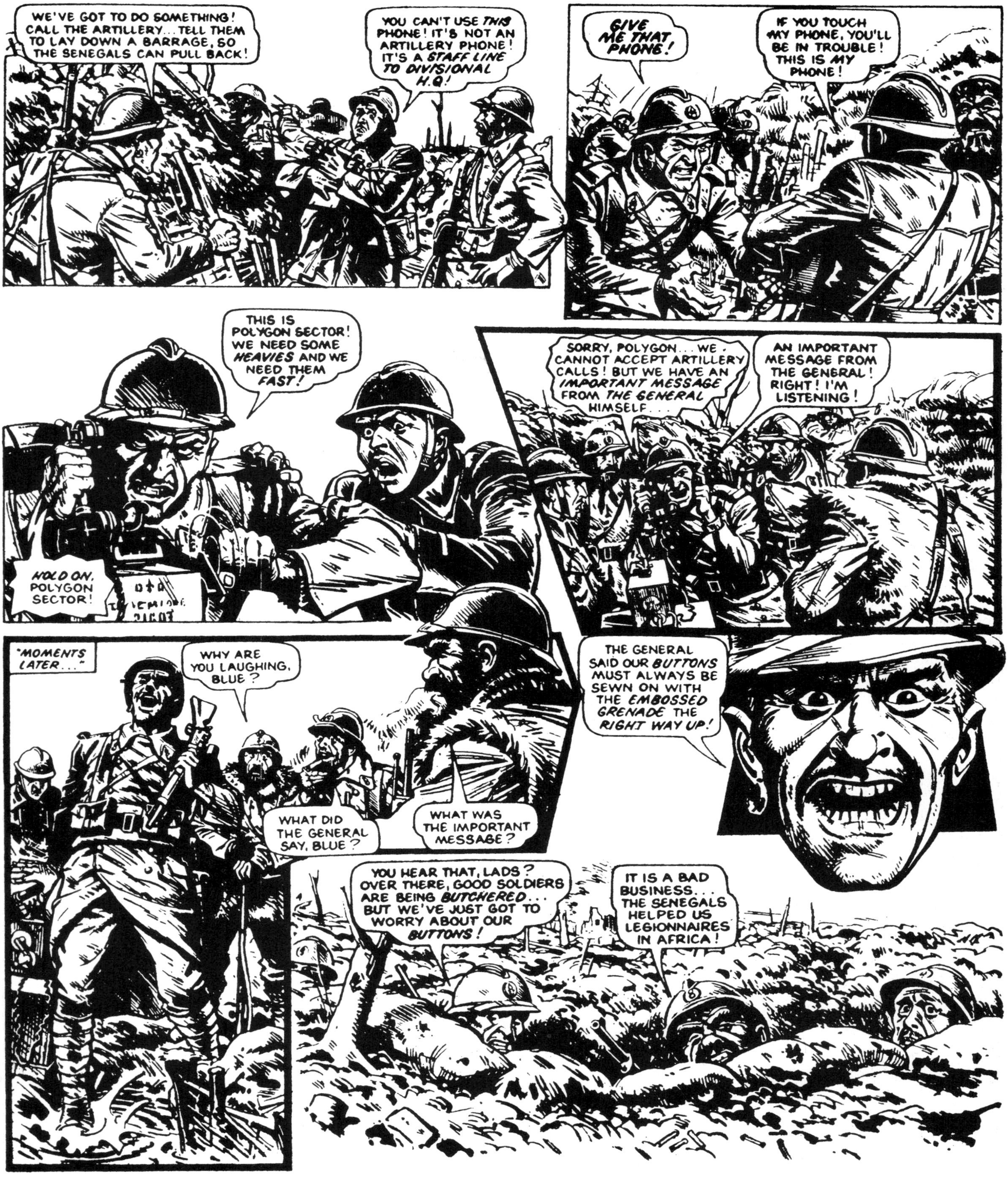
WE'VE GOT TO DO SOMETHING! CALL THE ARTILLERY... TELL THEM TO LAY DOWN A BARRAGE, SO THE SENEGALS CAN PULL BACK!
YOU CAN'T USE THIS PHONE! IT'S NOT AN ARTILLERY PHONE! IT'S A STAFF LINE TO DIVISIONAL H.Q!
GIVE ME THAT PHONE!
IF YOU TOUCH MY PHONE, YOU'LL BE IN TROUBLE! THIS IS MY PHONE!
THIS IS POLYGON SECTOR! WE NEED SOME HEAVIES AND WE NEED THEM FAST!
HOLD ON, POLYGON SECTOR!
SORRY, POLYGON... WE CANNOT ACCEPT ARTILLERY CALLS! BUT WE HAVE AN IMPORTANT MESSAGE FROM THE GENERAL HIMSELF...
AN IMPORTANT MESSAGE FROM THE GENERAL! RIGHT! I'M LISTENING!
"MOMENTS LATER..."
WHY ARE YOU LAUGHING, BLUE?
WHAT DID THE GENERAL SAY, BLUE?
WHAT WAS THE IMPORTANT MESSAGE?
THE GENERAL SAID OUR BUTTONS MUST ALWAYS BE SEWN ON WITH THE EMBOSSED GRENADE THE RIGHT WAY UP!
YOU HEAR THAT, LADS? OVER THERE, GOOD SOLDIERS ARE BEING BUTCHERED... BUT WE'VE JUST GOT TO WORRY ABOUT OUR BUTTONS!
IT IS A BAD BUSINESS... THE SENEGALS HELPED US LEGIONNAIRES IN AFRICA!

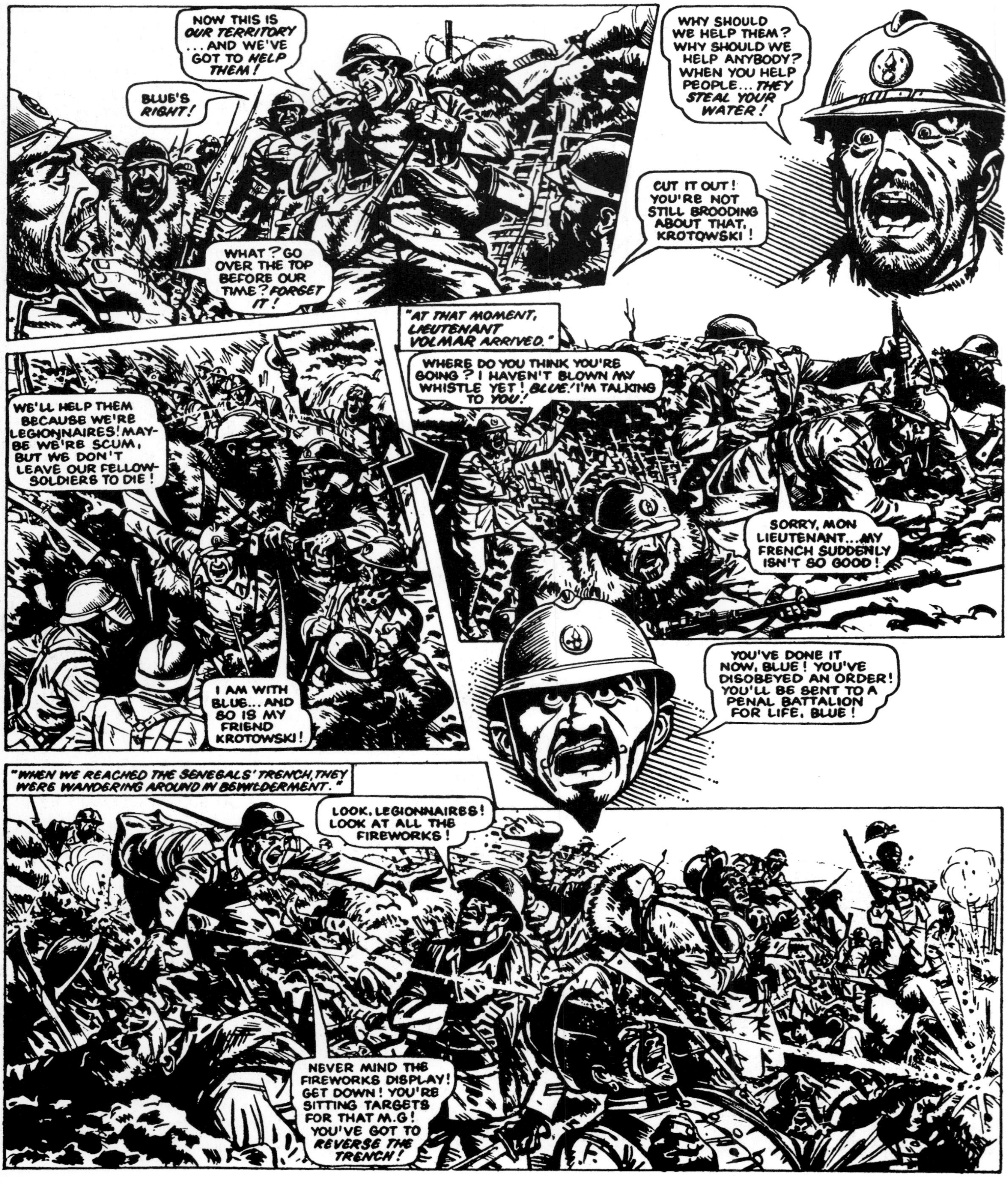
NOW THIS IS OUR TERRITORY ...AND WE'VE GOT TO HELP THEM!
BLUE'S RIGHT!
WHAT? GO OVER THE TOP BEFORE OUR TIME? FORGET IT!
WHY SHOULD WE HELP THEM? WHY SHOULD WE HELP ANYBODY? WHEN YOU HELP PEOPLE... THEY STEAL YOUR WATER!
CUT IT OUT! YOU'RE NOT STILL BROODING ABOUT THAT, KROTOWSKI!
WE'LL HELP THEM BECAUSE WE'RE LEGIONNAIRES! MAYBE WE'RE SCUM, BUT WE DON'T LEAVE OUR FELLOW-SOLDIERS TO DIE!
I AM WITH BLUE... AND SO IS MY FRIEND KROTOWSKI!
"AT THAT MOMENT, LIEUTENANT VOLMAR ARRIVED."
WHERE DO YOU THINK YOU'RE GOING? I HAVEN'T BLOWN MY WHISTLE YET! BLUE! I'M TALKING TO YOU!
SORRY, MON LIEUTENANT... MY FRENCH SUDDENLY ISN'T SO GOOD!
YOU'VE DONE IT NOW, BLUE! YOU'VE DISOBEYED AN ORDER! YOU'LL BE SENT TO A PENAL BATTALION FOR LIFE, BLUE!
"WHEN WE REACHED THE SENEGALS' TRENCH, THEY WERE WANDERING AROUND IN BEWILDERMENT."
LOOK, LEGIONNAIRES! LOOK AT ALL THE FIREWORKS!
NEVER MIND THE FIREWORKS DISPLAY! GET DOWN! YOU'RE SITTING TARGETS FOR THAT M.G! YOU'VE GOT TO REVERSE THE TRENCH!

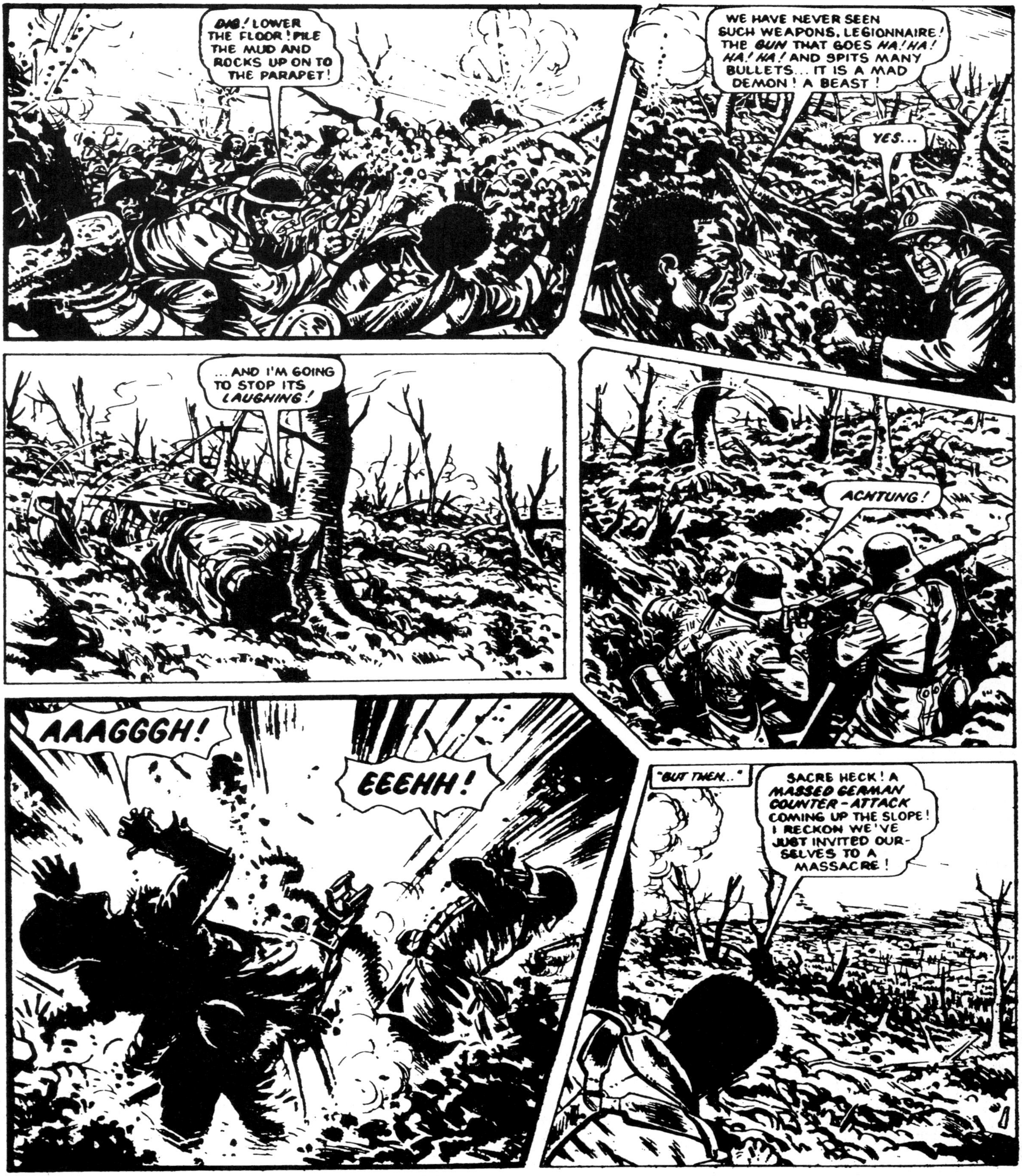
DIG! LOWER THE FLOOR! PILE THE MUD AND ROCKS UP ON TO THE PARAPET!
WE HAVE NEVER SEEN SUCH WEAPONS, LEGIONNAIRE! THE GUN THAT GOES HA! HA! HA! HA! AND SPITS MANY BULLETS... IT IS A MAD DEMON! A BEAST!
YES...
...AND I'M GOING TO STOP ITS LAUGHING!
ACHTUNG!
AAAGGGH!
EEEHH!
"BUT THEN..."
SACRE HECK! A MASSED GERMAN COUNTER-ATTACK COMING UP THE SLOPE! I RECKON WE'VE JUST INVITED OURSELVES TO A MASSACRE!

CHARLEY'S WAR

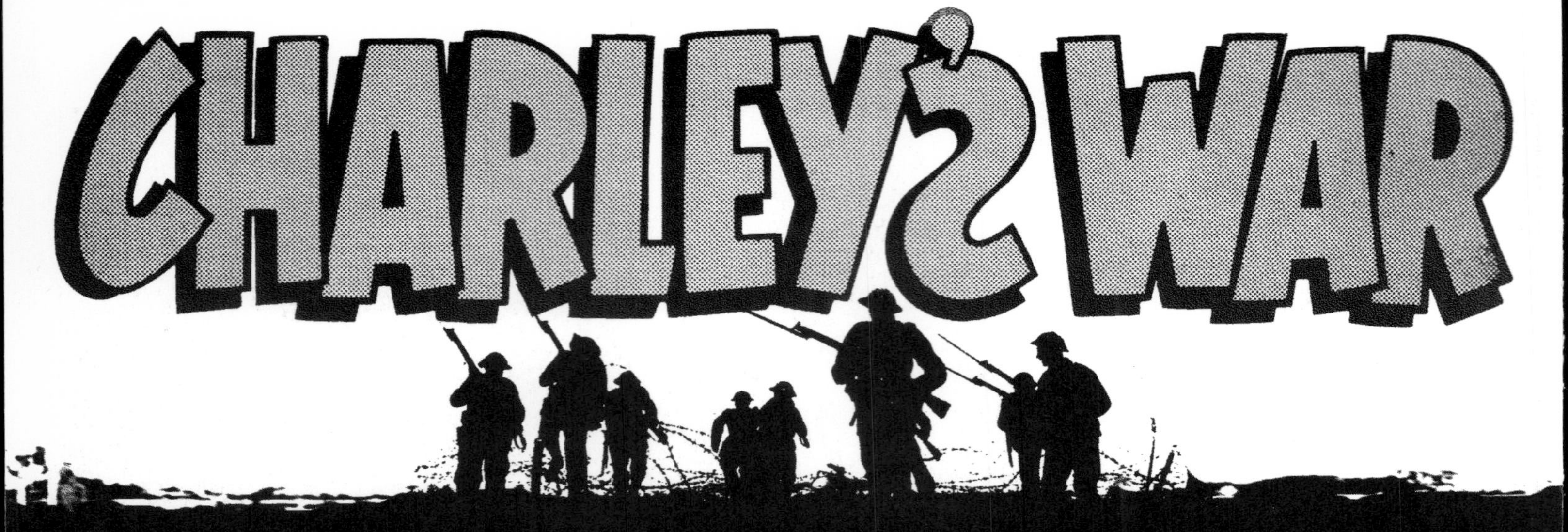

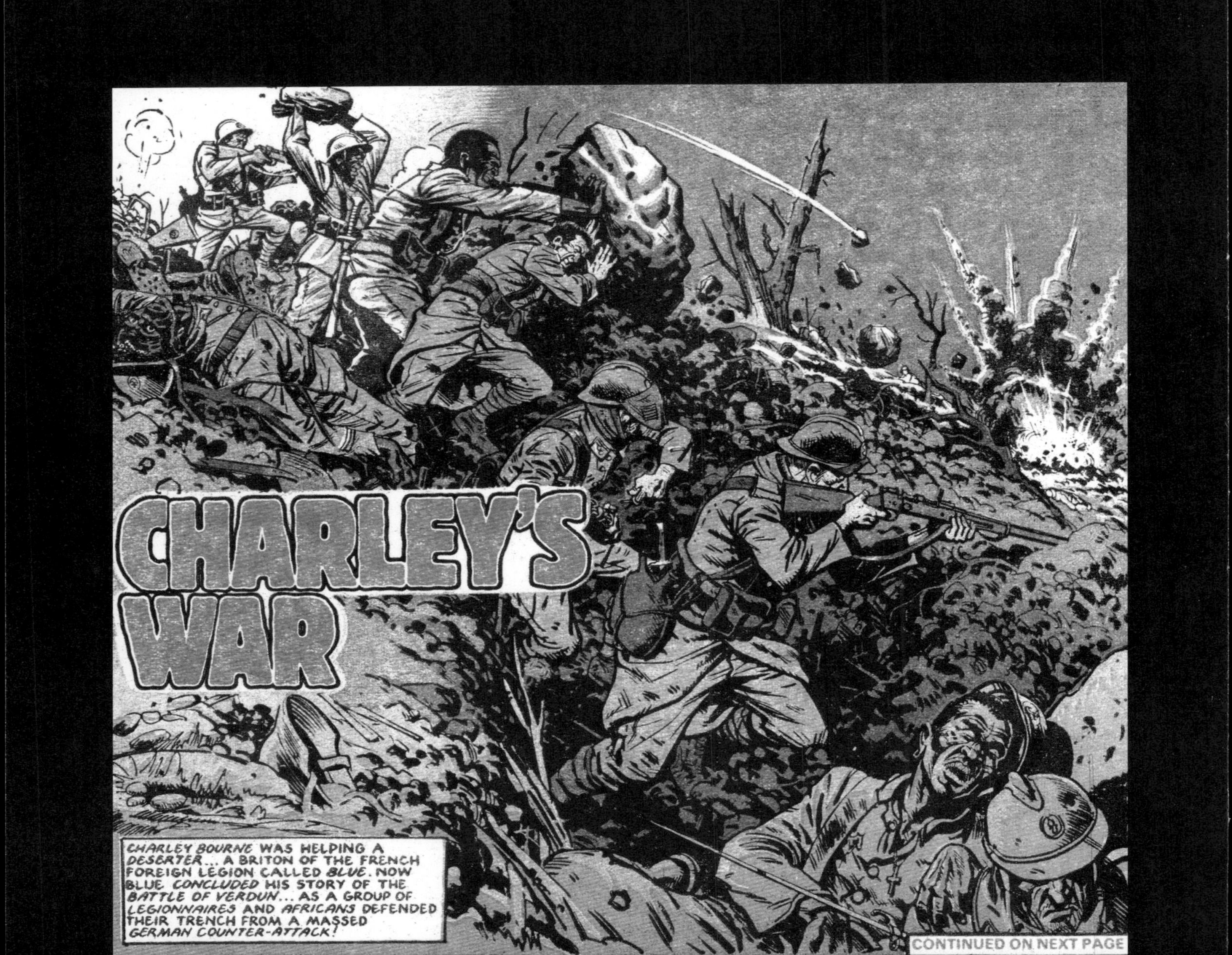
CHARLEY'S WAR
CHARLEY BOURNE WAS HELPING A DESERTER... A BRITON OF THE FRENCH FOREIGN LEGION CALLED BLUE. NOW BLUE CONCLUDED HIS STORY OF THE BATTLE OF VERDUN... AS A GROUP OF LEGIONNAIRES AND AFRICANS DEFENDED THEIR TRENCH FROM A MASSED GERMAN COUNTER-ATTACK!
CONTINUED ON NEXT PAGE

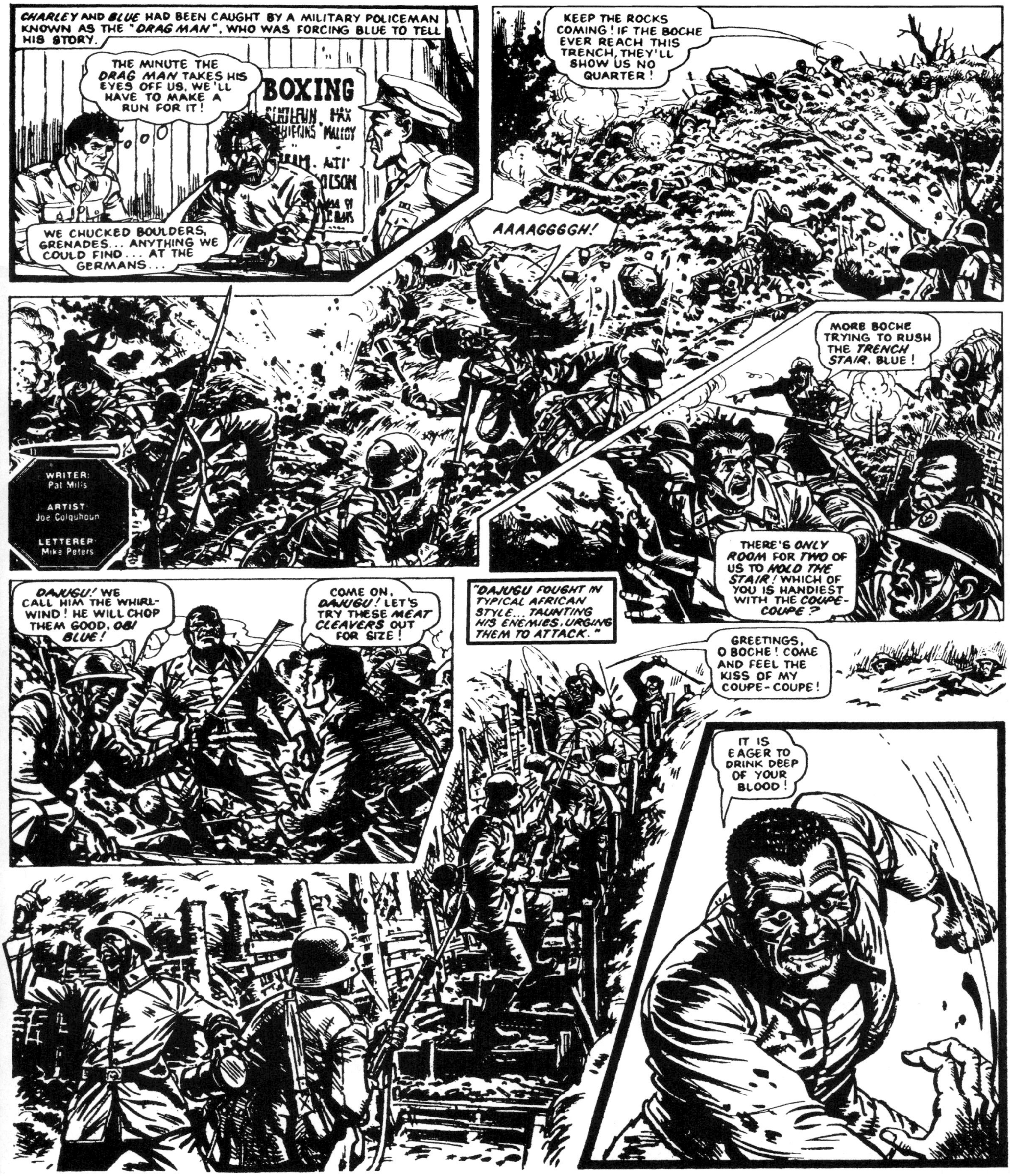
CHARLEY AND BLUE HAD BEEN CAUGHT BY A MILITARY POLICEMAN KNOWN AS THE "DRAG MAN", WHO WAS FORCING BLUE TO TELL HIS STORY.
THE MINUTE THE DRAG MAN TAKES HIS EYES OFF US, WE'LL HAVE TO MAKE A RUN FOR IT!
BOXING
WE CHUCKED BOULDERS, GRENADES... ANYTHING WE COULD FIND... AT THE GERMANS...
KEEP THE ROCKS COMING! IF THE BOCHE EVER REACH THIS TRENCH, THEY'LL SHOW US NO QUARTER!
AAAAGGGGH!
WRITER: Pat Mills
ARTIST: Joe Colquhoun
LETTERER: Mike Peters
MORE BOCHE TRYING TO RUSH THE TRENCH STAIR, BLUE!
THERE'S ONLY ROOM FOR TWO OF US TO HOLD THE STAIR! WHICH OF YOU IS HANDIEST WITH THE COUPE-COUPE?
DAJUGU! WE CALL HIM THE WHIRLWIND! HE WILL CHOP THEM GOOD, OBI BLUE!
COME ON, DAJUGU! LET'S TRY THESE MEAT CLEAVERS OUT FOR SIZE!
"DAJUGU FOUGHT IN TYPICAL AFRICAN STYLE... TAUNTING HIS ENEMIES, URGING THEM TO ATTACK."
GREETINGS, O BOCHE! COME AND FEEL THE KISS OF MY COUPE-COUPE!
IT IS EAGER TO DRINK DEEP OF YOUR BLOOD!

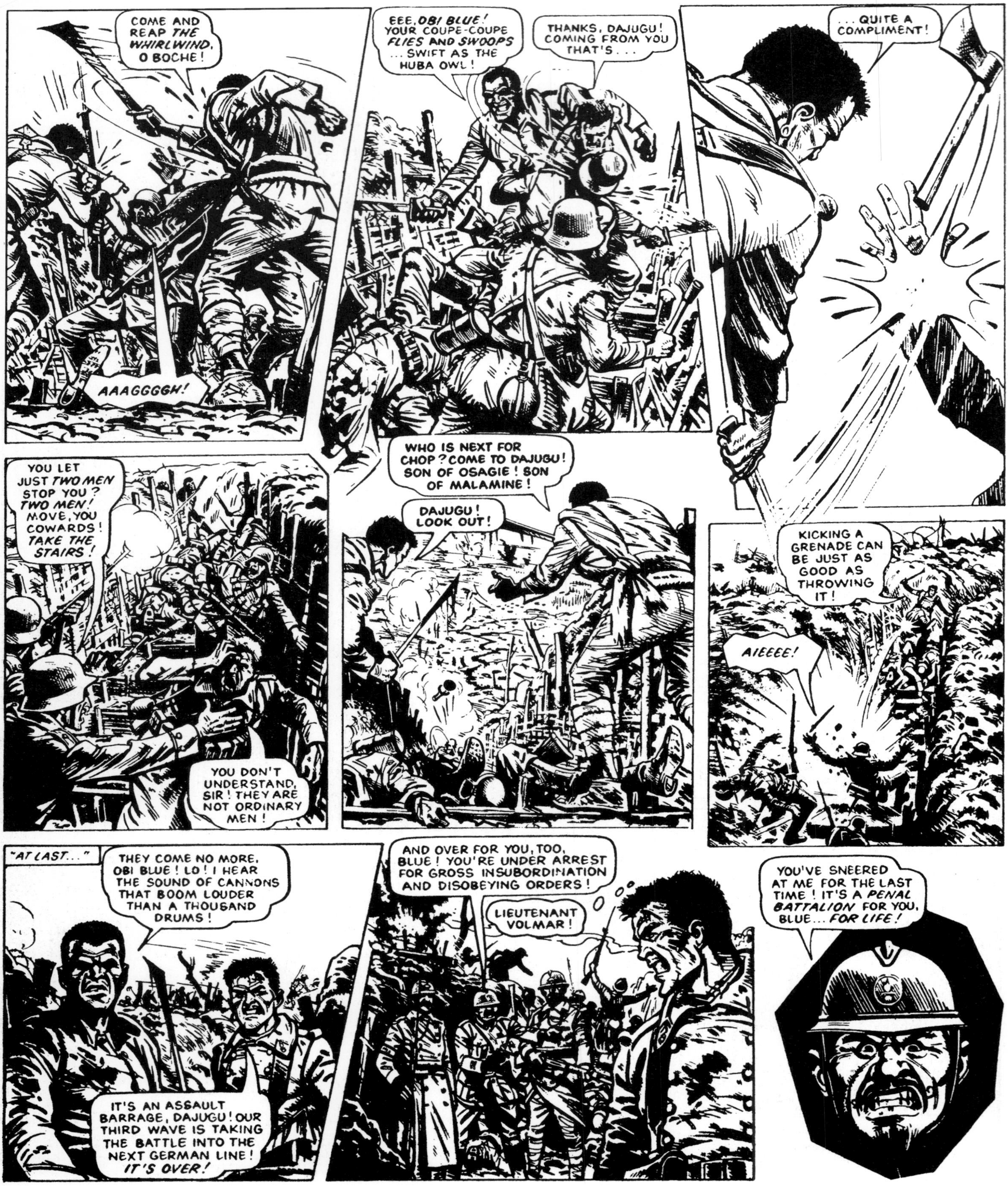
COME AND REAP THE WHIRLWIND, O BOCHE!
AAAGGGGH!
EEE, OBI BLUE! YOUR COUPE-COUPE FLIES AND SWOOPS ... SWIFT AS THE HUBA OWL!
THANKS, DAJUGU! COMING FROM YOU THAT'S...
...QUITE A COMPLIMENT!
YOU LET JUST TWO MEN STOP YOU? TWO MEN! MOVE, YOU COWARDS! TAKE THE STAIRS!
YOU DON'T UNDERSTAND, SIR! THEY ARE NOT ORDINARY MEN!
WHO IS NEXT FOR CHOP? COME TO DAJUGU! SON OF OSAGIE! SON OF MALAMINE!
DAJUGU! LOOK OUT!
KICKING A GRENADE CAN BE JUST AS GOOD AS THROWING IT!
AIEEEE!
"AT LAST..."
THEY COME NO MORE, OBI BLUE! LO! I HEAR THE SOUND OF CANNONS THAT BOOM LOUDER THAN A THOUSAND DRUMS!
IT'S AN ASSAULT BARRAGE, DAJUGU! OUR THIRD WAVE IS TAKING THE BATTLE INTO THE NEXT GERMAN LINE! IT'S OVER!
AND OVER FOR YOU, TOO, BLUE! YOU'RE UNDER ARREST FOR GROSS INSUBORDINATION AND DISOBEYING ORDERS!
LIEUTENANT VOLMAR!
YOU'VE SNEERED AT ME FOR THE LAST TIME! IT'S A PENAL BATTALION FOR YOU, BLUE... FOR LIFE!

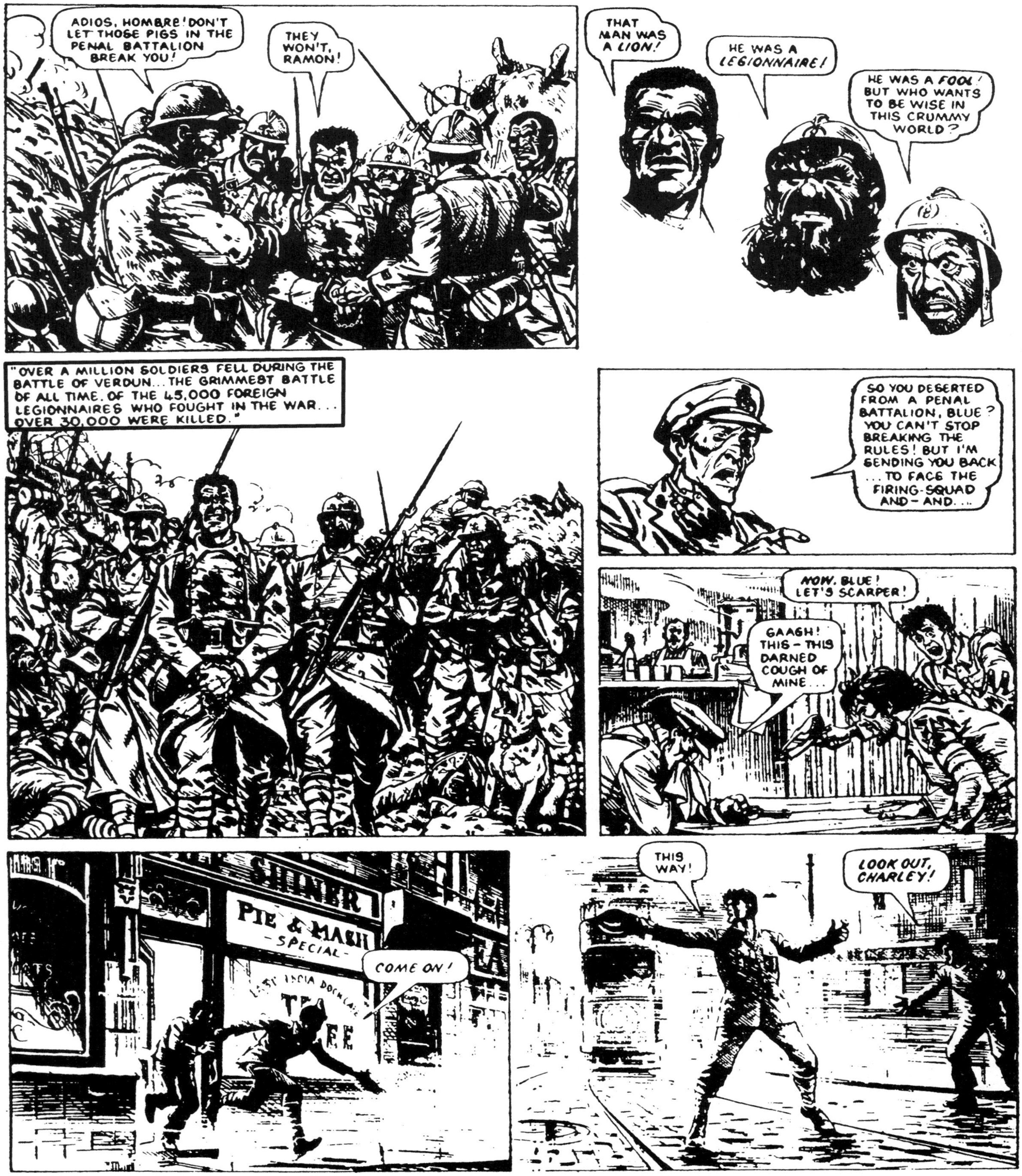
ADIOS, HOMBRE! DON'T LET THOSE PIGS IN THE PENAL BATTALION BREAK YOU!
THEY WON'T, RAMON!
THAT MAN WAS A LION!
HE WAS A LEGIONNAIRE!
HE WAS A FOOL! BUT WHO WANTS TO BE WISE IN THIS CRUMMY WORLD?
"OVER A MILLION SOLDIERS FELL DURING THE BATTLE OF VERDUN... THE GRIMMEST BATTLE OF ALL TIME. OF THE 45,000 FOREIGN LEGIONNAIRES WHO FOUGHT IN THE WAR... OVER 30,000 WERE KILLED."
SO YOU DESERTED FROM A PENAL BATTALION, BLUE? YOU CAN'T STOP BREAKING THE RULES! BUT I'M SENDING YOU BACK ...TO FACE THE FIRING-SQUAD AND - AND...
GAAGH! THIS - THIS DARNED COUGH OF MINE...
NOW, BLUE! LET'S SCARPER!
PIE & MASH
SPECIAL
COME ON!
THIS WAY!
LOOK OUT, CHARLEY!

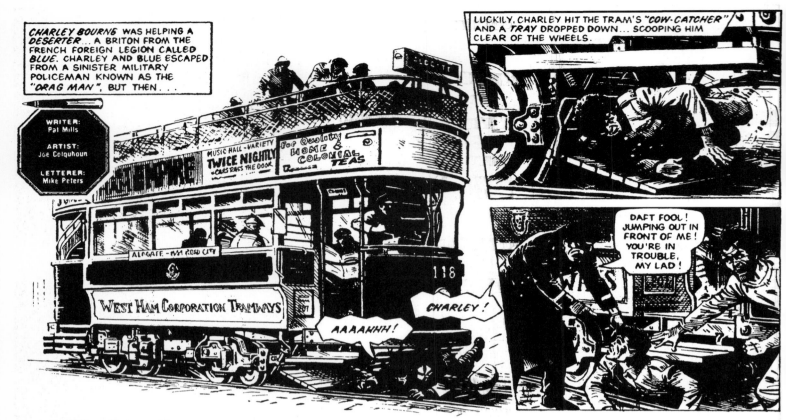

CHARLEY BOURNE WAS HELPING A DESERTER... A BRITON FROM THE FRENCH FOREIGN LEGION CALLED BLUE. CHARLEY AND BLUE ESCAPED FROM A SINISTER MILITARY POLICEMAN KNOWN AS THE "DRAG MAN", BUT THEN...
WRITER: Pat Mills
ARTIST: Joe Colquhoun
LETTERER: Mike Peters
MUSIC HALL - VARIETY
TWICE NIGHTLY
For Quality HOME & COLONIAL TEAS
118
WEST HAM CORPORATION TRAMWAYS
CHARLEY!
AAAAHHH!
LUCKILY, CHARLEY HIT THE TRAM'S "COW-CATCHER" AND A TRAY DROPPED DOWN... SCOOPING HIM CLEAR OF THE WHEELS.
DAFT FOOL! JUMPING OUT IN FRONT OF ME! YOU'RE IN TROUBLE, MY LAD!
Charley's War
HEY! IT'S BIG DAVE THE MOTORMAN! REMEMBER ME?
WHY, IT'S CHARLEY BOURNE WHO USED TO HELP OUT ON THE SOCCER SPECIALS WHEN WEST HAM WERE AT HOME! HOW ARE YOU, CHARLEY?
IN A SPOT OF BOTHER, BIG DAVE! THERE'S SOMEONE AFTER US... WE NEED TO GET OUT OF HERE FAST!
SAY NO MORE, CHARLEY BOY! CLIMB ABOARD! I'LL GIVE IT THE GUN!
WE'VE GIVEN THE DRAG MAN THE SLIP, BLUE! COR! HE DON'T HALF LOOK MAD!

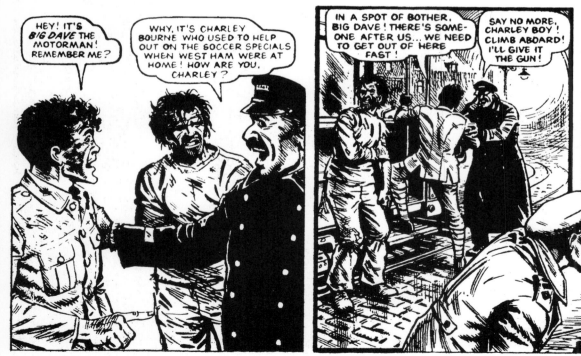

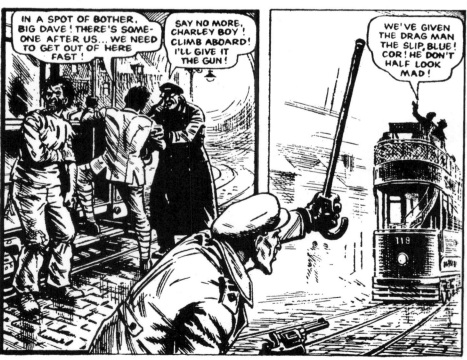

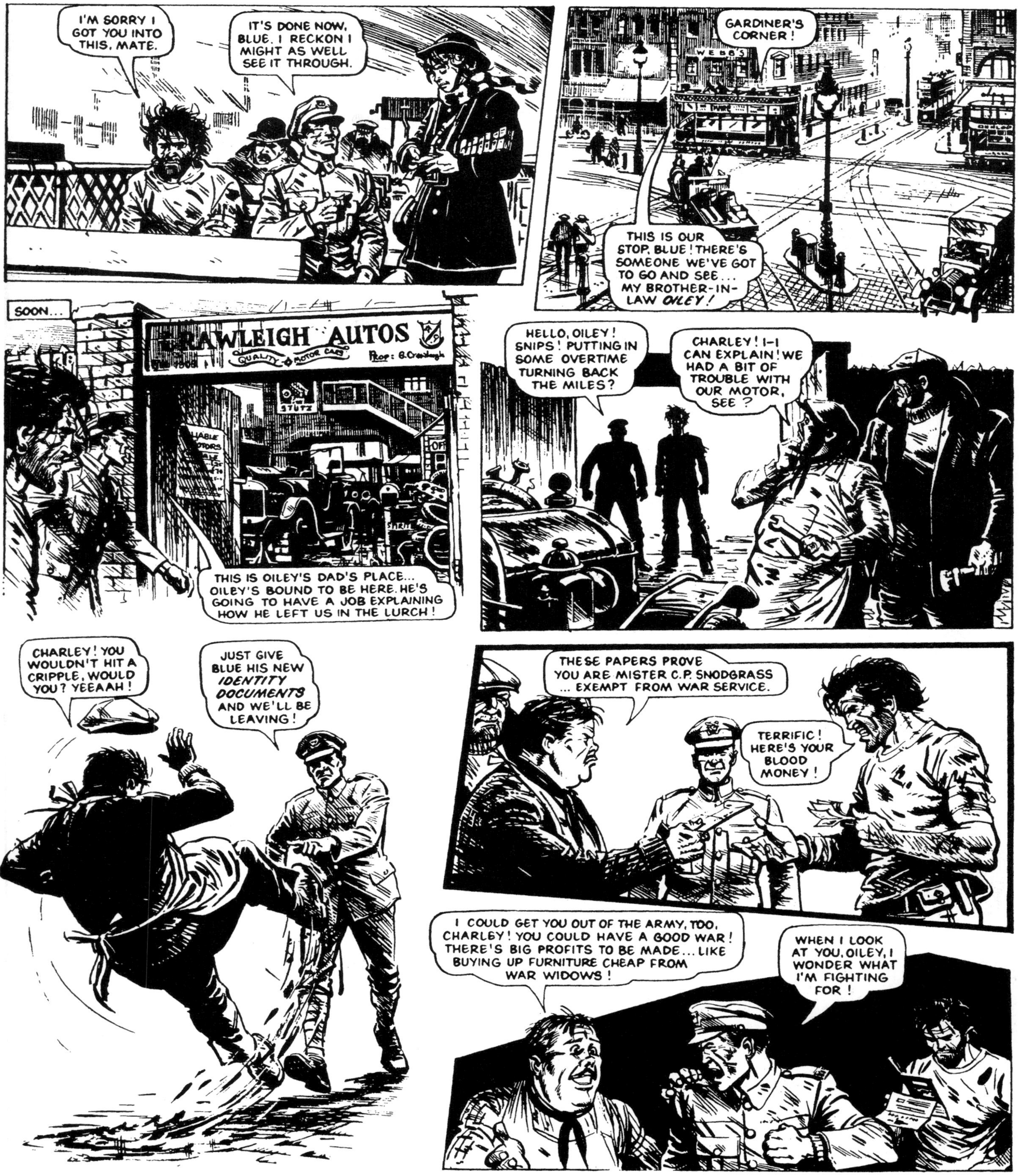
I'M SORRY I GOT YOU INTO THIS, MATE.
IT'S DONE NOW, BLUE. I RECKON I MIGHT AS WELL SEE IT THROUGH.
GARDINER'S CORNER!
THIS IS OUR STOP, BLUE! THERE'S SOMEONE WE'VE GOT TO GO AND SEE... MY BROTHER-IN-LAW OILEY!
SOON...
CRAWLEIGH AUTOS
QUALITY MOTOR CARS
THIS IS OILEY'S DAD'S PLACE... OILEY'S BOUND TO BE HERE. HE'S GOING TO HAVE A JOB EXPLAINING HOW HE LEFT US IN THE LURCH!
HELLO, OILEY! SNIPS! PUTTING IN SOME OVERTIME TURNING BACK THE MILES?
CHARLEY! I-I CAN EXPLAIN! WE HAD A BIT OF TROUBLE WITH OUR MOTOR, SEE?
CHARLEY! YOU WOULDN'T HIT A CRIPPLE, WOULD YOU? YEEAAH!
JUST GIVE BLUE HIS NEW IDENTITY DOCUMENTS AND WE'LL BE LEAVING!
THESE PAPERS PROVE YOU ARE MISTER C.P. SNODGRASS ... EXEMPT FROM WAR SERVICE.
TERRIFIC! HERE'S YOUR BLOOD MONEY!
I COULD GET YOU OUT OF THE ARMY, TOO, CHARLEY! YOU COULD HAVE A GOOD WAR! THERE'S BIG PROFITS TO BE MADE... LIKE BUYING UP FURNITURE CHEAP FROM WAR WIDOWS!
WHEN I LOOK AT YOU, OILEY, I WONDER WHAT I'M FIGHTING FOR!

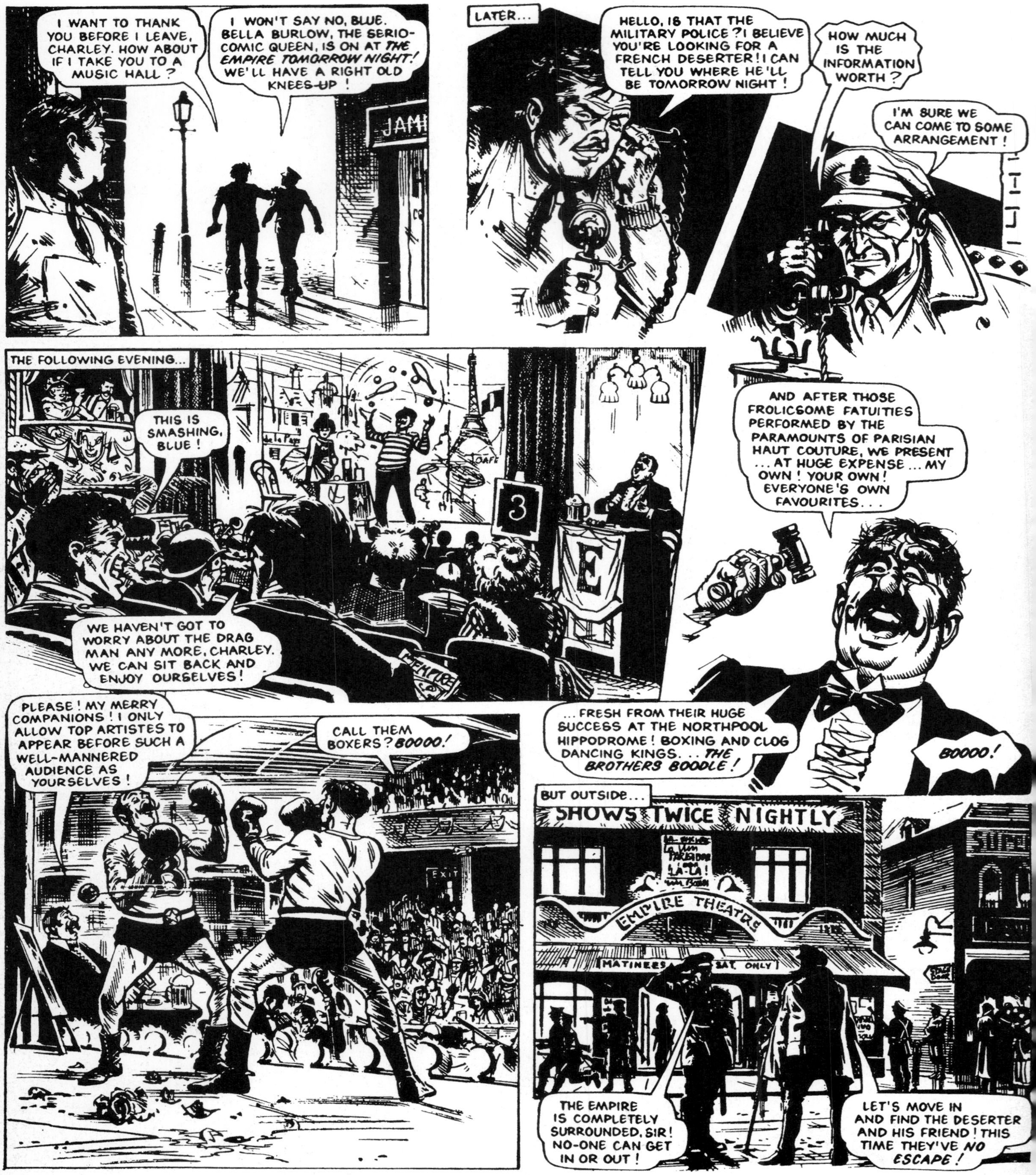
I WANT TO THANK YOU BEFORE I LEAVE, CHARLEY. HOW ABOUT IF I TAKE YOU TO A MUSIC HALL?
I WON'T SAY NO, BLUE. BELLA BURLOW, THE SERIO-COMIC QUEEN, IS ON AT THE EMPIRE TOMORROW NIGHT! WE'LL HAVE A RIGHT OLD KNEES-UP!
LATER...
HELLO, IS THAT THE MILITARY POLICE? I BELIEVE YOU'RE LOOKING FOR A FRENCH DESERTER! I CAN TELL YOU WHERE HE'LL BE TOMORROW NIGHT!
HOW MUCH IS THE INFORMATION WORTH?
I'M SURE WE CAN COME TO SOME ARRANGEMENT!
THE FOLLOWING EVENING...
THIS IS SMASHING, BLUE!
WE HAVEN'T GOT TO WORRY ABOUT THE DRAG MAN ANY MORE, CHARLEY. WE CAN SIT BACK AND ENJOY OURSELVES!
AND AFTER THOSE FROLICSOME FATUITIES PERFORMED BY THE PARAMOUNTS OF PARISIAN HAUT COUTURE, WE PRESENT ... AT HUGE EXPENSE ... MY OWN! YOUR OWN! EVERYONE'S OWN FAVOURITES...
... FRESH FROM THEIR HUGE SUCCESS AT THE NORTHPOOL HIPPODROME! BOXING AND CLOG DANCING KINGS... THE BROTHERS BOODLE!
BOOOO!
PLEASE! MY MERRY COMPANIONS! I ONLY ALLOW TOP ARTISTES TO APPEAR BEFORE SUCH A WELL-MANNERED AUDIENCE AS YOURSELVES!
CALL THEM BOXERS? BOOOO!
EXIT
BUT OUTSIDE...
SHOWS TWICE NIGHTLY
EMPIRE THEATRE
MATINEES SAT. ONLY
THE EMPIRE IS COMPLETELY SURROUNDED, SIR! NO-ONE CAN GET IN OR OUT!
LET'S MOVE IN AND FIND THE DESERTER AND HIS FRIEND! THIS TIME THEY'VE NO ESCAPE!

CHARLEY'S WAR

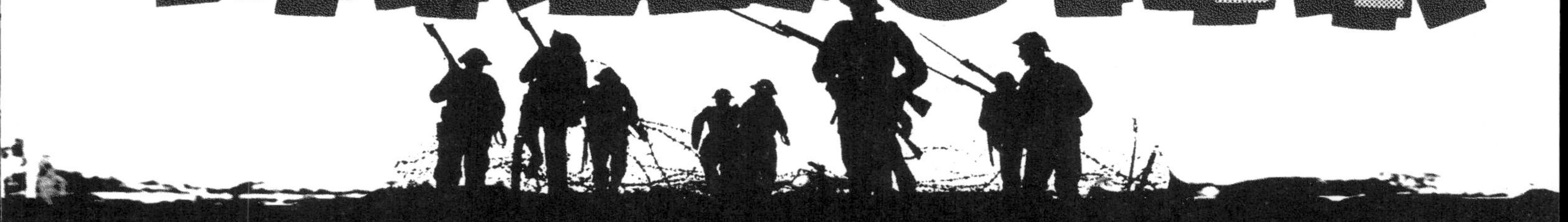

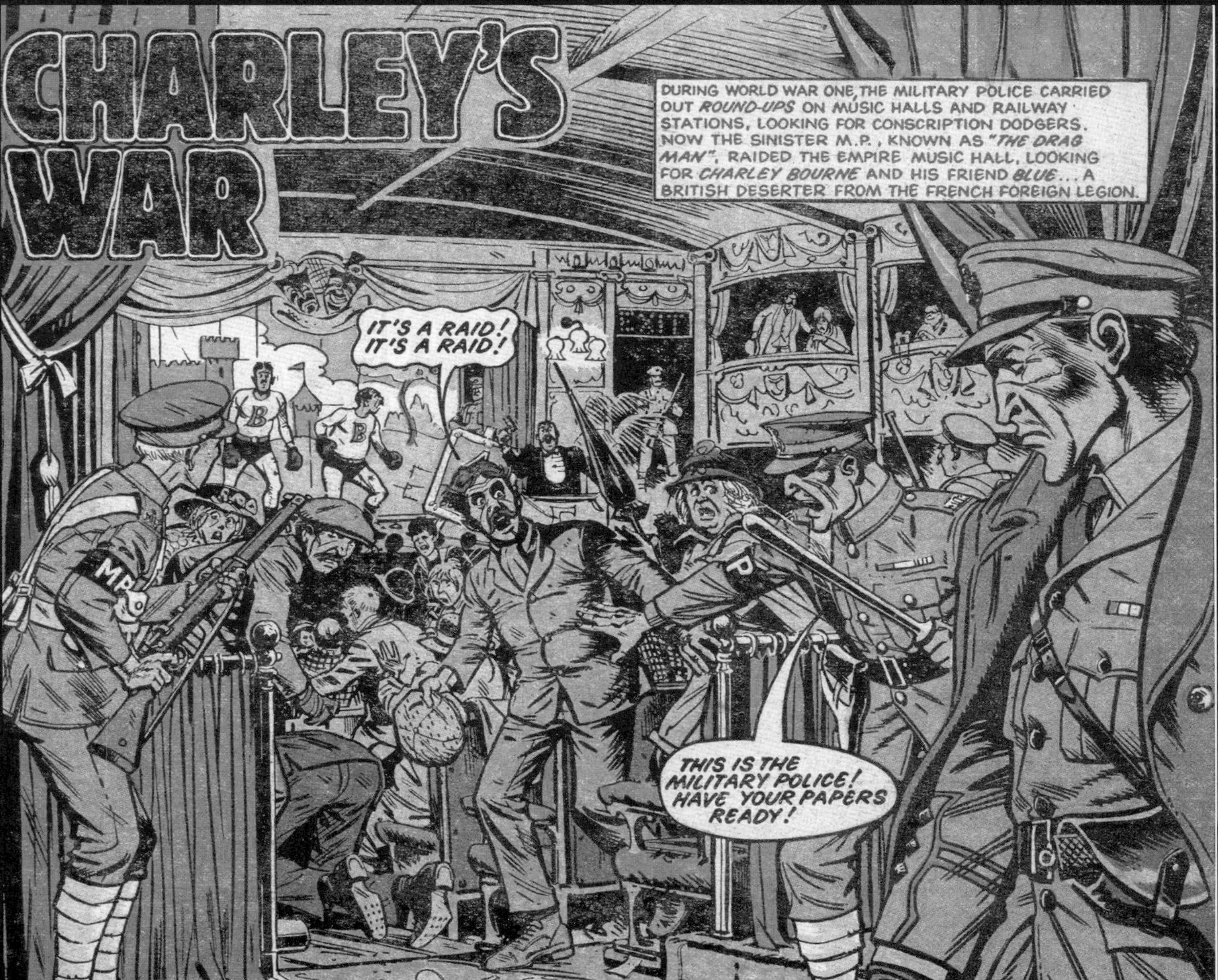
CHARLEY'S WAR
DURING WORLD WAR ONE, THE MILITARY POLICE CARRIED OUT *ROUND-UPS* ON MUSIC HALLS AND RAILWAY STATIONS, LOOKING FOR CONSCRIPTION DODGERS. NOW THE SINISTER M.P., KNOWN AS *"THE DRAG MAN"*, RAIDED THE EMPIRE MUSIC HALL, LOOKING FOR *CHARLEY BOURNE* AND HIS FRIEND *BLUE*... A BRITISH DESERTER FROM THE FRENCH FOREIGN LEGION.
IT'S A RAID! IT'S A RAID!
THIS IS THE MILITARY POLICE! HAVE YOUR PAPERS READY!

CONTINUED ON NEXT PAGE

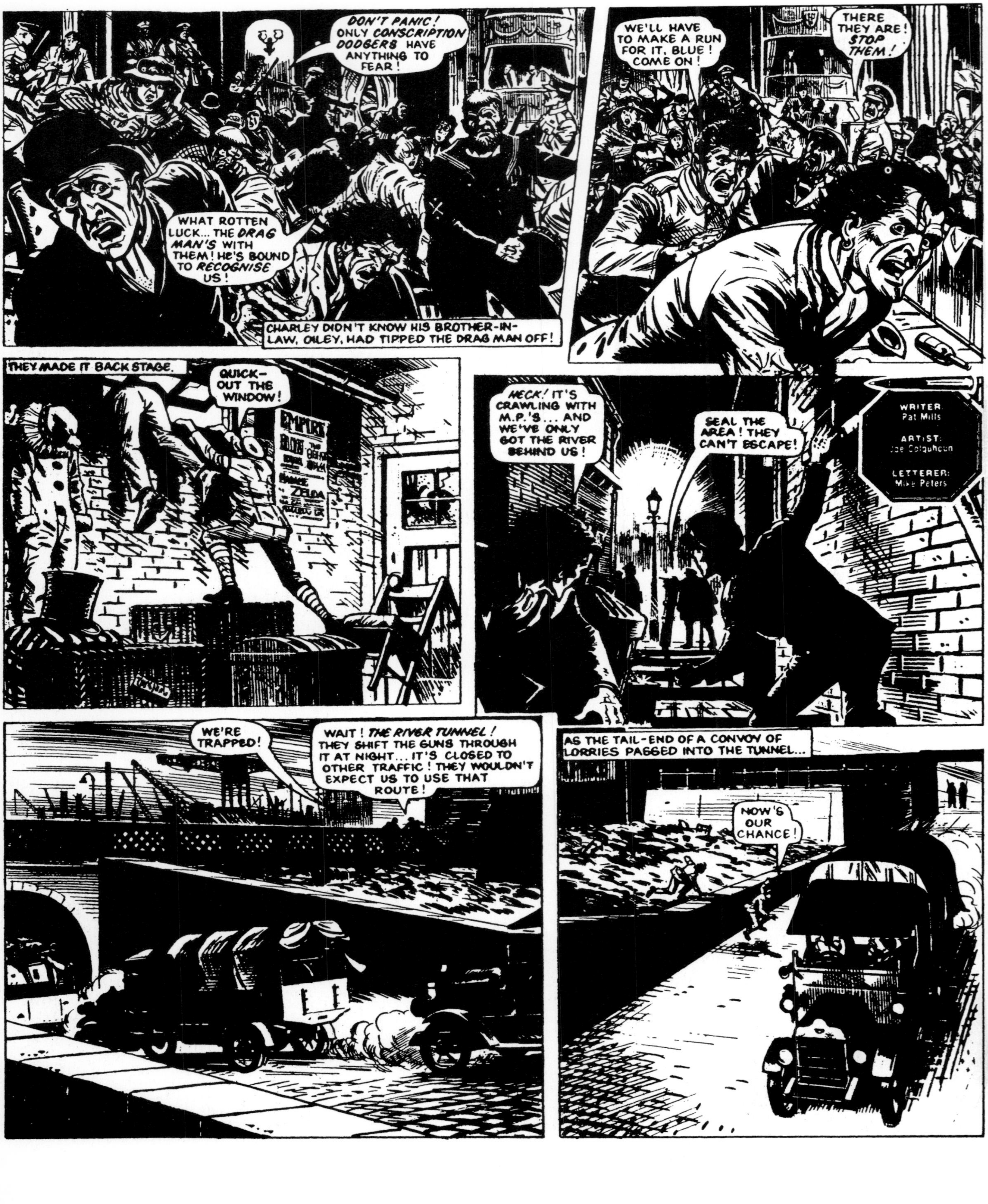
DON'T PANIC! ONLY CONSCRIPTION DODGERS HAVE ANYTHING TO FEAR!
WHAT ROTTEN LUCK... THE DRAG MAN'S WITH THEM! HE'S BOUND TO RECOGNISE US!
CHARLEY DIDN'T KNOW HIS BROTHER-IN-LAW, OILEY, HAD TIPPED THE DRAG MAN OFF!
WE'LL HAVE TO MAKE A RUN FOR IT, BLUE! COME ON!
THERE THEY ARE! STOP THEM!
THEY MADE IT BACK STAGE.
QUICK—OUT THE WINDOW!
HECK! IT'S CRAWLING WITH M.P.'S... AND WE'VE ONLY GOT THE RIVER BEHIND US!
SEAL THE AREA! THEY CAN'T ESCAPE!
WRITER: Pat Mills
ARTIST: Joe Colquhoun
LETTERER: Mike Peters
WE'RE TRAPPED!
WAIT! THE RIVER TUNNEL! THEY SHIFT THE GUNS THROUGH IT AT NIGHT... IT'S CLOSED TO OTHER TRAFFIC! THEY WOULDN'T EXPECT US TO USE THAT ROUTE!
AS THE TAIL-END OF A CONVOY OF LORRIES PASSED INTO THE TUNNEL...
NOW'S OUR CHANCE!

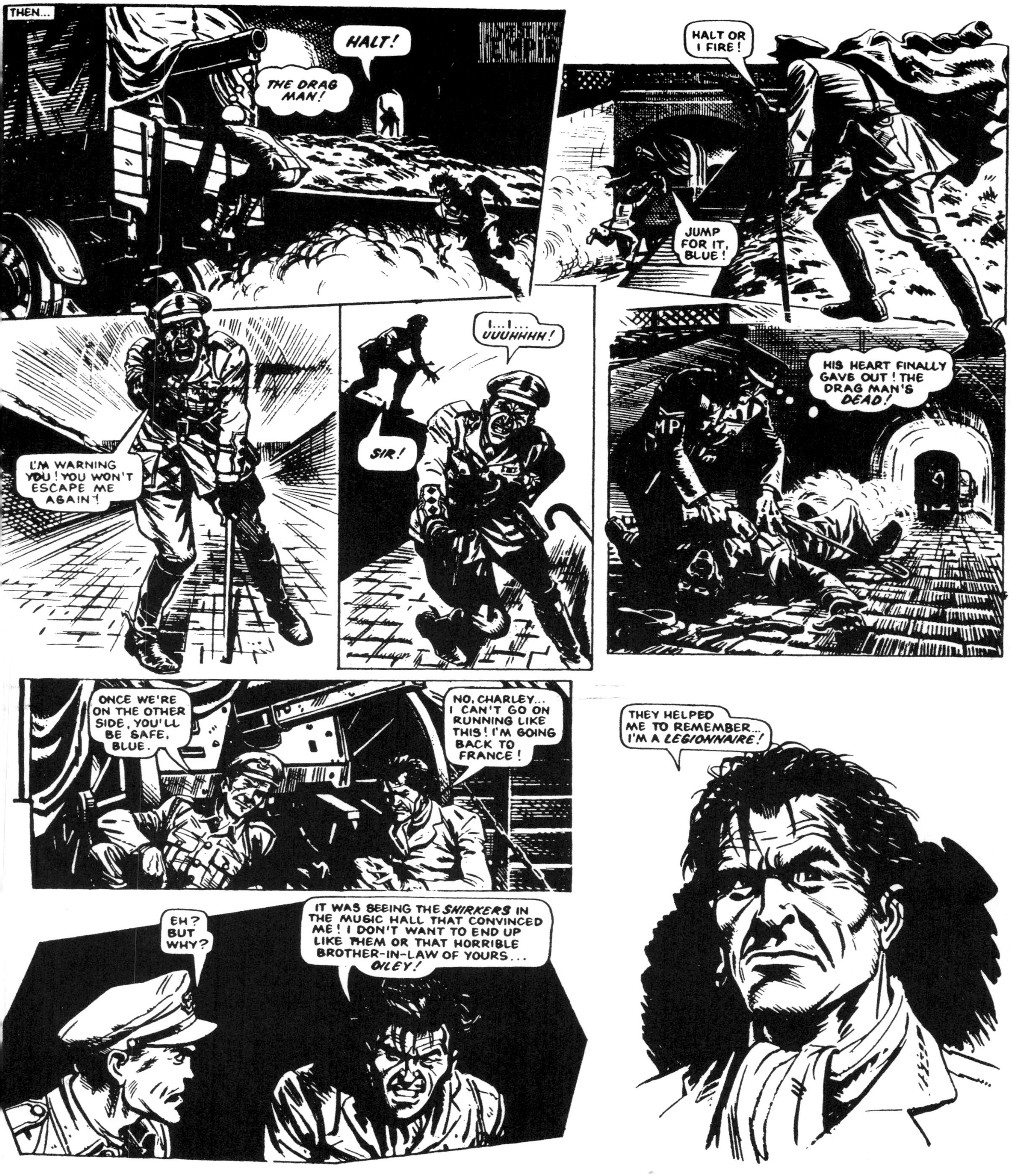
THEN...
THE DRAG MAN!
HALT!
HALT OR I FIRE!
JUMP FOR IT, BLUE!
I'M WARNING YOU! YOU WON'T ESCAPE ME AGAIN!
I...I... UUUHHHH!
SIR!
HIS HEART FINALLY GAVE OUT! THE DRAG MAN'S DEAD!
ONCE WE'RE ON THE OTHER SIDE, YOU'LL BE SAFE, BLUE.
NO, CHARLEY... I CAN'T GO ON RUNNING LIKE THIS! I'M GOING BACK TO FRANCE!
EH? BUT WHY?
IT WAS SEEING THE SHIRKERS IN THE MUSIC HALL THAT CONVINCED ME! I DON'T WANT TO END UP LIKE THEM OR THAT HORRIBLE BROTHER-IN-LAW OF YOURS... OILEY!
THEY HELPED ME TO REMEMBER... I'M A LEGIONNAIRE!

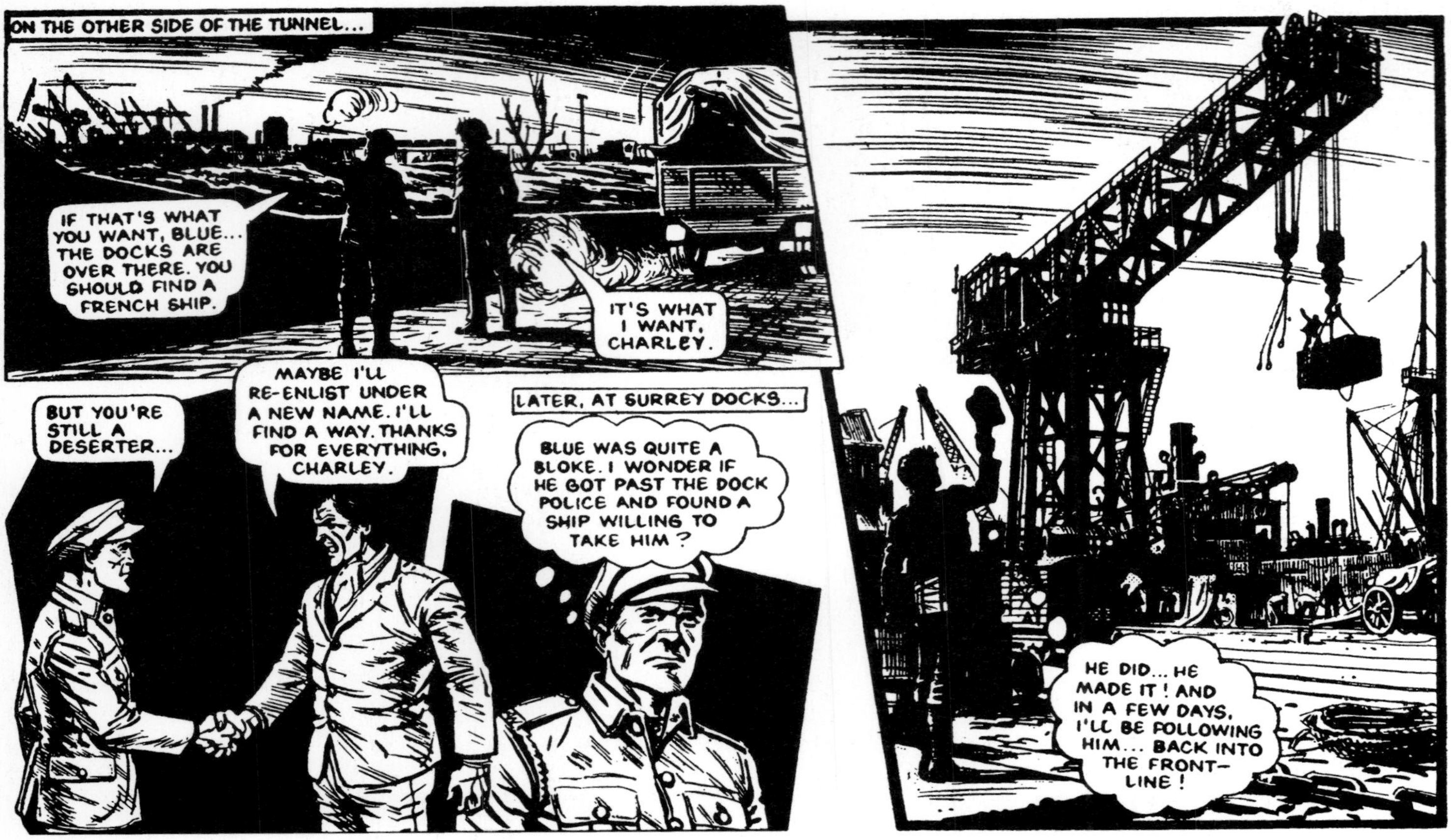
ON THE OTHER SIDE OF THE TUNNEL...
IF THAT'S WHAT YOU WANT, BLUE... THE DOCKS ARE OVER THERE. YOU SHOULD FIND A FRENCH SHIP.
IT'S WHAT I WANT, CHARLEY.
BUT YOU'RE STILL A DESERTER...
MAYBE I'LL RE-ENLIST UNDER A NEW NAME. I'LL FIND A WAY. THANKS FOR EVERYTHING, CHARLEY.
LATER, AT SURREY DOCKS...
BLUE WAS QUITE A BLOKE. I WONDER IF HE GOT PAST THE DOCK POLICE AND FOUND A SHIP WILLING TO TAKE HIM?
HE DID... HE MADE IT! AND IN A FEW DAYS, I'LL BE FOLLOWING HIM... BACK INTO THE FRONT-LINE!

STRIP COMMENTARY

by Pat Mills

EPISODE ONE

The death of the Zeppelin. These machines seem so bizarre – the stuff of science fiction – that it's easy to forget they were the weapons of mass destruction of their day, shortly followed by the aptly-named, giant "Gotha" bombers.

It's hard to imagine the "shock and awe" they must have created. One East End woman at the time exclaimed of the Zeppelins, "I don't think they ought to be allowed to make them things and go up there, prying into the Almighty's affairs."

EPISODE TWO

This is one of my all-time favourite episodes. Page 2, panel 3 is fabulous: Joe had a truly British sense of humour and this picture reminds me of the immortal *Just William* illustrations by Thomas Henry. As always, I am mesmerised by Joe's detailing. Take the scene that follows with the skeleton of the Zeppelin and the chap selling hot pies. It is one thing for me to write that in a script, the work of minutes; it is another for Joe to draw it with such engrossing precision.

EPISODE THREE

Because *Charley's War* was the most popular story in *Battle*, editorial wanted to run it on the cover to boost sales, but my ideas about what would make a good cover and theirs rarely coincided. So when they didn't like my idea, it would become the first picture of the episode inside. This is the case here. That image of Wilf outside the recruiting office is superb.

I wanted to establish Charley's brother Wilf as a character, ready for him to feature a year or so later in the serial. This was rather optimistic of me, given the state of British comics, because you never knew whether they would be around long enough; most were not. Many comics were merged into each other within months of their launch in order to artificially boost sales. It annoyed readers but their views were always ignored. This consciously ephemeral attitude greatly harmed British comics. It was summed up by the publisher's merger philosophy of "Hatch, match and despatch."

EPISODE FOUR

The hero, Blue, is introduced – and the Drag Man, who rounds up deserters.

I based Blue partly on Percy Toplis, the legendary mutineer who, to this day, has the establishment frothing at the mouth. Toplis was a deserter and the leader of the British army mutineers who rose up in revolt in 1917 . This was the subject of the book and TV series *The Monocled Mutineer*. This series, with its potentially subversive message to modern soldiers, has never been repeated after protests by Tory MPs. The establishment still does its best to debunk the findings of the book and drama, but I have studied the book carefully and its sources are impeccable. Toplis, to me, was a John Lennon character – a subversive,

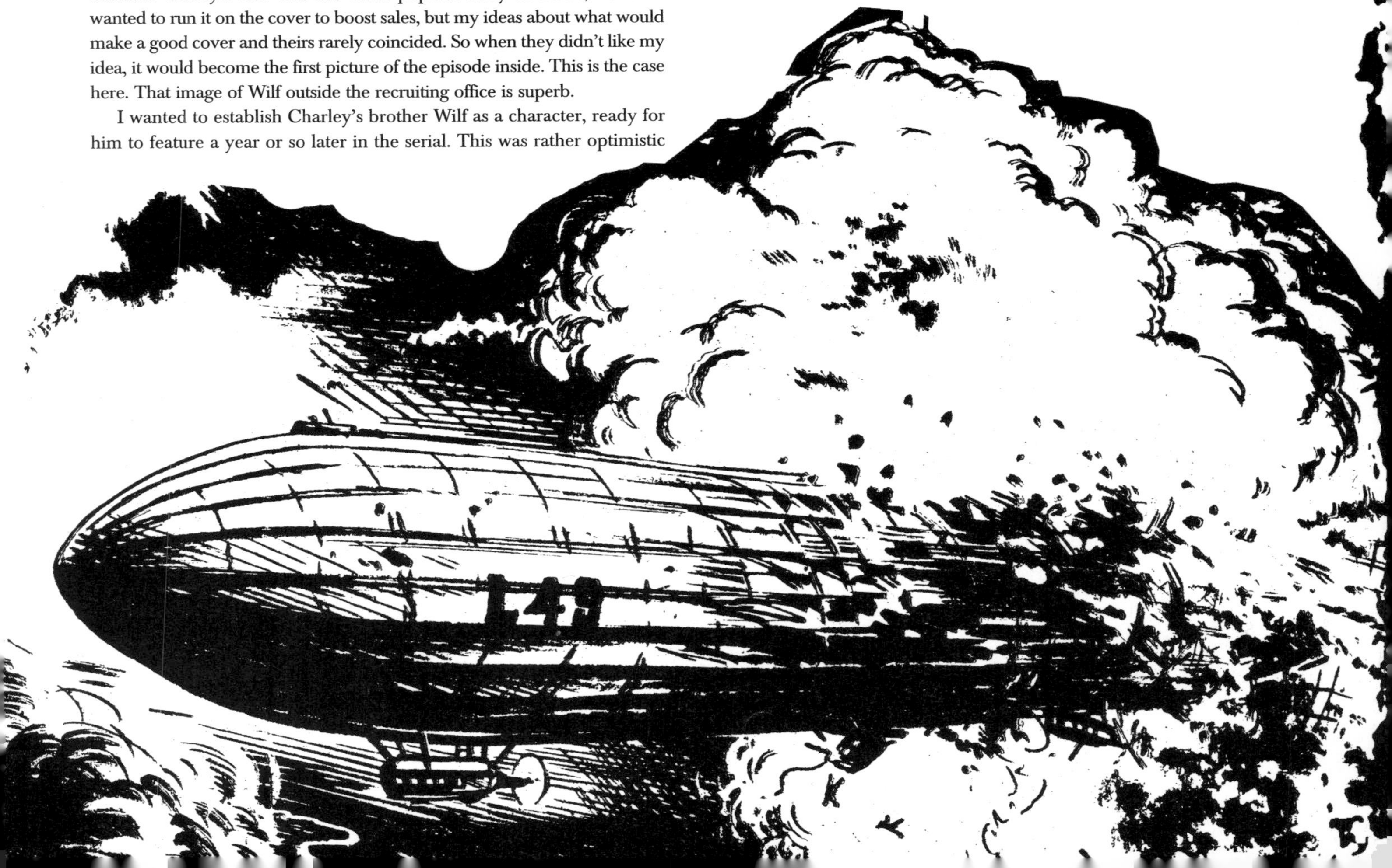

L49

working-class rebel and hero (I recall Roger Daltrey from The Who was originally going to play him in the film) and shared the same fate: assassination. Toplis was tracked down to Britain after the war and shot under questionable circumstances.

But the British army mutiny, in which Blue would play a significant role, similar to Toplis, was several years away in *Charley's War*. This story establishes Blue's character for that future serial.

EPISODE FIVE

The saga of Verdun begins – a story within a story. Although the dramatic device I used is not unknown in films and novels, it breaks the normal rules of comic-book drama whereby we normally follow only the adventures of the main character. Instead it deviates to feature the exploits of Blue. I was well aware of how risky this was and how many comic-book rules I was breaking. I also knew it might be unpopular to begin with, because of the sudden "change of gear". But I figured it would succeed in time, because of the astonishing nature of the battle of Verdun.

I would never get away with it today – there would be instant howls of complaint in cyberspace, and editors would have no choice but to tell me to can the story. Fortunately, in those days, there was more of a delay for reader feedback. Also, *Battle's* "mainstream" readers were more receptive to innovative ideas than some of today's cyber-pundits.

Frankly, I would write it exactly the same today because I have no choice. The muse that drives me to write is far more interested in content and subversive subtext than comic-book rules or appealing to purists and I have long given up arguing with her.

As always, it's an enormous compliment to Joe's patience and professionalism that he followed my sharp "U turn" without comment or complaint and went on to produce what many readers regard then – and now – as one of the most powerful, successful and beautifully drawn of all the *Charley's War* stories.

EPISODE SIX

Readers would generally follow the adventures of British and American comic-book war heroes. They might be forgiven for not realising that in the Great War, it was the French who bore the brunt of the fighting. It was important, therefore, that *Charley's War*, as an anti-war saga, should find a way to show the French perspective and – in that sense alone – Blue's story is a legitimate chapter in the *Charley's War* saga.

And the astonishing story of Verdun had to be told. To my knowledge it has never featured elsewhere, either in comics or in Anglo-American films. No *Saving Private Ryan* treatment for the French, I'm afraid. I think Stanley Kubrick's brilliant *Paths of Glory* is the only film I am aware of that chronicles the French experience during the Great War.

The Verdun battle was so ghastly that even today's establishment historians have never tried to do a revisionist job on it – unlike the Battle of the Somme, which was the subject of a recent television series. The message of the TV programme was that the Battle of the Somme was actually necessary, well-planned and was really a great victory; more or less what they were saying back in 1916. With such disturbing revisionist films and books

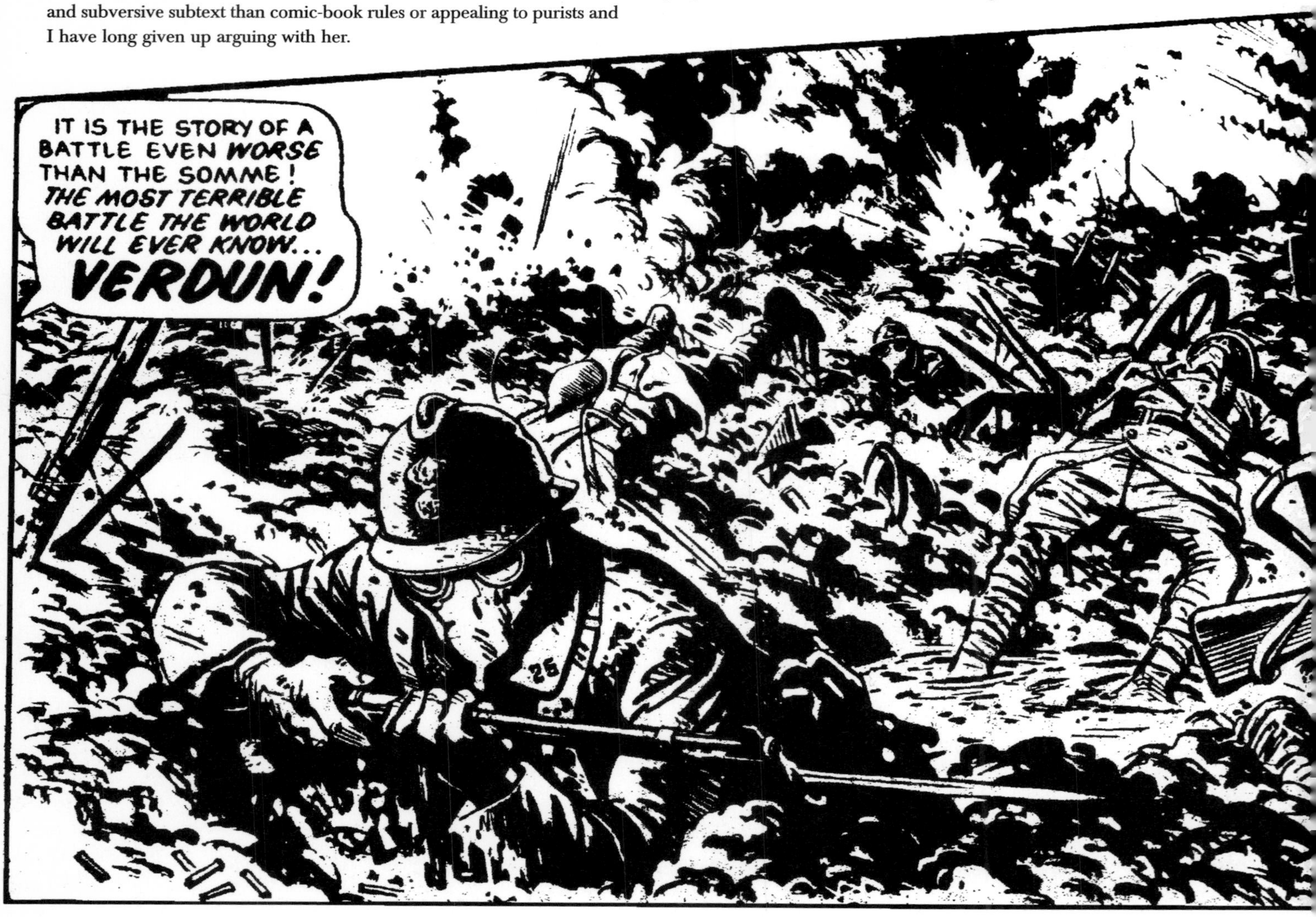
IT IS THE STORY OF A BATTLE EVEN WORSE THAN THE SOMME! THE MOST TERRIBLE BATTLE THE WORLD WILL EVER KNOW... VERDUN!

around today, it is valuable for stories like *Charley's War* to be out there to provide a counter-argument.

EPISODE SEVEN

Initially, with the introduction of Blue, there was a drop in the readers' votes as they adjusted to this "serial within a serial" and the *Battle* editor did became uneasy. I recall him telling me that if the votes continued to drop, I would have to axe Blue and send Charley back to the trenches.

But I knew it was normal for readers to take time getting into new and radical stories. Thus it was not until three months after the launch of *2000 AD* that Judge Dredd became the lead character. I knew the readers would come around and go for Blue. It was just too powerful a subject for them not to.

This episode probably marked the low-point in the votes. From the next episode onwards the votes quickly began to pick up. By the time the Blue saga was over, it would be one of the most popular *Charley's War* stories of all time.

EPISODES EIGHT TO TEN

Joe, as always, excels himself. He captures the claustrophobia of being inside the fort perfectly. Every one of Blue's companions is clearly defined and memorable.

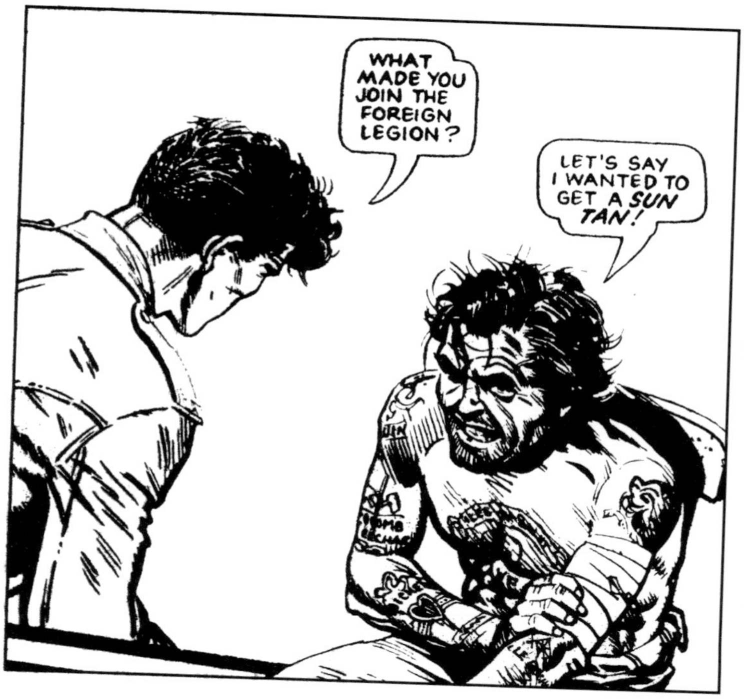
WHAT MADE YOU JOIN THE FOREIGN LEGION?
LET'S SAY I WANTED TO GET A SUN TAN!

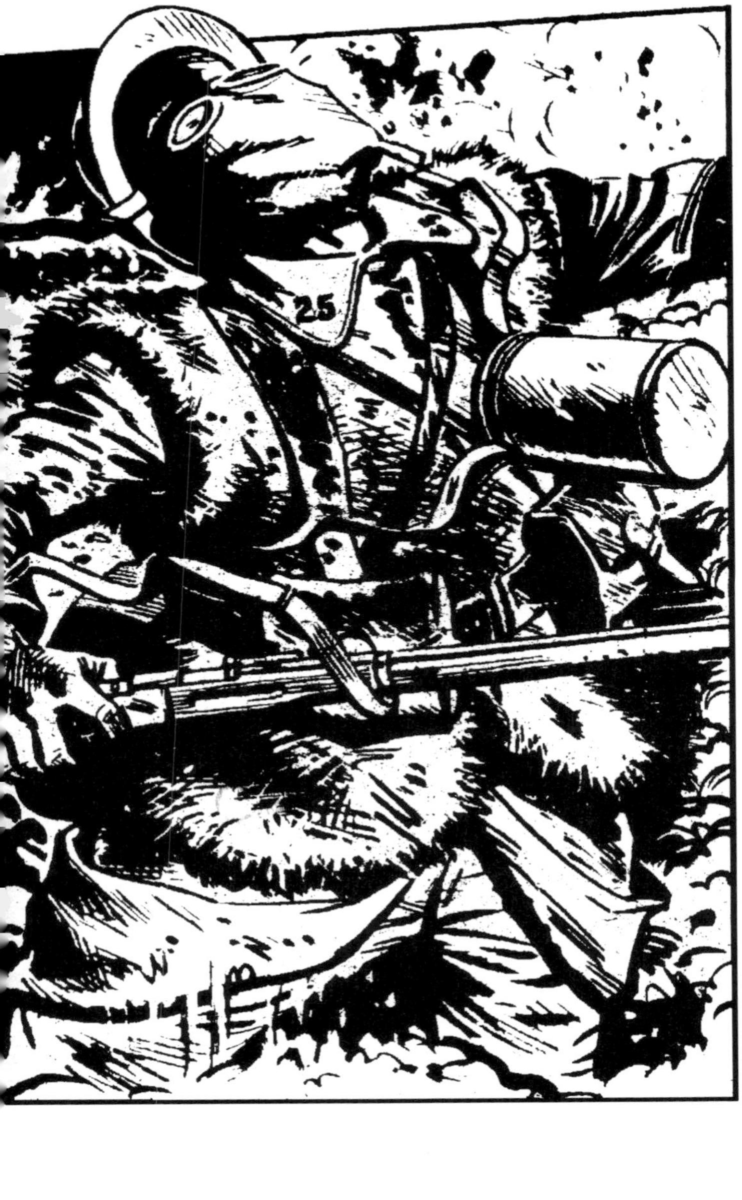

I asked Joe to base Blue on Jack Nicholson and you can see that comes through in many of the images. My *2000 AD* character Sláine was also based on Jack Nicholson; in both cases primarily on Nicholson's character in *One Flew Over the Cuckoo's Nest*. Who better for an anti-establishment hero?

Blue was also a catharsis for me personally. I couldn't have Charley coming out with my anti-authority views; it wasn't in his nature. Blue, on the other hand, I could identify with more and thus his dialogue was very easy to write.

EPISODE ELEVEN

In the back of my mind, I felt Blue had the potential to "spin off" into his own separate adventures, which is why I developed him with so much detail. And this could have been the case, but – alas – there was no artist around, apart from Joe, who could have done him justice. It's a shame, because whereas I eventually completed Charley's story and said everything I wanted to say, this was not the case with Blue. There were many more stories to tell about this mysterious character because he was a freebooter, troublemaker, mercenary and rogue who could turn up just about anywhere. Thus – apart from the British army mutiny – he might have gone on to appear in more French battles; he could have gone to Bolshevik Russia fighting for the Reds, then the Irish War of Independence up against the Black and Tans in a *Wind That Shakes the Barley*-esque drama; and finally featured in the British war of occupation in Iraq.

While Blue tells his story, the Drag Man continues his relentless hunt for Blue. He was based on the British officer in *Ryan's Daughter*, one of my favourite movies.

EPISODES TWELVE TO FOURTEEN

The desperate shortage of water culminates on the cover of episode fourteen, where a German soldier pours out water in front of a thirsty Frenchman's eyes. This is a cover I am particularly pleased with, and I recall describing it in the script in great detail. It was that rare occasion where my desire for subtle covers and editorial's desire for conventional action covers did not clash. I would have liked to have seen all the covers designed like this and to a similar high standard. But that would have required the involvement of an art editor, preliminary roughs, script meetings between editor, writer and artist, and additional strip footage so the cover didn't impede or artificially dictate the storyline. I'm afraid that British comic covers are rarely produced that way. Apart from budgetary considerations, their importance is rarely understood.

I found myself laughing when I read Krotowski's conversation with a German soldier about a watch in episode fourteen. He tells the German that he can have the watch in return for some water: "It's a good watch… it's German."

EPISODES FIFTEEN TO SIXTEEN

I particularly like Krotowski. I enjoyed his line in episode fifteen where he says, "I agree! I don't like it in here!" It's partly the way Joe has drawn him, but also his inane personality. I have no idea where he comes from; I suspect he is someone I made up entirely. Totally fictional characters like this, who come from some obscure corner of the writer's subconscious, are a joy to write.

EPISODES SEVENTEEN TO EIGHTEEN

The cover image for episode eighteen is truly excellent. Once again, a "cool" idea rather than a typical war comic cover. The problem with all subtle covers is they need great artists, whereas an action cover will still work when it is drawn by an average artist. This is why so many comic covers are "gung-ho". It's easier and safer. I can think of very few artists who could execute this cover as well as Joe; Brian Bolland and Dave Gibbons would be amongst those few.

EPISODE NINETEEN

That German band is incredible! Who but Joe could have captured that pompous but menacing militarism? I would have planned that as a cover, but editorial must have decided it wasn't exciting enough and relegated it to the opening picture instead. Another favourite image of mine is Blue's sneer in this episode. I had asked in the script for a 'Jack Nicholson' sneer, but Joe – being of an older generation – was possibly not that aware of Nicholson's movies, so he designed his own expression which is much more original. In many cases artists use a mirror to get such expressions. I can assure you Joe did not. He did not look anything like this!

EPISODE TWENTY

This is the kind of cover I like and Joe has conceptualised it so well. The dog makes it; he reminds me of Bill Sykes' dog in *Oliver Twist*. Working dogs were often used in the Great War, so the sight of dogs wearing gas masks was "normal" enough. However, around this time, the publishers hired a marketing firm at huge expense, to interview kids and ask them why they didn't buy comics anymore. The publishers were beginning to fear the progressive drop in comic sales and, rather than acknowledge that it was because of a lack of quality, they looked for other more convenient excuses; just as today's generation says the modern drop in comic sales is because of computer games (not true – look at French comic sales. They are colossal!) Anyway, one kid replied to the marketing firm that he didn't buy comics, "Because so many comic characters are stupid." (I know what he means!) "They're unbelievable." (Agreed!) "Look – here's one of a dog wearing a gas mask. That's ridiculous and impossible." (Alas, not…)

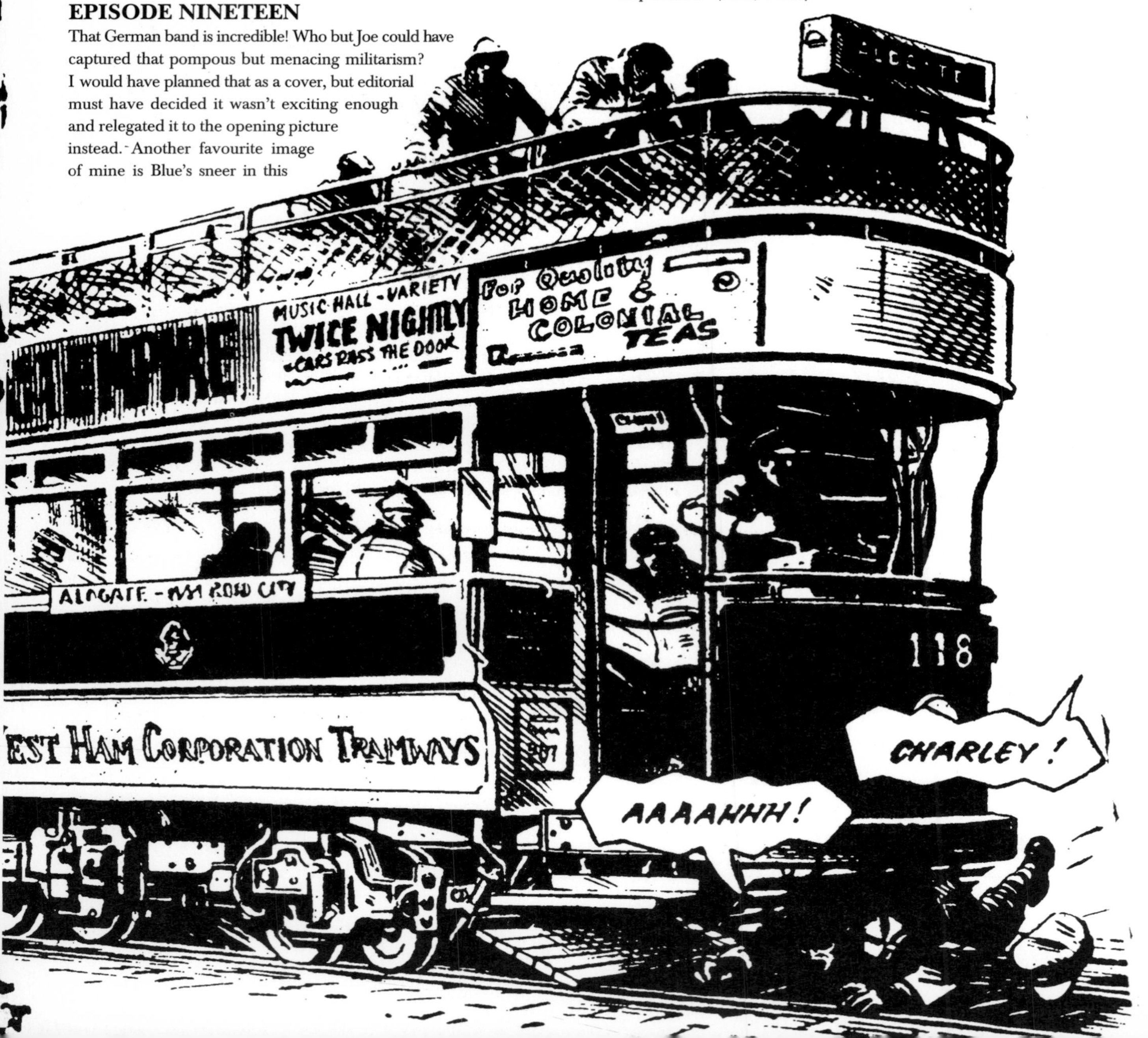
MUSIC HALL - VARIETY
TWICE NIGHTLY
CARS PASS THE DOOR
For Quality
HOME & COLONIAL TEAS
EST HAM CORPORATION TRAMWAYS
118
CHARLEY!
AAAAHHH!

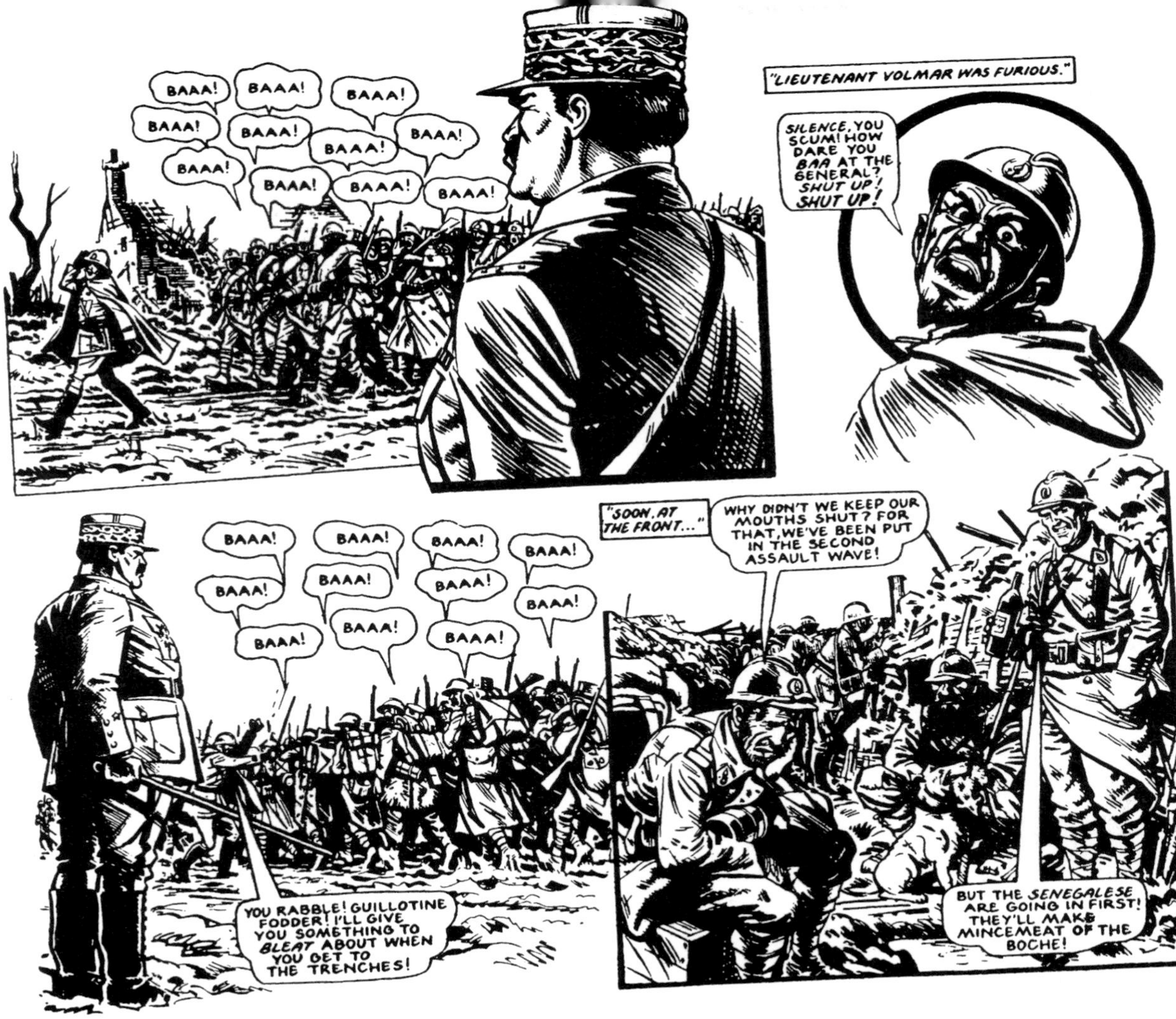
BAAA!
BAAA!
BAAA!
BAAA!
BAAA!
BAAA!
BAAA!
BAAA!
BAAA!
BAAA!
BAAA!
"LIEUTENANT VOLMAR WAS FURIOUS."
SILENCE, YOU SCUM! HOW DARE YOU BAA AT THE GENERAL? SHUT UP! SHUT UP!
BAAA!
BAAA!
BAAA!
BAAA!
BAAA!
BAAA!
BAAA!
BAAA!
BAAA!
BAAA!
BAAA!
YOU RABBLE! GUILLOTINE FODDER! I'LL GIVE YOU SOMETHING TO BLEAT ABOUT WHEN YOU GET TO THE TRENCHES!
"SOON, AT THE FRONT..."
WHY DIDN'T WE KEEP OUR MOUTHS SHUT? FOR THAT, WE'VE BEEN PUT IN THE SECOND ASSAULT WAVE!
BUT THE SENEGALESE ARE GOING IN FIRST! THEY'LL MAKE MINCEMEAT OF THE BOCHE!

EPISODE TWENTY-ONE

The triumph of Monkey Face. I seem totally incapable of writing sympathetic and heroic figures of authority, apart from Lieutenant Thomas, in an earlier volume of *Charley's War* – and he was executed by the establishment. Don't blame me, blame my muse. Someone told me the other day there is or was a punk band called Charley's War. I'm thrilled to hear it and I can guess why they chose that name.

EPISODE TWENTY-TWO

This was the episode why I had to write Blue: for that heart-rending scene of soldiers baa-ing like sheep as they go to the front. What an indictment of the generals of the Great War.

It is often harder to write deserters or pacifists as heroes. This is why Charley's War is a creative cul-de-sac. No story has ever followed its lead, despite its huge popularity. I once actively considered writing a pacifist character as a hero. I spent some time in Housmans, the pacifist bookshop in Kings Cross, looking at various options. No, don't all rush off, come back! Consider, for instance, the conscientious objectors in World War One. One objected to fighting on Christian grounds, saying that it was a sin to kill. The tribunal asked him, "Do you believe that the blood of Christ cleanses from all sin?"

"Yes."

"Then you would be forgiven if you took part in wars."

Er… right.

16,000 men refused to fight, many because they were socialists and felt it was a war for capitalism, which – of course – it was. Many objectors were sentenced to penal servitude. At Dartmoor, six were put on a treadmill. Thirty-one were driven insane by their inhumane treatment. Seventy-three died from their treatment. For me, these men are true heroes, worth a thousand "super" heroes.

Actually, I did later write a pacifist-hero story: when Charley becomes a stretcher-bearer in 1917, one of the most dangerous jobs on the Western Front.

EPISODES TWENTY-THREE TO TWENTY-FOUR

The story of the Africans who were shamefully used as cannon fodder. Their dialogue is authentic but would never be allowed in today's politically-correct world. Today, most editors might say, "Well, the Africans *may* have said the machine gun bullets were like magic but *you* can't say it, because you are reinforcing negative stereotypes." I would say that the context, the writer's intention and truth are more important than political correctness, allowing the readers to make up their own minds. I think it was necessary to show the Africans' innocence to contrast with the way they were cynically slaughtered as a test.

EPISODE TWENTY-FIVE

I remember sending Joe that reference of the tram. It's a beauty. Once again, it would have been scripted to appear as the cover. Some trams in the Great War even had searchlights on top and were used to track Zeppelins.

I hope, like me, you have been ignoring the strange Germanic *Charley's War* logos. That's why I am only mentioning them now when you are coming to the end of the story, in the vain hope that you may not have noticed. What on earth possessed editorial to do that?

EPISODE TWENTY SIX

So the scene is set for Blue to reappear later in the story of the British mutiny. Charley, too, returns to the trenches in 1917.

I still miss writing Charley and Blue and reading this volume reminds me just how much of a wrench it was when it all came to an end. And I miss Krotowski… and the Ratcatcher's dog.✢

ALSO AVAILABLE FROM TITAN BOOKS

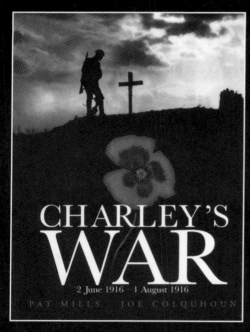
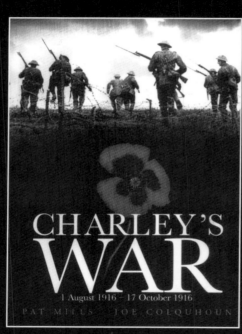
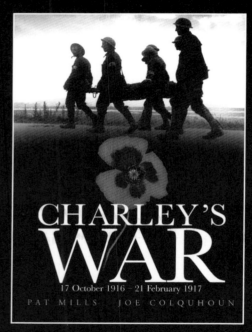